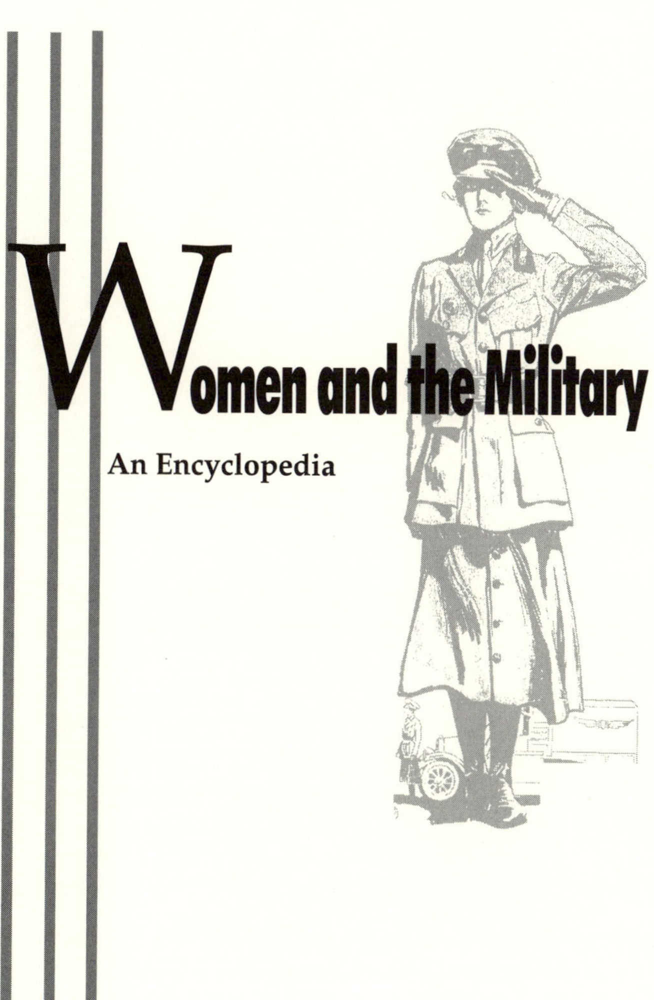

Women and the Military

An Encyclopedia

Women and the Military

An Encyclopedia

Victoria Sherrow

ABC-CLIO
Denver, Colorado
Santa Barbara, California
Oxford, England

Library of Congress Cataloging-in-Publication Data

Sherrow, Victoria.
Women and the military : an encyclopedia / Victoria Sherrow.
p. cm.
Includes bibliographical references and index.
1. Women and the military—Encyclopedias. 2. Women and war—Encyclopedias. I. Title.
U21.75.S54 1996 355′.0082—DC20 96-33459

ISBN 0-87436-812-X

02 01 00 99 98 97 96 10 9 8 7 6 5 4 3 2 1

ABC-CLIO, Inc.
130 Cremona Drive, P.O. Box 1911
Santa Barbara, California 93116-1911

This book is printed on acid-free paper ♾.
Manufactured in the United States of America

Contents

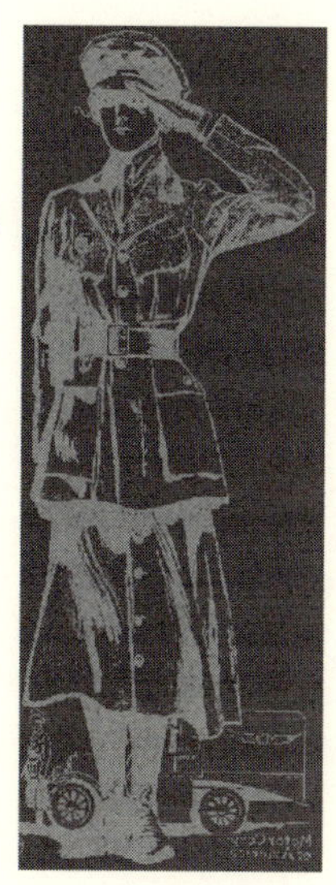

Introduction

During the 1980s, a popular military recruitment slogan exhorted potential enlistees to "be all that you can be—in the Army," but while men could take advantage of all the Army offered, some doors in the Army, as well as in the Air Force, Marines, and Navy, were closed to women. The scope of what women could be in the military has been changing through the decades, however, and continues to evolve as the United States moves into the twenty-first century.

In past centuries, women's roles have often been limited by what society, dominated by men, expected of them and wished them to be, not based on a clear assessment of their individual capabilities. Yet as individuals and groups have challenged the status quo, women's roles have been expanding. Women have been free to choose more traditional domestic roles as well as pursue occupations, professions, sports, and leisure activities that were dominated by men in the past.

Perhaps no area has been more resistant to full participation of women than the military. Here, as in no other sphere, long-standing ideas about the traits and abilities of the two sexes have kept the military predominantly male and male-controlled until well into the 1900s.

Since colonial days, roles for American women in the armed services have been only reluctantly expanded. Often, the contributions made by women have not been publicized or rewarded. Historians prefer to dwell upon women whose activities fit society's model of "feminine" behavior. Until after the 1960s, most school textbooks ignored the stories of women who had fought as soldiers, spied, or carried out other daring deeds during the Revolutionary War while containing the story of Betsy Ross, who supposedly made the nation's first flag (a story historians have since disputed).

Minority women and men experienced even fewer opportunities and less recognition. African Americans have fought in every war in American history, but there was no integration of African-American units with whites until the early 1950s. Both women and African Americans (both sexes) were given the chance to serve only when there were emergency conditions and shortages that required manpower not available from white men. As the crisis abated, they were once again shut out. Leadership positions were not open to them.

As in many other areas of life, women's roles in the military changed slowly, as ideas about their mental and physical capabilities have changed. In some cases, change has been forced by the courts, by new laws that promote equal access to education and employment, and by new laws and policies governing the military itself.

Debates over appropriate military roles for women have often been heated ones, with both women and men on various sides of the issues. Women who disagreed with conventional stereotypes have fought for a place in the military, whether as nurses, soldiers, physicians, journalists, pilots, missile operators, air-traffic controllers, or as crew members on naval ships. They have struggled for a place on the battlefield and in the air and at sea, as well as for the right to lead others. Writing about this struggle, in *Women in the Military: An Unfinished Revolution* (1992), Major General Jeanne Holm (Air Force–retired) says, "Acceptance of women as full and equal role participants in this masculine milieu is seen by many as the ultimate test of a society's willingness to compromise with long-established traditions."

Ancient Patterns

The purpose of the American military is to protect and defend the interests of the United States and its allies. From ancient times, men, who tended to be larger with more physical strength on average, have assumed the job of fighting for rights or territory and against others who would attack their homes, families, property, and lands. Women, with their biological capacity to bear and nurse offspring, carried out domestic duties, managing the household and raising children.

In some cultures, demonstrating courage and aggression in the field of battle was a way of demonstrating one's manhood, since combatants risked injuries and death. For taking those risks, successful warriors were praised as heroes and given many societal benefits.

It is not known whether women fought in conflicts during ancient times, but historians consider this unlikely. During those years, weapons consisted of spears, swords, axes, and bows and arrows wielded by sheer physical force. Greek mythology contains stories about the Amazons, a race of fierce women warriors with bows and arrows whose society excluded men, but many historians doubt that these women actually existed. In biblical stories, men assume the roles of leaders, fighters, and warriors, while women bear and raise children and tend to cooking, farming, and other home-related duties.

Despite these general patterns of participation, women have not always remained on the sidelines. Historians record that women leaders planned and executed attacks against enemy armies or oppressors. Angered when Romans seized property that belonged to England, Boudicca (first century A.D.) planned an armed rebellion against Roman troops occupying three major English cities. Her group, the Iceni, eventually were defeated but the central Roman government did instigate some reforms.

Other women leaders were active in planning battles or in handling defensive maneuvers or negotiating an end to war. Some personally led troops into battle. Perhaps the most famous female warrior was Jeanne d'Arc (Joan of Arc). In 1429, this 18-year-old claimed that "voices" had told her to lead French soldiers supporting the Dauphin Charles, heir to the French throne, against English troops. Charles, whose father had died five years earlier, had not been crowned king because the city of Reims, where the coronation must, by tradition, take place, was occupied by the British. They planned to make their leader, Henry VI, king of France.

Jeanne d'Arc organized and led two successful battles to oust the English at Orleans and Patay. In July 1429, she had led the French into Reims where Charles was crowned king, but, unable to overcome English defenses in Paris, she experienced military setbacks late in 1429 and in 1430. After English allies at Compiegne captured Jeanne, she was put on trial by officials of the Catholic Church. Church leaders berated her for wearing men's clothing and for claiming to receive divine guidance directly from God. After the "trial," Jeanne d'Arc was delivered to the English, who burned her at the stake on 30 May 1431.

Throughout Europe, Asia, and Africa, from time to time, there were stories of other women who defied conventions to fight in battle, often disguised as men. In North America, as a new nation fought for freedom during the late 1700s, women who were not satisfied with conventional roles would resort to the same tactics.

Home Front and Battle Front: Women of the Revolution

From the time of the Revolutionary War, American women have been involved in a wide range of activities, mostly nonaggressive, that supported the military. Women were expected to remain in roles defined as nonmilitary and noncombatant, yet many rejected those limits and found ways around the rules, and some found themselves in combat conditions despite military objections. In some cases, the military accepted the help of women who crossed the lines to enter the area of "combat." They were, however, unlikely to receive official recognition or the benefits accorded to male soldiers.

On the home front, women boycotted products made by the enemy, made clothing and other supplies for the Colonial Army, collected metal scrap to make bullets, and organized fund-raising efforts. They allowed military personnel to use their homes as headquarters and as stopping places for food and refreshments. They took over all the chores of homes and farms as their husbands and sons left to join the Army.

One woman expressed the patriotism felt by many women during those days, writing, "I know this—that as free I can die but once; but as a slave I shall not be worthy of life. These are the sentiments of all my sister Americans" [Utley 1968].

Women were authorized to follow along with the troops, some going as volunteers, and others receiving compensation in the form of food rations or a small amount of money. Among other tasks, camp followers, as they were called, nursed the wounded and the sick, cooked meals, carried water to the troops, and sewed and laundered their clothing.

A number of women volunteered to serve as spies, scouts, and couriers. Some, like Lydia Darragh of Philadelphia, were able to relay important information that could even determine the outcome of particular battles. Young couriers like Emily Geiger and Beth Moore cleverly made their way across enemy lines to deliver critical messages.

An unknown number of women disguised themselves as men in order to serve as soldiers in battle. Their reasons included patriotism, a desire to remain with husbands or fiancés who had enlisted, and the urge for excitement and new experiences. The best known of these women was Deborah Sampson, a tall schoolteacher who enlisted in Massachusetts under the alias Robert Shurtleff. Over a period of 18 months, Sampson fought in several battles and was wounded more than once. After becoming ill in Philadelphia, she was forced to reveal her secret. After marrying and raising her children, Sampson toured the country telling about her war experiences.

It was during this war that the military hired its first official women employees. In 1775, the Continental Congress passed a bill, sponsored by General George Washington, that created a hospital department for the Army. Under this law, civilian nurses could be hired at a pay rate of about 25 cents a day. Nursing duties—caring for the sick and nurturing—were viewed as women's work. In the years to come, the facts that most nurses were women and that the military needed nurses (the closer to the fighting the better) would collide with the military policy of keeping women in "safe" areas far from combat.

In the 1840s, nearly 75 years after the war had ended, a Frenchman named Alexis de Tocqueville traveled throughout America. He later wrote a book about his experiences called *Democracy in America*, in which he said, "If I were asked to what the singular prosperity and growing strength of Americans ought to be attributed, I should reply: To the superiority of their women" [Tocqueville 1969].

Women of North and South

Only partially in gest, President Abraham Lincoln once said to Harriet Beecher Stowe, "So you're the little lady who started this big war?" As the author of *Uncle Tom's Cabin* (1852), a novel that intensified the regional debate over slavery, Stowe had indeed stirred the embers that burst into civil war. Women had taken an active part in the bitter abolition movement that sought to end slavery; now, they would not stay on the sidelines after the first guns were fired in 1861.

Women from both North and South supported their military forces. A native of Georgia, Mary A. Ward, later said,

> The day that Georgia was declared out of the Union was a day of the wildest excitement in Rome. . . . Then we began preparing our soldiers for the war. The ladies were all summoned to public places, to halls and lecture rooms, and sometimes to churches, and everybody who had sewing machines was invited to send them; they were never demanded because the mere suggestion was all-sufficient. The sewing machines were sent to these places and ladies who were known to be experts in cutting out garments were engaged in that part of the work, and every lady in town was turned into a seamstress and worked as hard as anybody could work; and the ladies not only worked themselves but they brought colored seamstresses to these places, and these halls and public places would be filled with busy women all day long [Meltzer 1989].

Women also helped escaped slaves (called "contrabands") who came north for freedom before the war's end. Former slaves frequently aided the Union Army as blacksmiths, cooks, guides, laundresses, drivers, scouts, spies, nurses, and hospital workers. Some of the women who came to help and to educate the children and older people were former slaves themselves. Among those who sent boxes of clothing and food for fugitives were abolitionist women. Perhaps the most famous ex-slave to help the Union was Harriet Tubman, who risked her life hundreds of times during the war. Besides helping other slaves to escape along the Underground Railroad that stretched from the South through the North to Canada, Tubman nursed soldiers, led soldiers into enemy territory as an experienced scout, and spied on the Confederacy.

As in the Revolutionary War, women took an active part in many activities to support the military, raising money and supplies and working in numerous volunteer organizations. A number of daring women became couriers, saboteurs, gun-runners, scouts, and guides. Some especially colorful and clever women spies emerged during the course of the Civil War. There was alluring Belle Boyd, the Moon sisters, Harriet Wood (Pauline Cushman), Elizabeth Van Lew, and Rose O'Neil Greenhow, among others. Some, like Mrs. E. H. Baker, were professional espionage operators before the war. Some of these women became prisoners of war and one was nearly executed.

Several hundred women decided to "pass" as men in order to fight as soldiers. As "Franklin Thompson," Sarah Emma Edmonds, age 21, fought as a private in the Michigan Infantry. She also served as a spy (disguised, for example, as a black man, Irish peddlar, or rebel cavalryman), a dispatch rider, and a nurse over a period of three years with the Union Army. Later, Edmonds would say of her military experiences, "Patriotism was the true secret of my success" [Reit 1988]. Edmonds broke new ground for women when she applied for and finally received a veterans' pension.

Breaking new ground on another front, several women led the effort to bring medical care and better health conditions to those in the service. Mary Livermore was a leader in the United States Sanitary Commission, which inspected camps and made recommendations to improve food preparation and to prevent the spread of disease. Elizabeth Blackwell, America's first licensed physician, set up an organized training program for nurses who then went on to aid the Union Army, where nurses had been formally organized under the direction of social worker and advocate for the mentally ill, Dorothea Lynde Dix.

Early in the war, Clara Barton had begun taking supplies to the troops; then she nursed the wounded, moving closer and closer to the battlefields. At times, she worked under fire. Barton maintained an ongoing struggle with officials in Washington, D.C., to get the supplies and clearance she needed to carry on her work. After the war, she conducted a search to locate and identify veterans missing in action and founded the American Red Cross, serving as president of the organization until 1904.

Nurses from the Red Cross were among those who provided care to sick and wounded soldiers during the Spanish-American War of 1898, when a severe influenza epidemic took more lives than were lost in combat. This war pointed up the need for a permanent corps of nurses attached to the military.

The First Women's Corps Is Born

By the end of the 1800s, U.S. officials knew that many problems of caring for the wounded and sick during the Civil War and Spanish-American War had resulted from the lack of a unified nursing corps under military direction.

The Army Nurse Corps (ANC) was created in 1901, partly due to the efforts of a woman physician, Anita Newcomb McGhee, who had organized nurses during the Spanish-American conflict. The Navy followed suit in 1908 when it created its own nursing corps. These were the first women to be an official part of the military, and they were to be greatly needed during the next four decades as the nation found itself embroiled in two world wars. When the first of those wars began, only the United States and Great Britain had well-organized military nurses and excellent training programs for nurses.

Yet, although they were subject to military regulations and were responsible to military authorities, members of the nurse corps did not have military rank. This situation would continue for more than 20 years as other women joined the military in various capacities, also with an ambiguous status that allowed them to serve in limited ways but not with the same status, pay, or benefits that males in the military received.

In addition, military officials tended to downplay and even deny the contributions of women. The stories of women who had joined the Army during the Revolutionary and Civil Wars disguised as men had been published in books and newspapers and had become part of congressional records in some states. Throughout the nation were people who knew these women or who had heard them speak publicly about their experiences.

The military contended that such incidents were negligible, if they had happened at all. In 1916, the U.S. Army issued a statement saying,

> No official record has been found in the War Department showing specifically that any woman was ever enlisted in the military service of the United States as a member of any organization of the Regular or Volunteer Army. It is possible, however, that there may have been a few instances of women having served as soldiers for a short time without their sex having been detected, but no record of such cases is known to exist in the official files [Treadwell 1954].

Strides during World War I

World War I had been raging in Europe for two years when Josephus Daniels, the secretary of the Navy, asked a legal advisor, "Is there any law that says a yeoman must be a man?" [Holm 1992]. Looking ahead, Daniels believed that the United States would become involved in World War I, leading to manpower shortages in the Navy as well as in other branches of service. When the lawyers informed him that women could indeed join the Navy, Daniels directed that they be enrolled in the Navy Reserve, saying,

"We will have the best clerical assistance the country can provide" [Holm 1992].

As Yeoman (F) for "female," women were invited to join the Navy as of 19 March 1917. These "Yeomanettes," as they were popularly known, filled a number of clerical jobs in the United States, allowing more Navy men to go to sea. The Marines began enrolling their "Marinettes" about a year later, and about 13,000 women served in both groups. The Army chose not to form such a women's corps, even though some top Army officials supported one.

On 8 October 1917, General John J. Pershing cabled his need for 100 women telephone operators. Pershing faced a shortage of French-speaking operators in France, where he was leading the American Expeditionary Force (AEF). These American women went overseas at the request of the Army but still served with the AEF as civilian contract employees with a status and benefits like those given members of the Army Nurse Corps. Other people were also sent overseas to perform different jobs needed by the Army, but none with full military status.

While abroad, U.S. military officials were impressed by the variety of skilled and useful jobs performed by the British Women's Auxiliary Army Corps (WAAC), the largest auxiliary in the nation. U.S. servicemen commented on the women's efficient, well-disciplined units.

As station commanders in Europe continued to ask for women to do clerical work and other tasks in which they could replace men, the War Department finally agreed. They authorized sending mature women of "high moral character" as long as they had "careful supervision" [Treadwell 1954]. Women doctors were still not accepted by the military. Under the National Defense Act, men who wished to keep women doctors out could say that they were not physically qualified for that position, since the act required military physicians to be "physically, mentally, and morally qualified."

Women's groups continued to organize and protest, asking for change. In New York City, the Women's League for Self-Defense staged a demonstration. Five hundred women marched in bloomers doing drills with rifles while accompanying the 66th Regimental Armory. They wrote to the secretary of war offering to serve in the military, as did some other women's groups and individuals, including pilots.

Lack of Consensus

When World War I ended in 1918, the debate over women's service in the military was tabled—temporarily. Women could now vote, however, and they continued to press military officials to include women. In those days, women were to serve in nonaggressive jobs, since most people would have still regarded women unfit for any job involving combat.

In 1920, Secretary of War Newton D. Baker set up the position of Director of Women's Relations for the Army to handle public relations with women. The first woman to serve as director resigned within one year. The next director was Anita Phipps who fought for military status and a permanent place in the military for women during the ten years she served.

The year 1928 brought the Hughes Report, based on a study of potential roles for women in the military. It was one of several such reports submitted to the Department of Defense (DOD) during the 1920s and 1930s. The authors of this study recommended that women "be accorded the same rights, privileges, and benefits as militarized men" [Treadwell 1954]. Like the other plans, this one was filed away by the DOD.

Other plans for women's corps were devised then rejected, considered for a while only to be put aside. No organized military women's group was developed during peacetime; it would take another crisis to bring women other than nurses back into the military.

Sweeping Changes: World War II

Even before the United States entered World War II, American women offered to go to Europe to work for the war effort. After the fall of France and the Battle of Britain in 1940, women demanded in earnest that they be allowed to aid the nation's defense and demonstrate their patriotism and ability. The Women's League of Defense in Chicago set up an office to enroll and classify women who would be able to replace men in various types of jobs should the United States go to war. In other cities across the nation, ambulance corps, women trained in first aid and Red Cross work, and women's defense units wrote to the Army.

In March 1941, as war became imminent, the government began to acknowledge that women would be needed and should have an opportunity to serve. Congresswoman Edith Nourse Rogers prepared a bill that would give women full military status. Rogers had been in Europe during World War I and had seen that the lack of suitable quarters and training had caused problems for the women who served, as had the absence of veterans' benefits for those who were disabled in the service. She said, "I was resolved that our women would not again serve with the Army without the protection men got" [Anderson 1981].

In addition, the Air Corps asked that a women's volunteer defense corps be set up to serve with its Aircraft Warning Service. Support also came from First Lady Eleanor Roosevelt who suggested that American women could serve in antiaircraft barrage work. She urged that a pool of qualified women be developed to serve with the Army, Navy, and Marines.

Women were desperately needed in the nation's factories as well. With her coveralls and kerchief, Rosie the Riveter became the popular symbol of the millions of women who worked in defense plants building aircraft, ships, and munitions. Magazines, billboards, newspapers, and posters urged women to take defense jobs, replacing men who had left for the service.

Among the millions of women who entered the work force during the war, 2 million were married, making up 72.2 percent of the total increase in employed women. They outnumbered single women in the U.S. work force for the first time. Women whose husbands were away in the military were three times more likely to work than those whose husbands remained at home. Women over age 35 made up more than 60 percent of the increase in the female labor force, and those between ages 14 and 19 were 17.3 percent of the total [Anderson 1981].

The first WAAC officers were trained in 1942 after President Franklin Roosevelt signed Public Law 554, the so-called WAAC bill. Congresswoman Rogers had not been able to gain full military status for the corps, something that would come later in the war. Director Oveta Culp Hobby told the 360 women gathered for the first officer training class at Fort Des Moines, Iowa, "You are the first women to serve. . . . Never forget it" [Treadwell 1954].

Other branches of service developed their own women's corps: the Navy organized its Women Accepted for Voluntary Emergency Service (WAVES), the Women Marines were established, and the Air-WACS began serving with the Army Air Force. The Coast Guard, mobilized for military use during wartime, organized its SPAR—named for the Coast Guard motto, "Semper Paratis" (Always Ready).

Top women pilots found a place to use their talents for the military. From 1942 to 1944, nearly 2,000 of the best trained pilots in America flew with the Women's Airforce Service Pilots (WASPs). After training at Avenger Field in Texas, the WASPs flew all kinds of military aircraft, including the B-29 Superfortress, the YP-59, and the P-51 Mustang fighter. They ferried planes throughout the United States and Canada and inside England, sometimes flying missions that male pilots considered too risky. Thirty-eight WASPs died while serving. Of their achievements, the commanding general of the Army Air Forces would say in 1943, "If there was a doubt in anyone's mind that women can become skillful pilots, the WASPS have dispelled that doubt."

Women broke ground in other areas as well. During this war, a number of the top foreign correspondents, reporting from war zones in some cases, were women.

Demobilized

At the war's end, women seemed to have dispelled many doubts about their ability to handle difficult tasks, deprivation, physical and emotional stress, and danger. Military nurses had served with combat units in all theaters of operation. Some had died and been captured by the enemy, kept for months or years as prisoners of war. Members of the WAC had also served in every theater of operation and had received numerous decorations for their work. Thousands of WAVES, Women Marines, Air-WACS, and SPARs had performed numerous jobs never before assigned to women and had likewise earned high praise for their dedication and competence, including medals and other honors.

During the war, women had been urged to join these military organizations and to work in the nation's factories and in other nontraditional jobs, as truck drivers, pilots, and firefighters. With the end of the war, however, the idea that "a woman's place is in the home" returned. The women's corps were demobilized as traditional ideas about the roles of men and women dominated social attitudes once again. Women pilots found that no airline or military organization would hire them. Men took over jobs women had been doing in factories.

For the most part, many women agreed and were willing, even happy, to return to their prewar lives. Even those who had been leaders in some of the women's corps agreed. Others thought women should be a permanent part of the military so that the nation would never again be forced to reorganize such resources from scratch in the event of another crisis.

Some women bitterly resented being ousted from factory jobs that had provided higher wages and more satisfaction than they had known in previous types of work. One laid-off worker, a widow with a mother and son to support, wrote a plaintive letter to President Harry Truman, saying, "I would like to know why, after serving a company in good faith for almost three and a half years, it is now impossible to obtain employment with them. I am a lathe hand and was classified as skilled labor, but simply because I happen to be a woman I am not wanted" [Anderson 1981].

After much debate, those urging a permanent place for women in the military won out. In 1948, Congress passed the Women's Service Integration Act, making women an official part of the military. By 1950, there were nine women's components: (1) Army Nurse Corps, (2) Navy Nurse Corps, (3) Air Force Nurse Corps, (4) Army Medical Specialists Corps, (5) Air Force Medical Specialists Corps, (6) Women's Army Corps (WAC), (7) Women's Air Force (WAF), (8) Women's Naval Reserve (WAVES), and (9) Women Marines.

Toward Equal Opportunity

Throughout the 1950s and 1960s, the women's corps grew in size but there were still limits on what women could do, how many could serve, and what rank they might achieve. A ceiling of 2 percent had been set on how many women could join the military. Many military occupational specialties (MOSs) were closed to women. The Defense Advisory Council on Women in the Service (DACOWITS), a group of 50 prominent citizens that had been formed in 1951 by the president, continued to confront these issues. DACOWITS was also charged with promoting the military as a prestigious career for women and with recruiting.

When challenged about the limitations placed on the positions women could hold in the military, officials said that women had limited physical strength and could not handle heavy equipment or weapons. The possibility of pregnancy was also cited as a problem in deploying women to various locations, as were other physical conditions of women. In a statement made in 1942, Army planners referred to menstruation delicately as the "physiological handicap which renders her [women] abnormal, unstable, etc., at certain times" [Treadwell 1954].

Officials said it would be expensive to modify equipment, clothing, housing, and other facilities to accommodate women and that women and men needed privacy for sleeping and use of bathroom facilities.

In addition, it was said that women lacked the emotional stability, strength, and aggressiveness needed in many military jobs. Besides, the presence of women might disrupt the male bonding process that makes for efficient fighting units. Military officials warned that this could reduce men's motivation to fight since they have often been moved by the idea of fighting to defend women and children.

During the Korean War of 1950–1951 and throughout the fifties, the branches of service tried to expand their women's corps but had trouble recruiting the numbers they wanted. To meet quotas, recruiters began accepting people who did not meet the educational minimums, age limits, and other standards that had been set. The directors of the women's corps received numerous complaints from training facilities about the number of unqualified recruits.

To deal with this situation, some enlistment criteria were increased even more and female officers were allowed to give a final decision on new recruits. However, many factors worked against the goals of expansion. Jobs outside the military offered women better pay and working conditions. Women in the military still also suffered from an image problem, plagued by gossip about immoral behavior and the idea that women who joined were somehow less "feminine" than others. The mood of the country was also quite different than it had been during World War II when patriotism and a crisis motivated larger numbers of women to serve. Now, many Americans wanted to resume what they considered "normal" lives.

Higher standards made it even harder to find recruits. In the Air Force, for instance, women had to meet higher educational, physical, and mental standards than men. They underwent a psychiatric examination, and a search was done of police records, mental hospitals, and the applicant's former schools and employers. Yet directors supported high standards, believing they would make the women's programs more prestigious in the eyes of the public.

In October 1952 the number of women in the various branches of service reached 48,700, dipping to 35,000 by June 1955 [Holm 1992]. This was less than 1 percent of the total military, half the 2 percent ceiling that had been set in 1948. Although the women's programs continued throughout the 1950s and early 1960s, enthusiasm for developing these programs in peacetime diminished, and their survival was sometimes in doubt.

Women made significant gains in the military after the 1960s. The civil rights movement, women's liberation movement, and other social changes contributed to expanding opportunities for women in all jobs, including the military. In November 1976, President Lyndon B. Johnson signed Public Law 90-130, which removed significant restraints on women's career opportunities in the Army, Navy, Air Force, and Marines. The law abolished the 2 percent ceiling that had been set in 1948 and permitted the branches of service to promote women to the ranks of general and admiral. In 1970, the Army awarded stars to its first female generals: Anna Mae Hays, a 28-year veteran and chief of the Army Nurse Corps (ANC) and Elizabeth P. Hoisington, the director of the Women's Army Corps (WAC).

In 1971, the Air Force promoted Jeanne Holm, the director of the WAF, to brigadier general. That same year, E. Ann Hoefly, chief of the Nurse Corps, became the fourth woman general, and Alene B. Duerk, chief of the Navy Nurse Corps, was promoted to first female real admiral. Margaret Brewer became the first woman Marine brigadier general in 1974.

Women were now able to move up in the ranks as never before and to take on new military occupational specialties. As these changes were taking place, women were once again facing the hardships and horrors of war.

Courage under Fire

During the mid-sixties, as the United States became more embroiled in the Vietnam War, a debate ensued over whether and how women should serve in this region. Of course, military nurses were already serving in Vietnam, having been stationed there as the first U.S. troops arrived in the early sixties. By the time the war ended in 1973, more than 7,500 nurses had served in hospitals, evacuation units, and Mobile Army Surgical Hospitals (MASH) in Vietnam. These women were often exposed to combat conditions, sometimes operating when attacks were taking place. Some of these nurses died in Vietnam; many others suffered physical and emotional damage.

Nurses saw firsthand the ghastly wounds, burns, and broken bodies caused by modern weapons and guerrilla warfare. Within the space of an hour, a nurse might have to treat over 150 injuries, as well as deal with the appalling question of whom to save first. Some patients they worked on had live grenades embedded in their stomachs. Flight nurse Liz Allen recalled a night when she flew to a base hospital with a serviceman so injured he needed continuous mouth-to-mouth resuscitation, yet the helicopter had to fly in total darkness lest it be shot out of the air.

According to nurse Lynda Van Devanter, who wrote the critically acclaimed book, *Home before Morning*, about her war experiences, "We were the ones who were protecting the men who were the patients. In the operating room, if the attack was bad, we would lower the operating tables as low as possible so we could operate on our knees, but you had to keep going, so you did" [Holm 1992]. Another nurse said, "We never allowed them to die alone."

Women in the Air Force, Army, Marines, and Navy eventually served in Southeast Asia, although many more asked for assignments to Vietnam than were permitted to go. As they had withstood the climate and diseases of the South Pacific and the bucket latrines and lack of hot water in India during World War II, so did women manage to survive the Tet Offensive and other trials in Vietnam. A number of these women felt that if men were required to go, then women should also serve. A number of women veterans said they would choose to go to Vietnam again, given the same circumstances.

Women in the All-Volunteer Force

In February 1970, a report by the Gates Commission was released to the president and the public. The commission had been asked to explore the ways and means of developing an all-volunteer armed service in the United States, bringing an end to the draft. The commission concluded:

> We unanimously believe that the nation's interests will be better served by an all-volunteer force. . . . We have satisfied ourselves that a volunteer force will not jeopardize national security and . . . will have a beneficial effect on the military as well as the rest of society.

As plans for the AVF took shape, it was clear that women would play a larger and more vital role in the American military than ever before. Congressional subcommittees and think tanks, such as the Brookings Institute, which produced the Binkin-Bach report, were among those examining roles for women in this new kind of military organization. The branches of service were urged to take a closer look at the jobs that might be done by either men or women. The Department of Defense considered how to make military careers competitive with other careers and how to provide benefits that would attract qualified people of both sexes.

During the 1970s, women did not hesitate to go to court to challenge long-standing policies that discriminated against them. Women veterans, especially those who had served in Vietnam, began organizing groups to fight for better and more comprehensive mental and physical health care services. Another landmark for women veterans occurred in 1979 when the female members of the Women's Airforce Service Pilots (WASP) of World War II and the women who had served as Signal Corps operators in World War I were finally granted veterans' status.

That same year, the American Veterans Committee requested an Advisory Panel of Women Veterans at the Veterans Administration to provide equity for women veterans and to suggest policies and programs that met their specific needs. In 1983, Congress finally drafted a bill to make this a reality. Congressman Bob Edgar of Pennsylvania, a sponsor of the bill and chairman of the Subcommittee on Hospitals and Health Care of the House Committee on Veterans Affairs, said, "We intend to see that the equality of military service is matched by equal rights and benefits provided through the Veterans Administration, regardless of sex, age, or race" [Wilenz 1983].

Among the other changes that took place during the eventful seventies were the admission of women to all the military service academies (1976), the integration of women's corps into the regular military organizations with men (1978), and the development of integrated officer promotion lists that included both sexes, effective as of 1980. The services were forced to change their policies on pregnancy and motherhood, allowing women to continue in their careers after bearing or adopting children.

Women also demanded equal pay and benefits for themselves and their dependents. In some places, women and men have received co-educational training, and women trained in areas that had previously been closed to them, such as weapons.

Sea duty and flight training had also been closed to women, but changes were also occurring in these areas. The Navy began training its first women pilots, and in 1973, six women became the first female naval aviators. That same year, the Army opened its aviation program to women, one of whom, Lieutenant Sally Murphy, became the first female Army helicopter pilot. In 1976, the first group of women arrived for flight training at Lackland Air Force Base.

The Coast Guard made plans for mixed crews of men and women. In 1977, the USCGC *Morgenthau* and the USCGC *Gallantin*, both high-endurance cutters, became the first ships in which women were assigned as permanent crew members.

The Navy slowly moved toward assigning women to limited sea duty. The first group of women to join the crew of a Navy ship, a noncombatant vessel called the USS *Vulcan*, went aboard in 1978. A new law made it possible for women to receive permanent assignments on Navy ships.

By the late 1970s, there were more heated debates over whether or not women should be assigned to combatant ships, as well as to combat aircraft. Late in 1979, the Military Personnel Subcommittee of the House Armed Services Committee held hearings on a proposal from the Department of Defense (DOD) that would have repealed Sections 6015 and 8549 of the Women's Armed Services Integration Act of 1948. Among other things, these restrictions allowed the armed forces to ban women from flying combat planes, firing missiles and artillery, and serving on combat ships. The repeal would have permitted military personnel to assign people to where they were most needed on the basis of individual training, strength, and other qualifications.

During four days of hearings, various people stated their positions. The American Civil Liberties Union (ACLU) was among the organizations that supported the repeal, saying that it discriminated unfairly against women. Various men and women, both inside and out of the military, expressed opinions for and against the proposal. In the end, the restrictions were kept in place; the debate would continue for more than another decade.

Toward Greater Participation

By 1980, there were about 173,450 women in the military. When President Ronald Reagan took office in 1981, he announced plans to build up the nation's defenses and to expand the military as a whole by about 10 percent—about 200,000 more recruits. These men and women would need the education and skills to handle the highly technical equipment and weapons systems that characterized the U.S. military in the late twentieth century.

Yet, in 1981, the Army announced plans to cut back on its recruitment of enlisted women, maintaining that number at about 65,000. Army officials said they would conduct studies to determine how women functioned in the Army and the ways in which pregnancy, single parenthood, and other situations more common to women affected military readiness. The Air Force also proposed a moratorium on recruiting more women.

Critics of such proposals pointed out that problems more typical of male recruits—drug and alcohol abuse and going AWOL (absent without leave)—caused much more lost time at work and were potentially worse threats to military readiness. Others criticized the way the Army had dropped standards for male recruits, enlisting men without high school diplomas, some of whom could not read and comprehend standard training materials.

In July 1981, President Reagan asked a Military Manpower Task Force to study the manpower situation throughout the armed services. The committee, chaired by Secretary of Defense Caspar Weinberger, made its recommendations early in 1982. It stated that women were a vital part of the armed forces and that the administration expected the numbers of female recruits would increase in the future. Secretary Weinberger directed the secretaries of every service branch to eliminate barriers or unfair discrimination that might prevent the military from making the fullest use of women's capabilities.

As more barriers came down, women in the military received more equitable treatment and equal access to health care, training, and higher education through the military, as well as veterans' benefits. For some women, the goal was full participation, with no jobs closed to women. By the late 1980s, they had moved closer to that goal. A DOD task force devised the "Risk Rule" (1988), which forced the different service branches to standardize their approach in deciding what jobs were open to women. The standards were based on how likely a particular job was to involve exposure to direct combat, hostile fire, or capture.

As the 1990s began, women in the American military had broader roles than ever before, more than in some nations but less than others. In comparison, women in Canada, Belgium, Denmark, and Norway were permitted to choose from any position in their nation's military. In the Netherlands, women could serve in any assignments except the Dutch Marines and on submarines. British women were banned from ground combat assignments but could serve in combat aircraft or combatant ships. In Israel, some women were being drafted for a two-year period of service after reaching age 18. But far fewer women than men were drafted, and women were allowed to defer service if they were married, the mother of a small child, or if military service went against their strong religious principles. Women in the Israeli Defense Force (IDF) who were assigned to combat units were performing supportive jobs, not taking part in actual combat.

In 1991, America's all-volunteer army, which now contained the largest number of women in its history—11 percent of all those on active duty and 13 percent of those in the reserves—was put to the test. The Middle Eastern nation of Iraq had invaded its oil-rich neighbor Kuwait in August 1990. During the following months, President George Bush and other world leaders worked to aid Kuwait, a U.S. ally, and to prevent disruption of international oil markets. The situation led to the Persian Gulf War, and American military forces were deployed to fight in a desert region about 7,000 miles from home.

For the first time, on television and in the pages of newspapers and magazines, millions of Americans saw images of women in uniform performing a variety of military jobs. Women served in the air, at sea, and on the ground. They were pilots, military police, repairmen, nurses and physicians, weapons controllers, communications specialists, and operations officers; they launched missiles, drove jeeps and heavy trucks, flew C-141 transports, refueled tanks, delivered supplies, guarded harbors, and served on ships that brought vital supplies and ammunition to the region. Thirteen women died; two became prisoners of war.

The six-week-long war ended in defeat for Hussein, whose troops were driven out of Kuwait. The U.S. military was widely praised for its performance in the Gulf. Author Jeanne Holm, a retired major general in the Air Force, writes, "Throughout the war the women demonstrated that, like the men, they had the right stuff. They did the jobs they were trained to do and did them well. They asked for no special favors and received none" [Holm 1992].

Statistics from the U.S. Department of Defense (DOD) showed that 40,782 women, about 7.2 percent of the total number deployed to the Gulf, were women. By 1992, there were 3,130,200 people serving in the U.S. military. Of these, 2,002,600 were on active duty (full-time military employees) while 1,127,600 were in the reserves (part-time personnel). Women made up 11.4 percent of the active duty forces and 13.3 percent of the reserves.

That year, in the wake of the Gulf War, Presidential Commission on the Assignment of Women in the Armed Forces reopened the debate on whether women should still be banned from combat aircraft positions and ground combat positions. Deciding to continue the ban, the commission did recommend that women be permitted on combatant vessels other than submarines and amphibious vessels.

The early nineties saw gains for women in several areas. The Women's Veterans Health Program Act of 1992 directed VA hospitals to expand services for women. They began providing breast exams (including mammography), Pap smears, and reproductive health services, as well as medical care for menopause. Mental health services were increased, with more comprehensive care for post-traumatic stress disorder (PTSD) and the after-effects of sexual abuse in the military.

In 1993, under President Bill Clinton, Secretary of Defense Les Aspin ordered the armed forces to eliminate most restrictions barring women from aerial or naval combat. Women became eligible to fly aircraft in combat and to serve on combat vessels. The Marine Corps said that women could apply to serve as aircraft pilots or on the crews of aircraft. They said they would consider assigning women to ground combat duty, particularly to units unlikely to face combat—e.g. field artillery and air defense. After Aspin issued his directives, the Navy gave women assignments on combatant vessels and added women to other seagoing vessels.

By 1995, women had more opportunities than ever before. Within less than a century, military women had made incredible strides, reflecting other sweeping changes in women's legal rights, political power, and access to professions and activities that had once been closed to women. Women in every branch of the service had shattered myths and attitudes about what women can and should do.

Several questions remain as the United States moves into the twenty-first century. Should women and men serve in the military on terms that are completely gender-neutral, so that they face the same risks? Will women, like men, ever be obliged to register with the selective service? How can the nation maintain an efficient, top-notch military, one that draws talented people able to handle military jobs, many of which involve sophisticated technology? What standards can be used to choose the right people for the right jobs, regardless of gender? However these questions are resolved, women are clearly a permanent part of the U.S. military. They will continue to take an active role in shaping policy, as they continue to contribute to the nation's defense.

Academies

See Military Academies; United States Air Force Academy (USAFA); United States Military Academy (USMA); United States Naval Academy (USNA).

Adams, Charity (b. 1918)

During World War II, Charity Adams was commander of the first battalion of African-American women to serve in Europe. She later became the first African-American woman to achieve the rank of major.

Adams served in the Women's Auxiliary Army Corps (WAAC) during the war. Under pressure from African-American groups, units of black WAACs were directed to serve in the European theater. Eight hundred WAACS in the 6888th Central Postal Battalion, all chosen from the Air Forces and Service Forces, were charged with running a central postal directory. With Adams in command, the battalion arrived in Europe in February 1945 and stayed until six months after the war ended.

After the war, Adams was promoted to lieutenant colonel. She later wrote *One Woman's Army: A Black Officer Remembers the WAC*, a book about her army experiences, under her married name, Charity Adams Earley.

References

Charity Adams Earley, *One Woman's Army: A Black Officer Remembers the WAC* (1989); Martha S. Putney, *When the Nation Was in Need: Blacks in the Women's Army Corps during World War II* (1992); Mattie E. Treadwell, *U.S. Army in World War II: Special Studies–The Women's Army Corps* (1954).

Aerial Nurse Corps of America

See Volunteers.

Affirmative Action

The term *affirmative action* refers to efforts to make up for past discrimination that has caused a particular group of people to experience disadvantages. Programs of affirmative action have addressed long-standing discrimination and unfair treatment toward African Americans in business, education, and the workplace, for example.

In the military, individual women and women as a group have experienced discrimination through the years, being barred from many assignments and promotions. Since 1980, a unified promotion system has been in effect in the army so that women and men are promoted from the same lists. The written guidelines outlined in the Defense Officer Personnel Management Act (DOPMA) enacted in 1980, for those who have the power to implement promotions in the armed services, include instructions to look out for discrimination in the form of lower evaluation reports and assignments that involve less prestige and less authority. Leaders have been advised by the text of DOPMA, "The goal is to achieve a percentage of minority and female selections that is not less than the selection rate for the number of [soldiers] in the promotion zone (first time considered category)."

Affirmative action policies in the military are controversial, just as they are in civilian life. Critics have said that affirmative action programs lead to preferential treatment of certain groups and may not bring effective or positive results. Women have also said they do not want to be perceived as not deserving the promotions they receive.

Debating this issue, Army captain and social sciences professor Richard D. Hooker, Jr., has said, "As a group, women in the Army have enjoyed greater promotion success than men for almost a decade. Individually, some less-well-qualified candidates have inevitably been selected for promotion and command—an unavoidable price, perhaps, of a necessary and just commitment to the achievement of parity, but one with unpleasant side-effects just the same." Hooker believes that the Army has been carrying out "an aggressive and comprehensive affirmative action agenda."

References

Presidential Commission on the Assignment of Women in the Military 1980–90 (June 1990); Carol Wekesser and Matthew Polesetsky, eds., *Women in the Military* (1991).

African Americans

Since the earliest days in American history, black women have taken part in wars. During the American Revolution, 20-year-old Lucretia Emmons bravely stayed in the house in Monmouth County, New Jersey, where she worked as a servant, to defend it against 60 armed Tories. She and Captain Joshua Huddy outwitted the Tories by running from one window to another, shooting at their attackers. This led the Tories to believe a larger group of people were inside. As the Tories were about to set the house on fire, a rescue group arrived to save Huddy and Emmons.

African-American poet Phillis Wheatley, a former slave, was a loyal patriot. In October 1775, 23-year-old Wheatley wrote a poem praising General George Washington. The 42-line tribute was praised by the public, and Washington took time to write a letter personally thanking Wheatley. He invited her to visit army headquarters in Cambridge, Massachusetts. It was highly unusual in those days for a woman, particularly an African-American woman, to be received by a top military officer. Later, the *Pennsylvania Gazette* published Wheatley's poem, a stirring call for patriotism and victory for the colonists.

During the Civil War, black women served as nurses, spies, and couriers, as well as in other capacities, almost always for the Union Army. Some followed regiments of black soldiers to cook, do laundry, and nurse the sick and wounded. The remarkable Harriet Tubman, a leader in the Underground Railroad, performed numerous services, including nursing black soldiers and spying for the Union. Tubman helped Union military officers to plan attacks in territory she had grown to know during her numerous trips bringing escaped slaves out of the South.

Black women were eager to serve during World War I. However, prejudices against African Americans were so great, particularly among those raised in the segregated South, that the armed forces maintained official policies that discriminated against blacks. Servicemen were assigned to segregated units. Black nurses were denied jobs with the military, and many women who wished to volunteer with various organizations were also

An African-American welder in Daytona Beach, Florida, during World War II. Although African Americans made up a large part of the work force, they were often refused positions in defense plants. In 1941, civil rights activists prompted President Roosevelt to issue Executive Order 8802, which banned discrimination in defense industries.

rejected. A few outstanding African-American women managed to overcome these obstacles and serve overseas during the war.

Some progress was made during World War II. African-American women were already a major part of the work force; by 1941, more than 38 percent of black women in the United States were working outside the home, often as maids or cooks in private homes or institutions. Mobilized by various black leaders, including educator and civil rights advocate Mary McCleod Bethune, African Americans demanded their share of opportunity in defense plants and in military jobs. Bethune, a friend of President and Mrs. Roosevelt, used her personal and political influence to fight racism during the war. The black press and leaders such as labor organizer A. Philip Randolph called for a "Double V" campaign, stressing the need to win the war abroad and also to defeat racism at home.

Plants that refused to hire black workers were picketed by African-American citizens, and this caused some companies to change their policies. After black activists told the president they planned to send 100,000 protestors to march in Washington, D.C., Roosevelt issued Executive Order 8802, banning discrimination in defense industries. It also said that companies refusing to hire black workers would lose their government contracts.

In some defense plants, unfortunately, African Americans were assigned to the most difficult, dangerous, dirty, and uncomfortable jobs. Some plants continued to reject black applicants in order to avoid problems with workers who had racist attitudes.

African-American women officially joined the military during World War II. About 4,000 black women served in the Women's Army Auxiliary Corps (WAAC) and Women's Army Corps (WAC). As black women entered the service, many had new opportunities to travel and try different jobs, both at home and abroad.

Of the 440 women who reported for officer training in the first group of WAAC trainees (July 1942), 39 were African Americans. A quota of up to 10.6 percent had been set by the War Department. Like black men, the women served in units with other blacks. Following the then-segregated policies of the military, enlisted WAACs were assigned to a separate area of the dormitory and often were kept separate during sports and social functions. The women officers had integrated housing and mess service. Unlike the men's units, which were commanded by white officers, black women officers were in charge of African-American WAAC units.

Throughout the war, Bethune and another prominent African-American leader, Major Harriet M. West, continued to monitor the treatment of black servicewomen and to inform public officials about difficulties. They objected to special recruiting days held for black women only, as well as problems with transportation and the harassment that African-American Wacs endured in the South. In a letter to the editor of the *Houston Informer*, an African-American Wac stationed in Tennessee pleaded with the public for a show of democracy at home toward black servicepeople who were fighting in the war effort for that very cause. She wrote,

> Did not our forefathers fight and
> die
> For these United States.
> Have we not answered every
> cry
> To make this nation great?

She added, "I am really disheartened more than words can say, that I, and thousands of decent girls, abandoned colleges, clubs and friends who were most dear to us to join the Women's Army Corps to do a job and do it well, feeling that we were needed and could do our share to help the boys over there."

More than 500 black women eventually served as nurses in the Army during World War II, most assigned to duty stations with black servicemen and prisoners of war. Yet the Navy did not accept black nurses until January 1945. The Red Cross maintained segregated programs for the 252 black women who served overseas during the war.

In 1948, President Harry Truman ended segregation policies in the U.S. Armed Forces. This began the process that ended official policies of discrimination against African Americans and prevented them from having equal opportunities for jobs and promotions. Racial quotas were no longer permitted.

In 1973, the All-Volunteer Force (AVF) was enacted by Congress, ending the draft. By 1991, African Americans made up about 12 percent of the population of the United States, but accounted for more than 30 percent of the military. Of the women serving in the Persian Gulf War, 40 percent were African Americans.

African Americans are now a significant part of every branch of service and have proven their ability in every type of military job. Many black women have said the military offers them equal opportunities in all areas. Some have stated that during their military service, they experienced more discrimination as a result of being women than because of race.

See also

Adams, Charity; Army Expert Field Medical Badge; Army Nurse Corps (ANC); Bethune, Mary McCleod; Cadoria, Sherian Grace; Harris, Marcelite J.; SPAR; Taylor, Susie King; Tubman, Harriet; Volunteers; Young Women's Christian Association (YWCA).

References

Penny Colman, *Rosie the Riveter: Women Working on the Home Front in World War II* (1995); Jesse J. Johnson, *Black Women in the Armed Forces, 1941–1974* (1974); Jacqueline Jones, *Labor of Love, Labor of Sorrow: Black Women, Work, and the Family from Slavery to the Present* (1985); Sidney Kaplan, *The Black Presence in the Era of the American Revolution, 1770–1800* (1973); Judy Barrett Litoff and David C. Smith, eds., *We're in This War, Too: World War II Letters from American Women in Uniform* (1994); Joe H. Mays, *Black Americans and Their Contributions toward Union Victory in the American Civil War (1861–1865)* (1894); Martha S. Putney, *When the Nation Was in Need: Blacks in the Women's Army Corps during World War II* (1992); Mattie E. Treadwell, *U.S. Army in World War II: Special Studies–The Women's Army Corps* (1954); Carl Van Doren, *Secret History of the American Revolution* (1941).

Air Command and Staff College

See United States Army.

Air Force, United States

See United States Air Force.

Air Force Academy, United States

See United States Air Force Academy (USAFA).

Air Force Medical Specialists Corps

The Air Force Medical Specialists Corps was established in 1949 as one of nine women's components in the armed forces. Both the Army and Air Force had separate medical corps for women. Within a few years, the medical corps and nursing were integrated to include men and women.

Air Force Nurse Corps (AFNC)

The Air Force Nurse Corps (AFNC) was created in 1949, shortly after the Air Force became a separate branch of service from the Army. Many of the nurses in the AFNC had served during World War II in the Army Nurse Corps (ANC).

Nurses in the AFNC were praised for their exceptional performance during the Vietnam War. Flight nurses worked on med-evac planes that airlifted casualties from an area of about 6 million square miles. These nurses often worked difficult days lasting 12 hours or more. Their work included situations in which they might load a few dozen seriously wounded men into a plane as quickly as possible, even under fire. They were trained to use weapons in case they needed them in dangerous areas. Several Air Force nurses received medals for bravery in Vietnam.

During the war, 54 Air Force nurses worked in the Southeast Asia theater taking the wounded from Vietnam and Thailand to hospitals in Japan, Okinawa, and the Philippines. Other flight nurses accompanied the wounded from these medical centers to the United States in planes that were set up and equipped like hospitals. Most of these nurses worked on their own, since doctors did not usually fly on these planes.

See also

Army Nurse Corps (ANC); Vietnam War.

References

Jeanne Holm, *Women in the Military: An Unfinished Revolution* (1992); Lynda Van Devanter, *Home before Morning: The Story of a Nurse in Vietnam* (1983).

Air Medal

For their service in World War II, several women in the Women's Army Corps (WAC) received the Air Medal. One received the medal for helping to map the Hump, a region in India. Another who died during the crash of an aerial broadcasting plane received the medal posthumously.

Barbara Erickson, a member of the Women's Auxiliary Service Pilots (WASP), received this prestigious medal in 1944. In only five days, Erickson had managed to deliver a P-51, two P-47s, and a C-47 DC-3 cargo transport to their destinations. These flights covered a distance of 6,000 miles and 40 flying hours, six times the usual flying hours for most ferrying pilots. This made Erickson the first civilian to receive the Air Medal since Amelia Earhart.

See also

Avenger Field; Decorations.

References

Sally Van Wagenen Keil, *Those Wonderful Women in Their Flying Machines* (1990);

Mattie E. Treadwell, *U.S. Army in World War II: Special Studies–The Women's Army Corps* (1954).

Air Traffic Controllers

During World War II, members of the Women Accepted for Voluntary Emergency Service (WAVES) began working in this job, with new technology that was also unfamiliar to male controllers. At that time, simple radios and blinking lights were the major means by which controllers performed their jobs.

One problem that emerged as women took over these types of duties was their uniforms. Waves found that the skirts of their uniforms were designed in such a way that they could not gracefully climb up to control towers.

Most of all, though, they faced resistance from men who believed women did not have the intellectual and mechanical ability to learn how to understand charts, meteorology, and the use of the radio. Critics also complained that women were not emotionally strong enough to handle this high-pressure work. Women showed they could perform well as controllers, however; about 60 percent of all men in these jobs were replaced by women during the war.

Although women had shown themselves capable of this work, after the war it was assumed that they would no longer hold such jobs. Women who wished to work as control-tower operators, mechanics, and pilots were rejected in favor of men, just as women factory workers found themselves dismissed from their jobs. Those women who wanted to stay in the field of aviation were steered into jobs as clerks, secretaries, and stewardesses.

References

Sally Van Wagenen Keil, *Those Wonderful Women in Their Flying Machines* (1990); Doris Weatherford, *American Women and World War II* (1990).

Air-Wacs

During World War II, women became Air-Wacs (Army Air Forces Wacs) under the leadership of the Army, since the Army and Air Force were merged at that time.

General Henry "Hap" Arnold strongly supported the development of a women's corps. It was Arnold who had also asked aviator Jacqueline Cochran to organize the Women's Airforce Service Pilots (WASP) to ferry planes for the British war effort, then for the United States military. With the support of other high-ranking Air Force officials, Arnold urged training schools to open all areas except combat and flying school to women.

About 40,000 women served as Air-Wacs during the war. Some 50 percent of these women worked in more conventional clerical and administrative positions. Others worked as aerial photographers, flying radio operators, flight clerks, and aircraft mechanics. In addition, Air-Wacs were weather forecasters, teletype operators, radio mechanics, control tower specialists, parachute riggers, radar operators, dieticians, reporters, and chemists, among other things. One even served as a dog trainer.

When the war ended, most Air-Wacs returned to civilian life. Some returned to the service in 1948 after the Air Force became a separate branch of service and the Women in the Air Force (WAF) was established.

See also
Cochran, Jacqueline; Women's Airforce Service Pilots (WASP).

References
Jeanne Holm, *Women in the Military: An Unfinished Revolution* (1992); Helen Rogan, *Mixed Company: Women in the Modern Army* (1981).

Alcott, Louisa May (1832–1888)

Best known as the author of such classic books as *Little Women*, Louisa May Alcott served as a nurse for the Union Army during the Civil War. During that time, Alcott kept a diary that she later turned into a book called *Hospital Sketches*, published in 1863.

Alcott was born in Germantown, Pennsylvania, the daughter of Bronson Alcott, a famous educator. Bronson then moved the family to Concord, Massachusetts, a gathering place for innovative minds. Among the family's friends were Nathaniel Hawthorne, Ralph Waldo Emerson, and Henry David Thoreau. The Alcott children were reared to take an active interest in politics and social reform.

During her youth, Alcott worked as a seamstress, housekeeper, and teacher. Eager for adventure, in 1862 she left Concord for Washington, D.C., to nurse wounded soldiers in an army hospital. More than 250,000 soldiers were camping near the capitol at that time. She later said that her army experience included "painful duties all day long, & . . . a life of constant excitement. . . ."

Alcott began her duties in January 1863 at the Union Hotel Hospital, which had been converted from a hotel into an army medical center. Three days after she arrived, the Battle of Fredericksburg was fought in nearby Virginia and hundreds of wounded men began arriving at the hospital. Alcott was in charge of a ward with 40 beds for seriously wounded men, many of them missing arms or legs. Also at the hospital were men suffering from severe cases of pneumonia, measles, typhoid fever, and other diseases.

In her memoir, she described the scene at the hospital during those days: "In they came, some on stretchers, some in men's arms, some feebly staggering along propped on rude crutches, and one lay stark and still with covered face, as his comrade gave his name to be recorded before they carried him away to the death house. All was hurry and confusion; the hall was full of these wrecks of humanity, for the most exhausted could not reach a bed till duly ticketed and registered. . . ."

References
Louisa May Alcott, *Hospital Sketches* (1957); Cornelia Meigs, *Invincible Louisa* (1933); Joel Myerson and Daniel Shealy, eds., *The Journals of Louisa May Alcott* (1989).

Allen, Eliza (b. 1826)

A native of Eastport, Maine, Eliza Allen left home as a teenager after her family refused to let her marry a man with whom she had fallen in love. Disguising herself as a man, Allen went to fight in the war against Mexico, detailing her experiences in the memoirs she published in 1851. Allen described her autobiography, *The Female Volunteer; or the Life, and Wonderful Adventures of Miss Eliza Allen, a Young Lady of Eastport, Maine*, as "An Authentic and Thrilling Narrative."

All-Volunteer Force (AVF)

In 1973, under President Richard M. Nixon, Congress ended the military draft and created an all-volunteer military. Public opinion had been mounting during the late 1960s in support of this idea, which would end involuntary conscription of young men into the armed services.

After taking office in 1968, Nixon appointed former secretary of defense Thomas S. Gates, Jr., to head a commission to study the idea of an all-volunteer force (AVF). In addition to studying the way such a program would work, the Gates Commission looked at ways in which young people could be attracted to and retained by the military. Their report, submitted to the president in 1970, supported the idea of the AVF, saying that it would not threaten U.S. national security.

The report focused on men and did not discuss how women would fit into plans for an AVF. The commission pointed out, however, that most military positions would not be related to combat missions. This meant that many positions could be filled by either men or women, without any changes being made in the laws that excluded women from combat roles.

Late in 1971, the Central All-Volunteer Task Force, set up by the Department of Defense, studied the use of military women in the new system. In March 1972, several high-ranking military women and men testified before a congressional subcommittee about potential roles for women in the AVF. The subcommittee made a statement supporting a larger role for women in the military, saying, "We are convinced that in the atmosphere of a zero draft environment or an all-volunteer military force, women could and should play a more important role." The committee urged the secretary of defense to develop programs in line with this recommendation.

Each branch of service did develop such plans in the months that followed. The draft was eliminated early in 1973.

See also
Binkin-Bach Study; Draft.

References
Martin Binkin and Shirley J. Bach, *Women and the Military* (1977); Nancy Loring Goldman, ed., *Female Soldiers—Combatants or Noncombatants?* (1982); "One Way To Avoid a New Draft: Recruit More Females," *U.S. News and World Report* (14 February 1977); Helen Rogan, *Mixed Company: Women in the Modern Army* (1981).

American Expeditionary Forces (AEF)

The American Expeditionary Forces (AEF) were the U.S. Army's fighting units stationed in Europe during World War I. Finding itself with an acute manpower shortage, the AEF hired about 1,000 U.S. women as civilian contract employees. On 8 October 1917, General John J. Pershing cabled his need for 100 women telephone operators, since there was a shortage of French-speaking operators in France, where he was leading the AEF.

These women were sent overseas to serve with the AEF as translators, telephone operators, and in other positions as needed. As contract employees, they were accorded status and benefits similar to women in the Army Nurse Corps (ANC). They did not receive medical benefits or aid to their dependents while they were in the service or any veterans' benefits afterward. (Other groups of people were also sent overseas to perform different jobs needed by the Army under contract and none received full military status.)

Women who suffered from health problems due to their service with the AEF were not legally entitled to any compensation from the Army in later years. The War Department declared that "Female telephone operators have no military status whatever . . ." and that in their opinion, Congress did not intend to pay anyone who had not been an official member of the military. In some individual cases, however, Congress was moved to appropriate compensation for those who were clearly disabled as a result of their service in the war.

References

Dorothy and Carl J. Schneider, *Into the Breach: American Women Overseas in World War I* (1991); June A. Willenz, *Women Veterans: America's Forgotten Heroines* (1983).

American Red Cross (ARC)

The American Red Cross (ARC) was established in 1881 by Clara Barton, known for her work as a nurse on the battlefields of the Civil War. After the war, Barton was in poor health and traveled to Europe to recuperate. While there, she began working with the International Red Cross (IRC), founded by a nineteenth-century Swiss philanthropist, Jean Henri Dunant, to aid those involved in the Franco-Prussian War. Barton was impressed by the organized way in which the IRC was able to aid victims of the war.

After returning to the United States in 1871, Barton spent the next ten years convincing Americans that they needed a national version of the IRC to aid those in need during wartime and other large-scale emergencies or disasters.

On its own, with Barton at the head, the American Red Cross started its work in 1881. It began sending workers to the scenes of fires, hurricanes, and floods, including the devastating Johnstown, Pennsylvania, flood of 1889. Barton had not been able to garner widespread support for the ARC until the work of volunteers in Johnstown brought nationwide attention to the group and its work. In 1900, Congress officially chartered the organization, which supplied aid in the Spanish-American War.

During the 1900s, the American Red Cross was actively involved in both world wars. Of the thousands of volunteers who aided victims and soldiers, most were women. On the home front, the Red Cross ran blood drives and held first aid and home nursing courses for civilians.

Many women who volunteered to serve with the Red Cross during World War II worked overseas in Europe, Asia, and the South Pacific. They operated service clubs, snack bars, and recreation programs; served in hospitals and on hospital ships; and ran errands, among other things.

The arrival of Red Cross ships often meant survival, as when ARC representatives arrived in Manila early in 1944 to aid prisoners of war at the Santo Tomas prison. Hundreds of Army nurses and civilian women at the prison were going hungry as the Japanese curbed food rations to rice and

An American Red Cross hospital worker carries a supply box and a German ammunition box while in Italy in 1943.

one vegetable a day near the end of the war. The ARC brought the prisoners kits containing vitamins, canned and dried foods, cheese, and medicines.

Women working in the Red Cross during the Vietnam War continued to have auxiliary military status but were given military identifications and standard ranks. Some worked in a unit called Supplemental Recreational Activities Overseas. These auxiliary personnel were provided with medical insurance coverage while in the military, assistance that continued afterwards only for some women.

See also

Barton, Clara; Canteens; Clubmobiles; Volunteers.

References

William E. Barton, *The Life of Clara Barton, Founder of the American Red Cross* (1922); Foster Rhea Dulles, *The American Red Cross: A History* (1950); Patrick F. Gilbo, *The American Red Cross: The First Century* (1981); Judy Barrett Litoff and David C. Smith, eds., *We're in This War, Too: World War II Letters from Women in Uniform* (1994); Doris Weatherford, *American Women in World War II* (1990).

American Revolution

American women have been involved in the military since the American Revolution. In the years before the war, women expressed their rebellion against British rule by boycotting

British products, including sugar, wine, silk, linen, tea, paper, and glass. Abigail Adams, wife of patriot and future president John Adams, encouraged other women to forego certain domestic pleasures because of "the great and important duty you owe your country." She declared, "If our country perishes, it is as impossible to save the individual, as to preserve one of the fingers of a mortified hand."

Women took part in the Revolution in numerous ways—as nurses, spies, scouts, relief workers, fund-raisers, and camp followers. Many women hosted important meetings and prepared meals or other supplies for government officials and those serving on either side.

Some daring women pretended to be men and joined the army as soldiers or irregular fighters affiliated with local militia units. An unknown number of women enlisted in the army. Boys as young as 12 could be found serving as soldiers at that time, so while some women were discovered and discharged, many women were able to blend in and escape detection. The best-known of these women soldiers was Deborah Sampson. Another woman soldier, Sally St. Clair, was killed during the Battle of Savannah.

It was not unusual for wives, mothers, and daughters to accompany male relatives to camps. Usually, poorer people who went along were allowed rations of food in return for services—cooking, laundry, mending, molding bullets, and loading muskets. Around three to six of these helpers were authorized for each company.

Volunteers nursed the wounded, serving them broth, coffee, bread, and potatoes. Usually, women were not shot or arrested and could move about to get water and other supplies for the wounded. There were also paid employees in the army's medical service. On 27 July 1775, the Second Continental Congress addressed medical care for the 20,000 men serving in the army. They agreed that for every ten patients, one nurse and a matron would be hired. In the beginning, nurses received $2 per month and one ration per day; two years later, the pay increased to $8 per month. Although they received wages from the army, the nurses were viewed as civilian employees.

Women raised money to buy supplies and ammunition for the army and sent melted leaded windowpanes, family heirlooms made of pewter, and clock parts to make musket balls for guns. They held scrap drives, collecting pewter dishes, forks, fishnet weights, and any other materials that could be melted into shot. Some women's groups even made cartridges, such as the women from Litchfield, Connecticut, who managed to get possession of a statue of George III from New York, and then melted it for the lead. After pouring it into molds, they wrapped each bullet in oiled paper along with some gunpowder for a musket, producing more than 42,000 cartridges.

Because British goods were unavailable and cloth cost as much as $20 a yard, women struggled to feed and clothe their families. Those at home made sacrifices and worked many hours each day to supply the troops with clothing and other items. At Valley Forge during the harsh winter of

1777–1778 when General George Washington encamped there, women knit and spun for the troops and brought them blankets and used clothing, sometimes by horse.

One well-to-do woman wrote to a British officer, "I will tell you what I have done. . . . I have retrenched every superfluous expense in my table and family; tea I have not drunk since last Christmas, nor bought a new cap and gown since your defeat at Lexington; and what I never did before, have learned to knit, and am now making stockings of American wool for my servants. . . . These are the sentiments of all my sister Americans."

Women took to arms to protect their homes, families, and towns. In Groton, Massachusetts, after the local regiment had departed, Mrs. David Wright led a group of women, dressed in their husbands' clothing, to gather muskets and pitchforks. Stationed at the town bridge, they stopped the first enemy soldier who reached it—Captain Leonard Whiting, a Tory. "Sergeant" Wright and her group arrested him, searched him, and found dispatches for the British in Boston. He was taken to jail.

North Carolinian Jane Thomas fended off some Tories who had come to her home to take stored ammunition. While Thomas's daughters rapidly loaded and reloaded her husband's guns, she and a boy living at the house fired them so fast that the Tories thought a large group was inside and retreated. The ammunition was later used by the Continental Army in the battles of Rocky Mount and Hanging Rock. Thomas also once rode her horse for two days to warn her sons' regiment at Cedar Spring about a surprise attack after overhearing a Tory conversation. A number of other women spied, eavesdropping on enemy conversations at homes or inns, and carried their messages to the troops.

In Groton, Massachusetts, a Mrs. Wright and Mrs. Shattuck organized a women's militia when they heard British troops were coming. The women dressed in men's clothing and gathered muskets and other available weapons. They were able to scare away the British on Jewett's Bridge.

Some women defended their homes against attack or being taken over by British troops ("scavengers") who foraged homes for food and other items and stole horses and livestock. Enemy troops also burned a number of homes. In South Carolina, making a large sacrifice for the cause of liberty, Rebecca Motte told American soldiers to burn her house down. It was being used as a headquarters by the British and she preferred to have it destroyed rather than see the opposition profit from its existence.

Women organized groups to provide assistance to the troops. In Philadelphia, Esther Reed was the cofounder of a 35-woman committee that raised money to buy supplies and clothing for soldiers in the Continental Army.

After the men went to war, women took over their roles on farms and at other jobs. They also worked as gunsmiths, flag-makers, and blacksmiths, and they wrote military articles for the papers. Women published patriotic newspapers, some after their husbands had died and left them with the business. Anna Catherine Green (circa 1720–1775) took over the *Maryland Gazette* in 1767 and published articles supporting the resistance efforts of colonists at the Boston Tea Party and opposing the 1776 Townshend Acts, which taxed English products, including paper, glass, and tea.

During the Revolution, Mary Lindley Murray was among the quick-thinking women who helped the military. Murray was a rebel sympathizer. One September day in 1776, she saw a chance to help the army by delaying the progress of British General Howe. Known for her hospitality, Murray kept urging the general to consume more food and wine as she and her daughters charmed his entourage with conversation. As they delayed the British, rebel troops under General Israel Putnam moved ahead to safely join their group on the northern tip of Manhattan Island. Had Howe proceeded earlier along his planned route, his troops would have been able to apprehend Putnam and those with him. A portrait of Mary Murray entertaining the British was placed on display at the Museum of the City of New York for the Bicentennial Celebration of the nation's independence in 1976.

The 1777 death of a woman named Jane McCrea increased hostility toward the British and encouraged more patriots to join the colonial army. McCrea, the 24-year-old daughter of a Presbyterian minister, was brutally killed by Indians fighting under the direction of British General John Burgoyne at the Battle of Saratoga. McCrea was to be married that night to an officer in Burgoyne's regiment, but the Indians who were to escort her quarreled along the way and she became a victim during their fight. Both sides denounced the way McCrea had been scalped and stabbed to death. Speeches were also made in the English Parliament denouncing the practice of using Indians to fight in the war.

Historians have said that the outcry over McCrea's death led American troops to fight hard, winning a decisive victory at Saratoga. After that victory, France decided to aid the Americans in their struggle for independence from Great Britain.

African Americans took part in the war. Black historian William C. Nell compiled what is regarded as the first researched study of blacks in the Revolution. In *The Colored Patriots of the American Revolution*, Nell described the bravery of both men and women. One woman, a slave in Virginia, worked for the Continental Army running bullets. Yet after the war, Nell reported, the woman was kept in slavery until she managed to escape to Canada at about 80 years of age.

Women's efforts in the American Revolution were praised and appreciated by many. After the war, George Washington sent a letter to the Daughters of Liberty, which said, in part:

> The army ought not to regret their sacrifices or sufferings when they meet with so flattering a reward as the sympathy of your sex; nor can they fear that their interests will be neglected, while espoused by advocates as powerful as they are amiable.

See also
Bailey, Anne; Corbin, Margaret; Darragh, Lydia; Daughters of Liberty; Geiger, Emily; Hays, Mary Ludwig; Johnson, Jemima; Passing.
References
Katherine and John Bakeless, *Spies in the Revolution* (1969); Charles E. Claghorn, *Women Patriots of the American Revolution: A Biographical Dictionary* (1991); Linda Grant De Pauw, *Founding Mothers: Women of America in the Revolutionary Era* (1975); Elizabeth Evans, *Weathering the Storm: Women of the American Revolution* (1975); Catherine Fennelly, *Connecticut Women in the Revolutionary Era* (1975); Selma Williams, *Demeter's Daughters: The Women Who Founded America* (1976).

Antiaircraft Artillery (AAA)

During World War II, manpower shortages led to changing policies about what roles could be filled by women. In December 1942, General George C. Marshall, head of the American Expeditionary Force (AEF) in Europe, asked that the Army investigate whether women could perform certain antiaircraft artillery (AAA) duties.

During AAA testing, conducted on the East Coast, men and women worked together in a tactical unit. The experiment was classified. It represented the only instance up to that date in which women were tried in tactical combat roles. They were given the opportunity to try half the jobs in the experiment, which did not include firing weapons.

Those running the tests concluded that the women were competent to perform a number of AAA tasks, especially those involving manual dexterity. By the time the tests were over, military officials had concluded that there was no threat of enemy attacks on the East Coast, so women were not deployed in any AAA positions.

At Camp Davis in North Carolina, 25 of the top women pilots with the Women's Air Service Pilots (WASP) also flew in antiaircraft exercises during top-secret tests, towing targets at which men on the ground aimed antiaircraft guns.

See also
Casualties.
References
Jeanne Holm, *Women in the Military: An Unfinished Revolution* (1992); Ken Magid, *Women of Courage: The Women Airforce Service Pilots of World War II* (1993); Sally Van Wagenen Keil, *Those Wonderful Women in Their Flying Machines* (1990).

Appearance

As part of their training and ongoing supervision, men and women in the military have traditionally been told how to wear their uniforms and style their hair. Added to this, women have been given guidelines about how to apply makeup and wear jewelry in keeping with military rules. They are graded on their appearance during inspections.

For women in the Marines, the dress uniform requirements include having one's skirt at the proper length and a hairstyle that does not touch the bottom of the uniform collar. Long hair must be pinned or braided neatly to meet this requirement.

Appearance has been more of an issue for women in the military than for men. At times, critics have charged that women were rejected from various service branches on the basis of personal appearance issues that were not related to competence. This may be related to the issues of femininity of women in the military and a prejudice against women who appear "unfeminine" or who might not be heterosexual.

Official documents show that appearance was mentioned specifically while qualifying women. In 1964, for example, an Air Force board stated that it wished women recruited into that branch of service to be the "smallest group of women in the military service" and that they should be "the most attractive and useful women in the four line services," according to author Jeanne Holm, a retired Air Force major general. In 1966, the Air Force chief of staff asked the commander of the Recruiting Service to get "better-looking" recruits. Women applying to the Air Force were required to have four photos taken of four different views of their faces.

Training for women during these years included courses in manners, posture, hairstyling, and applying cosmetics—courses that some critics compared to finishing schools. Navy regulations stated that the women's hair should be "arranged and shaped to present a conservative, feminine appearance." Women were taught to be "ladylike" in appearance and behavior and were given specific instructions.

Since the 1970s, as women became integrated into the regular military and the segregated women's corps were disestablished, ideas about appearance underwent changes as well. Since that time, women have been subjected to fewer and fewer rules that make appearance more of an issue for women than men.

References
Betty Friedan, *The Feminine Mystique* (1963); Jeanne Holm, *Women in the Military: An Unfinished Revolution* (1992); Mattie E. Treadwell, *U.S. Army in World War II: Special Studies–The Women's Army Corps* (1954).

Army, United States

See United States Army; Women's Army Auxiliary Corps (WAAC); Women's Army Corps (WAC).

Army and Air National Guard

Also called the National Guard, this organization is under federal control during times of emergency. Women serve in the organization on equal terms with men.

Army College Fund

See GI Bill of Rights.

Army Expert Field Medical Badge

In 1967, Clara Adams-Ender, who began serving in the Army Nurse Corps (ANC) in 1961, became the first woman to receive the Army Expert Field Medical Badge. Adams-Ender, a graduate of North Carolina A & T University, was appointed chief of the Army Nurse Corps in 1987 by President Ronald Reagan. An African American, Adams-Ender once stated that she had found sexism to be "more pervasive than racism in the military."

References
Jessie Carney Smith, ed., *Notable Black American Women* (1992); Carol Wekesser and Matthew Polesetsky, eds., *Women in the Military* (1991).

Army Medical Corps (AMC)

Women were not accepted as military physicians until modern times. Before the mid-1800s, women were systematically kept out of U.S. medical colleges. As a result, some American women were trained in European medical schools.

In 1849, Elizabeth Blackwell became the first woman to earn a medical degree from a U.S. medical college. Gradually, medical colleges solely for women were set up in Boston, New York City, and Philadelphia. Still, many hospitals refused to grant female physicians staff privileges at their facilities. As late as 1875, there were state laws that kept women and others from acquiring licenses to practice, even after they had graduated from an approved medical training facility.

Although the Army rejected women physicians during the Civil War, some individual doctors and hospitals used their services. Some women physicians were hired as nurses in army hospitals but performed the functions of physicians when those services were needed.

The military continued to reject women physicians during World War I. A few were hired as contract employees but received less pay than their male counterparts serving in the Army Medical Corps. As contract employees, the women had no military status.

During World War II, military leaders contended that men would be embarrassed to be examined or treated by women doctors, and they also rejected women doctors based on the more familiar argument that women could not withstand the severe physical conditions and emotional stress of combat. Critics of these arguments pointed out that military nurses had already proven that women could function well in combat situations, and that female nurses already were examining and treating male soldiers.

In order to be military doctors, some American women went abroad and served in England during World War II. Others, led by Dr. Emily Barringer, worked to change laws and policies barring women military doctors. They organized a petition drive, testified before members of Congress, and tried to influence the public to accept and support their ideas. A shortage of military physicians increased support for their cause, especially after Congressman John Sparkman of Alabama presented a bill to Congress asking that women physicians be admitted into the Army.

President Franklin Roosevelt signed Sparkman's bill on 16 April 1943. It allowed women physicians to serve only with WAC units, however, and not on medical combat teams where they would have equal status with male physicians. Because of the barriers and limitations on what they could do, fewer than 100 women doctors enlisted during the war. One of the most prominent was Dr. Margaret Janeway, a surgeon who served with a WAAC unit in North Africa and WAC unit in the Mediterranean.

Understandably, the shortage of physicians on the home front during those years led to an increased demand for women doctors in civilian hospitals. Medical schools accepted more women students than ever before, and hospitals opened more internships and residencies to women. After the war, many institutions reverted to their former biases against women in the medical profession and imposed quotas on the number of women they would accept as students or staff members. Even so, women had made inroads and they continued to pursue medical careers.

As the armed services became integrated in the 1970s and discriminatory laws and policies were abolished, women physicians began serving on equal terms with men.

See also
Army Medical Specialists Corps; Barringer, Emily Dunning; Blackwell, Elizabeth Bradwell; Cornum, Rhonda; Craighill, Major Margaret D.

References
Ruth Abram, *Send Us a Lady Physician: Women Doctors in America, 1835–1920* (1985); E. A. Blacksmith, ed., *Women in the Military* (1992); Rhonda Cornum, as told to Peter Copeland, *She Went to War: The Rhonda Cornum Story* (1992); Esther Pohl Lovejoy, *Women Doctors of the World* (1957).

Army Medical Specialists Corps

The Army Medical Specialists Corps was established in 1949 as one of nine women's components in the armed forces, others being the three nursing corps—Army, Navy, and Air Force—and the Women's Army Corps (WAC), Women Accepted for Emergency Service (WAVES), Women's Air Force (WAF), and Women Marines. Both the Army and Air Force had separate medical corps for women. Within the span of a few years, the medical corps and nursing corps would be integrated to include men and women.

Army-Navy Nurse Act

Enacted in April 1947, the Army-Navy Nurse Act (Public Law 36-80C) established the Nurse Corps as a permanent component in both the Army and Navy. Henceforth, nurses in these corps would be integrated into the officer ranks of the regular Army and Navy, with lieutenant colonel/commander being the highest possible rank. This settled the question of whether or not nurses would be given membership in the Regular Officer Corps, a subject of debate during and after World War II.

See also
Air Force Nurse Corps (AFNC); Army Nurse Corps (ANC); Navy Nurse Corps.

Army Nurse Corps (ANC)

Since the American Revolution, women have worked as nurses for the military, assuming more duties and responsibility with each ensuing war. Nurses were the first women to serve in combat areas and the first to receive military rank.

In 1775, Congress passed a bill, sponsored by General George Washington, that created a hospital department for the Army. Under this law, civilian nurses could be hired to serve the military, paid at a rate of about 25 cents a day. Nurses also often performed other duties, such as doing laundry, sewing and mending, and cooking.

Before the 1900s, women often served informally as nurses or on an ad-hoc basis. During the Civil War, some, like Clara Barton, asked the War Department for special passes that allowed them to enter battle areas. Volunteer nurses saved thousands of lives, bringing food and other supplies as well as care and comfort to the troops. In all, about 6,000 nurses served the federal forces. Pay for nurses in military hospitals was about $12 per month.

During the Spanish-American War, 1,158 women served as military nurses, under contracts in which they were paid $30 per month and a daily ration of food. They served in Cuba, Puerto Rico, the Philippines, Hawaii, and China, as well as in the United States. A typhoid epidemic created more casualties than battle for those fighting in this war, also resulting in the deaths of 12 nurses. Another nurse, Clara Louise Maass, died in Cuba of yellow fever in 1901 after volunteering for a military experiment to test ways in which the disease might be transmitted.

By 1901, military officials recognized the need for a permanent corps of nurses, and the Army Nurse Corps (ANC) was created. Women were appointed as nurses in the regular Army for a period of three years. At that time, the corps numbered only a few hundred women. Army officials believed that in the unlikely event of war, American Red Cross (ARC) nurses could meet any extra need. The Navy Nurse Corps (NNC) was established in 1908, again increasing military opportunities for women.

In April 1917 during World War I, there were 403 nurses on active duty. That May, 400 Army nurses were sent to France to serve with the British Expeditionary Forces. They were highly praised for outstanding service in field hospitals and with mobile and evacuation units.

The number of nurses in the corps steadily increased, numbering about 20,000 by the war's end. About 10,000 nurses served overseas in France, Belgium, England, Italy, Serbia, Siberia, Hawaii (then not a state), Puerto Rico, and the Philippines. They served aboard hospital trains and transport ships, in evacuation and field hospitals, and at casualty clearing stations.

Although no nurses died as a result of enemy fire, more than 200 died from influenza and pneumonia. Many nurses received decorations for bravery: three earned the Distinguished Service Cross, and 23 were awarded the Distinguished Service Medal. Many also were honored with foreign decorations: the French Croix de Guerre was awarded to 28 American Army nurses, while the British Royal Red Cross went to 69.

In World War I, nurses worked without any official military rank. They were accorded what is called "relative rank" in 1920, followed by official rank during World War II. During that war, as in others, the vast majority of military nurses were women. Some American nurses began serving in the war before the United States joined the Allies in 1941, going overseas as volunteers to help the British Red Cross in 1940.

World War II saw a critical need for nurses, both in the military and on the home front. In 1940, there were only 700 women serving in the Army Nurse Corps. Those numbers increased dramatically as the Army began recruiting nurses shortly before the United States entered the war. More than 40 percent of all civilian nurses volunteered to serve in the ANC. By April 1941, there were about 700 new recruits each month. This was still not enough to meet the need, which the army estimated at more than 60,000 nurses.

Army nurses enter a trench at Fort Dix during intensive gas tests in June 1941.

Still, the Army continued to reject married nurses, African Americans, males, and those considered "too old" (usually around 45). Numerous qualified black nurses offered their services to the military. They met with discrimination from officials in the ANC, even though official Army policy was to treat all nurses as a single group with no segregation during training or discrimination as to promotions and assignments.

Mabel K. Staupers, executive secretary of the National Association of Colored Graduate Nurses (NACGN), worked hard on behalf of individuals and black nurses as a group. She contacted public officials, organized letter-writing campaigns, and urged that black nurses be integrated fully in the military. She and others protested about unfair treatment of African-American nurses who joined the ANC, some of whom were expected to perform menial jobs instead of giving professional nursing care. Also, disproportionate numbers of black nurses were assigned to care for prisoners of war instead of Americans. African-American nurses stationed at posts in the segregated South were often unable to move about freely or use facilities near their bases, since these were not open to blacks.

As civilian hospitals faced dire shortages, they relied more on volunteers and hastily trained nurses' aides to assume patient care duties. Industry enticed many nurses away from hospitals by offering higher wages and better working conditions, as well as free training programs. Entire units of some hospitals closed down, while nurses worked extra shifts and had ever-increasing patient loads.

The acute need for military nurses induced some politicians to propose drafting nurses. Polls showed that a majority of Americans favored this idea, contending that it was unjust to draft men to fight unless they could be assured of proper medical care while serving in the military.

The Cadet Nurse Corps (CNC) was formed in 1943 to attract more young people into nursing. Cadet nurses received an intensive training, shorter than the usual three years then required for registered nurses in a hospital training school. Their education was financed by the federal government, and upon graduation, they were assigned to active duty or to other service deemed essential.

Once in the military, nurses underwent stringent physical training to prepare them for combat conditions and build the strength they would need to set up hospitals with several hundred beds in remote locations. Like enlisted men, nurses trained on obstacle courses laced with barbed wire while instructors tossed out small explosives and fired live ammunition above them.

Nurses were the first women to see action in World War II and served wherever troops were stationed. Once overseas, they worked in mobile nurses' units as well as in evacuation hospitals where the wounded were received. Nurses near the battlefield could see close to a thousand new victims each day. They might care for 200 patients at a time, all needing high levels of care. The stress of their work compounded when dressings, medicines, stretchers, blood plasma, and other supplies ran out.

This war also marked the first time in which flight nurses served on evacuation flights. Ruth M. Gardiner, an Army flight nurse on such an air evacuation mission, was the first female killed in a theater of operations during World War II.

By 1945, the need for nurses was still so great that President Roosevelt and most members of Congress favored a bill to draft nurses into the military. The war ended that year, however, and the bill was abandoned. All told, during World War II, 201 Army nurses died, 16 as a result of enemy action. More than 1,600 received medals, including the Purple Heart. Among the other decorations nurses received were the Distinguished Service Medal, Silver Star, Distinguished Flying Cross, Soldier's Medal, Bronze Star Medal, Air Medal, Legion of Merit, and Army Commendation Medal.

After the war ended, the need for nurses was still great. Many injured soldiers were in veterans' hospitals. The Army continued to award nursing scholarships, along with stipends, to attract nurses to enlist after completing their education. In Congress, Representative Frances Bolton of Ohio, who had introduced the bill that formed the Cadet Nurse Corps (CNC), continued to support and work for women in the medical and nurse corps. The scholarship program that Bolton had advocated helped men and women to become nurses and physicians.

The Korean War brought nurses back to combat areas. Nurses began serving in Korea four days after the first troops arrived in July 1950. Over 100 nurses had arrived in South Korea within a month after the war began. By the year's end, there were 5,400 people active in the Army Nurse Corps, many of them World War II veterans. They served in 25 treatment facilities, including evacuation, field, and station hospitals, Mobile Surgical Army Hospitals, and hospital trains. No nurses died as a result of enemy action, but Major Genevieve Smith was killed in a plane crash while flying to her duty assignment as chief nurse in Korea. No nurses were taken prisoner by the enemy.

During the Vietnam War, nurses dealt with difficult field conditions in the jungles, and treated grave wounds resulting from booby traps, land mines, and high-speed rifles. As in the Korean War, nurses served in field and evacuation hospitals and Mobile Surgical Army Hospitals (MASH). They also worked aboard planes transporting the wounded and engaged in humanitarian work to aid Vietnamese citizens before and after the war. One nurse, Sharon A. Lane, died as the result of hostile fire.

Military nurses have also been active in peacetime. In November 1956, they cared for refugees after the Hungarian uprising against the Communist regime. In 1958, they worked in Lebanese hospitals while 10,000 troops were stationed there. Army nurses aided earthquake victims in Chile (1960), Iran (1962), Yugoslavia (1963), and Alaska (1964). They have also aided victims of airplane crashes and political strife. In 1982, Army nurses went to the Sinai to help operate two health clinics set up for the United Nations Peacekeeping Force.

In view of the long history of service by military nurses, many people considered it quite fitting that the first female general to receive her star (1970), Anna Mae Hays, was an officer in the nursing service branch.

The organization of health care services in the military has often enabled nurses to assume more responsibility than in civilian jobs. Top-notch facilities and equipment and chances for advanced training and advancement, maximum use of their skills, and further education have drawn women to join the Army Nurse Corps.

See also
African Americans; Army Medical Corps (AMC); Army-Navy Nurse Act; Bataan; Bickerdyke, Mary Ann; Blackwell, Elizabeth Bradwell; Blanchfield Army Community Hospital; Boulay, Donna-Marie; Brantley, Hattie Rilla; Cadet Nurse Corps (CNC); Casualties; Corregidor; Decorations; Dix, Dorothea Lynde; Navy Nurse Corps (NNC); Post-Traumatic Stress Disorder; United States Sanitary Commission; Van Devanter, Lynda; Veterans; Vietnam Women's Memorial.

References
Maj. Edith Aynes, A.N.C., *From Nightingale to Eagle: The Army Nurses History* (1973); Judith Bellefaire, *The Army Nurse Corps in World War II* (1976); Dorothy and Carl J. Schneider, *Into the Breach: American Women Overseas in World War I* (1991); Mattie E. Treadwell, *U.S. Army in World War II: Special Studies—The Women's Army Corps* (1954); U.S. Department of the Army, Medical Department, *Highlights on the History of the Army Nurse Corps* (1987); Lynda Van Devanter, *Home before Morning: The Story of an Army Nurse in Vietnam* (1983); Doris Weatherford, *American Women in World War II* (1990).

Arnold, Henry H. ("Hap")

See Air-Wacs; Cochran, Jacqueline; Women's Airforce Service Pilots (WASP).

Ashcraft, Juanita (b. 1921)

In 1976, Juanita Ashcraft became the first woman assistant secretary of the United States Air Force—the highest civilian appointive post that had ever been given to a woman in that branch of service.

Before this appointment, Ashcraft worked in California, serving for ten years on that state's employment board. She also served as the assistant appointments secretary to California governor Ronald Reagan. From 1970 to 1976, she served on the governor's commission on executive salaries. Ashcraft left that position to accept the appointment of President Gerald Ford to the Air Force post, becoming assistant secretary for manpower and reserve affairs.

Auxiliary Status

In the years before women were granted full or regular military status, they served in organizations classified as auxiliary. This was due, in part, to the idea that the use of women in the military was only temporary and that women's corps would exist only to fulfill short-term needs for supplemental personnel.

Auxiliary status offered fewer benefits than full military status. Women classified as auxiliary personnel did not receive free mailing, allotments for their dependents, government insurance, veterans' bonuses or pensions, or the right to be reinstated in their jobs after leaving the service.

When World War II began, women were still being offered only auxiliary status by the Army in the Women's Army Auxiliary Corps (WAAC). By contrast, the Navy offered full military status to its Women Accepted for Voluntary Emergency Service (WAVES). Army officials realized they might have trouble competing with the other branches that were offering more benefits. The WAC bill of 1943 gave Army women full military status.

References

Doris Weatherford, *Women and World War II* (1990); June A. Willenz, *Women Veterans: America's Forgotten Heroines* (1983).

Avenger Field

During World War II, Avenger Field became the site of the only all-female Army air base in history. Located in Sweetwater, Texas, the base welcomed 127 women with the Women's Airforce Service Pilots (WASP) for its first all-women's training class in March 1943. Coming from various parts of the country, the women arrived at the AAF Flying Training Detachment at Avenger, which was then under base commander Colonel Landon E. McConnell.

During the first few weeks, men were still training at the base, but the groups were kept separate. One of the training planes used most often was the 175-horsepower Fairchild PT-19. The students took classes in physics, aerodynamics, electronics and instruments, engine operations and maintenance, meteorology, navigation, military and civilian air regulations, and mathematics.

See also

Cochran, Jacqueline; Women's Air Force Service Pilots (WASP).

References

Sally Van Wagenen Keil, *Those Wonderful Women in Their Flying Machines* (1979).

B

Bailey, Anne (1758–1851)

After her husband was killed in 1774 during the first battle of the American Revolution, "Mad Anne" Bailey became a frontier legend. She rode from place to place in western Virginia recruiting soldiers for the colonial army. In addition, Bailey served as a nurse, scout, and messenger for the rebel forces. She carried messages into enemy territory numerous times. An excellent markswoman, she also knew how to defend herself against hostile Indians or British soldiers. Once she sneaked into an Indian camp at night to retrieve her favorite horse, which they had taken earlier that day.

When the war ended, Bailey continued to serve as a scout for the troops stationed at Fort Lee (now part of West Virginia). She undertook a courageous mission in 1791 to bring back needed gunpowder to the fort, which was about to face an attack. In 1795, after a peace treaty was enacted between Indians and settlers, Bailey set up a delivery service to bring supplies to settlers in wilderness areas of West Virginia. A memorial marks her grave in Point Pleasant, and a nearby museum features information about her life and times.

References

Patricia Edwards Clyne, *Patriots in Petticoats* (1976); Edith Patterson Meyer, *Petticoat Patriots of the American Revolution* (1976).

Bailey, Mildred (b. 1919)

Mildred Bailey served as director of the Women's Army Corps (WAC). She reached the rank of brigadier-general and was among the high-ranking officials who testified before Congress in 1972 about the roles women might play in the All-Volunteer Force (AVF) that was to replace the old system of drafting males into the armed services.

Baker, Mrs. E. H. (n.d.)

A professional spy for the Union Army during the Civil War (1861–1865), Mrs. E. H. Baker was an experienced agent who had been employed by the famous Pinkerton Detective Agency since the 1850s.

Baker lived in Richmond before the Civil War, at which time she moved to Chicago. During the war, the Union's war department hired the Pinkerton Agency to conduct spying activities. Knowing that she had contacts in the South, the agency asked Mrs. Baker to visit friends in Richmond while investigating some underwater ships the Confederacy was rumored to be building at the Tredigar Iron Works. Baker was able to tour the factory herself and see the ships being built there.

She provided the details of her visit when she returned to the North, and the war department was pleased to have this key information. As the first of the underwater ships came into use, the Union Navy was ready and could defend itself. No records or documents show what Mrs. Baker did after the war; she may have returned to private detective work or retired.

Baker, Genevieve and Lucille

See United States Coast Guard.

Ball, Mary Ann

See Bickerdyke, Mary Ann.

Bandel, Betty (b. circa 1913)

Betty Bandel served as the first director of the Air Force WAACs in World War II, when the Air Force was part of the U.S. Army. In this position, Bandel had the title Air-WAAC officer and the rank of lieutenant colonel, making her the second-ranking officer (next to Oveta Culp Hobby) in the Women's Army Corps (WAC) throughout the war.

Before assuming this post, Bandel had been Director Hobby's first aide. She came to the Army from Arizona, where she had been a woman's page editor for a newspaper and a drama and music critic. As Hobby's deputy, Bandel accompanied her on visits to Europe and on field trips to study WAAC units. She had also written many important staff papers for the WAAC.

Assuming the position of Air-WAAC officer in May 1943, Bandel was in charge of seeing that women were used efficiently in the Air-WAAC (later the Air-WAC) Division. She oversaw the deployment of women in new positions, such as air traffic controller.

Opponents had argued that women's voices might not be strong enough to be heard over the air as they gave landing instructions to pilots, and that women might become too nervous to perform well as air traffic controllers. The need for more controllers was so great, however, that Wacs were trained for the job, and they received praise for their efficient performance. As quoted by Mattie E. Treadwell, Bandel said, "Wacs love the work and have been highly commended. There seems to be no difference between men and women in adaptability to this work. . . . The WAC program in the Air Forces during World War II was a part of the natural evolution toward the full employment of a nation's manpower during a modern war."

Bandel was the first Wac to be promoted to the rank of lieutenant colonel. She resumed civilian life in December 1945.

References

Mattie E. Treadwell, *U.S. Army in World War II: Special Studies—The Women's Army Corps* (1954); Doris Weatherford, *Women and World War II* (1990).

Barkalow, Carol (b. 1958)

Carol Barkalow was one of the first women cadets to attend the United States Military Academy (USMA) at West Point. During her four years at the academy (July 1976 to May 1980), Barkalow kept detailed diaries that she later turned into a book, *In the Men's House*, about the experiences of the first women at the USMA.

After graduation, Barkalow served in Germany with the air defense artillery (ADA), switching to the Transportation Corps in 1983. In 1990, she volunteered to go to the Persian Gulf War as part of the 24th Infantry Division (Mechanized), where she functioned as a transportation officer in the Victory Division near the end of the war. Barkalow then became special assistant to Army Chief of Staff General Carl Vuono.

See also

United States Military Academy (USMA).

References

Carol Barkalow, "Women Really Are an Integral Part of the Military," *Army Times* (27 May 1991); Carol Barkalow with Andrea Raab, *In the Men's House* (1990).

Barker, Penelope

See Edenton Tea Party.

Barringer, Emily Dunning (1876–1961)

Emily Dunning Barringer, a physician, was a leader in the effort to have women physicians accepted in the military during World War II.

Barringer graduated from Cornell Medical School in 1901 and applied for a staff position in a New York City hospital. On the required test, Barringer scored higher than any other applicant but was rejected in favor of a male physician. After being turned down by another New York hospital, she accepted a position as an ambulance doctor, serving on the horse-drawn vehicles that were then used in the city. Barringer thus became the first woman ambulance doctor in the United States. She served as president of the American Medical Women's Association from 1941 to 1942.

When World War II began, Barringer headed the American Medical Women's Association committee that had been created to change policies that banned female physicians from military service. Their supporters included the American Legion and many state medical societies. Among the committee's major points was the shortage of male doctors and the fact that some male specialists being ac cepted into the military were not as qualified to deal with battlefield injuries as women applicants who were rejected. For example, a male pediatrician might be accepted while a woman surgeon or emergency room doctor was not.

On 16 April 1943, when President Roosevelt signed the Sparkman Bill into law, Barringer was among those present in the Oval Office. Introduced by Congressman John Sparkman of Alabama, the bill allowed women physicians to serve in the Army—only with Women's Army Corps (WAC) units, however, not on medical combat teams. Since female physicians were not given equal status with male physicians, many decided not to enter military service under those conditions.

Among Barringer's many credentials was membership in both the College of Surgeons and the New York Academy of Medicine. She headed the department of gynecology at a hospital in Brooklyn, New York.

References

Esther Pohl Lovejoy, *Women Doctors of the World* (1957); Geoffrey Marks and William K. Beatty, *Women in White* (1972).

Barton, Clara (1821–1912)

Known as the "Angel of the Battlefield," Clara Barton nursed wounded soldiers during the Civil War, going "directly in where the battle raged," as she later wrote. After the war, she founded the American Red Cross (ARC) and served as its voluntary president for 20 years.

Clarissa Harlowe Barton was born on 25 December 1821, on a prosperous farm in North Oxford, Massachusetts. Her two older sisters taught three-year-old Clara to read, and from two older brothers, she learned sports and horseback riding. Her father, Stephen, an ex–Army captain, shared with her his experiences under General "Mad Anthony" Wayne during the Indian Wars. He and Clara enjoyed laying out battle formations with toy

Clara Barton

soldiers, and she told her family that one day she would be a soldier.

Shyness made Barton uncomfortable at school, despite excellent marks. She hated public speaking, something she worked to overcome as an adult. When she was 11, her brother David was seriously hurt and she nursed him devotedly for two years. Later, she nursed neighbors during a smallpox epidemic.

In 1839 Barton became a rural schoolteacher. Although only five feet tall and slender, she gained the respect of male students when they saw how strong she was. In 1852, while visiting friends in Bordentown, New Jersey, Barton founded a school for poor millworkers' children. A great success, it was one of the first public schools in the state and is now a memorial to her.

Poor health and the loss of her voice led Barton to quit teaching and seek a warmer climate. While living in Washington, D.C., she became a clerk-copyist at the U.S. Patent Office, one of the first women to hold a civil service job. In her spare time, she attended congressional debates, becoming politically well informed and making friends in the nation's capital.

In 1861, after conflicts between North and South escalated into the Civil War, Barton volunteered to help the Sixth Massachusetts Regiment, which had come to Washington after a battle in Baltimore. Seeing their ragged condition, she sought donations of clothing, food, tobacco, and wine from Union supporters.

Barton began nursing the wounded in hospitals but quickly realized she could save far more lives on the battlefield. Supply trains often arrived at hospitals days after a battle ended. The wounded were transported in slow-moving wagons without adequate food or care. Before reaching a boat, train, or town, many died of thirst, hunger, or exposure to cold or heat.

After a long struggle with the War Department, Barton was finally allowed on the battlefield in March 1862, and she began delivering supplies to various army units. Until the war ended, she traveled with the Army of the Potomac to most of its major battles. She prepared and served food, nursed soldiers, and removed bullets when no surgeon was available. Barton and her assistants "followed the cannon" to places where fighting was the heaviest. She waded through muddy roads or dodged gunfire to reach the wounded. Her bed might be a blanket on the ground. With her childhood knowledge of military strategy, along with resourcefulness and courage, Barton was able to survive under these circumstances.

After the war, Barton nursed veterans and organized an office to find men who were still missing in action. She eventually located some 22,000 missing men and learned the identities of thousands who had died. Barton also lectured widely about her war experiences, using most of her earnings to finance her search for missing soldiers.

In 1869 Barton again lost her voice and became ill. While resting in Geneva, Switzerland, she learned about the Geneva Convention Treaty of 1864. This international agreement had approved the International Committee of the Red Cross, founded in 1863 by Swiss citizen Jean Henri Dunant. A volunteer organization, the Red Cross was dedicated to helping people in wartime.

Soon Barton felt well enough to organize relief efforts for combatants and refugees during the Franco-Prussian War. She received a decoration for this work, one of 27 decorations and citations she earned during her lifetime.

By 1877, Barton, having returned to America, began a fervent campaign to promote the Geneva Treaty and urge the United States to develop a version of the Red Cross. She spent thousands of dollars working to gain acceptance for the treaty, which was finally ratified in 1882.

The American Red Cross was founded in 1881, and Clara Barton was named first president. When the disastrous Johnstown flood occurred in Pennsylvania in May 1889, the Red Cross was ready. For five months, workers, including Barton, brought supplies and help to the flood victims.

Clara Barton was 77 years old when the Spanish-American War broke out. Once again, she set out on mule wagons to care for the wounded and carry supplies to those she called “my boys.” Barton died peacefully at her home in New York at age 91.

See also

American Red Cross (ARC); Civil War.

References

Clara Barton, *The Red Cross* (1899); William E. Barton, *The Life of Clara Barton*, 2 vols. (1969); Elizabeth Brown Pryor, *Clara Barton: Professional Angel* (1987); Ishbel Ross, *Angel of the Battlefield* (1958).

Bataan

In December 1941, during World War II, the U.S. military base in Manila was attacked by Japanese bombers, and U.S. forces fled to the nearby Bataan peninsula.

At the Sternberg General Hospital in Manila, Army and Navy nurses had been caring for the sick and wounded. When it became clear that U.S. forces could not withstand the oncoming attack, however, they decided to surrender. The nurses were ordered to prepare for evacuation. Dodging bombs, most were taken away at night by boat across the bay to Bataan to await the arrival of new U.S. troops.

On Bataan, the nurses subsisted on small meals of rice, oatmeal, and stew made of mule or horse meat. Operating from a hospital set up in the jungle, they faced danger and endured very primitive living conditions. Frequent shellings sent them into foxholes they had dug themselves. Most contracted malaria or dysentery or both.

A Navy nurse later said that she and her colleagues worked from seven in the morning until ten at night, assisting at seven operating tables to care for the lines of wounded men who waited helplessly on stretchers. By the time surrender was imminent, each nurse was responsible for between 200 and 300 patients.

The nurses were evacuated again a few months later, this time to the island of Corregidor. There, they worked in an underground hospital while bombing and gunfire raged above.

See also
Army Nurse Corps (ANC); Brantley, Hattie Rilla; Corregidor; Decorations.

References
Maj. Edith Aynes, A.N.C., *From Nightingale to Eagle: The Army Nurses History* (1973); Judith Bellefaire, *The Army Nurse Corps in World War II* (1976); Mark Murphy, "You'll Never Know," *New Yorker* (12 June 1943); Helen Rogan, *Mixed Company: Women in the Modern Army* (1981); Doris Weatherford, *American Women and World War II* (1990).

Bates, Rebecca and Abigail (1793–1875), (1797–1882)

Rebecca and Abigail Bates, at the ages of 19 and 15 during the War of 1812, became known as the "army of two" because of a daring and clever plan they put into action.

The daughters of Simeon Bates, a lighthouse keeper off the coast of Scituate, Massachusetts, Rebecca and Abigail had witnessed a British raid on Scituate in June 1814. On 1 September of the same year, after their father and the soldiers stationed at the lighthouse had all gone to town, the sisters saw a British ship heading toward the harbor. The Union Jack flew from the masthead of the *La Hogue*, which dropped anchor as two barges of soldiers were lowered into the water.

Concerned about the fate of the lighthouse and the town of Scituate, the girls decided to grab the fife and drum the soldiers had left behind. They began to make noise, marching back and forth behind the sand dunes and playing "Yankee Doodle" as loudly as they could. They hoped the soldiers would believe they were a group of soldiers practicing their maneuvers.

The British commander signaled the barges to return to the ship. He had evidently heard the music and decided not to risk sending his small landing party to shore.

References
Jane Atherton, "Society Acts To Restore Scituate Lighthouse," *The Scituate Historical Society Bulletin* (February 1968); Robert Carse, *Keepers of the Light* (1969); Scituate Historical Society Pamphlet; Scituate Town Report: Paper Read at a Meeting of the Chief Justice Cushing Chapter D.A.R. (5 September 1908); Edward Rowe Snow, *The Lighthouses of New England* (1973).

Battle Dress Uniform (BDU)

See Uniforms.

Battle Hymn of the Republic

See Howe, Julia Ward.

"Battle of the Black Stockings"

During World War II, a controversy over what type of stockings should be worn by women in the Navy led to the "Battle of the Black Stockings," a name given to the episode by Commander Mildred McAfee of the Women Accepted for Voluntary Emergency Service (WAVES).

Before the war, women had worn silk or nylon stockings in flesh tones. Stockings were hard to come by during the war, however; oriental silk was not available, and the military was using large quantities of nylon for parachutes. Nonetheless, the service branches decreed that women must wear hosiery as part of their uniforms. Women in the Army were issued cotton stockings in tan shades, but the Navy decided the WAVES would wear rayon stockings dyed black, like those worn by women in Canada's Women Royal Naval Service. The WAVES protested; they hated the idea of sheer black rayon stockings for daytime wear.

Despite their complaints, the chief of naval operations continued to insist on black stockings until he was advised that the dye used to make them was a vital ingredient in gunpowder, an essential material in the war effort. The WAVES thus won the battle to wear tan stockings.

Bell, Barbara

See Pilots; United States Navy.

Benefits

Until recent decades, women providing services to the armed forces often had an ambiguous status and did not receive the economic or fringe benefits given to men serving in the military. Having disguised themselves as men and fought as soldiers, the few women who were finally given pensions after the American Revolution and Civil War often pleaded their case for years. A few other women who provided services during these wars were awarded some kind of compensation by Congress, but there were no guarantees about what lawmakers would decide.

When the Women's Auxiliary Army Corps (WAAC) was formed in World War II, WAACs were not eligible for various benefits accorded to men in the military because they had auxiliary status as opposed to regular military status. They could not receive extra overseas pay, government life insurance, veterans' hospitalization or health-care benefits, or the death gratuity given to the families of those who were killed while in the service. As auxiliary personnel, they were also not entitled to be treated in conformity with international laws regarding the rights of prisoners of war if they were captured by the enemy.

The need to rethink this policy became more apparent during World War II as women moved into more dangerous situations. For instance, a ship carrying WAACs to England was sunk by enemy fire in December 1942. The women were rescued by a lifeboat and British battleship, but some could have been killed, injured, or captured.

Women's auxiliary status ended when the WAAC became the WAC—Women's Army Corps—but there was a debate over whether or not the women's dependents should be entitled to benefits. The comptroller of the armed forces had denied such benefits to the dependents of nurses and to the Navy's Women Accepted for Voluntary Emergency Service (WAVES). The decision was made to allow dependency allowances for the children and parents of Wacs, but not their husbands. The death gratuity was finally allowed late in 1943.

Members of the Army Nurse Corps (ANC) became eligible for all veterans' benefits at the end of World War II.

See also
American Expeditionary Forces (AEF); Auxiliary Status; Corbin, Margaret; Edmonds, Sarah Emma; GI Bill of Rights; Pensions, Veterans'; Sampson, Deborah.
References
Mattie E. Treadwell, *U.S. Army in World War II: Special Studies—The Women's Army Corps* (1954); Doris Weatherford, *American Women and World War II* (1990); June A. Willenz, *Women Veterans: America's Forgotten Heroines* (1983).

Berlin Airlift

In the years following World War II, the USSR (Soviet Union) took over several countries in Eastern Europe and built up its military forces and nuclear arsenal to become a world power. The so-called Cold War ensued between the United States and the Soviet Union.

In April 1948, troops from the Soviet Union cut off access to the city of Berlin, Germany. Hoping to avoid a Soviet takeover, the United States joined with Great Britain to conduct the largest airlift in history, transporting supplies to the people of Berlin. Short of manpower, the military asked male pilots to return to active duty in order to bring coal and other necessities to the city. Women pilots who had flown during World War II, however, were not invited to take part.

This crisis and other postwar events convinced lawmakers that there would be an ongoing need for more people in the U.S. military. Congress debated passing a new draft law for men and also creating permanent women's units in various branches of service. In response, the Senate proposed and passed Bill 1641, which, on 12 June 1948, became Public Law 625, The Women's Armed Services Integration Act. The act provided for women's corps in both the Army and Navy. The Selective Service Act of 1948, applying to men only, established the first peacetime draft in U.S. history.

See also
Women's Armed Services Integration Act of 1948.
References
Jeanne Holm, *Women in the Military: An Unfinished Revolution* (1992); Sally Van Wagenen Keil, *Those Wonderful Women in Their Flying Machines* (1990).

Bethune, Mary McCleod (1875–1955)

Well-known educator and civil rights activist Mary McCleod Bethune fought to improve the status of African-American women and to expand opportunities for them in defense plant jobs and the military during World War II.

Born to a poor family in South Carolina, the fifteenth of seventeen children, Bethune began working early in life, picking cotton and doing other people's laundry to help support the family. She was so eager to learn that she walked five miles to and from school each day and willingly repeated her lessons at night so her siblings could also get an education. Her hard work earned her a scholarship to Scotia Seminary in Concord, North Carolina. Later, after graduating from Moody Bible Institute in Chicago, she became a teacher.

With her husband, Albertus Bethune, she moved to Florida where the couple, both teachers, hoped to found a school for poor African-American children. To raise money, Bethune wrote articles and spoke at churches, schools, and other organizations.

Eleanor Roosevelt admired Bethune's work and staunchly supported civil rights. After her husband, Franklin Roosevelt, was elected president, he developed his New Deal programs to alleviate the grave economic problems of the Depression. Roosevelt asked Bethune to serve as director of the Division of Negro Affairs for the National Youth Administration (NYA), which created educational and employment opportunities for young people.

Concerned for oppressed people throughout the world, Bethune was among those who protested when Nazi Germany passed the Nuremburg Laws in 1935. Under Bethune's leadership, the National Council of Negro Women, which she founded in 1935, petitioned the president to aid German Jews, the main targets of Nazi persecution.

As World War II began, Bethune worked to open jobs to African Americans in the country's growing defense industry. She served as an advisor to Colonel Oveta Culp Hobby, head of the Women's Army Corps (WAC), on matters that related to African-American women in the WAC. Throughout the war, she helped to monitor the way black women were trained, treated, and deployed to duty assignments.

After the war, Bethune continued her crusade for civil rights, focusing on educational and job opportunities for minorities. Like Roosevelt, Presidents Harry Truman and Dwight D. Eisenhower asked Bethune to serve as an advisor on these matters. In 1955, as the modern civil rights movement was gaining momentum, Bethune died at the age of 80 after a lifetime of amazing achievement.

See also
Hobby, Oveta Culp.

References
Susan Altman, *Extraordinary Black Americans* (1989); John Hope Franklin and August Meier, eds., *Black Leaders of the Twentieth Century* (1982); Rackham Holt, *Mary McLeod Bethune;* Rayford W. Logan and Michael R. Winston, eds., *Dictionary of American Negro Biography* (1982); Juan Williams, *Eyes on the Prize: America's Civil Rights Years* (1987).

Bickerdyke, Mary Ann (1817–1901)

Mary Ann Bickerdyke, the large, friendly woman with the thick brown hair and Shaker bonnet, was known as "Mother" Bickerdyke to the soldiers she nursed during the Civil War. She was born Mary Ann Ball on a pioneer farm in Knox County, Ohio. Her mother died when she was a baby, and Mary Ann lived with relatives until she was 16 years old.

After attending school in Oberlin, Ohio, Mary Ann moved to Cincinnati to study at D. W. Cook's Physio-Botanic Medical College. There she earned a diploma in what was called "botanic medicine"—the use of herbs and natural remedies to alleviate sickness. Cook's school was not officially recognized as a medical college, but this forward-thinking man criticized bloodletting and purgatives (substances used to promote vomiting), two procedures used by doctors during those years and later abandoned. Cook advised ill people to eat a light diet with fresh fruits and vegetables and to take various herbal teas and preparations.

Mary Ann Bickerdyke

At age 30, Mary Ann Ball wed Robert Bickerdyke, a widower with several children. They had two sons together, and the family moved to Illinois where Robert died in 1859, leaving his widow to support the family. Known as a skilled healer, Bickerdyke set up a practice as a botanic physician.

Shortly after the Civil War began in 1861, a minister at Bickerdyke's church read his congregation a letter from a doctor stationed with Union troops in southern Illinois. The doctor said that many men were sick and needed care and better food. The congregation raised $500 to help the camp and asked Bickerdyke to deliver it and find out what was needed. When Bickerdyke arrived with supplies, she was moved to help. Aided by healthy soldiers, she cooked a chicken dinner and made sure each sick man received a hot bath, clean clothing, and a bed with fresh straw.

With the help of Mary Safford, a local girl who brought flowers and read the Bible to invalids, Bickerdyke nursed the wounded. (Safford would later become a physician.) Deciding to stay in the camp, Bickerdyke worked with an organization called the United States Sanitary Commission. The commission inspected conditions in camps and examined water supplies in order to prevent and control diseases, then reported their findings to the government.

After a battle in Belmont, Missouri, 200 wounded soldiers returned to Cairo where Bickerdyke and Safford cared for them in a hotel that was converted to a hospital. The doctor in charge wanted Bickerdyke out, but General Grant agreed she could stay. He appointed her hospital matron, and in that post, Bickerdyke tried to stop dishonest staff members from stealing clothing and food meant for patients. Eventually, the Cairo facility was cited as a model military hospital.

Bickerdyke then went to Fort Donelson on the hospital ship *City of Memphis*, accompanying wounded men during five trips. She visited other army hospitals in Illinois, St. Louis, and Louisville, all staffed by Catholic nuns and nurses hired by Dorothea Lynde Dix, the superintendent of female nurses of the army.

Moving on, Bickerdyke followed Grant's troops and nursed soldiers at the bloody battle of Shiloh where she brought much-needed supplies. Bickerdyke was not intimidated by men who tried to squelch her activities or overrule her. One night, when a surgeon asked her who had given her the authority to stay, she replied, "I have received my authority from the Lord

God Almighty. Have you anything that ranks higher than that?"

During this time, the U.S. Sanitary Commission began paying Bickerdyke a salary of $50 a month, which she was reluctant to accept. Shortly after, the head of a regional branch of the Sanitary Commission, Mary Livermore, asked her to make a series of fund-raising speeches. As a reward, the commission bought a large washing machine for Bickerdyke's hospital.

From time to time, Bickerdyke spent a few days visiting her sons in Galesburg, Illinois, where a kind neighbor was rearing them during her absence. Later, the boys attended a boarding school in Chicago run by friends of Mary Livermore's—a Presbyterian minister and his wife—and they received fine educations.

After the Battle of Fort Donelson on 16 February 1862, a poet in California wrote about Mother Bickerdyke, and newspapers told how she had worked tirelessly to save lives. In December 1862, Bickerdyke rejuvenated a smallpox hospital in Memphis that nobody else was willing to touch. She served at other battles and cared for former prisoners of war. In all, Bickerdyke served for four years and through 19 battles.

In 1865, 49-year-old Bickerdyke opened a boardinghouse and helped homesteading veterans in Kansas, where her sons had settled. From 1870 to 1874, she worked with a group in New York City trying to improve life in the slums. When grasshoppers destroyed crops in the Midwest, Bickerdyke collected grain, clothing, and food for poor farmers.

In poor health, she moved to California during the 1880s and worked as a clerk in the San Francisco mint while continuing to advocate for veterans. Bickerdyke also ran a home for neglected young people and did volunteer work for the Salvation Army. Near the end of her life, she lived with her son James in Bunker Hill, Kansas, where he served as superintendent of schools. Mother Bickerdyke died of a stroke on 8 November 1901.

References

Nina Brown Baker, *Cyclone in Calico* (1952); Sylvia G. L. Dannett, ed., *Noble Women of the North* (1959); Mary M. Roberts, *American Nursing: History and Interpretation* (1978).

Binkin-Bach Study

In 1976, the government asked for a priority study of the use of women in the military. By this time, the All-Volunteer Force (AVF) had been implemented, so men were no longer being drafted. Navy Commander Dr. Richard W. Hunter was asked to head the project, which was to be conducted by Martin Binkin and Shirley J. Bach, two researchers at the Brookings Institution in Washington, D.C. Brookings, an independent research institution specializing in national policy issues, had already completed a study on the all-volunteer army in 1973, with Binkin as coauthor.

The report, called *Women and the Military*, was published in June 1977. Binkin and Bach stated that women could potentially fill 33.3 percent of the total number of jobs then being carried out by enlisted servicepeople. In looking at the percentage of jobs women could perform in each service branch, their estimates were Air Force, 76.1 percent, Army, 25.9 percent; Navy, 9.2 percent; and Marines, 8.8 percent.

Since women had never before entered military careers in such high numbers, the Binkin-Bach study concluded that it was conceivable that the number of women could reach about 22 percent of the armed forces, or some 400,000 women. They suggested that these women could be attracted to enlist if the services publicized the opportunities available for women and encouraged women to take advantage of specialty training. They also suggested that developing standards that treated both genders alike would help attract more women, as well.

At the time the study came out, about 113,400 women were serving in the military on active duty. The Pentagon had stated that it foresaw increasing this number by about 44,000 by 1982. The Binkin-Bach study caused people to reevaluate these projections and to reconsider the roles women might play in the military.

References

Martin Binkin and Shirley J. Bach, *Women and the Military* (1977).

Black Americans

See African Americans.

Blackwell, Elizabeth Bradwell (1821–1910)

English-born Elizabeth Bradwell Blackwell was the first woman from the United States to earn a medical degree. When she was 11 years old, her family moved to the United States, first to New York, then Jersey City, and finally Cincinnati. In 1942, Blackwell began teaching school—first in Kentucky and later in the Carolinas.

In her spare time, Elizabeth studied medicine on her own, using medical books that practicing physicians lent her. After moving to Philadelphia, she found two Quaker physicians who offered to sponsor her application to medical school, but no medical college would accept a woman. Finally, Blackwell was accepted at the Geneva Medical School of Geneva College and received her medical degree in Switzerland in 1849.

With her sister Emily, also a physician, she founded the New York Dispensary for Poor Women and Children (later called the New York Infirmary). The hospital, incorporated in 1854, was staffed completely by women.

When the Civil War began, Blackwell realized the Union Army would need an organized way to receive and distribute supplies. In April 1861, she began organizing the Women's Central Association of Relief (WCAR). Thousands of women volunteers became involved in the group, collecting donations and medical supplies and transporting these to the army. They also ran a training course for nurses. (After the government set up the U.S. Sanitary Commission in July 1861, the WCAR became a part of that organization.)

In 1868, Blackwell organized a medical college for women, affiliated with the New York Infirmary and Cornell University Medical College (as of 1898). A year after founding the college, she moved to England where she organized the National Health Society of London and the London School of Medicine.

References

Ruth Abram, *"Send Us a Lady Physician": Women Doctors in America, 1835–1920* (1985); Elizabeth Blackwell, *Pioneer Work in*

Opening the Medical Profession to Women (1914); Ishbell Ross, *Child of Destiny* (1944); Elizabeth Schleichert, *The Life of Elizabeth Blackwell* (1992).

Blanchfield, Florence Aby (1882–1971)

Blanchfield was superintendent of the Army Nurse Corps (ANC) and the first woman commissioned in the regular army (1947). Born in Fort Royal, Virginia, Blanchfield graduated from South Side Hospital School for Nurses in Pittsburgh, Pennsylvania, in 1906. She took postgraduate courses at Johns Hopkins Hospital (Baltimore) and became a nurse supervisor in 1909.

In 1913, Blanchfield joined the staff at Ancon Hospital in the Panama Canal Zone, then worked in industrial nursing in the field of emergency surgery. During World War I, she served with the ANC in France. After departing the corps to work at a hospital in Pennsylvania, Blanchfield returned to the military in 1920 and completed tours of duty in San Francisco, Washington, D.C., China, and the Philippines, among other places.

She became part of the surgeon general's staff in 1935 and became first assistant to the superintendent of the Army Nurse Corps in 1939. She was promoted to the rank of colonel in 1942, at which time she became superintendent of the ANC. During World War II, in that demanding position, she was responsible for supervising the massive recruitment efforts and training and assignment of Army nurses. Blanchfield devised procedures for sending nurses to the front lines as part of medical teams performing emergency surgery, and she made numerous inspection tours of war areas.

After the war, Blanchfield received the Distinguished Service Medal and other honors. The Army-Navy Nurse Act of 1947 gave military nurses full military rank and permanent status as a corps, a goal she had strived for through the years.

In addition to her military duties, Blanchfield was active in national nursing associations and wrote extensively about her profession. She continued to pursue college studies and propose more effective ways to educate nurses, as well as pursuing many hobbies, among them dressmaking and auto mechanics. After retiring in 1947, Blanchfield began collaborating with author Mary W. Standlee on a history of the ANC. She was active writing and speaking about nursing and the military until her death in 1971.

References

Edith A. Aynes, "Colonel Florence A. Blanchfield," *Nursing Outlook* (February 1959): 78–81; Aynes, *From Nightingale to Eagle: A History of the Army Nurse Corps* (1973).

Blanchfield Army Community Hospital

Located at Fort Campbell, Kentucky, Blanchfield Army Community Hospital was named for Florence A. Blanchfield, who served with the Army Nurse Corps (ANC) during both world wars and was superintendent of the ANC during World War II. After serving in France during World War I, she remained in the ANC and became first assistant to the superintendent of the Army Nurse Corps in 1939. She assumed the rank of colonel, serving as

Evangeline Booth

superintendent as of 1 July 1943. Blanchfield received the Distinguished Service Medal after World War II, and she retired from the ANC in 1948.

See also
Blanchfield, Florence Aby.

Boot Camp

See Training, Basic.

Booth, Evangeline (1865–1950)

Born in England, Evangeline Booth was the daughter of Sir William Booth, who cofounded the Salvation Army. In 1896, Booth came to the United States and began working with the American branch of the organization, previously run by her brother Ballington.

From 1904 to 1934, Booth served as commander of the Salvation Army in the United States. The organization became known for its efforts to assist the poor and provide help during community emergencies, as well as its religious efforts. For her work in aiding relief efforts for the Allies during World War I, Booth became the first woman to receive the Distinguished Service Medal.

Booth became a U.S. citizen in 1932. Two years later, she was appointed general of the International Salvation Army, serving in that position from 1934 until 1939.

See also
Salvation Army.

Boulay, Donna-Marie (b. 1943)

A native of Massachusetts and a registered nurse specializing in trauma, Donna-Marie Boulay was completing her college degree when she joined the Army Nurse Corps (ANC) in 1966. She was moved to volunteer for service in Vietnam when a 19-year-old man she knew returned from Vietnam with severe injuries after serving with the Marines. Although personally opposed to the war, Boulay believed she must go to help those who needed care. In an interview with Shelley Saywell, Boulay recalled,

> All of a sudden, I knew where my talents were most needed. I went to the army recruiters in Boston and said, "I am a nurse, and I want to be sent to Vietnam." The recruiter said, "Raise your right hand and sign on the dotted line." And then, "What do you want to do that for?"

After six weeks of basic training at Fort Sam Houston, Texas, Boulay was assigned to the 36th Evac Hospital in Vung Tau on the coast of the South China Sea. She was later transferred to the 93rd Evac in Longbinh. In Longbinh, nurses had small, single rooms called hooches, big enough for a cot, footlocker, and chair. The area was regularly shelled by Vietcong troops.

During that phase of the war, troops were being sent into hills and other remote areas to search for North Vietnamese and guerrilla fighters. U.S. forces were incurring heavy casualties, and severely wounded men arrived regularly at Boulay's hospital. Only 12 of 150 men came back alive during the first of these missions she witnessed. When 12 people were brought in by helicopter, 10 of them dead, Boulay found it "the most gory thing I had ever seen in my life."

Boulay was serving at Longbinh during the Tet Offensive, which lasted about a month. Heavy fire occurred as the Vietcong attacked South Vietnamese and U.S. bases and major cities in the south. Boulay worked in intensive care and the postoperative recovery room.

While in Vietnam, Boulay learned to love the country's people and culture. She was able to communicate better with the Vietnamese after a professor from the University of Saigon, the capital of South Vietnam, came to the base to teach the staff the language. She was also impressed with the courage of the U.S. soldiers whom, she said, "had been through terrible things. . . . It was real courage, not that macho thing when you've got a gun in your hand."

Back home after her year of service, Boulay experienced the fear, anger, and depression that haunted many nurses who had served in Vietnam. For a while, she worked in a hospital in San Francisco. Later she and other nurses who had served in Vietnam helped organize the building of the Vietnam Women's Memorial.

See also
Army Nurse Corps (ANC); Post-Traumatic Stress Disorder; Vietnam War.

References
Shelley Saywell, *Women in War* (1985); June A. Willenz, *Women Veterans: America's Forgotten Heroines* (1983).

Bourke-White, Margaret (1906–1971)

During World War II, well-known photojournalist and photographer Margaret Bourke-White covered the war for *Life* magazine.

Bourke-White was born in New York City and graduated from Cornell University. She became the associate editor of *Fortune* magazine, a position she held from 1929 to 1933. In 1934, she traveled to the Soviet Union to photograph industrial sites and produced two documentary films about that country, as well as a collection called *USSR, A Portfolio of Photographs.*

Two years later, she joined the staff of *Life* magazine, continuing to produce books on her own and in collaboration with her husband, well-known author Erskine Caldwell. In the fall of 1942, Henry Luce, the publisher of *Life*, received permission from the Army for Bourke-White to accompany the troops in Europe. Her first stop was North Africa where she traveled with the first WAAC officers in December 1942. The boat was torpedoed, but all aboard survived. Bourke-White's skillful reporting and photographs made these events come alive for the people at home, who could see that women were deeply involved in the war and had serious military roles.

From Africa, Bourke-White flew with some U.S. bombing missions, becoming the first woman to photograph such action. She also photographed troops in Italy. A number of her photos showed brave acts by soldiers and medics and were inspirations to Americans back home.

Under an agreement the Army had made with Luce, it could use Bourke-White's photos in its literature and publicity materials. Several of her pictures appeared in a book called *They Called It "Purple Heart Valley": A Combat Chronicle of the War in Italy*, published in 1944.

At the end of the war, Bourke-White was present when the Allies advanced through Germany and Italy. She recorded conditions in the German death camp, Buchenwald, when it was liberated by Allied troops. These stark, haunting photos show starving prisoners and corpses and skeletons, the remains of those who had been killed or died from conditions in the camp. These photographs remain for all time documentary evidence of Nazi atrocities.

See also

Correspondents, War.

References

Eleanor A. Ayer, *Margaret Bourke-White* (1992); Margaret Bourke-White, "Women in Lifeboats," *Life* (22 February 1943): 48; Sean Callahan, ed., *The Photographs of Margaret Bourke-White* (1972).

Boyd, Isabelle ("Belle") (1844–1900)

Isabelle ("Belle") Boyd was probably the most famous female spy of the Civil War. One of her cousins and two uncles also spied for the Confederacy.

Born in Martinsburg, Virginia, where her father was a federal official, Boyd was 17 years old when the war began. When Union soldiers invaded Martinsburg, they hung a federal flag on the Boyd house, angering Boyd's mother, a devout Confederate.

When a Yankee soldier physically pushed her mother, Belle drew out a pistol and shot him. She later wrote, "My indignation roused beyond control; my blood boiling in my veins." The soldier died, but Belle was not prosecuted, as army investigators ruled that she had acted in self-defense.

Soon, federal officers and soldiers were occupying her hometown. Boyd could hear a great deal about the plans being made by the northern forces. Called "La Belle Rebelle" because of her appearance and charming mannerisms, Boyd circulated among Union officials and soldiers, then passed on the information she gained to Confederate leaders, sometimes dodging guards and bullets to deliver information in person. At other times, she convinced male friends to take this intelligence farther behind the Union lines.

On 23 May 1862, Boyd entered a battle zone in order to inform General "Stonewall" Jackson about the number of Union soldiers expected to attack his troops. Braving gunfire, she carried

Belle Boyd

the message herself. The information enabled Jackson to strengthen his forces and win the battle, and he later wrote a letter thanking his young helper.

Boyd managed to avoid being captured on several occasions, but was finally caught and put on trial as a spy. Secretary of War Stanton sent a member of the federal Secret Service to bring her back to Washington. Between 1862 and 1863, she spent 17 months in prison, during which time she defiantly hung a picture of Jefferson Davis, the Confederate president, in her cell.

Boyd regained her freedom after being exchanged for a Northern prisoner. Being arrested several times did not deter her from continuing as a courier and spy, however. During one imprisonment early in 1862, she passed information inside rubber balls she tossed out her cell window.

While under arrest on a Union ship near the end of the war, Boyd fell in love with a naval officer, Lieutenant Sam Wylde Hardinge. She married Hardinge, but he died in 1864.

Famous as a Rebel spy, Boyd toured the United States and England after the war. Dressed in a grey Confederate uniform, she lectured about her war experiences. In 1865, she wrote an account of her experiences, *Belle Boyd in Camp and Prison, Written by Herself*, which was published in New York City.

Boyd was married twice more during her lifetime and had three children. Her marriage to John Hammond ended in divorce in 1884, and she went on to marry Nathaniel High, Jr., 16 years her junior, the next year.

Boyd continued to make personal appearances and give readings from her book. At age 56, she died of a heart attack in Wisconsin where she was appearing on stage. The women's auxiliary of the Grand Army of the Confederacy paid for Boyd's burial. In 1919, a Confederate veteran paid for a new granite tombstone to mark the grave of the Rebel spy.

References

Ina Chang, *A Separate Battle: Women and the Civil War* (1991); Curtis Carroll Davis, ed., *Belle Boyd in Camp and Prison* (1968); Donald E. Markle, *Spies and Spymasters of the Civil War* (1994); Ronald Seth, *Some of My Favorite Spies* (1968).

Brant, Mary (Molly) (circa 1736–1796)

The daughter of a prominent Mohawk, Molly Brant helped the British government negotiate with Iroquois groups during colonial days and later spied for the British during the American Revolution. Her brother, Joseph Brant, was a famous Mohawk chief and diplomat.

Born in 1759 in what is now New York State, Brant began living as the common-law wife of Sir William Johnson, superintendent for Indian affairs of the Northern Colonies, with whom she had nine children. They occupied an elegant estate in what is now Johnstown, New York.

Women were highly regarded among the Iroquois, and their ideas were valued. Brant helped Johnson negotiate with the Mohawk and other members of the Iroquois Confederacy. She encouraged her fellow Native Americans to support the British side during the American Revolution.

During the war, Brant also served as a spy, providing information to British leaders about the movements of the colonial army. She and her commonlaw husband, a Loyalist, gave the British food and other supplies.

In 1783, the colonial army having defeated the British, Brant moved to Ontario, Canada. The British government paid her an annual pension of 100 pounds for her services during the war. She and her children had also inherited large tracts of land from Sir William Johnson after his death in 1774.

Reference

Lynn Sherr and Jurate Kazickas, *The American Woman's Gazetteer* (1976).

Brantley, Hattie Rilla (b.1918)

Lieutenant Colonel Hattie R. Brantley was one of 67 Army nurses who were captured when the island of Corregidor in the South Pacific was seized by the Japanese during World War II. She was imprisoned with 5,000 people, mostly civilians, at the Santo Tomas Internment Camp in the Philippines.

Brantley, who grew up on a cotton farm in east Texas, was stationed on the island of Manila before the war began. Manila fell to the Japanese in December 1941. On 24 December, General Douglas MacArthur ordered U.S. military personnel to evacuate, and they fled to the small Bataan peninsula. At Bataan, more than 100,000 people struggled to survive on half rations, then three-eighths rations. Brantley later recalled that they ate papaya, breadfruit, and roots and leaves from the jungle. With poor sanitation, contaminated water, and a limited diet, people suffered from malaria, pellagra, beriberi, dengue fever, and dysentery.

For over three months, more than 80,000 U.S. and Filipino soldiers tried to fend off the Japanese. Brantley and the other nurses worked in two crowded hospitals they had set up on Bataan. Abandoning their white uniforms, hose, and shoes, they appropriated size 42 Air Force coveralls as their dress.

With little equipment and running out of dressings and other supplies, the nurses had to improvise while caring for a total of 9,000 patients during those months. They worked 16 hours or more a day. Brantley later told author Helen Rogan that when she got to where her back would not straighten up, "I'd get down on my knees, finally not even bothering to arise, but crawling to the next cot." The Japanese deliberately bombed the hospital, wounding two nurses and killing a number of patients.

When U.S. troops surrendered on 8 April 1942, the nurses and other medics escaped while under fire to the nearby island of Corregidor. By then, Brantley was suffering from hepatitis. On the rocky island were underground tunnels about 12 feet high and 35 feet wide. They held 13,000 troops, while 2,600 patients and nurses were crowded into the underground hospital. "We were like a bunch of rats in a hole," recalled Brantley. They performed surgery using flashlights and sometimes without enough time to administer anesthesia.

Just before Corregidor fell, 32 nurses were evacuated, but Brantley was among those who stayed at the hospital. When the Japanese took over the island, they were surprised to find nurses working in the tunnel. The women were kept underground for the next six weeks and continued to care for their thousands of patients. Then Brantley and her colleagues were taken prisoner and sent to Santo Tomas, a prison camp that contained some 9,000 civilians, including businessmen and missionary families.

During 33 months of captivity, Brantley and the other nurses worked in the hospital, supplied with aspirin, some drugs for dysentery, and little else. She did other chores, such as cooking, cleaning, gardening, and laundry. Their main food was a cup of rice twice a day. The penalties for breaking rules, such as smuggling or aiding the resistance, included torture and beheading. The prisoners suffered from numerous hardships, including hunger, especially after December 1944. Nearing defeat, the Japanese cut their rations, and many people at the camp died of starvation. Brantley later recalled the struggle to find things to eat, including rats and grasshoppers. Toward the end of their captivity, Japanese guards held roll calls twice a day, forcing prisoners to stand for hours in the sun. They tortured and beheaded the prisoners who had served as leaders of the camp, which had tried to conduct itself like an organized town.

The nurses remained hopeful and committed to their work. Brantley said, "It was a matter of faith; we really believed that if we could get through today, help would be there tomorrow." The Japanese allowed almost no mail in or out of the camp. Brantley's father died in 1943 and she did not find out until a year later. Along with holding back mail, the Japanese also took items from Red Cross packages sent to the prisoners.

Help arrived in February 1945 when members of the First Cavalry Division of the Sixth Army liberated the camp after Allied troops under General MacArthur had driven Japanese troops from the Philippines. As Brantley left Santo Tomas, she saw tanks of gasoline outside the building in which they had been locked. Their captors had planned to burn the prisoners alive, but had not had enough time to light the wicks.

Returning to the United States, Brantley was awarded a Bronze Star, and her rank increased to first lieutenant. She continued to serve in the Army at Fort Sam Houston. She later told author Helen Rogan that women prisoners at Santo Tomas seemed to withstand their captivity better than the men, both mentally and physically.

See also
Bataan; Corregidor; Prisoners of War (POWs).

References
Jeanne Holm, *Women in the Military: An Unfinished Revolution* (1992); Judy Barrett Litoff and David C. Smith, *We're in This War, Too: World War II Letters from American Women in Uniform* (1994); Helen Rogan, *Mixed Company: Women in the Military* (1981).

Brassier, Deanna

See Fighter Pilots.

Bray, Linda L. (b. 1964)

Army Captain Linda Bray, of Butner, North Carolina, served during the invasion of Panama (Operation Just Cause) as commander of the 988th Military Police Company. On 20 December 1989, Bray led a platoon into battle against a Panamanian Defense Force position. Her troops were exposed to enemy fire at a Panamanian guard dog kennel. During the three-hour fight, her platoon killed three Panamanian soldiers. Describing the incident later, White House press spokesman Marlin Fitzwater said, "It was an important military operation. A woman led it, and she did an outstanding job."

The women in Bray's company were not assigned to combat, yet their jobs required them to function in hostile territory. This incident did not violate any military law or policy, but it intensified the ongoing debate over whether women should take part in combat.

References
"Women in Combat: The Same Risks as Men?" *Washington Post* (3 February 1990).

Brewer, Lucy (n.d.)

During the War of 1812, Lucy Brewer masqueraded as a man named George Brewer in order to serve with the crew of the USS *Constitution.* Brewer was aboard the ship during its famous victory over the British frigate *Guerriere* on 19 August 1812 at a battle east of Boston. Serving for three years, Brewer became known as the "first girl marine."

Brewer, Margaret A. (b. 1930)

A native of Lansing, Michigan, Margaret A. Brewer was the first woman to achieve the rank of brigadier general in the U.S. Marine Corps. After graduating from the University of Michigan at Ann Arbor, Brewer joined the Marines, serving with the Marine Corps Development and Education Command at Quantico, Virginia.

In February 1973, Brewer became director of the Women Marines. For five years, she served in this post, directing 2,000 women, until the women's corps merged with the men's in 1977. Then, in 1979, Brewer was stationed in Washington, D.C., as director of information of the U.S. Marine Corps. A year later, she was promoted to the rank of brigadier general.

See also
Women Marines.

References
Jeanne Holm, *Women in the Military: An Unfinished Revolution* (1992); N. R. Rowan, *The U.S. Marine Corps* (1994).

Broadwick, Georgia ("Tiny") (circa 1895–1960)

On 21 June 1913, Georgia ("Tiny") Broadwick became the first woman to free-fall parachute from a plane, making five jumps from a craft flying 30 miles per hour at an altitude of 1,000 feet. Broadwick's jumps, conducted at Griffith Field in Los Angeles, were done for the U.S. Army, which was testing a new type of 11-foot parachute called a "life boat." The results of the tests enabled the Army to implement the new chutes, which were then used in World War I.

Bronze Star

See Army Nurse Corps (ANC); Brantley, Hattie Rilla; Decorations; Women's Army Corps (WAC).

Brown, Mary-Agnes (n.d.)

Lieutenant Colonel Mary-Agnes Brown was the director of the Women's Army Corps (WAC) units serving in the South Pacific during World War II.

Brown was employed in the Army finance department during World War I, followed by ten years as executive secretary to high-ranking medical officers in the Army. The versatile Brown was also an attorney, and she served as an attorney for the Veterans Administration.

After World War II began, Brown was appointed staff director for the Eighth Service Command, then executive officer in the Office of the Director WAC. As Colonel Brown, she was placed in charge of WAC units in the South Pacific, where she arrived in March 1944 with her four officer assistants. (Women from the Red Cross and Army Nurse Corps [ANC] had been assigned to the South Pacific since 1942.) They began to prepare for the women scheduled to arrive in May at such stations as Port Moresby in New Guinea, then coordinated the work of these WACS until the end of the war.

References

Mattie E. Treadwell, *U.S. Army in World War II: Special Studies—The Women's Army Corps* (1954).

Cadet Nurse Corps (CNC)

During World War II, the Cadet Nurse Corps was formed to increase the number of American nurses, desperately needed both in military and civilian service. In 1942, the U.S. Public Health Service identified a need for 55,000 new nursing students, with that number rising to 65,000 in 1943. Nursing was dominated by women, but women were being attracted to other work, such as high-salaried jobs in defense plants that did not require the years of schooling that nursing did.

To motivate people to enter nursing, Representative Frances Bolton of Ohio proposed a bill to bring more young people into the profession. Under this bill, introduced early in 1943, the federal government agreed to pay the nursing school tuition of those who promised to serve for the duration of the war plus six months in any vital nursing job. The students also received uniforms and stipends during their period of schooling.

Schools were encouraged to accelerate their programs by operating year-round and enabling students to finish school in less time than the usual three years. Refresher courses were offered for retired nurses who wished to return to the profession. In addition, high school counselors were urged to steer qualified students into this career.

The resulting legislation, which went into effect in May 1943, created the Student Nurse Corps, later known as the Cadet Nurse Corps (CNC). The number of nurses did increase each year during the war, although shortages remained.

See also

Army Nurse Corps (ANC); Navy Nurse Corps (NNC).

References

Maj. Edith Aynes, A.N.C., *From Nightingale to Eagle: The Army Nurses History* (1973); Mary M. Roberts, *American Nursing: History and Interpretation* (1954); U.S. Department of the Army, *Highlights on the History of the Army Nurse Corps* (1987).

Cadoria, Sherian Grace (b. 1940)

As of 1990, Sherian Grace Cadoria was one of four female Army generals and also the highest-ranking African-American woman in the military. That year, Brigadier General Cadoria told journalist David Dent, “I had never actually considered joining the Army, but I wanted to do something exciting and different.”

Cadoria joined the Army in 1961 while she was still in college and served part-time in Anniston, Alabama. During the early 1960s, racial discrimination limited the kinds of jobs she could assume as well as her chances for promotion. Segregation laws and practices in the South meant that Cadoria, as a black woman working for the military, could not take her troops off the base. Limitations such as these prevented her from being a platoon leader, among other things.

After completing her college degree at the Southern University of Baton Rouge (Louisiana), she joined the service full-time. In 1967, after working hard for recognition and promotion, she was sent to Vietnam. Cadoria applied to work in protocol but was told that women could not handle various aspects of that job, such as lifting heavy luggage during travel. She persisted, saying, "Nobody said I couldn't carry those hundred-pound bags of cotton when I was just a little child." She was then appointed and served as a protocol officer in Vietnam.

Returning home after the war's end, she became the first African-American woman chosen to attend the Command and General Staff College, a high-level training course designed for majors and conducted at Fort Leavenworth, Kansas.

As deputy commanding general and director for mobilization and operations for the U.S. Total Army Personnel Command, Cadoria has the responsibility of providing replacements for overseas commanders on the field if a world war were to occur.

See also
African Americans; Discrimination, Racial.

References
David Dent, "Women in the Military," *Essence* (April 1990); Brian Lanker, *I Dream a World* (1989); Jessie Carney Smith, ed., *Notable Black American Women* (1992); Carol Wekesser and Matthew Polesetsky, eds., *Women in the Military* (1991).

Cammermeyer, Margarethe (b. 1942)

A highly decorated Army nurse, Colonel Margarethe Cammermeyer sued the military because she was discharged when she acknowledged she was a homosexual. At the time, she was the highest-ranking member of the military to be discharged for this reason.

Cammermeyer was born in Norway and fled from that country with her family after the Nazi invasion during World War II. Living in the United States, she became a nurse and joined the Army in 1961. For 15 months, Cammermeyer served in Vietnam where she was in charge of a hospital for wounded and dying soldiers, for which she was awarded the Bronze Star. In 1985, she was chosen as the Veterans Administration's Nurse of the Year in a nationwide competition among 34,000 others.

In 1989, while serving as an Army nurse in the National Guard, Cammermeyer was being interviewed for admission to the Army War College. Asked about her sexual orientation, she replied that she was a lesbian. While the military considered her case, she continued to serve as a chief nurse.

Cammermeyer was honorably discharged from the National Guard on 11 June 1992. She then brought her lawsuit, charging that the Army's policy was unconstitutional. Among those who supported her reinstatement and petitioned the military on her behalf was Governor Booth Gardner of Washington State. Federal District Court Judge Thomas S. Zilly agreed that the military's policy on homosexuality violated Cammermeyer's constitutionally protected right to equal protection of the law, under the Fourteenth Amendment. The judge ordered that Cammermeyer be reinstated.

After the verdict, Cammermeyer became a clinical specialist at a veterans' hospital in Tacoma. She told reporters that she felt "a bit like a general who has won a war."

See also
Sexual Preferences.

References
Margarethe Cammermeyer, *Serving in Silence* (1994); Eric Schmitt, "Pentagon Must Reinstate Nurse Who Declared She Is a Lesbian," *New York Times* (2 June

1994); Randy Shilts, *Conduct Unbecoming: Lesbians and Gays in the U.S. Military: Vietnam to the Persian Gulf* (1993).

Camp Followers

Women who accompanied military units during the American Revolution were known as camp followers. They were often the wives of soldiers (sometimes accompanied by their children), as well as other family members, laundresses, or prostitutes.

Camp followers took care of the sick and wounded and cooked, did laundry, ran errands, and performed a variety of other tasks. Keeping things clean was a major chore since men of that era regarded cleaning as "women's work" and had not been taught or prepared to do these things themselves. The camp followers maintained the troops' clothing by sewing, mending, and repairing ragged items.

Many camp followers also performed a key task during battles—carrying pitchers of water onto the fields to cool cannons that had just been fired. When the troops moved, the women had to travel with the baggage. Their rations were half the amount allocated to soldiers.

During the Revolution, the Continental Congress authorized a ratio of one woman camp follower per 15 men, but some officers permitted more than this, fearing that some of their soldiers would desert if their wives were sent away.

See also

Corbin, Margaret; Vivandieres.

References

Linda Grant De Pauw, *Founding Mothers: Women of America in the Revolutionary Era* (1975); Edith Patterson Meyer, *Petticoat Patriots of the American Revolution* (1976); H. Sinclair Mills, Jr., *The Vivandiere: History, Tradition, Uniform and Service* (1988); Mary Beth Norton, *Liberty's Daughters—The Revolutionary Experience of American Women, 1750–1800* (1980).

Canteens

To meet the social needs of those in the service, thousands of women volunteers—many of them teenagers who had never left home before—staffed canteens during World War I and World War II. A smaller number of men also volunteered in this capacity. In the United States, canteens were often located in church basements and other public buildings near military bases or places where servicemen were likely to congregate. Overseas, canteens were often set up in spaces provided by the military. They were staffed by members of groups such as the American Red Cross (ARC), Young Men's Christian Association (YMCA), the Salvation Army, and Knights of Columbus.

Canteens provided scheduled social activities, along with reading rooms and places where people could gather for refreshments, conversation, or card games. Volunteers were resourceful, finding furnishings and materials to create attractive rooms, sometimes decorated with colorful war posters.

Women at the canteens often found themselves providing help with mending, shopping for gifts, and writing letters, among other things. One World War I canteen worker later recalled that she and her partner often cooked as many as 2,500 doughnuts, 50 pies, 800 pancakes, and hundreds of gallons of cocoa and coffee in a single day.

Canteen work overseas was popular, and some sponsoring organizations received hundreds more applicants

American Red Cross canteen workers serve refreshments to returning soldiers at a New York pier in May 1945. During World War I and World War II, canteens, largely made up of women, organized social activities for servicemen.

each week than they could use. Women volunteers came from church groups, college alumnae associations, the Junior League, the Intercollegiate Committee, the American Federation of Women's Clubs, and other organizations. The volunteers' expenses were paid, but many received no salary for their services.

See also
American Red Cross (ARC); Clubmobiles; Young Men's Christian Association (YMCA).

References
Foster Rhea Dulles, *The American Red Cross: A History* (1950); Judy Barrett Litoff and David C. Smith, eds., *We're in This War, Too: World War II Letters from American Women in Uniform* (1994); Alma Lutz, ed., *With Love, Jane: Letters from American Women on the War Fronts* (1945); Dorothy and Carl J. Schneider, *Into the Breach: American Women Overseas in World War I* (1991); Doris Weatherford, *American Women and World War II* (1990).

Carroll, Anna Ella (1815–1893)

Politically active Anna Ella Carroll wrote pamphlets during the Civil War and became a friend of President Abraham Lincoln. She claimed to have planned the winning military strategy that was used by the Union Army in its Tennessee campaign, a turning point in the war.

Carroll was a native of Maryland, where her father, Thomas, had once served as governor. During the 1850s, she took part in numerous political causes, including campaigning for Millard Fillmore during his successful 1856 bid for the presidency. In 1860, she campaigned for Lincoln, writing and distributing pamphlets in support of his candidacy. Despite her emphatic support for the Union, Carroll did not believe the federal government had the power to abolish slavery.

After the war began, Carroll had a chance to speak to riverboat pilots who were familiar with Confederate encampments. She advised the war department and Lincoln that General Grant should move along the Tennessee River instead of the Mississippi, a course he followed during his 1862 campaign.

When Carroll and her friends later petitioned the government to recognize her contribution, officials declined to do so. She died in poverty, deaf and ill, at age 77. Carroll's supporters continued to press the government to acknowledge her contributions as a military strategist and believed that she was denied this recognition because she was a woman.

References
Jeanne Holm, *Women in the Military: An Unfinished Revolution* (1992); Joan and Kenneth Macksey, eds., *The Book of Women's Achievements* (1976); Lynn Sherr and Jurate Kazickas, *The American Woman's Gazetteer* (1976).

Casualties

Throughout U.S. history, women have died while serving with and for the military. Women veterans have returned with wounds, disabilities, and psychological scars as a result of their experiences. They have also been gravely affected by losing husbands and fathers who participated in the military.

Historically, although women were not often involved in direct combat, some have died as a result of enemy fire. During the American Revolution and Civil War, an unknown number of women who disguised themselves as men and became soldiers may have died without their identities being discovered. The bodies of women in soldiers' uniforms were occasionally found on Civil War battlefields.

Other women lost their lives because of illness or injuries suffered during their military service or as a result of accidents that occurred while they were on duty. In 1901, while serving with the Army during the Spanish-American War, nurse Clara Louise Maass died in Cuba of yellow fever. Maass had volunteered for a military experiment to test ways in which this deadly and contagious disease might be transmitted.

During World War I, nurses made up the largest percentage of women serving in the military. There were no casualties among these women due to enemy fire, but several members of the Army Nurse Corps (ANC) were wounded, and more than 200 died as a result of influenza and pneumonia, which took the lives of thousands of servicemen during that war.

In World War II, 201 Army nurses died, 16 as the result of enemy action. On 25 July 1943, Second Lieutenant Ruth M. Gardiner became the first Army nurse killed in a theater of operations during the war. Gardiner, a flight nurse, was on an air evacuation mission when her plane crashed over Alaska. In 1944, Gardiner General Hospital in Chicago was named in her memory.

Six other Army nurses died while working at a hospital in Italy on Anzio beachhead in February 1943 when it was bombed by German warplanes.

In 1943, Jane Champlin, a pilot with the Women's Auxiliary Ferrying Squadron (WAFS), became the first woman to die in a military plane crash. She was aloft with her instructor on the night of 7 June 1943 when the BT-13's engine caught fire, resulting in a fatal crash. Mabel Rawlinson, a pilot with the Women's Airforce Service Pilots (WASP), died during a top-secret antiaircraft training session when a plane she was riding in crashed and burst into flames. The plane had a faulty canopy mechanism, and Rawlinson was trapped inside.

During the Korean War, no nurses died as a result of enemy action, but Major Genevieve Smith was killed during a plane crash while flying to her duty assignment as chief nurse in Korea.

One nurse, First Lieutenant Sharon A. Lane, died as the result of enemy fire during the Vietnam War, in a rocket attack on 8 June 1969 at the 312th Evacuation Hospital in Chu Lai. In her memory, a life-size statue was placed at Aultman Hospital in Canton, Ohio, her alma mater. The Lane Recovery Suite in Fitzsimons General Hospital in Denver (Lane's first Army assignment) was named for her.

Captain Mary Klinger died on 4 April 1975 in Vietnam when her plane crashed on takeoff. A flight nurse, Klinger was serving on a C-5A Galaxy that was attempting to evacuate a large group of Vietnamese orphans just before the fall of Saigon.

During the Persian Gulf War, the number of female casualties rose higher than ever before: 13 women died, 6 due to enemy fire. This war saw a higher percentage of women in U.S.

military forces than ever before, all part of an integrated military. On 25 February 1991, a SCUD missile hit barracks near Dhahran, resulting in the deaths of 25 servicemen and the first 3 women to die in war since Vietnam: Specialist Beverly Clark, age 23; Specialist Christine Mayes, age 22; and Specialist Adrienne L. Mitchell, age 20. Sergeant Cheryl La Beau-O'Brien, age 24, died while serving on the crew of a Black Hawk helicopter that was shot down.

See also
Army Nurse Corps (ANC); Fort, Cornelia; Persian Gulf War; Pilots; Rossi, Marie T.; Vietnam War; Women's Airforce Service Pilots (WASP); World War II.

References
U.S. Department of the Army, "Facts on the U.S. Army Nurse Corps" (1983); Carol Wekesser and Matthew Polesetsky, eds., *Women in the Military* (1991).

Champion, Deborah (b. 1753)

In 1775, 22-year-old Deborah Champion rode on horseback for two days with a servant named Aristarchus to bring urgent messages to General George Washington, leader of the Continental Army during the American Revolution. Starting from her home in New London, Connecticut, Champion rode north, stopping once for fresh horses at her uncle's home in Pomfret before reaching General Washington in Boston.

Nicknamed the "female Paul Revere," Champion later wrote an account of her mission. She described how she had hidden the papers containing the messages deep inside her saddlebags beneath food her mother had packed for her. In her account, Champion notes that Washington praised "the courage I had displayed and my patriotism."

Reference
Catherine Fennelly, *Connecticut Women in the Revolutionary Era* (1975).

Chapelle, Dickey (Georgette Meyer) (b. 1919)

A pioneer woman war correspondent, Georgette "Dickey" Chapelle covered three wars and four revolutions during her amazing career. Born Georgette Meyer in Milwaukee, Wisconsin, she showed an adventurous spirit during her youth. When she was 18, she learned how to fly a plane. A mathematically gifted student, she had already attended the Massachusetts Institute of Technology (MIT) for two years as the recipient of a full-tuition scholarship.

After leaving MIT without graduating, she married her photography teacher, Anthony Chapelle, and began working for an airline in the field of public relations. Georgette Chapelle, nicknamed "Dickey," continued to fly and learned from her husband how to take professional-quality photographs. When Anthony joined the Navy during World War II, Dickey obtained accreditation from the War Department to travel as a correspondent for *Look* magazine.

Dickey Chapelle first went to Panama where her husband was stationed, then covered the war in the Pacific for Fawcett publications. In 1945, the Navy helped her travel to Iwo Jima with American nurses to cover the aftermath of that famous battle. Although their ship, *Samaritan*, was marked with red crosses and thus entitled to protection under the laws of the Geneva Convention, it was attacked by Japanese bombers at sea, one of which Chapelle boldly photographed.

The *Samaritan* managed to reach Iwo Jima and picked up wounded and dead Marines six days after the troops had landed. One of Chapelle's Iwo Jima photos, *The Dying Marine*, became famous. It featured a young Georgia private, Johnny Hood, whom Chapelle photographed in grave condition after her ship first arrived. She took another picture of a much-improved Hood the day after he had received 14 pints of blood. After these two pictures were publicized, blood donations swelled across the United States.

Chapelle was so impressed by the courage of the Marines that she devoted much of her time to photographing them in action. At times, she shot while under fire and from foxholes. She also took other pictures designed to increase blood donations. One of these showed a soldier receiving a transfusion at Brown Beach near Okinawa in April 1945.

While with the Sixth Marine Division on Okinawa, Chapelle slept with her helmet on and a knife in her hand in case of enemy attack at night. She helped medics find and rescue the wounded. Leaving Okinawa, the U.S. fleet with which she traveled endured what some have called the worst Japanese kamikaze attack of the entire war.

After 1945, Dickey and Anthony Chapelle photographed stories throughout the world, publicizing conditions in the postwar world and the suffering of refugees. Their work appeared in *Look*, *Life*, *National Geographic*, and other top publications.

Dickey Chapelle's marriage ended in the 1950s. She then worked for the Research Institute of America and traveled to Europe to photograph Hungarian refugees who had left their homeland after the uprising against the Soviet regime in 1956. On her own, she devised a risky scheme and dressed in Hungarian peasant clothing in order to photograph people who were escaping from Hungary over the Austrian border where the Soviets had put mine fields. Chapelle was arrested by Russian guards and imprisoned in Budapest for three months until Carl Hartman of the Associated Press in Vienna publicized her situation. The Communists then decided to let her go.

Chapelle risked her personal safety on other occasions. She photographed the Algerian revolution, which led to that nation's independence in 1962. She went to Lebanon with the Marines in 1958, and then to Cuba. She parachuted from an Air Force plane in Korea in 1959, and made about 30 more jumps during the early 1960s while covering the growing war in Vietnam and the conflict in Laos.

As more U.S. troops were sent to Vietnam, Chapelle photographed Marines in combat, focusing on their heroism and the plight of wounded men. Her trademarks were her camera, the small pearl earrings she wore, and sometimes a flower in her helmet. For her work in Southeast Asia, she received the George Polk Award from the Overseas Press Club in 1962 and, in 1963, the highest award given by the

U.S. Marine Combat Correspondents Association. Chapelle personally opposed war, yet she had great respect and admiration for the men who were fighting. Her sensitive photographs raised the morale of U.S. soldiers during the controversial Vietnam era.

In 1965, Chapelle was marching with Marines near Chu Lai Air Base when she stepped on a land mine and was killed. She became the first woman combat correspondent ever killed in action and one of 45 correspondents killed during the Vietnam War. In her obituary, fellow correspondent Richard Tregaskis wrote, "Dickey knew that the most dramatic and exciting stories in war are found where the action and danger are. That day, chance was against her. . . ."

References

Dickey Chapelle, *What's a Woman Doing Here?* (1962); Julia Edwards, *Women of the World: The Great Foreign Correspondents* (1988); Virginia Elwood-Akers, *Women War Correspondents in the Vietnam War, 1961–1975* (1988).

Chaplains

Men have historically dominated the clergy, so women were not official members of the military chaplaincy until recent years.

Ella F. Hobart broke the tradition to become the only official woman chaplain in the Civil War. Hobart, who served with the First Wisconsin Artillery, was refused a commission because of her gender, however.

During the two world wars, the military hired women to serve as hostesses at various posts or accepted volunteers to do this work. These military hostesses often worked with the Chaplain Corps to assist servicemen and their families during times of loss or family crises.

The Citadel

During the 1990s, a debate raged over whether or not the Citadel, an all-male military college in Charleston, South Carolina, should accept women cadets. The school, founded after the Civil War, receives some federal funding, so opponents of the all-male policy have said that it should be subject to federal civil rights laws, as well as the federal constitution provision of equal protection under the laws.

Shannon Faulkner filed a lawsuit after being denied admission to the school, which had accepted her before discovering she was female. During the 1994–1995 school year, Faulkner was permitted to attend the school as a day student but not as a regular member of the cadet corps.

In an effort to keep women out, in 1994, the Citadel worked on a plan that would give female cadets an alternative by subsidizing their training elsewhere. Together with the State of South Carolina, the Citadel offered to spend up to $5 million in order to develop women's leadership programs at two private women's colleges in the state, Converse College and Columbia College. Under this plan, women would enroll in the college under the Reserve Officer Training Corps (ROTC). They would take their summer training at Palmetto Military Academy in Columbia, which also trains National Guard officers. Those who wished to receive coeducational military training could attend the

ROTC program at North Georgia College.

Upon hearing this plan, Valerie K. Vojdik, attorney for Shannon Faulkner, said, "This is treating women as second class citizens. This makes a mockery of the desires of women who want to pursue a military education." Other critics also objected that a separate program could not duplicate the benefits of attending the Citadel itself.

In July 1994, a federal district court declared that the all-male admissions policy at the Citadel was unconstitutional. The Citadel appealed the verdict while allowing Faulkner to attend day classes. In June 1995, the Citadel finalized its alternative plan for women. Up to 20 women would be admitted to a special program called the South Carolina Institute of Leadership for Women at Converse College in Spartanburg, South Carolina, about 190 miles from the Citadel. The program would entail four years of ROTC training with once-a-week military classes and a four-week summer program. Special courses in leadership and physical education, as well as trips and seminars, would be available to women in the program.

When the case was being heard by the U.S. Court of Appeals for the Fourth Circuit, South Carolina Attorney General Charles M. Condon said that Faulkner's case represented an assault on single-gender education across the nation. He said, "Ms. Faulkner does not have the right to destroy single-gender education."

The Court of Appeals ruled that Faulkner was to be admitted to the school as a regular student for the fall term of 1995. As of 1996, women were to be admitted on the same basis as men.

See also

Faulkner, Shannon; Mellette, Nancy; Military Academies; Reserve Officer Training Corps (ROTC); Virginia Military Institute (VMI); Women in Support of the Citadel.

References

"Citadel Offers Plan To Avoid Female Cadets," *New York Times* (7 October, 1994); Catherine S. Manegold, "Appeals Panel Hears Case on Citadel's Ban on Women," *New York Times* (31 January 1995); Patrick Rogers et al., "Her War Is Over," *People* (4 September 1995).

Civil Rights Act of 1964, Title VII

See Title VII of the Civil Rights Act of 1964.

Civil War

During the Civil War (1861–1865), women were not authorized to serve as soldiers, but some, disguised as men, did enlist. Many women took part in the war as nurses and hospital workers, camp followers, clerks to military personnel, and volunteer relief workers. Others raised money and supplies to aid soldiers. A few daring women operated as couriers, scouts, and spies.

As in other wars, women were often left alone to manage their homes, as well as farms, mills, and factories. They had to defend their families when enemy troops came through. Most sewed clothing and rolled bandages to send to the troops and worked with churches and civic organizations to collect money for supplies.

Few women had official military roles, and those who served in the camps usually functioned as unpaid volunteers. They cooked and washed clothing, linens, and bandages, and nursed soldiers who were sick or wounded.

Approximately six million women served as nurses for the Union Army. Hundreds of women, from both the Union and Confederacy, worked in base hospitals. When the war began in 1860, there were still no training schools for nurses in this country. Women had learned nursing skills by caring for family members or neighbors and by working with local doctors.

The first woman to receive a medical degree in the United States, Elizabeth Blackwell, organized a training course for those who wished to nurse with the Union Army. Six hundred Catholic nuns also worked as volunteer nurses at Union Army hospitals during the war. Some doctors praised them as being the best trained of all the nurses.

The South had fewer organized relief organizations and less organized nursing services than the North, but individuals such as Sally Tompkins of Richmond, Virginia, provided outstanding care under difficult conditions.

Nurses struggled to care for the sick and wounded. During the war, more soldiers died from diseases than from bullets, but the toll was high for both. There were thousands of cases of dysentery, pneumonia, typhoid, and malaria. Armies were so eager for recruits that they did not screen applicants thoroughly for health problems. At that time, physicians knew little about bacteriology or ways to prevent the spread of germs. They had few effective drugs, medicines, or anesthetics for surgery. Sanitary conditions at the camps were often dismal. To help alleviate this problem, the Union government organized its United States Sanitary Commission, which employed a number of women inspectors.

A number of women aided both the Union and Confederate Armies as couriers, spies, saboteurs, guides, scouts, and gunrunners. Lila Greet of Alabama helped a group of saboteurs burn a railroad bridge that spanned the Tennessee River, thus preventing Union supplies from reaching their destination. Those who were caught spying or sabotaging the enemy were arrested and imprisoned. Mary Jane Green, a Union spy from West Virginia, was among those caught and sent to jail. The notorious spy Belle Boyd was apprehended more than once.

As in previous wars, some women disguised themselves as men and joined combat units. Historians believe that more than 400 women fought as soldiers during the war. They came from all parts of society, and some served as officers or sergeants. They were not detected during the cursory physical examinations given to new recruits as volunteer regiments were being organized in various states.

Among those who fought for the South was Amy Clark of Alabama, who posed as "Richard Anderson" and fought with her husband for seven months. Clark's husband was killed at the Battle of Shiloh, and after burying him, she continued to fight. At a battle in Richmond, Virginia, Clark was wounded; her identity was discovered and she was discharged. Malinda Black of North Carolina posed as her husband's younger brother so they could fight together. After three battles, he was wounded and Black admitted her true identity. They were discharged together. Mary Dennis, who stood 6 feet, 2 inches tall, served as an officer with the Minnesota Regiment.

See also
Alcott, Louisa May; Army Nurse Corps (ANC); Barton, Clara; Bickerdyke, Mary Ann; Boyd, Isabelle ("Belle"); Dix, Dorothea Lynde; Edmonds, Sarah Emma; Espionage; Greenhow, Rose O'Neal; Hawks, Esther Hill; Passing; Slater, Sarah; Taylor, Susie King; Tompkins, Sally Louisa; Tubman, Harriet; United States Sanitary Commission; Van Lew, Elizabeth; Velasquez, Loreta Janeta; Vivandieres; Wood, Harriet.

References
B. A. Botkin, *A Civil War Treasury of Tales, Legends, and Folklore* (1985); Ina Chang, *A Separate Battle: Women and the Civil War* (1991); Sylvia G. L. Dannett, ed., *Noble Women of the North* (1959); Richard Hall, *Patriots in Disguise: Women Warriors of the Civil War* (1993); Mary E. Massey, *Bonnet Brigades* (1966); Milton Meltzer, *Voices from the Civil War: A Documentary History of the Great American Conflict* (1989); Seymour Reit, *Behind Rebel Lines: The Incredible Story of Emma Edmonds, Civil War Spy* (1988); Wilbur H. Siebert, *The Underground Railroad from Slavery to Freedom* (1898); Stewart Sifakis, *Who Was Who in the Civil War* (1988); Francis B. Simkins and James W. Patton, *The Women of the Confederacy* (1936); John E. Stanchak, *Historical Times Illustrated Encyclopedia of the Civil War* (1986); Bell Irvin Wiley, *Confederate Women* (1975).

Civilian Employees

See American Expeditionary Forces (AEF); American Revolution; Army Nurse Corps (ANC); Civil War; Signal Corps; World War I; World War II.

Clarke, Mary E. (b. 1924)

In 1975, after serving in the Army for 30 years, Mary E. Clarke was appointed head of the WAC, replacing Mildred Bailey, who was retiring. The WAC was going to be phased out as military branches began the process of integrating women into the regular service, and Clarke oversaw the transition process.

Clarke was a major general in the late 1970s, when she was placed in charge of Fort McClellan, Alabama. This major U.S. Army post has a large coed training program and is the site of the Army's chemical warfare and military police schools.

When Major General Clarke retired in 1981, she was the highest-ranking woman in the military.

References
Jeanne Holm, *Women in the Military: An Unfinished Revolution* (1992); U.S. Department of the Army, "Background Information: The 50th Anniversary of the Women's Army Corps" (1992).

Clerical Workers

Efficient clerical workers were essential to the military efforts during World War I and World War II. Women eventually filled most of these roles, since they were already skilled at such tasks and it made more men available for combat. Both in the United States and overseas, women were typists and stenographers; they handled record-keeping and correspondence, ordered supplies, and served as secretaries for military officials. Overseas, women served as secretaries and clerks in the medical branches of the military as well. Some worked in dangerous conditions, serving in areas that were bombarded and shelled. They provided essential services for all branches of the armed services.

In January 1943 during World War II, a group of women—mostly clerical workers—who served in Algiers referred to themselves as the first "American Women's Expeditionary Force."

A number of female clerical workers also served at home and overseas for the American Red Cross (ARC), the Young Men's Christian Association (YMCA), the Young Women's Christian Association (YWCA), the Salvation Army, and other organizations.

See also
American Expeditionary Forces (AEF); Civilian Employees; Signal Corps; SPAR; Women Accepted for Volunteer Emergency Service (WAVES); Women's Army Auxiliary Corps (WAAC); Women's Army Corps (WAC).

References
M. C. Devilbiss, *Women and Military Service: A History, Analysis, and Overview of the Key Issues* (1990); Mattie E. Treadwell, *U.S. Army in World War II: Special Studies—The Women's Army Corps* (1954); Doris Weatherford, *American Women and World War II* (1990).

Clubmobiles

During World War II the American Red Cross (ARC) operated clubmobiles for Americans serving in Europe, Asia, and the South Pacific. Special trucks, driven and staffed by volunteers, held refreshments and recreational materials that were taken to troops located behind the battle lines. A group of clubmobiles formed a unit. A unit might operate out of Great Britain, then be transported to France and other locations where fighting was taking place.

Clubmobile workers were affectionately called "Doughnut Girls" or "Donut Girls" because they distributed coffee and donuts they made in the truck, along with cigarettes, chewing gum, candy, and other items.

Clubmobile volunteers had to be physically fit and resourceful. Their training included learning how to drive and repair heavy trucks used on the job. The women wore blue uniforms and were equipped with steel helmets and gas masks.

In a letter she wrote home in 1944 from Scotland, Mary ("Chichi") Metcalfe spoke of the machine on her truck that turned out "7 doughnuts a minute" and described her clubmobile:

> We have a push thing like for chocolate sauce in a drug store where we put our canned milk to serve with the coffee. Then at the other counter we have a tray which has life savers, gum, cigarettes, and some K ration chocolate in it. Also books like the Pocketbook editions, and postcards. . . . At the end and on the other side behind the driver's seat is a victrola, and records just above it. There is a microphone which carries the music out of the Clubmobile and which the boys can have fun with.

Some groups of Red Cross clubmobilers arrived in France within weeks of D Day, providing refreshments and music from their trucks set up near the beaches where Allied troops had landed at Normandy.

See also
Volunteers.

A woman serves soldiers doughnuts and coffee from her American Red Cross clubmobile while at a remote French farmhouse in 1945.

References
Judy Barrett Litoff and David C. Smith, *We're in This War, Too: World War II Letters from American Women in Uniform* (1994); Alma Lutz, ed., *With Love, Jane: Letters from American Women on the War Fronts* (1945); Oscar W. Rexford, *Battlestars and Doughnuts* (1989); Doris Weatherford, *American Women and World War II* (1990).

Coast Guard, United States

See United States Coast Guard (USCGA).

Coast Guard Academy

See United States Coast Guard Academy (USCGA).

Cochran, Jacqueline (1912–1980)

In 1953, Jacqueline Cochran became the first woman pilot to exceed the speed of sound. A top aviator who set more than 200 flying records during her lifetime, Cochran developed and headed the Women's Airforce Service Pilots (WASP) during World War II.

Born to a poor family in Pensacola, Florida, Cochran was orphaned when her parents died shortly after her birth. She lived with relatives who moved about seeking work in the sawmills of Florida and Georgia, camping in shacks set up for workers and often going hungry. At age eight, Cochran began working 12-hour shifts each night in a cotton mill for six cents an hour. She saved what she could to buy necessities like shoes, longing for a life free of poverty.

There was little time for school, even though she loved learning, so Jacqueline read in her spare time. At age 10, she found a new job and a new place to live with a beautician who taught her that line of work, which then led to a better job in Alabama.

Cochran changed careers again, completing three years of nursing training with the goal of helping those she had lived among as a child in the sawmill camps. For a while, she worked as a nurse, then returned to work as a beautician, traveling regularly between New York City and Miami.

On a business trip in 1932, Jacqueline met Floyd Odlum, a banker who enjoyed aviation. As they talked, Cochran became so interested that she soon enrolled in flight school in New York. In three weeks, she had earned a pilot's license. At the time, only a few thousand Americans had licenses, and among them were just a handful of women. Cochran's love of flying took her to California where she received a commercial pilot's license and bought her own plane.

Cochran moved back east in 1934 to open her own beauty shop and cosmetics manufacturing business. She married Floyd Odlum in 1936. The little girl who had once longed for a pair of decent shoes was now a glamorous woman with fur coats and designer clothes, as well as an up-and-coming pilot.

In 1938, Cochran persuaded Army officials to let her use a Seversky fighter plane in the 1938 Bendix Cup Air Race, which she went on to win. Despite her business schedule, she made time to enter and win races, sometimes setting records. Soon she was being asked to test new flight equipment for the Army.

During World War II, Cochran founded and served as director of the Women's Airforce Service Pilots (WASP) This civilian group of women pilots ferried planes and towed targets, thus freeing more male pilots for combat missions. More than 1,000 women pilots served in the WASP. In August 1945, she was present on the USS *Missouri* when the Japanese government surrendered to the Allies.

For her wartime service, Cochran was awarded the United States Distinguished Service Medal, the first civilian to receive it. After the war, she went on a world tour, meeting with prominent women and political leaders and witnessing part of the Nazi war crime trials held in Nuremburg, Germany. She became a correspondent for *Liberty* magazine, reporting on events in the Far East.

Cochran continued to serve in the U.S. Air Force Reserve until 1970, when she retired as a colonel. She also managed Jacqueline Cochran Cosmetics, which had become a million-dollar business by the early 1950s, and was named Business Woman of the Year in both 1953 and 1954.

In 1953, Cochran also tested a new type of plane called a jet. She became the first woman pilot to break the speed of sound. In 1962, she flew a jet across the Atlantic Ocean, again something no woman had done before. Her test flights added to the growing body of knowledge about jet planes and how pilots reacted to high speeds and altitudes.

Besides receiving honors in the field of aviation and from various American organizations, Cochran was honored by foreign governments. In 1971 she was elected to the Aviation Hall of Fame. In 1979, the year before Cochran's death, the WASPs were finally recognized as veterans. Overcoming childhood poverty and disadvantages, this amazing woman had succeeded in several careers and served her country during a critical time in history.

See also

Women's Airforce Service Pilots (WASP).

References

Eleanor Clymer and Lillian Erlich, *Modern American Career Women* (1959); Jacqueline Cochran, *The Stars at Noon* (1954); Jacqueline Cochran and Maryann Bucknum Brinley, *Jackie Cochran: An Autobiography* (1987); Jean H. Cole, *Women Pilots of World War II* (1992); Sally Van Wagenen Keil, *Those Wonderful Women in Their Flying Machines* (1990); Marianne Verges, *On Silver Wings, 1942–44: The Women's Airforce Service Pilots of World War II* (1991).

Coed Training

Since 1973, when a congressional law required the armed forces to integrate women and men into unified services, service branches have tried various programs in which men and women train together as well as separately. Those who support training women and men together (coed or integrated training) have claimed it can reduce sexism and sexual harassment in the military.

Coed training was implemented at the Navy boot camp in Orlando, Florida, where male and female recruits had their physical training, bunk and dress inspections, and firefighting training together. A substantial coed training program was also instituted at Fort McClellan, Alabama, a large Army post.

Critics of coed training claim it results in a less challenging physical training program for men, since most women do not exhibit the same degree of muscular strength in their upper bodies and many cannot run as fast as males. Some male recruits have also said that the presence of women "softens" training.

Scientists have studied the differences in physical capabilities of men and women. Looking at these studies, author Helen Rogan writes that men tend to be bigger by about 10 percent and stronger, on average, than women. Surveys at the United States Military Academy (USMA) at West Point have shown women to have less upper-body strength and leg strength than men, with about the same amount of strength in the abdomen. On average women have more acute hearing than men, are better able to withstand cold and remain buoyant in the water, and can burn up fat more efficiently, giving them more staying power during long runs. The average woman may also have an edge over the average man in leg wrestling.

Women are improving their physical performance in military training and tests, possibly because girls are now encouraged to be athletic and they have many more chances to play competitive sports than they did before the early 1970s. Title IX of the Education Act, passed by Congress in 1972, banned public schools from discriminating against girls' sports programs and required them to fund programs for girls as well as boys. By the 1990s, women at the military academies were able to do more pull-ups and push-ups than their predecessors. In 1980, Cadet Alice Berry, a member of the Reserve Officers Training Corps (ROTC), became the first woman to score a perfect 500 on the ROTC advanced physical training test, which measures all-around physical ability. Other women have since achieved this perfect score.

See also
Clarke, Mary E.; Military Academies; Training, Basic; Weapons Training.
Reference
Helen Rogan, *Mixed Company: Women in the Modern Army* (1981).

Coleman, Kit (n.d)

Kit Coleman was the first woman journalist known to have covered a war in the United States, the Spanish-American War of 1898. Born in Canada, Coleman was a correspondent for a Toronto newspaper, *The Globe and Empire.* At first, officials at the U.S. Secretary of War office in Washington, D.C., refused to sign her press card, but Coleman persisted. She managed to hitch a ride to Cuba on a fishing boat after being refused passage by both military and medical ships departing from the United States. The resourceful Coleman finally arrived in Santiago in time to report on the surrender of the Spanish troops and send back a story to the paper in Toronto.

Combat

Traditional views of women have assumed that they would not want to engage in combat or be capable of doing so. Males, viewed as physically and temperamentally suited for battle, were expected to fight and to perform other roles that require aggressive behavior. A woman's role was to wait for the men to return, keeping the home fires burning, so to speak, and providing support for those in the military. Many men also were inspired to fight because they prided themselves on protecting women and children.

During the American Revolution, Civil War, and Spanish-American War, however, hundreds of women defied social convention and fought alongside men—most always, if not always, in disguise. They challenged and disproved the idea that women could not perform as soldiers. As nurses, women served on and close to the battlefield in various wars, sometimes exposed to enemy fire.

When air and submarine warfare was introduced, more women were exposed to combat conditions in the form of bombing, antiaircraft artillery, and torpedoes, even though the military systems had not placed them in combat zones. In addition, civilian women and children have suffered from harsh treatment during war as the targets of enemy sieges, invasions, and occupations, or when they were taken to enemy prison camps.

Since World War II, women's occupational roles and legal rights have expanded. In that war, women worked in battle zones overseas and did heavy industrial work in factories at home. After the 1950s, women continued to perform jobs that had once been limited to men, working as police officers, firefighters, and in other nontraditional positions. Still, the idea that women should not take part in military combat persisted.

After the war, when women's divisions became a permanent part of the military, specific legislation, such as the Combat Exclusion Law, was passed to ban women from combat roles. Military traditions and policies in the various service branches also excluded women from these roles, which included ground combat, air combat, and serving on war vessels in the Navy. Nonetheless, women, especially nurses in the armed forces, were exposed to enemy action and sometimes became casualties.

During the Vietnam War, when men were being drafted and thousands were killed, some people contended that women should also be drafted and sent into combat. Some of these proponents reasoned that if women wanted all the same rights as males had in American society, they must have the same responsibilities and burdens. Others simply resented the idea of banning all women from a certain role in the military without considering individual differences. In addition, many military women were kept from advancing in rank and position because they were banned from certain assignments, such as sea duty in the Navy, that were required for certain promotions.

The debate over women in combat intensified after the 1991 Persian Gulf War. Several women were killed in the war, and two Army women became prisoners of war; this upset some members of the public. Others said it supported the idea that women could serve on an equal footing with men, taking risks that went along with combat assignments. During the war, women served in combat jobs and coped with the physical and emotional stress that went with those assignments. They worked with male colleagues to do what they had been trained to do. Said Captain Cynthia Mosley, who commanded a combat support company in Iraq,

"Nobody cares whether you're male or female. It's just: 'Can you do the job?'"

In the early 1990s, Pat Foote, who retired from the Army with the rank of brigadier general, supported the idea of removing all combat restrictions, as did Jeanne Holm, a retired Air Force major general and author of a definitive history of women in the U.S. military, *Women in the Military: An Unfinished Revolution.* Other high-ranking women officers disagreed, as did many male members of the military.

Congress reopened the debate about women in combat in 1991. In May, the House Armed Services Committee voted to allow women to fly combat missions in the Air Force, Marines, and Navy. The Senate Armed Services Committee, however, did not include this provision in its recommendations to the military. After more debate, the National Defense Authorization Act for Fiscal Years 1992 and 1993, signed into law by President George Bush in December 1991, did include a section that repealed the portion of the Women's Armed Services Integration Act of 1948 that barred women from flying combat missions. This opened the way for branches to assign women to combat aircraft, but at their own discretion.

The act also set up a presidential commission to study this matter and other issues affecting women in the military. In November 1992, the 15-member commission voted 8 to 7 against permitting women to fly combat aircraft.

The debate continued after President Bill Clinton took office in 1993. Secretary of Defense Les Aspin asked Congress to repeal laws that banned women from serving on combat ships and asked the Navy to increase women's assignments to sea duty.

All branches of the service were told to justify any policies that excluded women from combat duty, a process that could open up thousands more jobs for military women.

A poll taken by the Roper Organization in 1992 showed that the American public was divided about 50-50 on the issue of whether or not women should be assigned to combat jobs. Most of those who supported the idea did not believe women should serve in ground troops, only in the air or on combatant vessels. About half of those who favored the idea of lifting the ban on women in combat also thought their participation should be voluntary.

See also

Combat Exclusion Law; Combat Pilots; Cornum, Rhonda; Persian Gulf War; Pilots; Presidential Commission on the Assignment of Women in the Armed Services (1992); Prisoners of War (POWs); Rathbun-Nealy, Melissa; Sea Duty; Top Gun; Women's Armed Services Integration Act of 1948.

References

John Lancaster, "Nearly All Combat Jobs To Be Open to Women," *Washington Post* (29 April 1993): A1, A8; Helen Rogan, *Mixed Company: Women in the Modern Army* (1981); Eric Schmitt, "Women Ready To Fly for Navy, or Flee It," *New York Times* (23 April 1993): A14; Richard H. P. Sia, "Aspin Clears Way for Women To Fly in Combat, Prepares More Changes," *Baltimore Sun* (29 April 1993): 3A; Carol Wekesser and Matthew Polesetsky, eds., *Women in the Military* (1991).

Combat Exclusion Law

The Women's Armed Services Integration Act of 1948 contained provisions that excluded women from combat assignments in the military. By 1973, as women were being integrated into the various branches of service instead of remaining in separate corps, most of the 1948 act no longer remained law.

Still remaining, however, were Sections 6015 and 8549 of Title 10 U.S. Code—the provisions banning women from combat. These two provisions stated that women could not be assigned to Navy ships or to any Navy or Air Force aircraft that were likely to be involved in combat.

The different service branches tended to give a broad reading of these combat exclusion provisions, keeping women out of numerous positions only indirectly involved in combat. In the Navy, women were not allowed to serve on any combatant vessels. The Air Force did not permit women to fly certain kinds of fighter planes.

Critics complained that the combat exclusion provisions were being used for purposes of sexual discrimination and in order to restrict the number of women in the military. They asked that more careful distinctions be made between combat and combat support positions, which women could fill despite the exclusionary laws.

In 1987, the Department of Defense (DOD) Task Force on Women in the Military issued a report suggesting that a clear standard be set up for evaluating whether certain types of positions should be open to women. The DOD published its Risk Rule in 1988, aiming to give various service branches a standard rule for determining how women could serve. Under this rule, noncombatant positions may be closed to women when they involve "risks of exposure to direct combat, hostile fire, or capture . . ." if "such risks are equal to or greater than that experienced by associated combat units in the same theater of operations."

After the Risk Rule went into effect, about 30,000 more noncombatant positions were made available to women. The rule had many critics, however. Some critics, such as Jeanne Holm, pointed out that it was a fallacy that women could be protected from the risks of modern warfare. Said Holm, "Modern weapons do not distinguish between combatants and noncombatants."

On 28 April 1993, Secretary of Defense Les Aspin ordered an end to the ban on women in combat aviation jobs and asked Congress to repeal laws that banned women from serving on combat ships. He urged the Navy to increase women's assignments to sea duty and said that all branches of the service must examine and justify any existing policies that excluded women from combat duty.

The subsequent repeal of the combat exclusion law gave the branches of service more options in deciding how women could serve. It opened up thousands more jobs for women and gave them opportunities to be promoted to the highest military ranks.

See also

Bray, Linda L.; Combat; Combat Pilots; Combat Support Force (CSF); Direct Combat Probability Coding (DCPC); Pilots; Sea Duty; Submarines; Top Gun; United States Air Force; United States Navy; Women's Armed Services Integration Act of 1948.

References

Jeanne Holm, *Women in the Military: An Unfinished Revolution* (1992); John Lancaster, "Nearly All Combat Jobs To Be Open to Women," *Washington Post* (29

April 1993): A1, A8; Helen Rogan, *Mixed Company: Women in the Modern Army* (1981).

Combat Pilots

In modern times, as women's roles and legal rights changed, the idea that they should not take part in military combat persisted. The Combat Exclusion Law and long-standing policies within the Navy and Air Force were the bases for banning women from combat roles or combat support roles in the military. These roles included ground combat, air combat, and serving on war vessels in the Navy. In addition, these rules were used to keep women from jobs such as carpentry, masonry, and interior electrical work, among other specialty careers offered in the Army.

In 1990, Lieutenent General Thomas Hickey, the Air Force personnel chief, told the Senate Armed Forces Committee that he believed women were capable of doing any Air Force combat job. He said, "They can fly fighters, they can pull Gs, they can do all those things. . . . They are physically [and] emotionally capable. . . ." Although Hickey and some others favored lifting restrictions on women pilots, others did not, and Congress decided not to ban the restrictions.

During the Clinton administration, the issue was reopened. On 28 April 1993, Secretary of Defense Les Aspin issued an order to lift the ban on women in combat aviation jobs. Furthermore, Aspin urged all branches of the service to examine and justify any policies that excluded women from combat duty, a process that led to the repeal of the combat exclusion law.

Women pilots became eligible for more jobs, along with the chances for promotion that such positions entail. As of 1995, women in the Navy were flying combat jets, prop aircraft, and helicopters. They were assigned to the F-14, the A-6, and HM, among others; 77 women were Naval Flight Officers, and 43 women pilots were in training to fly combat aircraft. Women were also assigned to eight aircraft carriers.

See also
Combat Exclusion Law; Direct Combat Probability Coding (DCPC); Fighter Pilots; Hultgreen, Kara S.; Pilots; Top Gun; USS *Dwight D. Eisenhower.*

References
M. C. Devilbiss, *Women and Military Service: A History, Analysis, and Overview of the Key Issues* (1990); Deborah G. Douglas, *United States Women in Aviation, 1940–1985* (1991); Jeanne Holm, *Women in the Military: An Unfinished Revolution* (1992); Helen Rogan, *Mixed Company: Women in the Modern Army* (1981); U.S. Department of the Navy, "Facts on Women in the Navy" (1995); Jean Zimmerman, *Tailspin: Women at War in the Wake of Tailhook* (1995).

Combat Ships

See Combat; Combat Exclusion Law; Sea Duty.

Combat Support Force (CSF)

In 1986, the Navy reclassified its Mobile Logistics Support Force (MLSF) as the Combat Support Force (CSF). The Navy, along with other branches of the service, had been under pressure from the Department of Defense to open more positions for women in the armed services. By classifying six ships in the CSF as "other

A female Air Force pilot poses in front of a row of jet fighters in 1992. The following year, Congress repealed the exclusion law, which lifted the ban on women in combat aviation jobs.

combatant," the Navy could justify keeping women from serving aboard these vessels, since women did not serve on combat ships. This action came just before the Navy put a freeze on the number of women it would permit to enlist from 1987 through 1991.

See also
Combat; Combat Exclusion Law; Direct Combat Probability Coding (DCPC); Presidential Commission on the Assignment of Women in the Armed Services; United States Navy.

References
Jeanne Holm, *Women in the Military: An Unfinished Revolution* (1992); Helen Rogan, *Mixed Company: Women in the Modern Army* (1981).

Command and General Staff College

Located at Fort Leavenworth, Kansas, the Command and General Staff College offers further education for Army officers. Students are selected on the basis of achievement and merit. The program lasts a year and includes courses in military theory and practice, history, political science, and ethics. The Air Force has an equivalent school at Maxwell Air Force Base, Alabama, called the Air Command and Staff College.

Women have attended both schools. One well-known alumna of the Air Command and Staff College is flight surgeon and Persian Gulf War veteran Rhonda Cornum, who attended the college in 1992.

See also
Cadoria, Sherian Grace.

Commission on an All-Volunteer Force

Also called the Gates Commission, the Commission on an All-Volunteer Force, headed by former secretary of defense Thomas S. Gates, Jr., was appointed by President Richard M. Nixon in 1969. Nixon wanted to abolish the draft and asked the commission to provide plans for an all-volunteer military. The report, which stated that an all-volunteer military was feasible, was submitted to President Nixon in February 1970. The president then worked out a plan with Congress to end the draft system by mid-1973.

In its comments about attracting sufficient manpower and providing career incentives to retain people in the military, the commission talked about men, not women. It concluded, however, that only 20 to 30 percent of all active duty billets were directly related to combat missions, with many other positions available in the administrative, maintenance, training, and logistical support areas. These facts were later used to support the idea of enlisting more women and allowing them to choose from among a broad range of positions in the armed forces.

See also
All-Volunteer Force (AVF); Binkin-Bach Study; Draft.

References
Richard Cooper, *Military Manpower and the All-Volunteer Force* (1977); "One Way To Avoid a New Draft: Recruit More Females," *U.S. News and World Report* (14 February 1977).

Commission on the Assignment of Women in the Armed Forces

The 15-member Commission on the Assignment of Women in the Armed Forces was formed in 1991 under President George Bush. Congress had recommended that a special panel examine a number of issues regarding women in the military. Their report was intended to aid the president in developing a list of recommendations he would submit to Congress in December 1992.

Congress asked the commission to consider the current and potential roles of women in the military, including "what, if any, roles women should have in combat." In particular, Congress was concerned as to how any changes might affect combat readiness of the armed forces. The commission was to look at existing laws and policies that affected women and consider whether the laws "should be retained, modified, or repealed." It also was asked to study the social and military implications of expanding military roles for women. The commission could suggest legislative and administrative actions that would be needed in order to implement its recommendations.

In the wake of the Persian Gulf War, there was increased optimism among those who believed women should be working in more combat-related positions, including flying combat aircraft. Among those who hoped the commission would make such a recommendation was a group called the Women Military Aviators.

In November 1992, the commission completed its findings. By a narrow margin of eight to seven, it voted against the idea that women should fly combat aircraft, leaving the decision in the hands of individual service branches.

Reference
Jeanne Holm, *Women in the Military: An Unfinished Revolution* (1992).

Conduct Standards

Codes of conduct for women have often been stricter than those for men. When the first substantial numbers of women joined the women's corps that were formed World War II, they were subjected to more stringent and detailed regulations regarding their personal conduct than men and were not as free to come and go from their bases. These rules reflected widely held attitudes in society about protecting women from harm and keeping them from being morally corrupted.

Members of the Women's Army Corps (WAC) could be discharged for "undesirable habits and traits of character." Being pregnant and unwed or having an abortion were grounds for undesirable discharges from the WAC. Critics complained that these policies were discriminatory, applying a double standard to men and women. They also pointed out that, at that time, women in the military tended to be older and more mature than males in the armed forces.

See also
Pregnancy; Women's Army Corps (WAC).

Continental Army

See American Revolution; Camp Followers; Corbin, Margaret; Espionage; Hays, Mary Ludwig; Sampson, Deborah; Vivandieres; Washington, Martha.

Cooper, Polly

See Native Americans.

Corbin, Margaret (1751–1800)

Born in Pennsylvania, Margaret Corbin, also called Molly, later helped to defend Fort Washington during a battle in the American Revolution.

Molly was orphaned at age five when her father was killed in an Indian raid and her mother was captured. In 1772, she married John Corbin, who later enlisted as an artilleryman with the Continental Army against the British. Corbin became a camp follower with her husband's army unit, and she was with him at the Battle of Harlem Heights at Fort Washington on Manhattan Island in November 1776, when he was killed while attending a cannon. Margaret Corbin took over for him, loading and firing, as they fought against Hessian mercenaries.

Severely wounded, Margaret Corbin was transported by wagon to a Philadelphia hospital nearly 100 miles away. She was an invalid after the war, unable to use her left arm ever again. In 1777, she was enrolled in the Invalid Regiment, a group Congress had set up for disabled soldiers. As part of this regiment, she was assigned to West Point until the war ended in 1781.

Later, Congress granted her a military pension and other veterans' benefits, making her the first woman known to receive them. The benefits included half the monthly pay of a soldier and "one suit of clothes or the value thereof in money."

Corbin was known as "Captain Molly" in Highland Falls, New York, where she lived until her death. In 1926, she was reburied on the grounds of the West Point Cemetery near the Old Cadet Chapel at the United States Military Academy (USMA) in New York State. A statue marks her grave. A bronze plaque placed on a rock in Fort Tryon Park in New York City also honors Corbin, calling her "the first American woman to take a soldier's part in the War for Liberty."

References
Charles E. Claghorn, *Women Patriots of the American Revolution: A Biographical Dictionary*; Lynn Sherr and Jurate Kazickas, *The American Woman's Gazetteer* (1976); Selma Williams, *Demeter's Daughters: The Women Who Founded America* (1976).

Cornum, Rhonda (b. 1955)

Major Rhonda Cornum, an Army flight surgeon, became a prisoner of war during the Persian Gulf War, spending eight days in Iraqi custody before being released.

Born in Dayton, Ohio, as one of four children, Rhonda grew up in New York State. As a child, she was especially close to her grandfather, a farm owner and electrician who had served with the Marine Corps during World War II at Iwo Jima and Guadalcanal.

A strong student, she graduated from high school at age 16 and received a full scholarship to Wilmington College in Ohio. She later transferred to Cornell University where she received a bachelor of science degree in microbiology and genetics at age 20. She had married during her senior year and gave birth to a daughter, Regan, during her last year of college.

As a graduate student at Cornell, Rhonda did special studies on amino acids, the substances that make up proteins. She was invited to present a paper at a scientific conference in Atlantic City. There she met an Army official who urged her to consider working at the Letterman Army Institute of Research doing studies on amino acid metabolism. She visited Letterman, located at the Presidio in San Francisco, and began working there in 1978 after earning her Ph.D. in nutrition and biochemistry from Cornell. That same year, she received her basic training at Fort Sam Houston in San Antonio, Texas.

At the Presidio, Cornum joined the basketball and track teams, winning a bronze medal for the one-mile relay race in 1982. In the fall, she entered medical school at the Uniformed Services University in Bethesda, Maryland, after first completing more training at the Airborne School at Fort Benning, Georgia.

Rhonda's first marriage had ended. In spring 1983, she married fellow medical student Kory Cornum, who was in the Air Force. Rhonda Cornum also completed the Army's Aviation Medicine Basic Course required for those who wanted to become flight surgeons. She learned to fly a helicopter and graduated first in her class.

Cornum received her medical degree in 1986 and did her internship in general surgery at Walter Reed Hospital in Washington, D.C. She then served as a physician at Fort Rucker in Alabama, not far from a farm she and her husband had bought in Florida. In 1988, she was named Flight Surgeon of the Year at that base; two years later, she was named Flight Surgeon of the Year for the entire Army. In addition to practicing medicine, she studied how pilots responded to new and existing technologies and evaluated experimental equipment.

When the Persian Gulf War began, Cornum was assigned to go as a medic with the 101st Airborne Division. On 27 February 1991, she was serving as a flight surgeon aboard a Black Hawk helicopter that was attempting to rescue a downed F-16 fighter pilot. The helicopter was shot down, and five of the eight people aboard were killed. Cornum and two others were taken as prisoners.

Cornum sustained numerous injuries. Both arms were broken between the shoulder and elbow and one finger was crushed. A bullet was lodged in her shoulder, causing her to lose a great deal of blood. Her Iraqi captors moved her from place to place, including a hospital where she received some care for her injuries. She later told a presidential commission that she had been sexually molested by an Iraqi guard, but that she had not been raped, a concern that has often been raised in regard to problems women might encounter as prisoners of war.

After eight days, Cornum was placed on a bus with other prisoners, blindfolded, and taken from Baghdad to Riyadh. There, she learned that she had been released. She was flown to Bahrain in Saudi Arabia, then taken to the U.S. Navy hospital ship *Mercy*, where she was reunited with her husband before flying home.

At Fort Rucker, Cornum and her husband Kory, who had also served in the Gulf, were honored with a parade and messages from many well-wishers. A featured speaker at halftime ceremonies of the 1991 Army-Navy football game, she has also received several awards for her courage.

Cornum later served at Brooke Army Medical Center in San Antonio as a urology resident and attended the Air Command and Staff College. An accomplished horseback rider, she has a steeplechase jockey's license. She also enjoys skydiving and piloting and has flown F-15s and an F-16 as a member of the Air National Guard.

Reference

Rhonda Cornum, as told to Peter Copeland, *She Went to War: The Rhonda Cornum Story* (1992).

Corps of Engineers

Early in 1943, during World War II, 422 Wacs were assigned to the Corps of Engineers at Los Alamos, New Mexico, where top scientists were working on the secret project to build the atomic bomb. When they were being recruited for this assignment, the Wacs were told that their work would be secret and they would have to live in an isolated region and not be able to go overseas. They were forbidden to discuss their work with outsiders or receive public acclaim during the project.

Most of the Wacs served in supportive roles traditionally assigned to women; they were secretaries, stenographers, typists, and clerks. Others were telephone operators and teletype and cryptographic technicians. A number of the Wacs worked with top-secret classified papers and communications. Some served in a technical capacity, as engineers, or in chemical laboratories. Wacs with special qualifications received technical training at Los Alamos, working on ceramic, plastic, electrical, or metallurgical aspects of the job.

Morale was low among some Wacs at Los Alamos, who felt they were not being used to the fullest of their training or ability—particularly when they were expected to baby-sit children living at the camp and serve as servants and waitresses in other nonmilitary jobs.

General Leslie Groves, head of the Manhattan Project, later praised the WAC units that served in Los Alamos, saying that "no WAC assignment anywhere exceeded in importance their mission with the Atomic Bomb project." In a congratulatory message directed to these women, Groves wrote, "You can well be proud of your service with the Manhattan Project and the part you played in saving countless American lives."

The WAC units in the Corps of Engineers received the Meritorious Unit Service Award, and 20 members of the corps were awarded the Army Commendation Ribbon. One received the Legion of Merit.

Reference

Mattie E. Treadwell, *U.S. Army in World War II: Special Studies—The Women's Army Corps* (1954).

Corregidor

Corregidor, an island in the South Pacific, was the site of a dramatic siege during the early months of U.S. involvement in World War II. In 1942, members of the Army Nurse Corps (ANC) were stranded on the nearby Bataan peninsula where they had been awaiting the arrival of U.S. troops while caring for hundreds of wounded and sick men. The nurses had been removed from Manila after the Japanese bombed the Philippines in December 1941. They had already endured numerous hardships, including illness and inadequate staff, food, and supplies.

On 9 April 1942, anticipating that Bataan would fall to the Japanese, commanders evacuated the nurses by boat to the island of Corregidor where an underground hospital was located in a deep tunnel. While on Corregidor, the nurses often faced electrical power outages and other problems as, above them, U.S. troops fought a losing battle against Japanese gunfire.

On 19 April, when it became clear that Corregidor would also fall, plans were made to evacuate the nurses by boat at night and take them to Australia. Only a few overcrowded boats were able to escape, carrying 21 nurses. They safely reached Australia and then the United States, then became the first American women to receive decorations for bravery during this war.

There were still 50 nurses and 50 doctors at Corregidor when Japanese troops arrived. One boatload of medics was also captured by the Japanese, which raised the total to 66 captured nurses. They were taken to Manila where they spent three years in Japanese prison camps along with thousands of British and American civilians.

Chief nurse First Lieutenant Josephine Nesbitt (left) and nurse Mary Moultrie pose for a picture before leading a group of nurses serving in Bataan to the island fortress of Corregidor on 11 April 1942.

See also
Army Nurse Corps (ANC); Bataan; Brantley, Hattie Rilla; Navy Nurse Corps (NNC); Prisoners of War (POWs); World War II.

Correspondents, War

Women had written for periodicals and operated newspapers in America since colonial days but were not often welcomed in these jobs. After the Civil War, women writers staffed new magazines written specifically for women and families. They also began working as editors of the women's pages of newspapers.

As time went on, women showed they could write well about serious political, labor, and social issues of the day. In the beginning, some used male pen names, but the idea of female journalists and editors slowly gained more acceptance.

As late as World War I, women were regarded as unfit to cover such grim subjects as war, particularly if it meant going to the battlefront. A few obstinate women persisted. Among them was the pioneer journalist Nelly Bly (pen name for Elizabeth Cochrane), who had become a reporter for the *New York World* newspaper and had done investigative reporting on unsafe factories and mental asylums, among other serious topics. Bly served as a correspondent in Europe during the war.

Some women found themselves in Europe when the war broke out and decided to record the action they could observe and investigate. A number of women kept diaries that were later published. Mildred Aldrich, a retired journalist, wrote a series of articles from France where she lived from 1914 to the end of the war. Among her reports was a description of the damage caused by the Battle of Marne.

Professional women journalists who wanted to cover the war in Europe often found innovative ways to get the job done. Some joined volunteer groups such as the Young Men's Christian Association (YMCA) and asked considerate supervisors to send them to places where they could report on important events. Others, like Sophie Treadwell, a reporter for the San Francisco *Bulletin,* and Ellen LaMotte, a writer for *The Masses,* went abroad as nurses after trying and failing (because they were women) to get permission to cover the war. LaMotte's hospital experiences formed the basis for her book, *The Backwash of War.* Her candid, opinionated look at the war did not always present the military in a good light and was banned by the French, British, and U.S. governments.

Several women journalists wrote about the activities of women during the war. They described the courage of women in battle zones and their work on behalf of refugees and sick and wounded soldiers. Among those who described daily life in war-torn Europe was Corra May White Harris, a correspondent for the *Saturday Evening Post,* who described conditions behind the battle lines of France.

Madeleine Zabriskie Doty reported from Europe for the *Chicago Tribune* and *New York Tribune.* She described the fate of foreigners in Germany and the desperate condition of German war orphans during two trips she made to Germany during the war. Some German women met with her secretly to confide their negative feelings about the war and about their nation's political leaders. Mary McAuley also reported on the war in Germany, where she had been studying art in 1915. She described the lives of German women, many working in factories and living on limited rations.

One of the best-known correspondents of the 1930s was Sigrid Schultz, manager of the *Chicago Tribune* office in Berlin. After meeting Adolf Hitler and other Nazi leaders during the 1930s, Schultz wrote articles warning Americans to regard the Nazis as a serious threat to world peace. She believed Hitler was getting ready for a massive war. Dorothy Thompson, another American journalist, was ordered by Hitler to leave Germany because her articles for the *New York Herald Tribune* criticized the Nazis and their anti-Jewish policies.

When World War II broke out, some American women were already working abroad as foreign correspondents. They began filing reports on political events, as well as the lighter subjects they had been assigned to cover. Eager for news and eyewitness accounts of the war, editors were no longer so concerned about whether these articles were being written by men or women. Some women radio commentators broadcasted from Europe.

Back in the United States, women journalists sought permission from the War Department to accompany troops in order to file on-the-scene reports. Sonia Tomara, a reporter for the *New York Herald Tribune,* asked to report from Asia. The War Department rejected her requests until 1942. Tomara reached China in August of that year and began reporting on bombings by Japanese. She made requests for months before being allowed to join a bombing mission, flying on a B-25 out of Kweilin.

Martha Gellhorn was aboard a British ship that crossed the English Channel during the Allied invasion of Normandy on D Day. She hid on a water ambulance in order to reach troops at Easy Red Beach. There, Gellhorn talked with some of those who had taken part in the battle, and she is believed to be the first woman to have gone ashore on D Day.

In January 1943, Ruth Cowan, a reporter for the Associated Press, became the first woman to be assigned to a specific military unit fighting in North Africa in World War II. After she arrived in Africa, Cowan faced the hostility of several Army officials and male war correspondents who did not want to work with a woman.

Rather than struggle with the U.S. War Department, Helen Kirkpatrick of the *Chicago Daily News* received permission to travel with French combat troops in Africa and Italy during World War II. She had become acquainted with influential French leaders during her years as a correspondent in France before the war started. Kirkpatrick receive bylines for many of her articles, which was considered a great compliment. By 1944, she was so highly regarded that the Allied troops asked her to help organize press coverage of the planned invasion of France. Through hard work and skillful reporting, Kirkpatrick was one of the first journalists to arrive in Paris after the Nazis were forced out on 25 August 1944.

Among the other famous women journalists of World War II were Margaret Bourke-White, Marguerite Higgins, and Ann Stringer. The reports and photographs sent back by women helped inform Americans about the war and build support for the trials held at Nuremburg for Nazi leaders accused of crimes against humanity.

See also

Bourke-White; Margaret; Chapelle, Dickey (Georgette Meyer), Coleman, Kit; Higgins, Marguerite ("Maggie"); Rinehart, Mary Roberts; Stringer, Ann; Trotta, Liz.

References

Barbara Belford, *Brilliant Bylines: A Biographical Anthology of Notable Newspaperwomen in America* (1986); Julia Edwards, *Women of the World: The Great Foreign Correspondents* (1988); Martha Gellhorn, *The Face of War* (1988); Mary McAuley, *Germany in War Time: What an American Girl Saw and Heard* (1918); Antoinette May, *Witness to War: A Biography of Marguerite Higgins* (1983); Dorothy and Carl J. Schneider, *Into the Breach: American Women and World War I* (1990).

Coughlin, Paula (b. 1962)

In September 1991, Paula Coughlin, a Navy lieutenant and admiral's aide, was one of dozens of women who claimed that they were assaulted by male officers attending the Tailhook convention in Las Vegas, Nevada. After Coughlin decided to speak out about the abuse, the Pentagon launched investigations into Tailhook and the problems of sexual harassment and sexism in the Navy. During these investigations, several top naval officials resigned and nearly 200 men faced some kind of disciplinary action.

Coughlin grew up in Virginia where her father, a career naval aviator, was stationed. Strong and athletic, she was at one time the only woman lifeguard working on Virginia Beach. She later joined the Reserve Officer Training Corps (ROTC) program at Old Dominion University in Norfolk, Virginia, and joined the Navy in 1984. Coughlin had strong feelings of patriotism and had long wanted to serve in the military.

In 1987, Coughlin graduated first in her helicopter school class and began serving as an H-2 helicopter commander, instructor pilot, and maintenance check pilot. She was deployed twice in the west Pacific and spent 12 months at sea. She enjoyed working on a hydrographic research ship that was charting the ocean floor. In addition, she flew supplies to Navy Seabees who were working on out-islands around Australia, Bali, the Philippines, and Singapore.

In 1990, Rear Admiral Donald Boecker, commander of the Naval Air Test Center in Patuxent River, Maryland, chose Coughlin as his new aide. Among Coughlin's jobs was evaluating old and new planes and helicopters to make sure they were ready at all times. She described it as a "great job," saying, "I got to fly maybe 20 different kinds of aircraft, and I was working for a man who without a doubt was the finest officer and gentleman I have ever met in my life."

In July 1991, Admiral Boecker was transferred and Coughlin began serving as the aide to his replacement, Admiral John W. Snyder, Jr. Shortly thereafter, she accompanied Snyder on a working trip to the Tailhook convention (named for the aircraft landing hook that catches onto carrier-deck cables) in Las Vegas. The association of naval aircraft-carrier aviators had held this convention annually for over a decade.

About 2,500 Marine and Navy fighter pilots attended the convention that September. The mood at the convention was influenced by the fact that five weeks earlier, the Senate had passed a bill asking a presidential commission to review combat restriction laws applying to women and another bill that would remove combat restrictions for female pilots. Coughlin hoped for such a ruling because she had applied to fly H-60s in a combat squadron based on the West Coast. There were a few other female pilots at the convention.

As a naval officer among other naval officers, Coughlin did not expect any problems as she arrived at the third floor of the convention hotel to attend evening parties with friends. Along the corridor on the third floor, she saw lines of pilots standing in the halls outside the suites, forming what was called a "gauntlet." Coughlin later reported that as she walked down the hall, she was pushed and lifted from the ground, and that pilots grabbed her breasts and other parts of her body. Coughlin described their behavior as aggressive and hostile. She fought back physically, fearing the group intended to rape her. After breaking free, she left the floor, deeply disturbed.

After the convention, Coughlin decided to tell her boss, Admiral Snyder, and others what had happened. As she later explained, "This was not my navy. People needed to know there was something seriously screwed up here." She had expected them to share her outrage, but some Navy officials simply shrugged off the incident as the behavior one would expect of drunk and rowdy fliers who were letting off steam. Some people told Coughlin she should have stayed away from the group if she wanted to avoid such experiences.

Coughlin viewed things differently and later said,

> I saw the men in that hallway as the future leaders of the navy. That wasn't boy play but malicious, counterproductive, unprofessional, criminal behavior. . . . If

I had walked into a sleazy biker's bar in San Diego and been abused, I could have handled that. I could almost accept the idea that I was in the wrong place at the wrong time. But I could never accept being abused by my peers, the naval aviators. . . .

Coughlin received a new assignment in the Bureau of Naval Personnel in Washington, D.C., that October. During the Tailhook investigation, she was asked to identify the men who had assaulted her at the convention. The stress of the case took its toll as Coughlin experienced health problems and felt isolated and ostracized.

Critics called the first Tailhook investigation a weak attempt to cover up the incidents and protect those who had taken part, including several top-ranking officers who had been on the floor where Coughlin reported being assaulted. After receiving numerous complaints, Congress insisted that the Pentagon conduct a more thorough investigation. The secretary of the Navy resigned in June 1992 shortly before it began.

The Navy settled its lawsuit with Coughlin for an undisclosed amount, and in 1994, a jury awarded her $6.7 million in damages in a lawsuit her attorney filed against the Las Vegas hotel where the Tailhook convention had been held.

Coughlin was harassed and labeled a "whistle-blower" by her critics, while supporters praised her courage in standing up to a powerful organization. Some women worried there would be reprisals against other women in the Navy, where men outnumbered women ten-to-one in the early 1990s. The hostility Coughlin experienced from fellow officers finally led her to leave the Navy. She later told journalist Linda Bird Francke, "What I wanted from day one was for the navy to realize there was a huge problem out there, to have someone—anyone—in the chain of command admit that the navy was broken and then start to fix it."

See also
Tailhook.

References
Linda Bird Francke, "Paula Coughlin: The Woman Who Changed the U.S. Navy," *Glamour* (June 1993): 159ff; Marie-Beth Hall, *Crossed Current: Navy Women from World War II to Tailhook* (1993); Tom Morgenthau et al., "The Military Fights the Gender Wars," *Newsweek* (14 November 1994): 35–37; Eloise Salhoz, "Deepening Shame: A *Newsweek* Investigation into the Scandal That Is Rocking the Navy," *Newsweek* (10 August 1992): 30–36; Jean Zimmerman, *Tailspin: Women at War in the Wake of Tailhook* (1995).

Cowan, Ruth

See Correspondents, War.

Craighill, Major Margaret D. (b. 1907)

Margaret Craighill, a medical doctor, was the dean of Woman's Medical College in Philadelphia, Pennsylvania, before joining the Army Medical Corps. She was appointed the first woman's Medical Corps officer in 1943 when the Women's Army Auxiliary Corps (WAAC) became the Women's Army Corps (WAC). Craighill was in charge of planning medical services for the 160,000 Wacs and Army nurses at that time.

As she began her duties, Craighill heard from training center personnel that many newly admitted Wacs had to be discharged for psychiatric and gynecological reasons. The latter included pregnancy, ovarian tumors, and uterine tumors. Other Wacs were being discharged early due to arthritis, diabetes, tuberculosis, and other health problems. Craighill found that women applying to join the WAC were not being given adequate gynecological and psychiatric examinations.

Craighill appointed a committee to set the standards of acceptability in these areas. As part of the newly authorized exam, an applicant's menstrual history was recorded and more complete medical histories and exams were given. Craighill then examined how menstruation affected women while they were in the Army. She found that some women did complain about more difficult and painful menstrual periods while others said theirs remained the same or improved. Some studies were then conducted to determine what effect different kinds of military jobs had on menstrual problems, but they were inconclusive.

Under Craighill's direction, women received regular physical exams, sometimes on a monthly basis. Her staff noted that women were more modest than male recruits when undergoing physical examinations, yet most examining physicians in the Army were men. Many WAC recruits continued to object to the physical exams, even though a female officer was required to be present during all exams.

As of 1943, training for Wacs included discussions of menstruation and films showing proper hygiene. The program aimed to get rid of old and incorrect ideas, substituting factual information and proper care.

Policies for handling women suffering from serious menopausal symptoms were also discussed. Medical personnel were concerned that some menopausal women might experience severe depression or other symptoms that would keep them from functioning well in their units and that might lower morale. Craighill was among those who said that the military could give such women an honorable discharge, as it would for a pregnancy or health disability. The surgeon general, however, countered that menopause was a normal condition.

The Army also considered lowering the age limit for recruits to 38 rather than 50, the previous limit, in order to reduce the number of women who might begin menopause while they were in the service. Since the WAC needed recruits so badly, Director Oveta Culp Hobby and other officials rejected this idea. They did implement a policy of treating menopausal symptoms for six months, then authorizing a discharge if treatment did not relieve symptoms sufficiently by that time.

Reference

Mattie E. Treadwell, *U.S. Army in World War II: Special Studies—The Women's Army Corps* (1954).

Crawford v. Cushman

In 1976, in *Crawford v. Cushman*, the Second Circuit Court declared unconstitutional a Marine Corps regulation that required that a pregnant Marine be discharged as soon as the pregnancy was revealed. The court said that this rule violated the due process aspects of the Fifth Amendment to the United States Constitution. It viewed pregnancy as a "temporary disability" and said that no other comparable conditions resulted in discharge.

The court also argued that all pregnant women were being treated alike with this rule, regardless of individual differences. It ruled that the Marines must make an effort to determine how fit each individual pregnant woman was to serve, rather than apply a mandatory discharge.

Cushman, Pauline

See Wood, Harriet.

D Day

During World War II, on 6 June 1944, thousands of Allied troops landed on the Normandy coast as part of a massive effort to oust the German troops that occupied France. The Allied invasion, commonly known as the D Day invasion, then swept inland to liberate Paris.

Women serving in the nurse corps reached Normandy within four days after the invasion, and women with the American Red Cross (ARC) arrived later the same week. Nurses and medical teams set up field and evaluation hospitals, and Red Cross clubmobiles began operating for the benefit of servicepeople in the region.

A number of women war correspondents in Europe were eager to cover the Normandy invasion, as some male correspondents were doing. From their offices in Britain, about 100 women from the United States, Britain, France, and several other nations repeatedly asked military officials for clearance to go to the front. None were given official permission to accompany troops to France, however. The U.S. War Department also stated that no women could go to Normandy.

Resourceful women journalists managed to gather news about the invasion in other ways. Martha Gellhorn was aboard a British ship that crossed the English Channel during the invasion. By hiding on a water ambulance, she reached Easy Red Beach where troops were located and interviewed some soldiers who had taken part in the fighting. Gellhorn is thought to be the first woman to have gone ashore on D Day.

Ruth Cowan of the Associated Press and British journalist Iris Carpenter were allowed to join the 91st Evacuation Hospital unit, which was setting up an 800-bed field hospital in a grassy area. The two correspondents shared a tent with Army nurses. Although international laws banned the bombing of hospitals, German planes repeatedly bombed the area. Carpenter suffered from a shattered eardrum during one bombing.

While male correspondents were given jeeps to use on the job and were briefed each day by military officials, the women who managed to get to Normandy received less consideration. They had to wait for the men to finish using communication equipment before they could file their stories. Nonetheless, Cowan and Carpenter managed to get to the front and were able to report on the battle of Saint-Lô as well as other significant events surrounding D Day.

In August 1944, journalist Lee Carson joined an official Army tour of Normandy, then abandoned the group in order to reach Paris on the 24th to report on the city's liberation. Sonia Tomara of the *New York Herald Tribune* had already arrived in Paris, and Ruth Cowan and British reporter Iris Carpenter joined them shortly thereafter.

Carpenter reported back to the British Broadcasting Company (BBC) about the triumphant celebration that took place in the French capital after the Germans were defeated. She also spoke to top military officials about the discriminatory treatment of female correspondents. According to author Julia Edwards, Carpenter told General Eisenhower's top aides, "I am going to get my story. I am going to go whether you accredit me or not." Although the women still were not accredited to war zones, they did finally get the military to authorize them to join specific military units.

See also
Correspondents, War.

References
Barbara Belford, *Brilliant Bylines: A Biographical Anthology of Notable Newspaperwomen in America* (1986); Julia Edwards, *Women of the World: The Great Foreign Correspondents* (1988); Martha Gellhorn, *The Face of War* (1988).

Darragh, Lydia (1729–1789)

Called the "Fighting Quaker," Lydia Darragh served the Continental Army as a spy in Philadelphia. She was born Lydia Barrington in Ireland and moved with her husband, William Darragh, to Philadelphia. There they joined the Religious Society of Friends (Quakers) and raised a family of nine children.

During the American Revolution, Darragh's son Charles was serving as a lieutenant in George Washington's unit camped at Whitemarsh. It is said that Darragh sent information to the army by means of folded pieces of paper with coded messages on them so that they fit into large buttons she sewed on the jackets of another son, John. Fourteen-year-old John could then carry these messages into camp when he visited his older brother.

Quakers are pacifists and are expected to take a neutral stance in a war, so British General Howe sometimes met with officers in the Darragh home to discuss their strategy. Howe also took over rooms in the house when his soldiers did not have lodgings. One night in December 1777, Howe and his men met at the Darragh home, and the general held an important conference in a room on the ground floor. When Howe asked if the whole family was in bed as he had ordered, Darragh said yes. A friend later asked how she could have told a lie, and Darragh is said to have remarked, "Husband and wife are one, and that one is the husband, and my husband was in bed."

That night, while eavesdropping on the conference, Darragh heard important information about plans for a surprise attack on Washington's encampment. The next day, after telling her family and General Howe that the household was in need of flour, Darragh set out on foot to warn the American troops. Along the way, British sentries who stopped her believed they need not fear the middle-aged woman in the Quaker dress and bonnet. Darragh got close enough to the troops to get her message to Colonel Boudinot, who hastened to tell Washington the news. She returned home, stiff with cold—and with the sack of flour in tow.

When British troops arrived at Whitemarsh, they were met by substantial troops and were soundly defeated. The loss dampened British morale and led some high-ranking officers to conclude that their side could not defeat the colonists.

References
Elizabeth Anticaglia, *Heroines of '76* (1975); Katherine and John Bakeless, *Spies in the Revolution* (1969); Patricia Edwards Clyne, *Patriots in Petticoats* (1976).

Daughters of Liberty

Daughters of Liberty groups were formed by women throughout America during prerevolutionary days. As men had formed the Sons of Liberty, so women patriots had their own groups, sometimes referring to themselves as "associations of ladies."

One of the major tasks of these women's groups was to spin cloth for the new American nation and its fighting men. Textiles were a major export industry in England; by boycotting British cloth, the colonists were hurting the British economy. As Abigail Foote of Cochester, Connecticut, wrote in her diary in 1775, "I carded two pounds of whole wool and felt Nationly."

The first Daughters of Liberty meeting took place in 1766 in Providence, Rhode Island, where 17 women gathered to spin thread and make homespun cloth that would replace British goods. The women also agreed to boycott tea and certain other products.

On 31 January 1770, 300 women in Boston announced they would totally abstain from serving or drinking tea. It is said that this one group made 13,000 overcoats and thousands of pairs of spatterdashes (leggings) for the cavalry, as well as thousands of skirts and garters for infantrymen and frocks for riflemen during the war.

In enforcing boycotts, Daughters of Liberty groups sometimes formed mobs and used force to persuade local merchants. Some mobs of women tarred and feathered Tories (British loyalists) in their communities.

See also
American Revolution; Edenton Tea Party.

References
Elizabeth Boutwell, *Daughter of Liberty* (1967); Patricia Edwards Clyne, *Patriots in Petticoats* (1976); Mary Beth Norton, *Liberty's Daughters: The Revolutionary Experience of American Women, 1750–1780* (1980).

Death Gratuity

See Benefits.

Decorations

In war and peace, women have won a number of military decorations. These include combat decorations and decorations for service or special acts of bravery.

During World War II, members of the Army Nurse Corps were highly decorated—1,600 received one or more of the following: Silver Star, Distinguished Flying Cross, Distinguished Service Medal, Soldier's Medal, Bronze Star, Air Medal, Legion of Merit, Commendation Medal, and Purple Heart. In 1943, nurses who escaped from the island of Corregidor became the first American women to receive decorations for bravery during the war.

After a hospital in Italy on Anzio beachhead was bombed by German warplanes, six Army nurses died. The four who survived the attack were awarded the Silver Star, the first women ever to receive this honor.

The Fifth Army WAC, the first unit to set foot in Europe during World War II, arrived in Italy on 17 November 1943 under First Lieutenant Cora M. Foster. The women often worked out of tents or in mobile units as telephone operators, clerks, typists, stenographers, and switchboard operators. They followed the Fifth Army throughout the peninsula of Italy and were later awarded the Meritorious Service Unit Plaque (the only WAC unit to receive this award) and 27 Bronze Stars.

For her wartime service, Jacqueline Cochran, aviator and director of the Women's Airforce Service Pilots (WASP), was awarded the United States Distinguished Service Medal, the first civilian thus honored.

The WAC units that served with the Corps of Engineers received the Meritorious Unit Service Award. Twenty members of the corps were awarded the Army Commendation Ribbon, and one received the Legion of Merit.

In 1953, Barbara Olive Barnwell became the first woman to receive the U.S. Navy–Marine Corps medal for heroism. A native of Pittsburgh, Pennsylvania, Staff Sergeant Barnwell was serving in the U.S. Marine Reserve when she rescued a drowning soldier, thus earning the medal.

During the Vietnam War, First Lieutenant Jane A. Lombardi, a flight nurse, managed to enplane 38 battle casualties at a base at Da Nang while it was under attack. All but 12 of the men were on litters. Acting under fire, Lombardi achieved this feat with remarkable speed. She was later awarded the Bronze Star medal for her "extraordinary and outstanding professional skill" and calmness under life-threatening conditions.

During that same war, four Navy nurses who were injured during an enemy bombing were the first women in Vietnam to receive the Purple Heart.

See also
Army Nurse Corps (ANC); Hobby, Oveta Culp; Purple Heart.

References
Jeanne Holm, *Women in the Military: An Unfinished Revolution* (1992); Sally Van Wagenen Keil, *Those Wonderful Women in Their Flying Machines* (1990); Mattie E. Treadwell, *U.S. Army in World War II: Special Studies—The Women's Army Corps* (1954); June A. Willenz, *Women Veterans: America's Forgotten Heroines* (1983).

Defense Advisory Council on Women in the Services (DACOWITS)

In 1951, the U.S. Department of Defense created the Defense Advisory Council on Women in the Services (DACOWITS) in order to increase the number of women being recruited into the military. Secretary of Defense George Marshall had supported the formation of the council. The 50 members of DACOWITS were prominent civilian women appointed by the president. They included retired military officers, educators, businesswomen, attorneys, politicians, and women from the arts. Led by their chairwoman, Mrs. Oswald Lord, DACOWITS met for the first time on 18 September 1951.

DACOWITS, throughout the 1950s, examined the reasons that an inadequate number of women were joining the military. They held hearings on this subject and worked to publicize the need for more servicewomen, promote the military as a desirable career for women, and raise the social status of these careers. In addition, DACOWITS committed itself to ensuring that quality was not sacrificed in the process of recruiting larger numbers of people.

The Department of Defense (DOD) carried out a nationwide recruitment program along the lines suggested by DACOWITS. Funds were allocated for a public relations campaign, advertising, and larger recruitment staffs. The DOD hoped that an additional 72,000 women would enlist by the summer of 1952.

The recruitment goals set by DACOWITS and the DOD were not met. Barriers to recruitment included widespread attitudes about acceptable careers for women. Prejudices against women in the military persisted, including the idea that such women were not really "feminine" or that they might be of low moral character. In addition, there were no national crises at the time that aroused strong feelings of patriotism and the desire to serve.

Many women also did not qualify for the armed services. To maintain the prestige of the women's corps, the services set higher educational, mental, and physical standards than those that male recruits had to meet. Background checks and psychiatric exams were also more thorough.

Since its inception, DACOWITS has remained active, although the goals of the council have changed somewhat through the years as the roles of military women have changed. During the years of the Vietnam War, DACOWITS again confronted the problems of recruiting and deploying enough women. At that time, qualified recruits were being turned away because the various service branches had set quotas on the number of women they would accept.

Through the years, DACOWITS has been an advocate for opening more jobs in the military to women. The council recommended that the DOD give the various service branches more latitude in assigning people based on their skills and ability regardless of gender. During the early 1970s, DACOWITS suggested that Sections 6015 and 8549 of the Women's Armed Services Integration Act of 1948 be repealed so women could fly combat aircraft and serve aboard combat sea vessels. During the 1990s, DACOWITS continued to consult with the Department of Defense on a variety of matters regarding women in the military.

References

E. A. Blacksmith, ed., *Women in the Military* (1992); M. C. Devilbiss, *Women and Military Service: A History, Analysis, and Overview of the Key Issues* (1990); Marie-Beth Hall, *Crossed Current: Navy Women from WW II to Tailhook* (1993).

Defense Officer Personnel Management Act (DOPMA)

Enacted on 12 December 1980, the Defense Officer Personnel Management Act (DOPMA) put women in all service branches on the same promotion lists as men. Although Air Force promotion lists had combined men and women for years, the Army, Navy, and Marines were still promoting women and men separately until DOPMA was enacted.

The idea of a unified promotion list was not a new one. By the time DOPMA was passed, the Army had disestablished the Women's Army Corps (WAC) and had begun integrating women into male promotion lists.

From 1973 until the enactment of DOPMA in 1980, the Department of Defense (DOD) planned how it would implement the consolidation of officer promotion systems. The DOD developed a set of uniform laws to help the various service branches use the new system. It informed every service branch about the provisions of DOPMA that banned separate promotion lists for men and women and showed them how to integrate men and women into one list.

DOPMA met with some resistance in Congress. Women also debated the pros and cons of the new system, wondering how they would be treated or if they would have equal chances for promotion.

References
Jeanne Holm, *Women in the Military: An Unfinished Revolution* (1992); Dorothy and Carl J. Schneider, *Sound Off! American Military Women Speak Out* (1992).

Defense Plant Workers

During World War II, a record six million women entered the labor force. About two million took jobs in heavy industry, working in defense plants and other factories, with about 300,000 women in the aircraft industry. Women were metalworkers, draftsmen, welders, and machinists; they made ammunition and built planes, ships, tanks, and ammunition.

Individuals and families moved to cities such as Detroit or San Diego where defense jobs were available, and some settled in those places permanently. It is estimated that 25 million Americans relocated during the war to take new jobs.

Industries began a serious effort to train and hire more women after 7 December 1941, the day the Japanese bombed Pearl Harbor and the nation entered the war. Some companies admitted a limited number of women to programs that trained people for jobs in the aircraft and shipbuilding industries. In auto plants and other places where women had been barred from employment, discriminatory practices were ended. In February 1943, women made up about 90.8 percent of the newly hired autoworkers in Detroit.

Hiring women meant overcoming several obstacles. A number of companies had contracts with unions, such as the United Steelworkers of America, and had promised not to hire nonunion workers. Unions, however, had been reluctant to let women join. Besides the prejudices that some men held against women workers, they feared women might accept lower pay than men and be less willing to fight for better wages and working conditions. As the need for defense plant workers became critical, though, many unions changed their policy and accepted women as members.

In order to recruit more women factory workers, there was an organized effort to convince them that holding a "man's job" would not diminish their femininity. Working with the Office of War Information, the media contributed to this effort. Newsreels of women workers portrayed attractive, capable workers aiding a vital national cause. In *Yank*, a servicemen's magazine, the glamorous Marilyn Monroe appeared in a pinup photo dressed in overalls and working in a defense plant.

A filmstrip called *Glamour Girls of '43* featured workers transferring their skills as homemakers to various jobs in a factory. The narrator explained that "instead of cutting the lines of a dress, this woman cuts the pattern of aircraft parts." Another woman showed how she used her sewing skills to make parachutes. The Office of War Information declared that the performance of women workers "disproved the old bugaboo that women have no mechanical ability and that they are a distracting influence in industry."

An ad for a cleaning product lauded the femininity of defense plant workers in this song:

Oh, aren't we cute and snappy
in our coveralls and slacks?
And since the tags say: "Sanforized"
we'll stay as cute as tacks.

As the war continued, companies promoted the idea that women were capable of doing factory jobs and that they had a patriotic duty to their country. A Boeing Company advertisement pointed out that U.S. fighting men were defending those at home, and then asked, "Are you doing your part?"

Not only did women want to be patriotic, they found these jobs interesting, exciting, higher paying, and challenging. For women who had never worked outside the home, being in the work force provided a social circle, eased loneliness, and helped to ease the worry of having a spouse or other loved ones overseas. Many women later said that their wartime jobs greatly increased their self-confidence and led to more career opportunities.

In defense plants, women earned about 40 percent more than they did in civilian jobs. A typical job in a laundry, office, or shop paid around $24 a week at that time, while women in defense plants could earn $40 (still less than men were paid). Earning a dollar an hour was a great improvement for most women, and some were able to lift themselves and their families out of debt or poverty during the war. Others put their children through school with their earnings. African-American women had a harder time getting these well-paying jobs, since they still faced long-standing patterns of discrimination.

Many wartime jobs involved heavy, dangerous work. In a munitions plant accident in Maryland in May 1943, 15 women were killed and 54 sustained serious injuries. During the war, 37,000 defense plant workers of both sexes were killed and more than 210,000 were permanently disabled. Deaths and accidents occurred in about the same proportions for men and women.

After the war ended in 1945, factory women were usually fired to make room for returning male veterans. Within two months of the war's end, 800,000 workers had been laid off in the aircraft industry alone. The percentage of women in the auto industry fell from 25 percent during the war to 7.5 percent by the end of 1945.

Women who wished to stay in the labor force or in heavy industry found few openings. Just as wartime publicity had urged women to work in defense plants, postwar propaganda urged them to focus on roles as wives and mothers. Those who insisted on working outside the home were steered into fields viewed as more feminine—teaching, nursing, bookkeeping, and secretarial work.

See also

African Americans; Douglas Aircraft; Executive Order 8802; Kaiser Shipyard; "Rosie the Riveter"; War Manpower Commission (WMC).

References

Teresa Amott and Julie Matthaei, *Race, Gender, and Work: A Multicultural Economic History of Women in the United States* (1991); Karen Anderson, *Wartime Women: Sex Roles, Family Relations, and the Status of Women during World War II* (1981); Sherna Berger Gluck, *Rosie the Riveter Revisited: Women, the War, and Social Change* (1987);

Women inspect propellers produced at a defense plant in 1942. Following the conclusion of World War II, the majority of the estimated 300,000 female aircraft workers were laid off to make room for the returning male veterans.

Elaine Tyler May, *Pushing the Limits: American Women: 1940–1961* (1994); Nancy Baker Wise and Christy Wise, *A Mouthful of Rivets: Women at Work in World War II* (1994); Karen Zeinert, *The Incredible Women of World War II* (1994).

Demobilization

Prior to the World War II, women involved in military service were always demobilized after a war ended. Since women traditionally participated in the military as civilians and in women's corps, their services were viewed as temporary and their jobs were terminated when a given crisis had ended.

During World War I, women in the Signal Corps were praised for making necessary and useful contributions. Some military officials, civilians, and legislators recommended that women's corps be made a permanent part of the military, ready to serve quickly in an emergency. In 1921, Anita Phipps was appointed as director of women relations for the U.S. Army. She worked on a plan to mobilize civilian women as aides for the military, but it was never adopted by Congress. In addition, Phipps's position was never given full military status.

When World War II began, the military again experienced a manpower shortage. Army officials took a fresh look at the plan Anita Phipps had devised for a women's corps and organized one, largely along the lines she had proposed. Women's groups were also formed to work with the Army Air Force, Marines, Navy, and Coast Guard. At the end of the war, a process of demobilization began once again as most women were discharged. For those in the Women's Army Corps (WAC), the official demobilization policy stated that they would be removed from their duty stations when there was no longer a "military necessity."

The first women's group to demobilize was the Women's Airforce Service Pilots (WASP), which was terminated at the end of 1944. Women in the WAC, the Navy's Women Accepted for Voluntary Emergency Service (WAVES), Women Marines, Coast Guard SPAR, and Air-Wacs (women in the Air Force) were officially regarded as veterans and therefore entitled to postwar benefits, such as funding for education under the GI Bill of Rights. Discharge meetings were conducted as part of demobilization, but they were often brief and vague. Veterans' organizations tended to ignore women, who made up a relatively small percentage of veterans.

Many women reported that families and the general public showed far more concern and understanding for returning male veterans than for returning servicewomen. After demobilization, most women tended to take up their former lives, returning to their hometowns and previous occupations or getting married and raising families.

See also

American Expeditionary Forces (AEF); Signal Corps; Veterans.

References

Jeanne Holm, *Women in the Military: An Unfinished Revolution* (1992); Nancy McInerny, "The Woman Vet Has Her Headaches, Too," *New York Times Magazine* (11 February 1946): 18; Doris Weatherford, *American Women and World War II* (1990).

Dependency Entitlements

See Benefits; Pensions, Veterans'.

Direct Combat Probability Coding (DCPC)

In November 1982, the Army developed Direct Combat Probability Coding (DCPC) as a tool for deciding and identifying which positions would be closed to women. DCPC is sometimes called a combat exclusion rule, since it states that women cannot be assigned to positions that are likely to be involved in direct combat situations.

Using the DCPC system, each position in the Army is ranked from P1 to P7, according to the probability that the position would involve routine engagement in direct combat. The lower the number, the more risk of direct combat. Under the DCPC system, P1 positions are completely closed to women.

DCPC arose from recommendations made by the 1982 Women in the Army Policy Review. The review committee stated that such a system would help military officials assign the best-qualified soldiers to a given job, regardless of their gender.

The DCPC process has been reviewed and altered from time to time. In 1988, the "risk rule" was added. It states that "*noncombat* units should be open to women unless the risk of exposure to direct combat, hostile fire or capture is equal to or greater than that experienced by associated *combat* units in the same theater of operations."

See also
Combat.

References

Helen Rogan, *Mixed Company: Women in the Modern Army* (1981); Carol Wekesser and Matthew Polesetsky, *Women in the Military* (1991); "Women in Combat: The Same Risks As Men?," *Washington Post* (3 February 1990).

Discrimination, Racial

Throughout history, American women of all races have experienced discrimination from the military, and black women have endured even more obstacles and lack of recognition. They were long denied the chance to serve on equal terms with white women.

During World War I, a number of black women offered to serve overseas with the military and with various volunteer groups, but only a handful were able to do so. Two resourceful women, Addie Hunton and Kathryn Johnson, were among four who managed to work overseas under the sponsorship of the Young Men's Christian Association (YMCA). Hunton and Johnson operated a canteen in France for black soldiers, 200,000 of whom served abroad during the war. In a memoir they wrote about the experience, the two women recalled thinking as they arrived in Europe: "Would blind prejudice follow us even to France where men were dying by the thousands for the principles of truth and justice?" In France, the black canteen workers were honored by the French and treated with great respect. They said that black soldiers and social welfare workers enjoyed a "most cordial and friendly" relationship with the French people.

A professional pianist, Helen Hagan, was not permitted to entertain the troops until near the end of the war. After her performance, she received grateful letters from servicemen who enjoyed hearing her play.

African-American nurses were also the victims of discrimination during World War I. Well-trained, experienced black women were available to answer calls from the Red Cross and other organizations for nurses. Despite the need for nurses and a campaign by churches and other organizations to change racist policies, these women were not given the chance to work overseas.

Although more than 500 black women eventually served in the Army Nurse Corps (ANC) during World War II, most were assigned to duty stations with black servicemen and prisoners of war. The Navy did not accept black nurses until the war was nearly over, in January 1945. The Red Cross kept the 252 black women who served overseas during the war separate from white programs. During both world wars, segregation by race was an official policy of the military, reflecting practices that existed in other areas of American life during those years.

Despite protests from a number of groups, black women were not admitted to serve in the Navy WAVES or Coast Guard SPAR until November 1944. Members of black sororities and alumnae associations, joined by other African-American women around the country, launched letter-writing campaigns to these service branches. By the end of the war, there were 2 African-American women officers and 72 enlisted women in the Navy and 4 African-American Spars. There were no African-American women serving with either the Marines or Women's Airforce Service Pilots (WASP).

In 1948, President Harry Truman set in motion the process that would end official discrimination against African Americans that prevented them from having equal opportunities for military jobs and promotions. Racial quotas were banned. In 1954, separate units for African Americans were abolished.

The military draft ended in 1973, and the All-Volunteer Force (AVF) was approved by Congress. By 1991, African Americans made up about 12 percent of the population of the United States, and more than 30 percent of the military. Forty percent of the women serving in the Persian Gulf War were African Americans. Black Americans have become a significant part of the Army, Navy, Marines, Air Force, and Coast Guard. They have proven their ability in every type of military job.

See also

Adams, Charity; African Americans; Army Expert Field Medical Badge; Army Nurse Corps (ANC); Cadoria, Sherian Grace; Civil War; Defense Plant Workers; Harris, Marcelite J.; Volunteers; Young Women's Christian Association (YWCA).

References

Penny Colman, *Rosie the Riveter: Women Working the Home Front in World War II* (1995); Adele Hunton and Kathryn Johnson, *Two Colored Women with the American Expeditionary Forces* (1971); Jesse J. Johnson, *Black Women in the Armed Forces, 1941–1974* (1974); Jacqueline Jones, *Labor of Love, Labor of Sorrow: Black Women, Work, and the Family from Slavery to the Present* (1985); Sidney Kaplan, *The Black Presence in the Era of the American Revolution, 1770–1800* (1973); Judy Barrett Litoff and David C. Smith, eds., *We're in This War, Too: World War II Letters from American Women in Uniform* (1994); Joe H. Mays, *Black Americans and Their Contributions toward Union Victory in the American Civil War (1861–1865)* (1894); Martha S. Putney, *When the Nation Was in Need: Blacks in the Women's Army Corps during World War II* (1992); Emmet J. Scott, *Official History of the American Negro in the World War* (1969); Mattie E. Treadwell, *U.S. Army in World War II: Special Studies—The Women's Army Corps* (1954); Carl Van Doren, *Secret History of the American Revolution* (1941).

Discrimination, Sexual

American women have traditionally experienced discrimination from the military because of their gender. Opponents of sexual discrimination say that it penalizes people based on an inborn trait (gender) instead of taking into account individual merit, performance, or qualifications.

Until recent decades, women were not accepted in the military in any official role. The policies developed by the men in charge of military affairs reflected beliefs about how men and women should behave in society and what they were capable of doing. The long-standing history of sexual discrimination in the military was rooted in widely accepted ideas that men should protect women and children, while women cared for homes and families. Women were viewed as physically, mentally, and emotionally inferior to men. Custom and social norms defined these roles, and few women challenged them. Even as more women gradually assumed roles and occupations that had once been viewed as masculine, the military remained a male arena since it involved fighting, weapons, combat, aggression, and war.

Even beginning with the American Revolution, however, some women did defy social customs to fight as soldiers and serve as spies. During the Civil War, nurses like Clara Barton fought for permission to serve on the battlefield where quick aid would save more lives. In this and later wars, military nurses were exposed to the dangers of combat, yet officials continued to insist that women would not serve in any roles connected with combat conditions.

After the Spanish-American War, the Army acknowledged its ongoing need for nurses, a field made up almost entirely of women. The Army Nurse Corps (ANC) was created in 1901 and the Navy Nurse Corps (NNC) followed in 1908. Still, nurses with these corps were not given official military status or benefits that men had in the military.

After World War I, women became increasingly part of the U.S. military. Throughout the years, laws specified ways in which women were to be treated differently from men in terms of rank, salary, and veterans' benefits. The Women's Armed Services Integration Act of 1948 contained provisions that excluded women from combat assignments.

By 1973, as women were being integrated into the various branches of service, most of the 1948 act was no longer law. Still remaining, however, were Sections 6015 and 8549 of Title 10 U.S. Code, which banned women from combat, so they could not be assigned to Navy ships or to Navy or Air Force aircraft that were likely to be involved in combat. Section 6015 banned women from permanent assignment to any combat aircraft or naval vessels. Some male officers applied this law so broadly that they did not permit women even to visit the vessels. The rules against combatant units prevented women from achieving certain increases in salaries, bonuses, and extra pay.

Although the services had been integrated, women continued to be treated differently in numerous ways. Restrictions applied to how many women could be recruited, the percentage of female officers, and the areas in which they could serve. Women who were married or had dependent children were ineligible, and those who became pregnant could not stay on active duty.

Competition for assignments and promotion was among women only. In the late 1960s, the highest permanent rank a woman in the Navy could achieve was captain, and women could not be promoted to a position in the top four pay grades.

With the end of the draft and creation of the All-Volunteer Force (AVF) in 1973, most discriminatory policies ended one by one. During the 1970s, women became eligible for promotion to the general officer ranks. They began serving as commanders of units and service groups made up of both women and men. As part of integrated units, women and men now came under the same command and were measured against the same standards and rules of discipline. Women also began receiving equal pay and benefits under this new structure. No longer were married women, pregnant women, or those with dependents under age 18 ineligible for military service.

Women's roles and opportunities continued to expand during the 1980s. After the Defense Officer Personnel Management Act (DOPMA) was passed in 1980, women were assigned to more leadership positions and high-visibility jobs. They began serving on missile crews, in units closer to the battlefront, and on peacekeeping forces. They could join the crews of more types of aircraft and participate in spy and surveillance missions. They joined two-person missile crews for Minuteman and Patriot missile systems. These began as same-gender crews, but women were assigned to mixed-gender crews as of 1988. That same year, the Air Force opened security jobs to women.

The year 1988 also marked the first time the Navy allowed women to serve on combat logistics units in ships that traveled with battle groups near combat areas. That year also saw the first time a woman was assigned to command a sea vessel. Women became commanding officers at initial training schools and technical schools. Jobs as senior-level technicians were opened to women, but they were still kept off submarine duty. The lack of substantial sea duty continued to hinder women's chances for increased status and some promotions.

During the 1990s, the barriers against sea duty and flying combat planes were also repealed. In the Marines, women could train in battle skills, survival, and defensive combat operations. The Marines became the first branch to let women work as security guards in selected locations overseas, but not in "hardship" posts—those still deemed too dangerous or harsh for women.

See also
Defense Advisory Council on Women in the Services (DACOWITS); Defense Officer Personnel Management Act (DOPMA); Direct Combat Probability Coding (DCPC); Draft; Executive Order 10240; Flores, Anna; Persian Gulf War.

References
Carolyn Becraft, *Women in the Military 1980–1990* (1990); Jean Zimmerman, *Tailspin: Women at War in the Wake of Tailhook* (1995).

Dispatch Riders

See Edmonds, Sarah Emma.

Distinguished Service Medal

A number of women have received the Distinguished Service Medal because of their services to or with the military. Among them was Jacqueline Cochran, aviator and director of the Women's Airforce Service Pilots (WASP) of World War II. Cochran was the first civilian to receive the medal.

See also
Decorations.

Dix, Dorothea Lynde (1802–1887)

At age 59, Dorothea Lynde Dix volunteered to serve the Union cause in the Civil War as superintendent of all female nurses employed by the armies.

Born in Maine, Dix had been a teacher who published a popular science textbook for elementary students in 1924. After 1941, she devoted most of her life to helping the mentally ill. For decades, Dix lectured throughout the United States and Canada about the shoddy treatment of the mentally ill. She also set up hospitals where they could receive humane care.

After Secretary of War Edwin Stanton appointed Dix superintendent of nurses in 1861, she made strict rules that caused some to call her "Dragon Dix." She scrutinized potential nurses carefully to make sure they understood the difficulties they would encounter. To deter those who wanted to nurse soldiers because they sought romance or adventure, she set a bottom age limit of 30 for her nurses and required

Dorothea Lynde Dix

them to be "plain in appearance." Their dresses had to be brown or black with no bows or other adornments; jewelry and hoopskirts were not allowed. Dix also rejected people when she did not approve of their religious affiliations.

Known for her attention to detail and willingness to challenge medical authorities, she was also criticized by male officials during the war. Nonetheless, Dix served, without pay, for the duration of the war, overseeing approximately 10,000 women. In 1866, she returned to her work on behalf of the mentally ill until poor health caused her to retire in 1881.

References

Helen Marshall, *Dorothea Dix: Forgotten Samaritans* (1937); Elizabeth Schleichert, *The Life of Dorothea Dix* (1991).

Doty, Madeleine Zabriskie

See Correspondents, War.

Double Standards of Behavior

See Conduct Standards.

Double V Campaign

See African Americans.

"Doughnut Girls"

See American Red Cross (ARC); Canteens; Clubmobiles; Young Men's Christian Association (YMCA).

Douglas Aircraft

Located in Santa Monica, California, Douglas Aircraft hired women for the first time for defense projects during World War II. By 1943, women made up 45 percent of the work force at Douglas. Those numbers continued to grow, and Douglas became the largest wartime private employer of women in the nation. The company was one of several war industries to develop daycare for employees' children.

Dowdy, Betsy (b. circa 1759)

At age 16, Betsy Dowdy made a courageous horseback ride to warn Patriot troops that British loyalists planned to attack them and destroy homes along the eastern shore of Virginia.

Dowdy grew up on a farm on the northern tip of North Carolina's eastern shore known as the Outer Banks. In the early months of the American Revolution, she witnessed the destruction caused by British raids, and her family's barn was burned by British loyalists.

An experienced horsewoman at the time of her ride, Dowdy set out on her

Banker pony on a cold, foggy night in early December. She covered nearly 50 miles of steep cliffs, banks, and dunes, as well as parts of Great Dismal Swamp, in order to reach General Skinner's camp.

Dowdy's timely warning enabled Skinner to organize his men and join the Virginia Continental troops to defeat Governor John Dunsmore's 1,200-strong forces.

Draft

Women serving in the United States military have always done so as volunteers rather than being subject to conscription.

During World War II, the government considered three separate proposals to draft women into the military, something that was being done in Great Britain and the Soviet Union. Most urgently needed were nurses, almost all of whom were women, and there was a swell of political and public support to draft them for military service.

Gallup polls taken in late 1943 showed that 73 to 78 percent of the American public believed single women should be drafted ahead of men who were fathers. The same polls showed that 75 percent of the single women in the age group designated for the draft would favor such a measure. Statistics from the Bureau of the Census showed that there were about 18 million American women between the ages of 18 and 49 who did not have dependent children under age 18. Army officials estimated that of those women, at least 5 million could meet the high requirements of becoming Wacs. The number of women who would be needed by the draft was estimated at 631,000.

In the end, no women's draft was enacted. The idea of drafting nurses also became a moot point as the war drew to a close.

As the women's liberation movement grew during the 1960s, men were still being drafted into the military. The debate over whether women, too, should be subject to conscription continued, with some saying that women should have the same duties and responsibilities as men.

The All-Volunteer Force (AVF) was established in 1973, however, ending the draft for males. In its 1992 report, the Presidential Commission on the Assignment of Women in the Armed Services recommended that women not be subject to a draft, even if it were ever reinstated. The commission also did not favor having women register with the Selective Service.

The debate on this subject has continued. Many who advocate equal treatment for both sexes say that women must have the same responsibilities in this area as men do, as well as the same privileges and benefits.

See also
H.R. 2277; *Rostker v. Goldberg*.

Dual Service Couples

Dual service couples are married couples in which both partners are serving in the military. Military regulations have been set up regarding the conditions under which both people can be sent on active duty when the couple has minor children. Parents must designate a specific guardian to care for the children while both parents are deployed overseas on active duty.

Duerk, Alene B. (b. 1920)

In July 1972, Alene B. Duerk became the first woman to attain the rank of admiral in the United States Navy, a rank comparable to that of brigadier general in the Army.

A native of Ohio, Duerk graduated from the Toledo Hospital School of Nursing in 1941. In 1943, she was commissioned as an ensign in the Navy, serving both in the Pacific theater and in stateside naval hospitals during World War II.

Moving to reserve status after the war, Duerk returned to school and earned her bachelor of science degree in nursing from Case Western Reserve University in Cleveland, Ohio. She returned to active duty during the Korean War, then went back into the regular Navy where she served as a nursing instructor and in other assignments.

In 1965, Duerk moved to California, where she became the director of nursing at the San Diego Naval Hospital Corps School. From 1968 to 1970, she served as chief of nursing services at Great Lakes Hospital. She was named head of the Navy Nurse Corps in 1970, and was promoted from captain to rear admiral two years later. (By then, the passage of Public Law 90-130 had opened the way for women to be promoted to the ranks of general and admiral.) Duerk retired from the Navy in 1975.

References

Marie-Beth Hall, *Crossed Current: Navy Women from World War II to Tailhook* (1993); Jeanne Holm, *Women in the Military: An Unfinished Revolution* (1992); U.S. Navy, *White Task Force: History of the Nurse Corps* (1946).

E

Earhart, Amelia (1898–1937)

A pioneer aviator, Amelia Earhart broke many women's flying records and inspired women to become pilots.

Earhart was born in Atchison, Kansas, on 24 July 1897 and grew up in several towns in Kansas and Iowa. Her parents encouraged Amelia and her sister Muriel to be athletic and adventurous, eager to learn. A science-lover, Amelia focused on biology and chemistry when she went to college and first planned to become a doctor.

Shortly after World War I, Earhart became a nurse's aide in a Toronto hospital for veterans. She enjoyed watching the Royal Flying Corps, admiring the fascinating loops and spins undertaken by stunt pilots. Later she wrote that after her first time watching a stunt pilot, "his little red airplane said something to me as it swished by."

Earhart took a brief course in engine mechanics. A year later, in 1920, she made her first flight. While working at a telephone company, she began taking flying lessons with Neta Snook, one of the first American women to become a pilot. In 1921, she soloed for the first time. She then set out to beat the women's altitude record in 1922, and did so on October 22, reaching 14,000 feet (4,267 meters).

For the next six years, Earhart worked as a social worker and barnstormed (performed air stunts) for the Kinner aircraft company. In 1929, she cofounded the Ninety-Nines, an organization of women pilots, and became the group's first president. A number of these women would later serve in World War II with the Women's Airforce Service Pilots (WASP). Thrilled by Earhart's exploits, more women became pilots during these years.

In 1932, President Herbert Hoover presented Earhart with the National Geographic Medal, a symbol of having made scientific contributions through her flying achievements. That same year, she received the Distinguished Flying Cross.

In June 1937, Earhart and her navigator, Freddie Noonan, embarked on a trip around the world in Earhart's Lockheed Electra. They were en route to Howland Island in the Pacific Ocean when radio contact was lost on 2 July 1937. The plane and its two occupants disappeared without a trace, resulting in years of speculation about the fate of Earhart and Noonan. It was rumored that they might have been taken prisoner by the Japanese, who then occupied islands in that region. In recent years, historians have concluded that the plane probably ran out of fuel, and Earhart and Noonan died in the crash that followed.

Of her sister's legacy, Muriel Earhart Morissey told interviewer Harry Gardiner in 1990, "She embodied the spirit of adventure and she was sincere in her desire to contribute to our understanding and knowledge of the science of aviation. It's nice to know that others are still inspired by her adventurous spirit."

References

Randall Brink, *Lost Star: The Search for Amelia Earhart* (1994); Amelia Earhart, *20 Hrs., 40 Min.* (1928); Harry Gardiner, "A Conversation with Muriel Earhart Morissey," *Cobblestone* (July 1990): 10–13; Doris L. Rich, *Amelia Earhart, A Biography* (1989).

Edenton Tea Party

In October 1774, on the eve of the American Revolution, a group of women in North Carolina organized a

A British cartoon ridicules a group of North Carolina women who organized a boycott of tea and other British imports in October 1774.

boycott of British imports. The leader of the group, Penelope Barker, wrote a declaration that was signed by more than 50 women. They agreed to do "every thing as far as lies in our power" to support the "publick good." They later decided not to wear clothing made in Britain or to buy British tea or other goods.

News of the women's activity spread, and their October gathering became known as the Edenton Tea Party. In England, the king noted this new rebellion from the colonies, and cartoonists tried to make light of the fact that women had joined men in openly defying British rule.

Later, Barker continued to support the rebel cause. When British soldiers came to her home to take the family's horses, she confronted them with a sword, cut the horses' reins, and led them back into the stables. Impressed with her courage, the British officer said she could keep her horses.

The site of the "tea party" is marked by a monument in the form of a bronze teapot on top of a cannon. The tea caddy used by the women that October day is displayed at the North Carolina Museum of History in Raleigh. Barker's former home in Edenton is open to the public.

References

Patricia Edwards Clyne, *Patriots in Petticoats* (1976); Mary Beth Norton, *Liberty's Daughters: The Revolutionary Experience of American Women 1750–1800* (1980).

Edmonds, Sarah Emma (1841–1889)

Pretending to be a man, Sarah Emma Edmonds worked as a nurse and fought as a private in the Michigan Infantry during the Civil War. Over the three war years, she also served as a dispatch rider and spy, using various disguises.

Born on a farm in Nova Scotia, Canada, Edmonds grew up doing physical labor, hunting, fishing, and riding horseback with her brothers. In 1858, 16-year-old Emma—she had dropped her first name—left home to settle in the United States. Her mother had died, and she dreaded staying at home with her hot-tempered, critical father. The family may also have been planning an arranged marriage for Emma. She disguised herself as a man and moved to Connecticut where she called herself Franklin Thompson. She found work in a publishing company. Later, she moved to Flint, Michigan, again posing as a man.

When war broke out in 1861, Edmonds, now 21 years old, at once volunteered to serve as a male nurse. Her fellow soldiers knew her as Frank. Edmonds nursed the wounded at the first Battle of Bull Run and accompanied the regiment into several other battles.

Early in 1862, Edmonds took on the dangerous job of regimental mail carrier, which sometimes meant crossing enemy lines on horseback. She then decided to spy for the Union Army. While stationed with the Ninth Corps near Louisville, Kentucky, she undertook secret missions. Disguised as Charles Mayberry, a Confederate sympathizer, she tried to find out who was spying for the South in that region. Later, in her memoirs, Edmonds described some hair-raising adventures during these months. She claimed to have gone behind rebel lines numerous times, disguised as a black man, slave, or old peddler woman.

Edmonds was serving in a military hospital under General Grant's command when she became seriously ill with malaria. That illness, and a fall from her horse, left Edmonds in poor health. Her request for a leave of absence from the army early in 1863 was denied, so Edmonds left without permission in April. Since she was actually a woman, and therefore not eligible to serve, Edmonds did not feel guilty or think she had deserted. Unable to join her unit after she recovered, in 1864 Edmonds served as a nurse in army hospitals.

After the war, she resumed her true identity and wrote about her experiences in a book called *Nurse and Spy in the Union Army*. In one story, she described having nursed a dying woman soldier who was also disguised as a man and asked Edmonds not to reveal her identity. She revealed the reasons she had joined the army, writing, "But the great question to be decided was, what can I do? What part can *I* myself play in this great drama?" Edmonds admitted that a desire for ambition and success had been one reason for her ruse, but said, "Patriotism was the true secret of my success."

The book sold thousands of copies, making it a bestseller in its day. Edmonds donated the proceeds to relief organizations that helped Union soldiers and veterans. Homesick, she visited Canada and became reacquainted with Linus Seelye, a friend from childhood. The two were married in 1867 and had three sons. The Seelye family lived in Ohio, Michigan, and Illinois before settling in Fort Scott, Kansas.

In 1882, Edmonds decided to clear her army record and seek a government pension. She had never fully recovered her health after contracting malaria during the war. She contacted Damon Stewart and several other former campmates, who agreed to write letters to the war department on her behalf. The men swore that they had served with Edmonds, whom they believed to be Frank Thompson at the time. They also verified that Edmonds had been forced to leave the service because of serious illness.

Congress examined the evidence and concluded that Edmonds had shown herself to be Frank Thompson "by abundance of proof and beyond a doubt." By a special act of Congress on 5 July 1884, Edmonds received an honorable discharge and the charge of "desertion" was stricken from her record. She was awarded a veterans' bonus payment and $12 monthly pension.

Thus Edmonds became the first woman ever granted a soldier's pension. She also became the first and only female member of the Grand Army of the Republic (GAR), an organization of Union Army veterans that numbered more than 4,000. Edmonds died in Texas on 5 September 1889 and was buried in the military section of Washington Cemetery in Houston.

See also

Benefits; Civil War; Passing; Veterans.

References

Sarah Emma Edmonds, *Nurse and Spy in the Union Army: Comprising the Adventures and Experiences of a Woman in Hospitals, Camps, and Battlefields* (1865); Richard Hall, *Patriots in Disguise: Women Warriors of the Civil War* (1993); Seymour Reit, *Behind Rebel Lines: The Incredible Story of Emma Edmonds, Civil War Spy* (1988).

Emblem Ceremony

At graduation at the end of basic training, Marines take part in the emblem ceremony where they receive their Marine emblem pin and any special honors, awards, or promotions they have earned during their 13-week training period. This graduation ceremony marks the first time they may officially use the title "Marine."

Emmons, Lucretia

See African Americans.

Enemy Prisoners of War

See Prisoners of War (POWs).

Engel, Connie

See Pilots.

Equal Employment Opportunity Act (EEOA)

See Equal Employment Opportunity Commission (EEOC).

Equal Employment Opportunity Commission (EEOC)

Established by Title VII of the Civil Rights Act of 1964, the Equal Employment Opportunity Commission (EEOC) enforces the provisions of the act, which bans discrimination in employment on the basis of race, color, religion, national origin, or sex. The commission also handles complaints based on the Equal Employment Opportunity Act, the Age Discrimination in Employment Act, and the Equal Pay Act. It has developed guidelines for employers explaining how to comply with these laws.

When it was set up in 1964, the EEOC was limited to investigating charges brought against employers and working with the parties to reach an agreement. By 1972, the powers of this agency had been broadened to include seeking judgments in the federal court system. Called the Equal Opportunity Act of 1972 (EEOA), the new act included an amendment, Title II, that included "military departments" among the list of employers.

References

Susan Gluck Mezey, *In Pursuit of Equality: Women, Public Policy and the Federal Courts* (1992).

Espionage

Since American colonial days, women have been active in gathering both tactical and strategic information to give to the military cause they supported. They have worked both on their own and officially, as part of the military or professional detective agencies. Some women led rings consisting of numerous other operators.

To gather information, women used their social and political contacts, went about in disguise, and crossed enemy lines, often risking imprisonment or other serious penalties. Information was carried in person or sent in the form of coded or written messages. During the American Revolution, loyalist Lorenda Holmes of New York worked as a courier for British troops. Captured while carrying letters through British lines, she was stripped and searched but not imprisoned. She continued to help the British until she

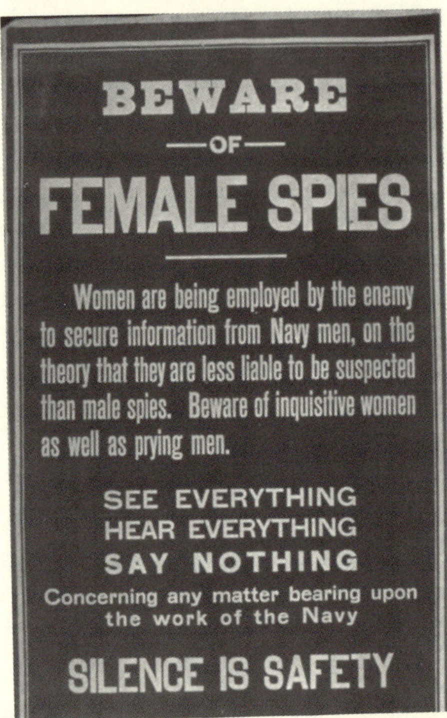

A World War II poster warns of women spies.

was captured a second time and Patriot soldiers burned her feet with hot coals.

Some women spies adopted clever ruses. A hatmaker from Philadelphia named Margaret Hutchinson carried letters to the British in her hats and told them what she observed during trips to Valley Forge. Ann Bates, a Philadelphia schoolteacher, was perhaps the best-known female spy. Posing as a peddler selling thread, needles, combs, and other items, she moved about various American camps to gather information about positions, numbers of cannons, and the like, which she communicated to the British.

Women also operated as spies during the Civil War. Some were professional agents, such as Mrs. E. H. Baker, a woman who had been working for the famous Pinkerton Agency before the war began. Others were asked by officials to begin spying, while still others took up spying on their own. Many men did not even suspect them, believing women were too innocent and not clever enough to conduct espionage activities.

Male spies were sometimes executed by hanging or treated harshly, but women received less punishment. None were executed, and several of those who were imprisoned, including the notorious Belle Boyd, were exchanged for prisoners from the other side.

Some women spies worked without their husband's cooperation or knowledge. Jeanette Laurimer Mabry was married to a colonel in the Confederate Army, but staunchly supported the Union and sent information to Union officers during the war. Mabry transmitted a steady flow of information to the spies and messengers operating in her area of east Tennessee.

Women took great risks to work as spies and couriers. At times, their efforts helped the military to win battles or avoid disaster. While some of these women's names are known, many remain anonymous to this day.

See also

Baker, Mrs. E. H.; Boyd, Isabelle ("Belle"); Darragh, Lydia; Edmonds, Sarah Emma; Greenhow, Rose O'Neal; Guerrero, Joey; Slater, Sarah; Tubman, Harriet; Van Lew, Elizabeth; Wood, Harriet.

References

Katherine and John Bakeless, *Spies in the Revolution* (1969); George Baker, *World's Greatest Military Spies and Secret Service Agents* (1917); Richard Hall, *Patriots in Disguise: Women Warriors of the Civil War* (1993); Donald E. Markle, *Spies and Spymasters of the Civil War* (1994); Seymour

Reit, *Behind Rebel Lines: The Incredible Story of Emma Edmonds, Civil War Spy* (1988).

Evans, Diane Carlson

See Vietnam Women's Memorial.

Executive Order 8802

During World War II, after defense plants began offering jobs to women, African Americans faced discriminatory hiring practices. Blacks had also been denied opportunities within the military. Prominent organizations and individuals planned a large march on Washington, D.C., to protest this inequality and demand the right to serve the nation both in the armed forces and the defense industry. President Roosevelt had been considering action to end discriminatory hiring practices. His wife, Eleanor, was an ardent spokesperson for civil rights, and the Roosevelts had influential African-American friends, including educator Mary McCleod Bethune. In 1941, Roosevelt signed Executive Order 8802, which banned discrimination in defense industries. Those companies that refused to comply with the order could lose government orders for their goods and services.

See also

African Americans; Bethune, Mary McCleod; Defense Plant Workers; Discrimination, Racial.

Executive Order 10240

Signed by President Harry S Truman on 27 April 1951, Executive Order 10240 permitted military officials to discharge women from the service if they were pregnant or were responsible for minor children. It applied to women on active duty or in the reserves, regardless of rank, grade, or length of service. While the law did not force military officials to terminate the service of women in these situations, all the service branches adopted such a policy throughout the 1950s and 1960s.

Opponents of this policy stated that it discriminated against women solely on the basis of their gender, while men who had family responsibilities were not affected. They especially protested the policy of discharging women who had minor children living with them, since this situation was common to both men and women.

See also

Discrimination, Sexual; Motherhood; Pregnancy.

F

Faulkner, Shannon (b. 1975)

In 1993, Shannon Faulkner, a native of Powdersville, South Carolina, applied to and was accepted by the Citadel, a prominent all-male military college in Charleston with an enrollment of about 2,000 students. Founded in 1842, the Citadel accepted Faulkner, the daughter of a fencing company owner and high school social studies teacher, without knowing her gender. After discovering she was a woman, the school reneged and Faulkner sued for discrimination. Since the school receives state funds, it comes under the province of federal laws regarding discrimination.

In 1994 a federal court ordered that the Citadel admit Faulkner as a student. After the court order, Faulkner received death threats, hate mail, and phone calls from harassers. Her family's home was vandalized.

There were fierce debates about whether women should be admitted. Those who opposed their admission included retired Lieutenant Colonel T. Nugent Courvoisie, who said, "That girl says she wants to come in and be one of the boys. But the minute she comes in, the atmosphere changes. She ruins the whole concept of getting everyone together and working on the same team."

In the wake of the decision, officials and concerned citizens questioned how to provide an equal educational experience for women at the Citadel without undue risk or excessive discomfort. People also expressed concern about Faulkner's safety and said she should not suffer more than male students. They discussed whether certain requirements for freshmen (called "knobs")—such as crew cuts, being forced to walk in gutters instead of sidewalks, and doing push-ups until they vomited—should apply to a female student.

Faulkner's attorney, Sara Mandelbaum, said that Faulkner should be excused from head-shaving because it would make her look odd and stigmatize her as a woman. The school argued that this was the whole point of shaving, to subjugate cadets and teach them to give up individual interests in favor of the group. On 1 August 1994, Judge C. Weston Houck ruled that Faulkner need not be exempt, saying, "The Citadel is perfectly at liberty to treat the hair on her head the same way it treats the hair of every other cadet."

In August 1994, an appeals court ruled in favor of a stay for the Citadel until arguments in the case could be heard later in the year. This meant that Faulkner could attend classes during the day only and would not be admitted as a regular cadet in 1994.

The Citadel lost its appeal, in which it presented alternative educational plans for Faulkner. In 1995, the court ruled that Faulkner must be admitted as a regular cadet. She arrived with the other cadets on 12 August to begin what is called Hell Week. Shannon experienced heckling and name-calling and no other cadets talked with her. During the first week of training, marching in 100-degree heat, she became severely nauseated and could not eat or drink. Faulkner was treated in the infirmary for dehydration, at one point receiving intravenous therapy. On Friday, she asked for her father and her attorney, Suzanne Coe, and told them she had decided to drop out of the Citadel.

Shannon Faulkner, the first woman to attend classes at the Citadel, is escorted to the gift shop by a senior cadet on 20 January 1994. Faulkner had won her discrimination suit against the Citadel in 1994 and had started the first week of training before dropping out due to dehydration.

Of Faulkner's departure, critics claimed that she seemed overweight and out of shape. Yet 4 other students had also left because of heat sickness and 20 others had dropped out by that time. Typically, about 15 percent of all new students leave the Citadel each year.

Faulkner later made several public appearances discussing her experience and told one interviewer, "I'm disappointed I wasn't able to stay, but I've got a full life ahead of me."

See also
Mellette, Nancy; Virginia Military Institute (VMI); Women in Support of the Citadel.

References
Catherine S. Manegold, "Judge Allows Head Shaving for Woman at Citadel," *New York Times* (2 August 1994: A-14); Patrick Rogers et al., "Her War Is Over," *People* (4 September 1995: 76–80); David Van Biema, "The Citadel Still Holds," *Time* (22 August 1994: 61).

Fifth Amendment

The United States Supreme Court has ruled that the Fifth Amendment to the United States Constitution, which includes an Equal Protection Clause, can be applied to the federal government. The clause says that people who are similarly situated must be treated similarly by state and federal governments, thus giving people "equal protection of the laws." In applying this law, the courts have said that employers are banned from making unreasonable classifications that deny classes of people fair treatment.

This law has often been cited by those who oppose laws and policies that prevent women from holding any military jobs or positions that are open to men. They believe that assignments should be made based on the qualifications and capabilities of individuals.

See also
Combat; Combat Exclusion Law; *Rostker v. Goldberg.*

Fighter Pilots

Combat exclusion laws and policies kept U.S. women from flying fighter planes in the military until the 1990s. Then, women could complete fighter pilot training but were not permitted to work in the field. Two Canadians, Captain Jane Foster and Major Deanna Brassier, became the first women jet fighter pilots in 1987. During one exercise, after Foster "shot down" a simulated missile being carried by a U.S. Marine AV-8B Harrier, Captain Pierre Ruel of the Canadian Forces Base Cold Lake commented that people could no longer regard flying fighter jets as solely "a man's job."

In the United States, one pioneer, Lieutenant Jeanne Flynn, graduated first in her fighter pilot training class. In 1993, after Secretary of Defense Les Aspin lifted the ban against women flying combat missions, Flynn became the first woman fighter pilot in the Air Force.

See also
Combat; Combat Exclusion Law; Hultgreen, Kara S.; Tailhook.

References
Jeanne Holm, *Women in the Military: An Unfinished Revolution* (1992); John Lancaster, "Nearly All Combat Jobs To Be Open to Women," *Washington Post* (29 April 1993): A1, A8.

FitzGerald, Frances (Frankie) (b. 1940)

Journalist and foreign correspondent Frances ("Frankie") FitzGerald wrote numerous articles about the Vietnam War for *The Atlantic* and other magazines during the late 1960s. In 1967, she won the Overseas Press Club award as the journalist who had best interpreted foreign affairs. FitzGerald, the daughter of an author and diplomat, wrote a highly acclaimed book about Vietnam, *Fire in the Lake*, published in 1972. Among other awards, it won the Pulitzer Prize and National Book Award.

Flight Surgeons

See Army Medical Corps (AMC); Cornum, Rhonda; Physicians.

Flores, Anna (b. 1947)

In 1970, Anna Flores, a seaman stationed in Florida, was discharged by the Navy because she had become pregnant. Flores and her fiancé, an enlisted man in the Navy, were planning to marry when Flores suffered a miscarriage. Base officials, now aware that Flores had been pregnant, began the process of discharging her. They said that if they did not follow this long-standing policy, it would appear that the Navy condoned unwed pregnancy and would lower moral standards for women in the service.

Represented by the American Civil Liberties Union (ACLU), Flores filed a lawsuit in the U.S. District Court at Pensacola, Florida. Flores's attorneys maintained that women were the victims of unconstitutional discrimination in that they were treated differently from male servicemen. Men could be party to a pregnancy and remain in the Navy without repercussions. The lawsuit expanded into a class action suit that challenged other military policies that treated women differently from men. It questioned Executive Order 10240, the 1951 law that enabled the military to dismiss women who became pregnant or had responsibility for minor children.

Rather than go to court, the Navy decided not to discharge Flores and stated that her naval career would not be affected by the incident. The Flores case was one of several lawsuits women brought during the early 1970s to challenge military policies. The Department of Defense reevaluated its policies and asked that Executive Order 10240 be repealed. This change took effect on 15 May 1975.

Flying Jobs

During World War II, besides serving as pilots with the Women's Airforce Service Pilots (WASP), about 50 Army women worked in other flying jobs. They served as radio operators during training flights and as mechanics and photographers. In the last months of the war, women served as flight clerks on planes running from Paris to London and on other noncombat trips.

See also
Air Medal; Air-Wacs; United States Air Force; Women's Airforce Service Pilots (WASP).

Flynn, Jeanne

See Fighter Pilots.

Foote, Evelyn (Pat) (b. circa 1939)

Evelyn (Pat) Foote joined the Army in 1969 at age 30. After completing her training, she served as a WAC company commander and a public affairs officer in Vietnam before joining the faculty of the Army War College. Her next assignment was commander of the Military Police Group in Mannheim, West Germany. Her final position in the service was commanding general of Fort Belvoir, Virginia.

During the 1980s, Brigadier General Foote supported the idea of opening all military roles, including combat roles, to women. She said that individuals who have the ability to do the job well should be permitted to do it. When Foote retired from the Army in 1989, she expressed strong views in a letter to Staff General Carl E. Vuono, saying, "I know of no more dysfunctional military policy in effect today than the much-despised and unquestionably inoperable [Direct Combat Probability Coding (DCPC),] which places gender-based restrictions on the assignments of highly-trained Army Women. . . ."

See also
Direct Combat Probability Coding (DCPC).

Reference
Jeanne Holm, *Women in the Military: An Unfinished Revolution* (1992).

Fort, Cornelia (1919–1943)

A native of Nashville, Tennessee, Cornelia Fort became a pilot in 1939 after she graduated from college. She worked for the Civilian Pilot Training Program in Colorado and served as a flight instructor at Pearl Harbor for the Andrews Flying Service. She was at Pearl Harbor during the surprise attack by Japanese bombers on 7 December 1941.

Fort left Hawaii three months later to return home, then sought a way to help the war effort. Early in 1942, Nancy Harkness Love, founder of the Women's Auxiliary Ferrying Squadron (WAFS), invited her to fly with the group. With the WAFS, Fort flew different types of aircraft, building a reputation as a premier aviator and an example of what women pilots could accomplish.

In March 1943, Fort became the first woman pilot to die while serving in the U.S. military. She was flying over Texas in formation with six BT-13s when one of the other pilots elected to pull away and perform a nosedive. His landing gear destroyed the left wing of Fort's plane, which then crashed to the ground.

References
Deborah G. Douglas, *United States Women in Aviation, 1940–1985* (1991); Sally Van Wagenen Keil, *Those Wonderful Women in Their Flying Machines* (1990).

Foster, Jane

See Fighter Pilots.

Frontiero, Sharron A.

See *Frontiero v. Richardson.*

Frontiero v. Richardson

In *Frontiero v. Richardson*, the Supreme Court ruled that the dependents of women in the military should receive the same entitlements as those given to the dependents of male servicemen.

Lieutenant Sharron A. Frontiero, a 23-year-old physical therapist in the Air Force, filed a lawsuit alleging sex discrimination. Because the military did not regard her husband as a dependent (as it did for female spouses of male servicemen), Frontiero was not eligible for the economical housing on Maxwell Air Force Base where she was stationed. Her husband was denied medical care, and the couple could not receive other benefits since Frontiero was basically classified as a single officer.

After the federal district court ruled in favor of the Air Force, Frontiero sought a reversal of their judgment from the United States Supreme Court. She was represented by attorney Ruth Bader Ginsberg, who later became the second woman ever appointed to the United States Supreme Court.

On 14 May 1973, the Supreme Court ruled in Frontiero's favor. The Court said that the military could not require women to prove their civilian spouses were dependent upon them for more than one-half of their support unless they required the same proof from men. In explaining its decision, the Court said that the policies denying benefits to the spouses of women in the military denied them equal protection under the law. In reaching its decision, the Court rejected an argument made by Air Force attorneys that the male role is to protect women. Calling this "romantic paternalism," the Court said that such ideas can put women "in a cage" rather than on a pedestal.

As a result of Frontiero's case, the Department of Defense (DOD) changed its policies regarding entitlements to dependents so that female and male servicepeople were treated the same. The words "wife" and "husband" were changed to read "spouse" in documents pertaining to these matters. Further, the DOD granted payments to women who had not been able to receive such benefits in the past.

See also

Benefits; Discrimination, Sexual.

References

Harry G. Beans, "Sex Discrimination in the Military," *Military Law Review* (Vol. 67, Winter 1975: 19–83); Barbara Brown et al., "The Equal Rights Amendment: A Constitutional Basis for Equal Rights for Women," *Yale Law Review* (Vol. 80, No. 5, April 1971): 871–979; Robin Rogers, "A Proposal for Combating Sexual Discrimination in the Military: Amendment of Title VII," *California Law Review* (Vol. 78, No. 1): 165–196.

G

Gallina, Julianne (b. 1970)

In 1991, Julianne Gallina, a native of Pelham, New York, became the first woman named brigade commander by the United States Naval Academy. After graduating from Pelham Memorial High School, Gallina entered the academy where she joined the track and lacrosse teams and became coxswain of the women's crew team.

Only one other woman had achieved the position of brigade commander at a service academy—the United States Military Academy at West Point—when Gallina was given that responsibility during her junior year at the Naval Academy. As leader of the 4,300 members of her brigade, Gallina was charged with presiding over ceremonies, parades, and daily formations, as well as serving as a liaison between midshipmen and the officers at the academy.

Gardiner, Ruth M.

See Army Nurse Corps (ANC); Casualties.

Gates Commission

See All-Volunteer Force (AVF).

Geiger, Emily (b. circa 1763)

South Carolina teenager Emily Geiger became a heroine of the American Revolution after she carried an important message from General Nathaniel Greene, commander of the colonial army's southern forces, to General Thomas Sumter. Greene's men were under attack by the British, and he needed reinforcements and immediate help from Sumter's troops.

While en route by horseback, Geiger was stopped by Peter Simons, a British scout under the direction of a Redcoat leader, Lord Rawdon. A local woman was summoned to search Geiger's body for any messages. Geiger was forced to wait at the guard station where she quickly memorized the message, then broke the paper into bits and swallowed it before the woman arrived.

When the British found nothing on her, Geiger was released. She took a more indirect and less suspicious route to Sumter and succeeded in reaching his encampment in three days. She delivered the message verbally, asking that he send troops to Orangeburg. There, colonial forces went on to win the Battle of Eutaw Springs.

After the war, Geiger married Captain John Threwitz. During the 1780s, she died shortly after giving birth to her daughter, Elizabeth.

References

Donald Barr Chidsey, *The War in the South* (1969); Elizabeth Ellet, *Women of the Revolution* (1884); M. Foster Farley, "Emily Geiger's Ride," *South Carolina Magazine* (May/June 1976): 10–11; Edith Patterson Meyer, *Petticoat Patriots of the American Revolution* (1976); Mollie Somerville, *Women of the American Revolution* (1974).

GI Bill of Rights

Near the end of World War II, the military created the GI Bill of Rights—formally known as the Serviceman's Readjustment Act of 1944—to thank veterans for their wartime service and enable them to rebuild their civilian lives. Among other things, the bill provided for unemployment and education allowances and help in obtaining loans for homes, farms, and businesses. A limit was set on the time during which educational benefits could be used.

The bill, directed by the Veterans Administration (VA), had widespread support. It financed thousands of college educations, leading to upward mobility for many Americans and their families.

Many women who served with the armed forces during the war, such as those in the Women's Airforce Service Pilots (WASP), were not eligible for the benefits offered by the GI Bill. Among those who were eligible, such as members of the Women's Army Corps (WAC), the percentage of women using the GI Bill to attend college was much lower than for male war veterans. Many women returned to their former jobs or became wives and mothers—the most acceptable roles for women in those years. Some analysts also believe women veterans were not as well informed about their rights under the bill.

A revised GI Bill was adopted in 1981. It stated that members of the armed forces who served at least two years and contributed $100 each month for 12 months can receive $10,800 later on for further education. The money is paid out by the Veterans Administration. The Army offers additional funding to high school graduates who score in the top half of an intelligence test and enlist in a critical military specialty. They are entitled to a total of $25,200 from the GI Bill and the Army College Fund.

See also

Demobilization; Veterans.

References

Sally Van Wagenen Keil, *Those Wonderful Women in Their Flying Machines* (1990); June A. Willenz, *Women Veterans: America's Forgotten Heroines* (1983).

Gordon, Gale Ann

See Pilots.

Grable, Betty

See Pinups.

Grade

See Rank.

Grand Army of the Republic (GAR)

See Boyd, Isabelle ("Belle"); Edmonds, Sarah Emma.

Grasshopper Squadron

The Grasshopper Squadron was a group of pilots who flew for the U.S. Army during World War II, scouting enemy territory and spotting artillery fire. The pilots were all men, but the Army hired skillful women pilots to test planes used by the squadron. Among them was Alma Heflin, who had spent five months in Alaska in 1942 as a bush pilot. During one training exercise, Heflin was injured after her parachute did not open properly. After spending several months recovering in a hospital, Heflin returned to flying.

Greenhow, Rose O'Neal (n.d.–1864)

A prominent member of Washington, D.C., society, Rose O'Neal Greenhow

Civil War spy Rose O'Neal Greenhow poses with one of her daughters in this undated photograph.

operated as a spy during the Civil War. Born to a wealthy family in Maryland, she was the aunt of Stephen A. Douglas and was acquainted with many prominent politicians and diplomats.

Even before the war began, a military officer stationed in Washington, D.C., recruited Greenhow as one of the spies he was assembling for the Confederacy. A competent organizer herself, Greenhow went on to direct a ring of spies that included more than a dozen others, including both men and women.

Greenhow's many social connections enabled her to gather information of use to the Confederacy. Her mansion in the capital city received numerous important visitors, including military leaders. In July 1861, Greenhow informed General Beauregard that Northern troops under General Irvin McDowell were coming south into Virginia near Manassas. Greenhow hid a coded message in the hair of a girl who carried it to Beauregard's encampment while pushing a vegetable wagon.

Suspicious federal agents began watching Greenhow and her mansion on Sixteenth Street. In August 1861, they entered and searched the house, to arrest Greenhow and a Union officer who was visiting her. Greenhow was allowed to remain in her home but was placed under constant surveillance, a form of house arrest. Nonetheless, she continued her spying activities. Early in 1862, federal officers took her to the Old Capitol Prison, where she stayed for six months. Even from jail, Greenhow managed to send and receive messages.

After being exchanged for a Union prisoner, Greenhow toured Europe to raise funds for the Confederacy. She also wrote a book about her spying experiences. On the voyage home, her ship ran aground in a severe storm off the coast of North Carolina. Greenhow's lifeboat capsized in the turbulent waters. Inside the hem of her dress, she had stashed the heavy gold coins she had collected in Europe for the army, and the weight of them caused her to drown. A state funeral was held in Richmond, the Confederate capital, with public viewing of Greenhow's body.

See also
Civil War; Espionage.

References
Ina Chang, *A Separate Battle: Women and the Civil War* (1991); Donald E. Markle, *Spies and Spymasters of the Civil War* (1994); Francis B. Simkins and James W. Patton, *The Women of the Confederacy* (1936).

Greenwood, Edith

See Medals.

Grenada, Invasion of

The invasion of Grenada began on 25 October 1983, when President Ronald Reagan ordered U.S. military forces to that island in the Caribbean. Called "Operation Urgent Fury," the invasion ended in mid-December that same year. It marked the first armed conflict to occur after men and women were integrated in the U.S. military.

During the relief operation to rescue hundreds of American students, 170 women in the Army, most of them from Fort Bragg, North Carolina, took part in various ways. As military police, women soldiers guarded prisoners of war, patrolled in armed jeeps, and served as roadblock and checkpoint guards. Others served as helicopter pilots, crew chiefs, intelligence specialists, and signal and communications specialists.

Twenty-six women stevedores were charged with loading captured weapons and ammunition on ships and aircraft. Women in the Air Force served on crews that delivered troops and supplies to the island, and women also served in medical units during the invasion. Interviewed later by military historian and retired Major General Jeanne Holm, some of the women who served in Grenada said they had enjoyed the challenge of their jobs and that women and men had not been treated differently as they went about their work.

References

Jeanne Holm, *Women in the Military: An Unfinished Revolution* (1992); "Women GIs in Grenada," *Houston Post* (8 December 1983): 12A.

Guarding Prisoners

During the 1970s, after men and women were integrated into one service, some women were trained in weaponry and as military police. The 1983 invasion of Grenada marked the first time women in the U.S. military were charged with guarding prisoners of war. In previous years, this was among the jobs that had been closed to women. Women continued to receive this duty assignment during the invasion of Panama in 1989. The Persian Gulf War saw more women in charge of guarding enemy prisoners of war than in any previous conflict.

See also

Grenada, Invasion of; Panama, Invasion of; Persian Gulf War.

Guerrero, Joey (b. 1918)

Phillipine-born Josefina (Joey) Guerrero served as a spy for the Allies in Manila during World War II. She is credited with having saved hundreds of American lives and contributing to the Allied victory in her homeland.

As a child, Guerrero endured many hardships, including the loss of both parents, and suffered from tuberculosis and other illnesses herself. She was raised first by her grandmother, who managed a coconut plantation, and then by an uncle in Manila. She married a young doctor, Renato Maria Guerrero, and gave birth to daughter Cynthia in 1939.

In 1941, Guerrero became seriously weak and unable to eat or care for her child. An American doctor diagnosed her with the dreaded Hansen's disease—leprosy—which meant she had to leave her child, who might contract the illness. As Guerrero and her husband were making plans for her care and treatment, the Japanese bombed Pearl Harbor. Japanese troops invaded the Philippines a few days later.

Impressed by Guerrero's courage in the face of the invasion, the Filipino Underground invited her to join them as a guerrilla. At that time, the Underground was gathering intelligence about the Japanese and sending it to Australia so General Douglas MacArthur, Allied Commander in the Pacific, could return to expel the invaders. Later, Guerrero was to call her work "my quiet war."

Assigned to watch the waterfront, she began at once making notes about the movements of Japanese troops and the locations of their buildings, supplies, and aircraft. Guerrero drew pictures and maps for the Allies, showing key information such as the location of mine fields. Some messages she memorized. Others, such as reports and photographs, she hid in the hollow soles of her wooden shoes. Japanese soldiers sometimes stopped her but did not spend much time questioning a woman who bore the telltale sores of leprosy.

Guerrero also joined a group of Filipino women who took food to American and Filipino prisoners of war at two large camps in Manila. She worked long hours, with little food and in pain from recurring headaches and sores on her feet.

Early in 1945, Guerrero undertook a crucial and dangerous mission. Japanese soldiers had set up mines in an area the Allies believed to be mine-free, and a new map had to be sent to them at once. Guerrero, the map taped between her shoulder blades, walked 40 miles in two days and two nights in an area where fighting was taking place. She delivered the map to American headquarters at Calumpit and managed to return to Manila safely.

As the war came to an end, Guerrero nursed the wounded until her own health collapsed. She entered a government-run hospital for lepers but it was ill-staffed and poorly supplied, with no real treatments. Through her efforts and the resulting publicity, the hospital was improved and modern drugs were made available there.

The Americans Guerrero had helped did not forget her. For her wartime service, she received the Medal of Freedom with Silver Palm, the highest honor the U.S. government can award a civilian. Friends asked the government to arrange for her to receive free treatment at a hospital in Carville, Louisiana, a facility that had specialized treatments for Hansen's disease. After leaving the hospital with her health much improved, Guerrero settled in California.

Reference

Thomas M. Johnson, "Joey's Quiet War," in The Reader's Digest Association, *Secrets and Spies: Behind-the-Scenes Stories of World War II* (1964).

Gulf War Syndrome

Gulf War Syndrome refers to a wide range of symptoms and health problems exhibited by some of the military personnel who served in the Persian Gulf War. Among the symptoms these veterans have identified are rashes, extreme fatigue, vision problems, lowered immunity, cancer, and birth defects in their children. One theory holds that they were exposed to a toxic substance, such as a nerve gas, that Iraq might have used during the war.

After becoming ill or giving birth to children with deformities, some

U.S. Army MP Liz Milliken holds a M-16 rifle and a M-60 machine gun at a sandbag post in St. George's, Grenada, on 14 December 1983.

veterans filed claims against the military for compensation and health benefits. Military officials have said that further studies are needed to determine if these problems arise from the Persian Gulf War or are random in nature.

Victims have disputed this notion, saying that they and their families suffer from rates of these problems that far exceed the rates in the general population. Some families point to the fact that their children born before the Persian Gulf War had no problems, while those born afterwards have had serious deformities. Research studies that were undertaken after the war have been interpreted differently by the opposing sides.

Between 1994 and 1996, scientists reported on the results of several studies of the syndrome. They suggested that the various types of health problems experienced by Persian Gulf War veterans were the results of several kinds of illnesses. Dr. Boaz Milner identified five syndromes, one caused by radiation, one by experimental medications given to some soldiers, a third by environmental contaminants, a fourth from chemical compounds, and a fifth that seems to be linked to chemical weapons used by Iraq. By 1996, Persian Gulf War veterans' groups claimed that more than 70,000 vets and their dependents have suffered from health problems related to service in the Gulf. By August 1996, Congress was investigating the situation and considering ways the government could help victims.

References

Philip Hilts, "Researchers Say Chemicals May Have Led to War Illness," *New York Times* (17 April 1996): A17; Kenneth Miller, "The Tiny Victims of Desert Storm," *Life* (November 1995): 46–52; Sarah Richardson, "Chemicals at War," *Discover* (January 1996): 19; Kenneth Timmerman, "The Iraq Papers," *The New Republic* (29 January 1996): 12+.

H

Hallaren, Mary Agnes (b. 1907)

A native of Lowell, Massachusetts, Mary Agnes Hallaren became director of the Women's Army Corps (WAC) in May 1947. In 1948, the WAC moved from auxiliary to full military status, becoming part of the regular Army. Hallaren was thus the first nonmedical woman in the Army to serve as a regular officer rather than an auxiliary officer.

Before joining the military, Hallaren had been a schoolteacher and women's rights advocate and lecturer. She was part of the first officer training class for the WAC in 1942 and led the first group of Wacs who were sent to the European theater during World War II. She then served as WAC director of the Air Forces in Europe.

As the ranking woman in the military after the war, Colonel Hallaren fought vigorously for a permanent role for women in the armed forces. The petite Hallaren, who was 5 feet tall, was nicknamed "the Littlest Colonel," and she developed a reputation for persistence and assertiveness. In 1948, Hallaren testified before members of the House Armed Services subcommittee that was considering legislation that was later passed as the Women's Armed Services Integration Act of 1948. She pointed out how much women would be needed in other wars, saying, "When the house is on fire, we don't talk about a woman's place in the home. And we don't send her a gilt-edged invitation to help put the fire out."

During the 1950s and following decades, Hallaren worked to increase the number of women in the military. In striving to help open more opportunities for women in the military, she also stressed the need to maintain quality.

References

Carolyn Becraft, *Women in the Military 1980–1990* (1990); Mattie E. Treadwell, *U.S. Army in World War II: Special Studies—The Women's Army Corps* (1954); Jean Zimmerman, *Tailspin: Women at War in the Wake of Tailhook* (1995).

Hancock, Joy Bright (1898–1986)

Serving in the Navy during both World War I and World War II, Joy Bright Hancock later became director of the Navy's Women Accepted for Volunteer Emergency Service (WAVES).

During World War I, Hancock joined the Naval Reserve Force as a Yeoman (F), after which she worked as a civilian in naval aviation for more than a decade. During those years, while working at the Navy's Bureau of Aeronautics, she earned a pilot's license and learned to maintain aircraft. She was also widowed twice, having been married to naval aviators both times.

In October 1942, Hancock joined the newly formed WAVES and was the official representative of that group in the Bureau of Aeronautics in Washington, D.C. Later, she was appointed special assistant for the Women's Reserve to the deputy chief of Naval Operations (Air), a position she held until the war ended.

In 1945, Hancock was promoted to the rank of commander, and a year later she became the director of the WAVES, serving in that position until she retired from the Navy in 1953. In 1948, she was an ardent supporter of a permanent role for women in the

Navy, believing they would fill essential roles during peacetime. She developed a plan that would integrate women into both the regular and reserve Navy. Hancock later wrote a memoir, *Lady in the Navy: A Personal Remembrance.*

See also
United States Navy; Women Accepted for Voluntary Emergency Service (WAVES); Yeomen (F).

References
Marie Bennett Alsmeyer, *The Way of the WAVES: Women in the Navy* (1981); Joy Bright Hancock, *Lady in the Navy: A Personal Remembrance* (1972); Nancy Wilson Ross, *The WAVES: The Story of the Girls in Blue* (1943); Doris Weatherford, *American Women in World War II* (1990).

Harassment, Sexual

See Sexual Harassment.

Harris, Marcelite J. (b. 1942)

Among other firsts for women in the military, Major General Marcelite J. Harris became director of maintenance, deputy chief of staff, logistics, at Headquarters U.S. Air Force in Washington, D.C. This position entails organizing, training, and equipping a work force of more than 125,000 technicians and managers, and maintaining the $260+ billion Global Reach-Global Power aerospace weapons inventory.

A graduate of Spelman College in Atlanta, Georgia, Harris was commissioned through Officer Training School, Lackland Air Force Base, Texas, in 1965. In 1983, she attended Air War College seminar at Maxwell Air Force Base in Alabama. She went on to earn another bachelor's degree in 1986, this time her degree was in business management.

From 1965 to 1967, Harris was assigned to Travis Air Force Base in California where she served as assistant director for administration. From January 1967 through September 1970, she served at Bitburg Air Base in Germany, working as an administrative officer and then maintenance analysis officer. The first woman aircraft maintenance officer, Harris received her training in 1970 at Chanute Air Force Base in Illinois, then went on to serve as a maintenance supervisor.

Harris was a personnel staff officer and White House aide from 1975 until May 1978. She was then assigned to the U.S. Air Force Academy at Colorado Springs where she served as an air officer, commanding one of the first two women air officers ever chosen for this position.

Major Harris and her husband, Maurice, have a son, Steven, and a daughter, Tenecia. Among her numerous honors are being chosen Outstanding Young Woman of America (1990); Woman of the Year, National Organization of Tuskegee Airmen (1990); and Woman of Enterprise, Journal Recording Publishing Company (1992). Harris has received the Legion of Merit with oak leaf cluster, the Bronze Star, a Presidential Unit Citation, the Air Force Commendation Medal with oak leaf cluster, the Vietnam Service Medal with three oak leaf clusters, and the Republic of Vietnam Campaign Medal.

References
"Major General Marcelite J. Harris: Biography," Fact Sheet: United States Air Force; *Who's Who Among Black Americans* (1992).

Hart, Nancy (circa 1740–1830)

A housewife and mother living in Georgia during the American Revolution, Nancy Hart outwitted the British on numerous occasions. Hart stood 6 feet tall, unusually tall for a woman of her day, and used this as an advantage to spy. She used various male disguises, such as that of a madman, while gathering information for the colonial army.

Hart grew up in Georgia where she excelled at the approved feminine arts of cooking, nursing, and the use of herbal remedies. In 1771, she married Benjamin Hart and they settled in a cabin in northern Georgia, above Augusta. When the war began, Indians fighting for the British avoided the Harts' cabin, since Nancy Hart was known for miles around as "War Woman" because of her sharpshooting ability.

Between 1778 and 1781, Hart went on several spying missions in northern Georgia and South Carolina. While scouting for the rebels, she also captured several British sympathizers.

On one occasion, Hart outwitted British soldiers who burst into her home demanding food. The men had shot a turkey in Hart's yard and ordered her to prepare it. While they were eating and drinking the glasses of homemade wine she kept pouring, Hart sent her daughter off to signal colonial soldiers. One by one, she secretly pushed all of the family's and the soldier's guns out a hole in the side of the cabin. Hart then kept a rifle aimed at the British to prevent their escape until they could be captured and taken away.

In 1853, the State of Georgia named a county after Hart, and Nancy Hart State Park was also named in her honor. Later, during the Civil War, when a group of women organized themselves as soldiers to protect the town of La Grange, Georgia, they called themselves the "Nancy Harts."

References

Elizabeth Anticaglia, *Heroines of '76* (1975); Lynn Sherr and Jurate Kazickas, *The American Woman's Gazetteer* (1976); Selma Williams, *Demeter's Daughters, the Women Who Founded America* (1976).

Hawks, Esther Hill (b. circa 1836)

A physician trained at the New England Female Medical College in Boston, Esther Hill Hawks tried unsuccessfully to serve as a volunteer army doctor during the Civil War. When she then applied to become a nurse, superintendent Dorothea Dix also refused to accept her, possibly because she was not yet 30 years old, the minimum age Dix had set for her nurses.

In 1862, Hawks gave up her quest and found a post in Beaufort, South Carolina, as a teacher of newly freed slaves. Her husband, also a physician, was working in Beaufort and was named director of a hospital for black soldiers in 1863. Together, they treated members of the First South Carolina Volunteers, the first official African-American regiment in the Union Army.

In July 1863, the hospital received 150 wounded soldiers from the 54th Massachusetts regiment after a battle at Fort Wagner. While caring for these black soldiers, Hawks met men from all walks of life—college graduates, farmers, former slaves. In her diary, she wrote, "They are intelligent, courteous, cheerful and kind, and I pity the

Revolutionary War heroine Nancy Hart shot British loyalists at her dinner table in 1778.

humanity which, on a close acquaintance with these men, still retains the unworthy prejudice against color!"

During the rest of her life, Hawks promoted medical education for women and worked to open opportunities for them to practice in hospitals and other settings.

References

Gerald Schwartz, ed., *A Woman Doctor's Civil War: Esther Hill Hawks' Diary* (1984).

Hays, Anna Mae (b. circa 1920)

On 11 June 1970, Anna Mae Hays, then chief of the Army Nurse Corps (ANC), became the first female brigadier general in U.S. history. Hays, a veteran of World War II, the Korean War, and the Vietnam War, had been serving in the ANC since 1942. General William Westmoreland awarded Hays her new stars moments before honoring Elizabeth P. Hoisington, the second female brigadier general to be promoted to this rank by the Army.

Hays was a brilliant organizer and was known as an advocate for women in the military and for her efforts to improve health care for all servicepeople. Near the end of the Vietnam War, when large numbers of injured servicemen required care, it was Hays's job to organize about 5,000 nurses to serve in hospitals in Vietnam and stateside, where returning veterans needed a great deal of rehabilitative care.

See also

Public Law 90-130; Rank.

References

Maj. Edith Aynes, A.N.C., *From Nightingale to Eagle: The Army Nurses*

History (1973); Jeanne Holm, *Women in the Military: An Unfinished Revolution* (1992).

Hays, Mary Ludwig (1754–1832)

The woman who became known in legend as "Molly Pitcher," famed as the "Heroine of Monmouth," was probably Mary Hays, a camp follower who accompanied her husband, artilleryman John Hays, during the Revolutionary War. As part of the Seventh Pennsylvania Regiment, her husband served under General George Washington.

At the Battle of Monmouth Courthouse on 28 June 1778, Mary Hays moved around the field with her water pitcher, giving thirsty soldiers drinks, a task often performed by women camp followers. After John Hays and his crew lay wounded (or, in some accounts, collapsed after being overcome by the heat), she put down her water pitcher, cleared the gun barrel, and fired it herself. She continued to function as a "rammer"—loading and reloading the cannon—until another artilleryman replaced her.

A man named Joseph P. Martin claimed to have witnessed her heroic act and later wrote, "While in the act of reaching for a cartridge, and having one of her feet as far before the other as she could step, a cannon shot from the enemy passed between her legs without doing any other damage than carrying away all of the lower part of her petticoat. Looking at it with apparent unconcern, she is said to have commented that it was lucky it did not pass any higher."

After the war, John and Mary Hays lived in Pennsylvania, where he died several years later. She then married John McCauley, another war veteran. Hays worked as a domestic servant and charwoman at the Carlisle County Courthouse. She was awarded a military pension in 1822 by a special act of the Pennsylvania state legislature, which cited her "services during the Revolutionary War." The pension provided Hays with $40 in cash a month and an annual payment of the same amount until her death ten years later. In 1876, a special marker was placed on her grave.

There is some controversy about the actual identity of "Molly Pitcher." Some say she was Mary Hays, while others believe she was Margaret Corbin.

See also
Corbin, Margaret.

References
Elizabeth Anticaglia, *Heroines of '76* (1975); Linda Grant De Pauw, *Founding Mothers: Women of America in the Revolutionary Era* (1975); Mary Beth Norton, *Liberty's Daughters: The Revolutionary Experience of American Women, 1750–1800* (1980).

Hazing

Hazing refers to physical punishment and verbal abuse, usually perpetrated on lowerclassmen by upperclassmen, and has been a tradition in some organizations and educational settings, including military academies. Hazing has been justified by those who say it helps to prepare people for the often brutal conditions of war. Supporters of hazing traditions in the military also have claimed that they enhance bonding among those who are in the service together. At some institutions, including the Citadel, the need for hazing as a means of ensuring bonding has been given as another reason to exclude women from the school.

During the early 1990s, Congress passed legislation banning these practices at the United States Naval Academy. Legislators defined hazing as "an unwarranted assumption of authority resulting in cruelty, indignity, humiliation, hardship, or the deprivation or abridgement of rights."

This legislation came in the wake of incidents reported by female cadets. Women claimed that male students insulted them, called them obscene names, and left pieces of meat lying on the floors of their rooms. Many incidents combined hazing with sexual harassment. In 1989, Gwen Dreyer, a second-year student at the naval academy, was taken into the men's bathroom by two midshipmen and chained to a urinal. These men and eight others proceeded to expose themselves to Dreyer and to photograph her in the humiliating situation. The story was reported nationally on the front pages of the *New York Times* and *Washington Post*, among other new papers. Dreyer left the academy that year, and her family claimed that they were warned not to make a public case of her experiences.

In the wake of Dreyer's experience, the naval academy conducted four separate reviews and assessments and concluded that they must take action to improve relations between male and female students. An order was given that banned any physical touching of plebes—new students—except "for their own safety or during approved athletic contests." This meant that a number of traditional hazing practices were forbidden. Counselors were told to inform students about these rules and help them understand how to behave appropriately. More female commanders were appointed to leadership roles at the academy.

Among those who oppose hazing is Paul E. Roush, a retired Marine colonel and professor at the naval academy, who writes, "Hazing diminishes both the practitioner and the recipient. It is a lose-lose arrangement—an equal-opportunity, moral vacuum." Roush views hazing as "a surrogate for leadership."

See also

Sexual Harassment; United States Naval Academy (USNA).

References

Paul E. Roush, "Women Serving in Combat Would Strengthen America's Defense," in Carol Wekesser and Matthew Polesetsky, eds., *Women in the Military* (1991); Gregory L. Vistica, *Fall from Glory* (1996); Jean Zimmerman, *Tailspin: Women at War in the Wake of Tailhook* (1995).

Health Care

Prior to the 1900s, women served as nurses providing care of those in the military. Women serving in an auxiliary capacity with the armed services were not eligible for military health services themselves. During World War I, women were often on their own or dependent on volunteer organizations such as the Red Cross for care.

During World War II, health care for the thousands of newly recruited women became a major issue, and a special department was set up in the Army to deal with medical care and evaluations. It was not until 1944 that military medical supply catalogs were updated to include drugs and hormones that women needed. Prior to that time, these catalogs only contained items needed for the treatment of men. In cases where their conditions were specific to being female, enlisted women had been obliged to purchase their own health-care items and medications.

As women became a permanent part of all branches of the service, medical departments expanded to include gynecologists and other specialists to provide care specifically needed by women. Women in the service, notably Sharron A. Frontiero, also fought for the right to have their dependents receive medical benefits comparable to those available to the dependents of men in the service.

See also
Benefits; Craighill, Major Margaret D.; *Frontiero v. Richardson*; Menopause; Pregnancy; Women's Army Corps (WAC).

References
Jeanne Holm, *Women in the Military: An Unfinished Revolution* (1992); Dorothy and Carl J. Schneider, *Into the Breach: American Women Overseas in World War I* (1991); Mattie E. Treadwell, *U.S. Army in World War II: Special Studies—The Women's Army Corps* (1954).

Heflin, Alma

See Grasshopper Squadron.

Higgins, Marguerite (Maggie) (1920–1966)

A graduate of the Columbia School of Journalism, Marguerite (Maggie) Higgins worked as a war correspondent during World War II and was among the first reporters to cover the arrival of U.S. troops that liberated the concentration camp at Dachau. In later years, Higgins covered the Nuremburg war crimes trials and won a Pulitzer Prize for her reporting of the Korean War. Once, when told to leave a dangerous front in Korea, she said, "Trouble is news and the gathering of news is my job."

The daughter of a French mother and a military pilot, Lawrence Higgins, Marguerite was born in Hong Kong and lived in Vietnam before the family settled in Oakland, California. There she had a difficult childhood with an alcoholic father and a mother prone to fainting spells. Although the family had little money, she attended a private school as a scholarship student among wealthier classmates. Higgins then earned her college degree at the University of California.

After earning her master's degree at Columbia in 1942, Higgins worked for the *New York Herald Tribune*. She was also married briefly to a philosophy professor. Higgins longed to serve as a foreign correspondent, but faced opposition from male journalists. Later, she would state that the biggest obstacles she faced were being a woman who was young and also blonde, a combination that led some men to view her as dumb, sly, or both. Those who met Higgins often commented on her good looks and sex appeal.

As the war went on, Higgins continued to request an overseas assignment and received her credentials as a war correspondent in 1944. The *Herald Tribune* sent her to Paris in 1945, where her knowledge of the language was an asset. She worked to understand the political situation and meet people who could inform her about ongoing events.

For a closer look at the action, Higgins accompanied a group of reporters who flew with the Eighth Air Force to bombed-out areas of Germany. Her articles about the liberation of various countries at the end of the war made the front page of her paper.

Higgins and Sergeant Peter Furst, a military journalist, were the first correspondents to reach the Nazi concentration camp in Dachau, Germany, shortly before it was liberated. They made their way into the camp, which was still manned by armed Germans who tried to surrender and give up their weapons. Higgins and Furst were nearly crushed by the crowds of prisoners who rushed out of the barracks after realizing they would finally be freed.

Higgins also recorded the reactions of German citizens who were ordered by American military leaders to tour the concentration camp, where they witnessed evidence of torture and cruel treatment, death, and devastation perpetrated by the Nazis. Higgins wrote that several German women fainted while viewing the crematorium where hundreds of prisoners had been burned to death each day. Several half-burnt bodies remained in the oven.

For her courage that day, Higgins was awarded the U.S. Army Campaign Ribbon. The New York Newspaper Women's Association named her story about Dachau's liberation the best foreign reporting of 1945. Higgins, however, also had many detractors who called her overly competitive, uncooperative, and petty. Her enemies claimed that she exaggerated some of her stories and achievements.

After boldly driving alone to Poland to report on the ongoing civil war there, Higgins remained in Europe after the war to cover the Nuremberg trials. She was named Berlin bureau chief for the *Herald Tribune* in 1947. She reported on the Russian blockade of Berlin in 1948 and described the developing Iron Curtain in Eastern Europe in 1949, then left for Japan as a correspondent in Tokyo the next year.

When the Korean War began in June 1949, Higgins flew to Seoul to cover that action for her paper. She was often in danger there and had to find ways to get her stories back to the United States despite a poor communications system and limited access to telephones. At the front, she endured physical hardships, including exhausting hikes, no place to sleep, and not enough food. At one point, Higgins met the U.S. supreme commander, General Douglas MacArthur, who was leading American troops.

An order came from General Walton H. Walker that Higgins was to leave Korea. She was told that the facilities (meaning bathrooms) were lacking for women and that, besides, women did not belong in battle zones. Walker was also concerned that if anything happened to Higgins, he would be sharply criticized for letting her stay in the region.

Unwilling to leave, Higgins asked Helen Rogers Reid, president of her paper, to intervene on her behalf with General MacArthur, who agreed to quash the order. In the meantime, she received support from the troops she had met at the front. After she was sent back to Tokyo by Army officials, word came that MacArthur had issued an order to reverse Walker's demand that she leave. In his cable, the general said, "Marguerite Higgins [is] held in highest professional esteem by everyone." Walker agreed that Higgins could continue reporting with the same conditions as male journalists.

When people urged her not to take such risks, Higgins said it was part of her job. She argued that if she conducted herself any differently than men did in the same situation, "it would prove that a woman as a correspondent was a handicap to the *Herald Tribune*."

Her coverage of Korea brought Higgins the Overseas Press Club Memorial Award and a Pulitzer Prize in journalism, shared that year among five writers. When the war ended, she continued to write and lecture about her experiences. Meanwhile, she had married Major General Wilson Hall, with whom she had three children, the first of whom died at birth. Higgins continued to travel as a correspondent, covering the 1954 departure of the French colonial government in Vietnam. She also authored six books.

Higgins joined the staff of *Newsday* in 1963 as a columnist. Her final trip abroad as a journalist took place in 1965, when she visited India, Pakistan, and Vietnam, where the war was heating up. It was her tenth trip to that nation. A parasitic infection she contracted during the trip led to an illness and her death in January 1966 at the age of 45. Higgins was buried in Arlington National Cemetery.

See also

Correspondents, War.

References

Jean R. Collins, *She Was There: Stories of Pioneering Women Journalists* (1980); Marguerite Higgins, *News Is a Singular Thing* (1955); Marguerite Higgins, *Our Vietnam Nightmare* (1965); Marguerite Higgins, *War in Korea* (1951); John Jakes, *Great War Correspondents* (1967); Richard Kluger, *The Paper: The Life and Death of the* New York Herald Tribune (1986); Antoinette May, *Witness to War: A Biography of Marguerite Higgins* (1983).

Hobart, Ella F.

See Chaplains.

Hobby, Oveta Culp (1905–1995)

The first director of the Women's Army Auxiliary Corps (WAAC), Oveta Culp Hobby later directed the Women's Army Corps (WAC), which was set up during World War II to meet the need for more military personnel.

Born in Killeen, Texas, on 19 January 1905, Oveta attended Mary Hardin Baylor College in Belton, Texas, and studied law at the University of Texas in Austin, unusual for a woman of her day. From 1925 to 1931, she served as parliamentarian for the Texas House of Representatives.

In 1931, she married 56-year-old William P. Hobby, a widower and former governor of Texas, with whom she had two children. Oveta Hobby was known as a civic leader, and in 1938, she took on the challenging job of executive vice president of her husband's newspaper, the *Houston Post.* By age 35, Hobby had served as president of the Texas League of Women Voters, a member of the Houston Symphony Orchestra Committee, and regional chairman of the Mobilization for Human Needs.

In 1941, she became the head of the Women's Interest Section of the War Department, part of its public relations division. The section was developed to handle problems and concerns of women whose husbands were drafted into military service. Hobby was asked to help plan a women's auxiliary corps, with an organizational chart and description of the ways women could serve. General George Marshall then asked her to direct the corps when it was officially set up on 14 May 1942. Her rank at that time was major.

Hobby worked quickly to recruit the thousands of women needed in the WAAC, then the WAC. She began by finding highly qualified and well-educated women for officer training classes. The WAC grew to include about 100,000 women, and 17,000 served overseas.

By the end of World War II, Hobby had been promoted to the rank of colonel. She received the Army's Distinguished Service Cross Medal, becoming the first woman to receive this highest noncombat award given by the Army. Some had argued that Hobby should be given the rank of major general, but this was never done. The citation accompanying her medal praised Hobby for her ability to develop the women's corps "without the guidance of precedents in United States military history to assist her. . . ." It pointed out that she had "established sound initial policies, planned and supervised the selection of officers and the preparation of regulations."

Returning to work at the *Houston Post* after the war, Hobby became coeditor and publisher. She also became the director of KPRC radio and television stations. In 1952, Hobby became the second woman (after Frances Perkins) ever appointed to a president's cabinet and the first secretary of health, education, and welfare, under Dwight D. Eisenhower. While in that post, she developed nurses' training programs and a hospital reinsurance plan. As research on the long-awaited Salk polio vaccine was completed, Hobby oversaw the testing process that was required before the vaccine could be released to the public.

Hobby left her cabinet post in 1955 to return home to Houston where her husband was ill. The two worked together to run the *Houston Post*, she as president and editor. Hobby was named chairman of the board in 1965, a year after her husband's death. In 1968, she was also chosen to serve on the board of the Corporation for Public Broadcasting. She also served on the board of H&C Communications, Inc., the family enterprise, from 1978 to 1983, chairing its executive committee as of 1983. The company eventually included five television stations.

In 1983, Hobby sold the *Houston Post* to the Toronto Sun Publishing Company for about $130 million. She suffered a stroke in 1995 and died at age 90, survived by her son and daughter, eight grandchildren, and twelve great-grandchildren.

See also

Women's Army Auxiliary Corps (WAAC); Women's Army Corps (WAC).

References

Army Center of Military History, *History of the Women's Army Corps, 1942–1978* (1989); James Barron, "Oveta Culp Hobby, Founder of WAC's and First Secretary of Health, Dies at 90," *New York Times* (17 August 1995): B13; Judith Freeman Clark, *Almanac of American Women of the 20th Century* (1987); Bettie J. Morden, *The Women's Army Corps 1945–1978* (1990); Karen Salisbury, "The Women's Army Corps," *Newsweek* (21 May 1951); Dorothy R. Spratley, *Women Go to War: Answering the Call in World War II* (1992); U.S. Department of the Army, Fact Sheet: "Oveta Culp Hobby."

Hoefly, Ethel Ann (b. circa 1920)

In 1972, Ethel Ann Hoefly became the first woman in the United States Air Force to reach the rank of brigadier general and the fourth woman in

American history to be promoted to the rank of general. During World War II, Hoefly served as a nurse with the Army Nurse Corps (ANC). In 1949, she transferred to the newly established and separate U.S. Air Force Nurse Corps (USAFNC), becoming its chief in 1968. Hoefly retired in 1974.

References

Jeanne Holm, *Women in the Military: An Unfinished Revolution* (1992); U.S. Department of the Air Force, *History of Women in the Air Force* (semiannual reports, 1948–1976).

Hoisington, Elizabeth P. (b. 1918)

On 11 June 1970, Elizabeth P. Hoisington, the director of the Women's Army Corps (WAC), became one of the first two women promoted to the rank of general in the U.S. Armed Forces. Along with Anna Mae Hays, director of the Army Nurse Corps (ANC), Hoisington received her stars from General William Westmoreland, the Army chief of staff, and became a brigadier general.

Elizabeth P. Hoisington

Hollen, Andrea (b. 1959)

Andrea Hollen was a member of the first coeducational class at the Army's United States Military Academy (USMA) at West Point. In 1980, she graduated tenth in her class with a major in engineering. Hollen was assigned to command a signals company in West Germany, and she attained the rank of major.

In 1992, Hollen, a homosexual, decided to leave the Army, which has always maintained the right to discharge any homosexual serviceperson. Hollen thus gave up the chance to teach at West Point and began working as an environmental consultant.

See also

Cammermeyer, Margarethe.

Holm, Jeanne (b. 1921)

In 1965, Jeanne Holm became the youngest commander of women in the Air Force; six years later, she became the first woman general officer in that service branch.

Jeanne Holm was born in Portland, Oregon. She joined the Army in 1942, serving with the Women's Army Auxiliary Corps (WAAC), and became a second lieutenant the following year. Holm continued to serve when the WAAC became the Women's Army Corps (WAC).

Retiring after the war, Holm attended Lewis and Clark College in Portland until being recalled to active duty in 1948. She then transferred from the Army to the Air Force, which had become a separate branch of service. From 1957 to 1965, she was in charge of determining manpower needs for the Allied air forces. Holm then served as director of women in the Air Force from 1965 to 1972. For the three following years, she was director of the Secretariat of Air Force Personnel.

Holm was promoted to the rank of brigadier general in the Air Force in 1971. The next year, she began urging her service branch to allow women to become pilots, saying the Air Force should lead the way. In 1974, however, the Navy opened this job to women, followed by the Army, while the Air Force waited until 1976.

When Holm reached the rank of major general in 1975, she became the first woman in the military ever to achieve this high rank. She retired from the United States Air Force that year but remained active in political and military affairs. From 1975 to 1976, under President Gerald Ford, Holm served as a special assistant for women to the president. She then served as a member of the Defense Advisory Council on Women in the Services (DACOWITS).

A noted military author, Holm wrote and revised a comprehensive history about women in the United States military and continued to do public speaking on this subject. After the Persian Gulf War, she reiterated her belief that women can perform well in a variety of jobs that once were closed to them, saying, "[Women] have earned the right to be treated like members of the first team rather than as a protected sub-class on the fringes of their profession. As citizens, they deserve the opportunity to be all they can be."

References

Jeanne Holm, *Women in the Military: An Unfinished Revolution* (1992); United States Air Force, "Major General Jeanne M. Holm" (1973); U.S. Department of the Air Force, *History of Women in the Air Force* (semiannual reports, 1948–1976).

Holmes, Lorenda

See Espionage.

Home before Morning: The Story of an Army Nurse in Vietnam

See Van Devanter, Lynda.

Homosexuality

See Sexual Preferences.

Hook, Frances

See Prisoners of War (POWs).

Hooker, Olivia

See SPAR.

Hopper, Grace Murray (1907–1992)

Computer specialist Grace Murray Hopper, the "Grand Old Lady of Software," had in 1982 the distinction of being the oldest officer on active duty in the U.S. Armed Forces.

During World War II, Hopper joined the Naval Reserve and was commissioned as a lieutenant, junior grade. An expert mathematician, she was assigned to the Bureau of Ordnance Computation at Harvard University, where she learned to program Mark I, the first large-scale digital computer. Hopper went on to invent the first practical compiler and helped to develop the widely used computer language, COBOL.

In 1966, Hopper retired from the Naval Reserve with the rank of commander. The next year, the Navy called her to active duty to standardize its computer programming languages. Hopper remained on duty and was promoted to captain in 1973. In 1983, the 76-year-old Hopper was promoted to commodore. At that time, she was serving as special advisor to the commander of the Naval Data Automation Command.

To honor the woman who brought them into the computer age, the Navy christened a new warship the USS *Hopper* after her death in 1992. It was the first time since World War II and the second time in history that a warship was named after a female member of the Navy.

Reference

Paula Studios, *Women of Computer History: Forgotten Heroines* (1990). U.S. Department of the Navy, Fact Sheet: "Grace M. Hopper" (1992).

Housing for Women

See Women's Army Auxiliary Corps (WAAC); Women's Army Corps (WAC).

Howe, Julia Ward (1819–1910)

Julia Ward Howe was an abolitionist, women's rights activist, and poet whose husband, Samuel Gridley Howe, had helped to arm John Brown and his raiders for the antislavery battle at Harper's Ferry. She believed strongly in the Union cause, but said she had nothing to give: "My husband was beyond the age of military service, my eldest son was a stripling. I could not leave my nursery to follow the march of our armies."

During a trip to Washington, D.C., in 1861, Howe visited a Union Army camp and watched McClellan's troops marching to the tune of "John Brown's Body." That night at the Willard Hotel, she awoke and began composing a poem to go along with that melody. The result was "The Battle Hymn of the Republic," a stirring song that became the theme of the Union Army. Howe later recalled, "As I lay waiting for the dawn, the long lines of the desired poem began to twine themselves in my mind." The poem, which she sold for $4, was published in the February 1862 issue of the *Atlantic Monthly*. It received wide acclaim and was often played by military bands.

After the war, Howe worked tirelessly for women's suffrage, a cause she led for more than 50 years. When she died in 1910, 4,000 mourners at her funeral joined together to sing "The Battle Hymn of the Republic."

References

G. J. Barker-Benfield and Catherine Clinton, *Portraits of American Women* (1991); Catherine Clinton, *The Other Civil War: American Women in the 19th Century* (1984); Julia Ward Howe, *Reminiscences, 1819–1899* (1899).

H.R. 2277

The serious shortage of nurses during World War II led to the introduction of H.R. 2277, which would have drafted nurses into the military. The bill was presented by Congressman Andrew May of Kentucky early in 1945.

Julia Ward Howe

Critics of the bill did not want women to be drafted. Some said the draft might discourage women from choosing a career in nursing. In addition, some accused the armed services of not using available nurses already, since, in some cases, black nurses and male nurses had not been used effectively. Called the Nurses Selective Service Act of 1945, the bill was passed in March by a margin of 347 to 42 (with 43 people abstaining).

As it became clear that the war would be ending by early May, however, Congress realized it no longer needed to consider this bill, and no further action was taken.

See also
Army Nurse Corps (ANC); Draft.

H.R. 4906

Also called the WAAC Bill, H.R. 4906 was formally titled "A Bill to establish a Women's Army Auxiliary Corps for Service with the Army of the United States." The law set up the Women's Army Auxiliary Corps (WAAC), which took part in World War II.

H.R. 4906 was introduced by Massachusetts Congresswoman Edith Nourse Rogers on 28 May 1941. Rogers had unsuccessfully tried to have women enlisted as a part of the Army—and given full military status with pensions and disability benefits comparable to those of men. When this proved fruitless, Rogers agreed to compromise with the wording of H.R. 4906, which was then revised as H.R. 6293.

The bill was 14 pages long and described plans for the WAAC, which would be a corps of about 25,000 women taking part in noncombatant service. Its mission was "making available to the national defense the knowledge, skill, and special training of the women of the nation." The goal of using women was "to increase the efficiency of the Army." The corps thus planned to recruit women with strong educational and technical qualifications "in order that it may quickly attain the highest reputation for both character and professional excellence."

The WAAC was to be under the command of a woman director who would "operate and administer the Corps in accordance with the normal military procedure of command." Women serving in the WAAC were to receive medical care while in the service, but no veterans' benefits.

See also
H.R. 6293; Rogers, Edith Nourse; Women's Army Auxiliary Corps (WAAC).

Reference
Mattie E. Treadwell, *U.S. Army in World War II: Special Studies—The Women's Army Corps* (1954).

H.R. 6293

A revised version of H.R. 4906, H.R. 6293 incorporated proposed amendments suggested by the War Department. Congresswoman Edith Nourse Rogers introduced this revised bill on 31 December 1941. Despite much opposition in Congress, it was quickly considered, debated, and passed. Strong support from the Army chief of staff and secretary of war influenced both the House of Representatives and Senate to pass the bill, thus creating the Women's Army Auxiliary Corps (WAAC).

See also
H.R. 4906; Rogers, Edith Nourse; Women's Army Auxiliary Corps (WAAC).
Reference
Mattie E. Treadwell, *U.S. Army in World War II: Special Studies—The Women's Army Corps* (1954).

Hughes, Everett S. (n.d.)

In 1928, Major Everett S. Hughes was appointed as chief Army planner for the development of a women's Army corps. A member of the General Staff, Hughes was convinced that if another major war occurred, women would play a significant role. He managed to bring together the various factions that could not agree on a plan, urging men in the military to accept this idea and develop an effective scheme for militarizing women. Among his suggestions was the proposal that women should begin training so they would be familiar with the military way of thinking and operating before any new wars took place.

Hughes also proposed combining men's and women's military organizations, with women being integrated into the current Army rather than being in separate units. He believed this would be more economical and efficient.

These proposals for women in the Army, like those made earlier by Anita Phipps, were delayed by red tape for years. Hughes's plan was tabled in 1931 and was ignored until 1939, when the inevitability of World War II reopened the issue under crisis conditions.

References
Mattie E. Treadwell, *U.S. Army in World War II: Special Studies—The Women's Army Corps* (1954).

Hultgreen, Kara S. (1965–1994)

Lieutenant Kara S. Hultgreen, who died on 25 October 1994 when her F-14 crashed during a training exercise, was one of the first two female combat jet pilots in the United States.

Hultgreen, a native of Texas, fought long and hard to be cleared for flying combat jets on aircraft carriers. She joined the ROTC while attending the University of Texas and decided to become a Navy flier. During flight training, the tall, aggressive Hultgreen was dubbed "the Incredible Hulk" after a male television character of that era.

After graduating from flight training school in August 1989, Hultgreen was stationed as a junior officer at Naval Air Station Key West in Florida. During her training, she had mastered the same skills as male pilots, in some cases exceeding their performance, and was frustrated by policies that kept her from serving in the same fleets. Instead of flying combat jets, she was assigned to fly the EA-6B, which was not equipped to drop bombs. Her regular requests to be transferred from this job to the TacAir division were always denied.

Hultgreen joined other women lobbying Congress to end the ban against women pilots in combat. She attended the April 1993 meeting of the Defense Advisory Commission on Women in the Service (DACOWITS), urging members to continue asking the services to assign women as fighter pilots and in other combat positions. Congress had voted more than 18 months previously to lift that ban, but the service branches had not taken action. At the DACOWITS conference, Hultgreen asked General Merrill A. McPeak, chief of staff of the Air Force, when women would be assigned to combat aircraft, but she did not receive a clear answer. As the military continued to hedge on this issue, Hultgreen said their attitudes might force "women like me . . . to leave the Navy."

In 1994, after the Navy ended the ban against women fighter pilots, Hultgreen qualified in a combat-ready F-14 Tomcat, popularly known as the Top Gun fighter. Her unit, the Black Lions of VF-213, was scheduled to leave for the Persian Gulf that November. During a training exercise in San Diego on 25 October, Hultgreen's F-14 crashed as she prepared to land on a carrier, the USS *Abraham Lincoln.* Radar officer Lieutenant Matthew Klemesh ejected and was rescued, but Hultgreen ejected as the plane rolled upside down and was killed.

Her commanding officers rated Hultgreen as an "average to above average" pilot. Yet after her death, rumors arose that Hultgreen was incompetent and had been promoted and cleared for combat because she was a woman, not because of her flying ability. Anonymous faxes, originating from inside the Navy, falsified her flying record to make her look inept. This was unprecedented, since traditional naval etiquette forbids challenging the ability of a fallen pilot. Since 1992, ten male F-14 pilots have died, and they were not criticized in this way.

To quell the rumors, Hultgreen's family made her flight records public. These records had been given to the family after Hultgreen's death, along with her other personal belongings. The records, published in several newspapers, showed that Hultgreen had received an overall score of 3.10 on a scale of 4.0, ranking her third among the pilots in her class of seven, all of whom qualified to fly F-14s. An investigation into the cause of the crash indicated problems with the F-14's left engine, not pilot error.

Hultgreen was buried in Arlington National Cemetery with full military honors.

References

Steve Komarow and Gordon Dickson, "Female Aviator, a Navy Pioneer, Killed in Crash," *USA Today* (27 October 1994); Tom Morgenthau et al., "The Military Fights Its Gender Wars," *Newsweek* (14 November 1994): 35–37; "Navy Records Highly Rated Woman Pilot Who Crashed," *New York Times* (21 November 1994): A16; Gregory L. Vistica, *Fall from*

Glory (1996); Jean Zimmerman, *Tailspin: Women at War in the Wake of Tailhook* (1995).

Huyler-Gillies, Betty (b. 1908)

A pioneer aviator during the 1920s and 1930s, Betty Huyler organized women pilots in the United States and urged her group, the Ninety-Nines, to gain the kind of flying experience they would need in case of war.

Huyler had planned a career in nursing and entered the prestigious nursing program at Columbia Presbyterian Hospital in New York City. While in training in 1928, she met and fell in love with a naval aviator. After reading an article in *Cosmopolitan* magazine called "Try Flying Yourself," written by Amelia Earhart, Huyler decided to take flying lessons. She earned a pilot's license at Roosevelt Field on Long Island, and then left nursing to work for the Curtiss-Wright Corporation, demonstrating the flight instruction program and showing prospective customers a new trainer plane, the American Moth.

In November 1929, Huyler was a driving force in organizing the Ninety-Nines, the first national group for U.S. women pilots. After marrying Bud Gillies, the aviator she had met in nursing school, she continued to fly, working as a utility pilot for Grumman Aircraft on Long Island where her husband was an executive. She also reared three children. As president of the Ninety-Nines during the late 1930s, Huyler urged her fellow members, now numbering about 500, to gain the flying experience they might need in case of war, which threatened the entire world by that time.

As Betty Huyler-Gillies, she was one of 28 women pilots invited to join the Women's Auxiliary Ferrying Squadron (WAFS) in 1943. Her first military assignment was to fly PT-26s a distance of about 2,500 miles from Hagerstown, Maryland, to Calgary in Canada. In September 1943, she became one of the first women pilots in the world to fly a four-engine bomber. Standing 5 feet, 1½ inches tall and weighing 108 pounds, she impressed male pilots with her ability to handle this aircraft.

As one of the more mature and experienced women pilots, Betty often served as a mentor to the younger pilots and was nicknamed Mother. A leader known for her sense of humor and inspirational qualities, she served as a squadron leader for the WAFS and the Women's Airforce Service Pilots (WASP), the organization that merged with the WAFS later in 1943.

See also

Love, Nancy Harkness; Women's Auxiliary Ferrying Squadron (WAFS).

References

Deborah G. Douglas, *United States Women in Aviation, 1940–1985* (1991); Sally Van Wagenen Keil, *Those Wonderful Women in Their Flying Machines* (1979); Ken Magid, *Women of Courage: The Women Airforce Pilots of World War II* (1993).

Ingraham, Mary Shotwell (1887–1981)

The founder of the United Services Organization (USO), Mary Shotwell Ingraham was born in Brooklyn, New York. She graduated from the prestigious women's college, Vassar, and then worked for the Brooklyn Young Women's Christian Association (YWCA). From 1922 to 1939, Ingraham was president of this community organization, going on to serve as president of the national board of the YWCA in 1940. An advocate for education, she also served as a volunteer from 1938 to 1968 on the New York City Board of Higher Education.

In 1941, as World War II began, Ingraham envisioned a service group that would provide social, recreational, and welfare aid to servicemen around the world. Toward that end, she founded the USO and served as its vice president.

At the request of the War Department, Ingraham was also part of the committee that selected the women who entered the first officer's training class for the Women's Auxiliary Army Corps (WAAC) in 1942. In 1946, Ingraham became the first woman to receive the U.S. Medal of Merit, a tribute to her creation of the USO as well as her service on the selection committee.

See also
United Services Organization (USO).
Reference
Doris Weatherford, *American Women and World War II* (1990).

Integration Act

See Women's Armed Services Integration Act of 1948.

Intelligence Operators

See Espionage.

Intercontinental Ballistic Missiles (ICBMs)

Work with intercontinental ballistic missiles (ICBMs), an important element in the nation's strategic defenses, became open to women during the early 1970s. Women's involvement in the launching of ICBMs had been controversial, since some military leaders felt it violated the ban against women in combat positions. The Air Force, however, began training women in missile maintenance and other support-related positions with the Minuteman and Titan systems.

By 1980, women were part of missile crews and were being trained as missile launchers. In 1979, Captain Patricia Fornes became the first woman to qualify as a member of a missile crew and be assigned to a position. By 1991, during the Persian Gulf War, women were serving in all areas of missile operations.

Interpreters

See American Expeditionary Forces (AEF); World War I.

J

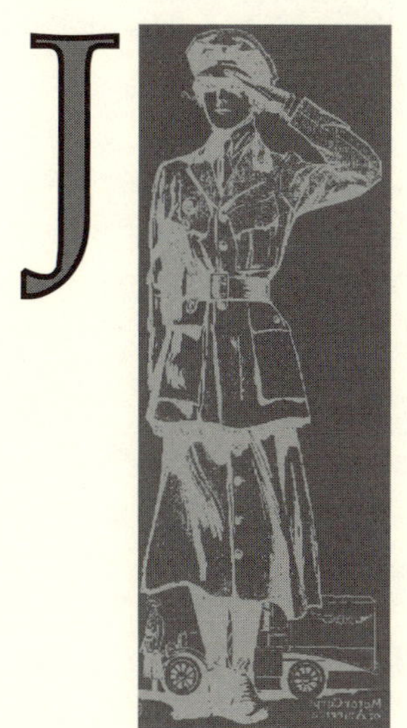

Johnson, Jemima (n.d.)

Jemima Johnson became renowned for her courage during the American Revolution. On 15 August 1782, a group of more than 600 British soldiers and Indians surrounded a stockade at Bryan's Station near Lexington, Kentucky. Inside were Johnson, her neighbors, and some colonial soldiers.

The colonists were running out of water, so Johnson suggested that she, along with 27 other women and girls, would go through the back door to the creek, carrying their water buckets, and acting unconcerned about the presence of the troops. The astonished soldiers did not hurt or arrest the women, and they were able to return to the stockade with sufficient water to sustain those barricaded inside until soldiers from Lexington arrived to end the siege.

Johnson, Opha

See Marine Corps Reserves.

K

Kaiser Shipyard

As women workers became the majority in defense industries during World War II, Kaiser Shipyard, or Kaiser Shipbuilding, was known for its support systems, especially for working mothers. Located in Portland, Oregon, Kaiser had determined by 1943 that about 30 percent of all shipbuilding tasks could be performed by women. The company, led by Henry Kaiser, decided to recruit women and develop programs that addressed the needs of women workers. Some companies had lost workers or experienced lower productivity because women were struggling to perform double duty at home and on the job.

Working with public authorities, Kaiser built a planned community in nearby Vanport City where nearly 40,000 workers and family members could live. The company operated a cafeteria and kitchen that sold hot meals that workers could take home when they finished their shifts. It also gave working women weekly menus that featured nutritious meals they could prepare quickly at home.

Kaiser was noted for its child-care center, which cost 75 cents per day for the first child and 50 cents for each additional child in a family. Available for workers' children ages 18 months and older, it operated at night as well as during the day and would take sick children. According to *Architectural Record*, "The Kaiser Child Service Centers are among the first places where working people, people of average means, have been able to afford good nursery education for their children."

See also

Defense Plant Workers; "Rosie the Riveter."

References

"Designed for 24-Hour Child Care," *Architectural Record* (March 1944): 75; Lora Swartz, "Child Service Centers," *Journal of Home Economics* (February 1944): 75; Doris Weatherford, *American Women and World War II* (1990).

Kelley, Beverly Gwinn (b. 1952)

Beverly Gwinn Kelley, a Coast Guard lieutenant (junior grade), was the first woman captain of a U.S. military vessel. The Florida native commanded the patrol boat *Cape Newagen*, a 95-foot vessel, from April 1979 to July 1981.

Kelley grew up in a seafaring family, the daughter of a former captain in the merchant service. In 1977, she was one of the first two women to serve along with men on an armed vessel, the *Morgenthau*, a cutter charged with arresting those who violated fishing limits.

The news that a woman had been placed in command of a military ship made headlines in April 1979. One newspaper headed its story "Yo-ho-ho and a Bottle of Chanel No. 5."

In 1980, Kelley and her 14-man crew on the *Cape Newagen* were awarded a citation for professionalism after they rescued 12 people who were at sea in a dangerous storm off the coast of Hawaii. Their search-and-rescue work earned the crew a Meritorious Unit Commendation.

Reference

John A. Tilley, *A History of Women in the Coast Guard* (1996).

Kendleigh, Jane

See Navy Nurse Corps (NNC).

Kilgore, Margaret (Maggie) (n.d.)

In 1968, journalist Margaret Kilgore offered to go to Vietnam to cover the

Tet Offensive. When H. L. Stevenson, her boss at United Press International (UPI), asked male correspondents to volunteer, Kilgore asked, "How about me, coach?"

In January 1970, UPI officials finally agreed that Kilgore could cover the war in Southeast Asia. During her 20 months on this assignment, she covered events in the South Vietnamese capital of Saigon and in the demilitarized zone (DMZ) near Da Nang.

Kilgore was one of a handful of women correspondents to cover the Vietnam War. She later told author Hayton-Keeva about the many difficulties of surviving day to day during those two years—the rats in the news bureau office, the trouble getting necessities, and "lousy plumbing, lousy sewers, lousy lighting, nothing working." She said, "It was hard to be there and hard to live there." Still, Kilgore called this experience "the single most interesting thing I've ever done in my life."

See also

Correspondents, War.

References

Virginia Elwood-Akers, *Women War Correspondents in the Vietnam War, 1961–1975* (1988); Sally Hayton-Keeva, *Valiant Women in War and Exile: Thirty-Eight True Stories* (1987).

King, Micki (Maxine) (b. 1945)

As a captain in the United States Air Force, Micki King won a gold medal in springboard diving at the 1972 Olympic Games held in Munich, Germany.

King grew up in Pontiac, Michigan, and began swimming at an early age. At age four, she was able to dive but did not begin studying it seriously until she was ten years old. She also became a skillful figure skater and played softball and baseball. Competing at a diving meet in Ohio at age 15, King, the only girl present, won first place. She began to work more intensely on her sport but did not make the Olympic team that year.

King entered the University of Michigan where she was named all-American in water polo, playing the position of goalie. She also competed as part of the university's women's swim team and continued to train as a diver.

At the 1968 Olympic Games in Mexico City, King was favored to win a medal. She had completed eight of her ten dives and was in first place when she began a reverse one-and-a-half layout. An error in her takeoff led her to hit the board with her left arm, causing a painful injury. Despite her discomfort, King finished her last dive but was only able to reach fourth place in the competition, which meant she received no medal. She then learned that her arm was broken.

After taking a break from competitive diving, King entered the World Military Games in 1969. Against a field that consisted entirely of men, King captured third place in platform diving and fourth in the springboard competition. On the heels of that event, she won first place in the U.S. women's diving championship and took top honors at that year's Pan American Games.

King then changed her mind and decided to compete at the next Olympic Games. In her late twenties and competing against younger divers, she nonetheless gave a performance in the springboard competition that was described as flawless by many

U.S. Air Force captain and Olympic diver Micki King

onlookers. At last, she had won her gold medal. Retiring from competition, King was named diving coach at the U.S. Air Force Academy, the first woman ever to coach sports at a service academy. She coached only men until 1976, when the academy began admitting women.

In 1977 King married Jim Hogue, also a member of the Air Force. She was then assigned to develop sports and recreation programs for servicepeople and their families. Along with motherhood, she continued her career in the Air Force into the 1980s.

References

Phyllis Hollander, *American Women in Sports* (1972); Robert Markel and Nancy Brooks, *For the Record: Women in Sports* (1985); David Wallechinsky, *The Complete Book of the Olympics* (1984).

Korean War

Also called the Korean Conflict, the Korean War lasted from 1950 to 1953. Although the Women's Army Corps (WAC) had become part of the regular Army in 1948, there were not enough Wacs on active duty to meet the increased need for wartime personnel. Hundreds of reservists either volunteered or were called back to the service. From a total of 7,300 Wacs in June 1950, the WAC increased to 12,000 women in 1951.

No entire WAC unit was sent to Korea, although a few women served there in 1952 and 1953. Of the 49,000 women serving in the military during the war, nurses were the only personnel stationed in Korea. Others served in administrative, communication, and supply jobs for the U.S. military in Japan and Okinawa. The Women in the Air Force (WAF) also sent some women to other bases in the Far East during the war. The maximum number of women allowed to serve was not reached during the conflict.

In 1956, a permanent WAC unit was set up in Seoul, Korea, and by 1974, 280 Wacs were serving there.

See also

Army Nurse Corps (ANC); Higgins, Marguerite ("Maggie"); Mobile Army Surgical Hospital (MASH).

References

Herbert K. Barnett, "A Date with Destiny: The Women's Army Corps Museum" (1992); Carol Wekesser and Matthew Polesetsky, eds., *Women in the Military* (1991).

L

Ladies' Gunboat Fair

In spring 1862, women volunteers in Charleston, South Carolina, organized a large raffle to raise money to buy supplies for the Confederate Army. They sold 4,000 raffle tickets, each giving the buyer a chance to win prizes such as silverware, watches, and a diamond ring, all donated by Confederate supporters.

Lady Washington

A row galley (small wooden river gunboat), the *Lady Washington* was the first American-armed ship named for a woman. Its namesake, Martha Washington, was the wife of George Washington, who commanded the colonial army and became the nation's first president. The boat was built in 1776 and used in New York State, under General Washington's command, to defend the Hudson River until June 1777.

See also
American Revolution; Washington, Martha.

Lambine, Janna

See United States Coast Guard.

Lane, Anna Maria

See Passing; Pensions, Veterans'.

Lane, Sharon A.

See Army Nurse Corps (ANC); Casualties; Vietnam War.

Lanham Act (1943)

Passed in 1943 during World War II, the Lanham Act provided federal funds for child-care programs for the families of workers in defense industries. Before this time, the only other federally funded child care had been provided for those employed by the Works Progress Administration (WPA) during the Depression.

More than a million women went to work in defense plants and other places after men left for the service during World War II. It was difficult to recruit enough women since many were responsible for young children and there were not nearly enough private child-care centers to fill the need. The act required that a center be set up "for one child for every ten working women in a defense plant."

Pressure from working women, labor unions, and others led Congress to extend the act until March 1946, after which time communities received no more federal funding. Faced with the option of closing down or increasing their fees, most of these child-care centers ceased to operate after the war.

See also
Kaiser Shipyard

References
Karen Anderson, *Wartime Women: Sex Roles, Family Relations, and the Status of Women During World War II* (1981); Miriam Frank, Marilyn Ziebarth, and Connie Field, *The Life and Times of Rosie the Riveter* (1982); Mattie E. Treadwell, *U.S. Army in World War II: Special Studies—The Women's Army Corps* (1954).

Lewis v. United States Army

In 1988, (plaintiff) Lewis filed suit against the U.S. Army because she was denied the chance to enlist. Her education did not meet the Army's requirements, although she had a G.E.D. (General Education Development) certificate and some college credits. In her suit, she charged that the policy was unconstitutional since men with the G.E.D., sometimes called a high school equivalency, were permitted to enlist.

Lewis v. United States Army, 697 F. Supp. 1385 (E.D. Pa. 1988), was dismissed by the federal district court, which did not agree that the policy violated the Fourteenth Amendment Equal Protection Clause. The court claimed that the policy of combat exclusion meant there were fewer openings in the military for women, so the military was justified in setting higher admission requirements for women than men. Their legal argument maintained that men and women were not "similarly situated" in the military.

Reference

Robin Rogers, "A Proposal for Combating Sexual Discrimination in the Military: Amendment to Title VII," *California Law Review* (January 1990): 165–196.

Libya, Raid on

In 1986, the U.S. military took part in a raid on Libya, a country in the Persian Gulf. Libyans had arranged for the bombing of a disco in West Berlin, Germany, and U.S. planes dropped bombs on Tripoli and Benghazi in Libya in retaliation. Hundreds of military women were involved in the raid, with about 258 sailing to the Persian Gulf on the *Arcadia*. Women served on the crews of tankers that refueled bombers in midair and as military police, munitions specialists, and signal operators. Some were copilots on noncombat airplanes.

Lighthouse Keepers

Women lighthouse keepers have been called the first women to perform duties of the Coast Guard. Historians believe that between 1828 and 1947, 138 women were hired as lighthouse keepers. Others took over as keepers after their fathers or husbands died or could no longer perform the job.

During the American Revolution, Hannah Thomas took over her husband's job as keeper of Garnet Point Light near Plymouth, Massachusetts, after he joined the army.

One of the most famous women lighthouse keepers was Idawalley (Ida) Lewis (1842–1911), who tended Lime Rock Light near Newport, Rhode Island, for 54 years, beginning at age 15 when her father became disabled. A courageous and skilled rower, Lewis rescued 18 to 24 people from the sea over the years. After one famous rescue in 1869, her picture appeared on the cover of *Harper's Weekly*.

From 1886 to 1919, Kate Walker operated Robbins Reef Light off Staten Island, New York. A widow, Walker and her son and daughter carried out the arduous work of running a lighthouse—carrying the kerosene up the steps to the lantern, keeping the lantern filled and lit, polishing the glass around the light. In her years as lighthouse keeper, Walker saved a total of 50 people from drowning.

As steam foghorns replaced traditional fog bells and electric lighting became available in the early 1900s, the number of lighthouse keepers, both men and women, declined.

See also

Bates, Rebecca and Abigail; United States Coast Guard.

Lillybridge, Anny

See Civil War.

Livermore, Mary (1820–1905)

A social reformer, Mary Livermore was a nurse and executive in the United States Sanitary Commission during the Civil War. As she traveled in the Midwest and other regions doing war work, she kept notes and documented the ways in which women were contributing to the war effort. Her notes were later published.

In 1863, Livermore was involved in collecting fruits and vegetables to distribute among Union troops in order to prevent scurvy, a disease caused by a lack of Vitamin C. She noted that during the harvesttime, "Women were in the field everywhere, driving the reapers, binding and shocking, and loading grain, until then an unusual sight."

See also
United States Sanitary Commission.
References
Mary Livermore, *My Story of the War* (1888); Milton Meltzer, *Voices from the Civil War: A Documentary History of the Great American Conflict* (1989).

Long-Range Aid to Navigation (LORAN)

During the 1940s, LORAN, or long-range aid to navigation, was the most highly classified navigation system used by the armed services. Although women had always been barred from highly classified projects, they began working in LORAN during World War II, a time when both the Navy and Coast Guard lacked enough men to fill such positions. The Coast Guard staffed one LORAN station entirely with members of the SPAR, its all-women corps. The Navy assigned members of Women Accepted for Voluntary Emergency Service (WAVES) to serve at LORAN stations, such as the one in Washington, D.C. Having proven their competence in these jobs, women were no longer automatically excluded from similar positions.

Reference
Jeanne Holm, *Women in the Military: An Unfinished Revolution* (1992).

Love, Nancy Harkness (b. 1914)

Nancy Harkness Love was the first woman commander of the Women's Auxiliary Ferrying Squadron (WAFS), a group of women pilots who served during World War II.

Love began flying as a teenager in 1930, earning her license at age 16. While attending Vassar College, she set up flying clubs for students. She later married a deputy chief of staff for the air transport command of the Army Air Force, and together they established Inter-City Airlines in Boston.

Before the war, Love worked for the Bureau of Commerce as an air marker (a person who decides where to place rooftop signs that guide pilots from the air). She served as a test pilot at a flying school she helped manage and was among the pilots who helped test tricycle landing gear, later used on medium and heavy bombers.

When the war began in Europe in 1939, Love joined some women pilots who ferried planes from the United States to Canada, where they would be used by the British air force.

Through her efforts, the government approved the establishment of the WAFS on 10 September 1942. A salary of $3,000 a year was given to each of these expert women pilots,

Statue of Revolutionary War heroine Sybil Ludington

who were classified as civilian contract employees rather than members of the military. Pilots in the squadron flew various types of military aircraft to bases in noncombat zones. As commander, Love was in charge of the training program.

Love's command ended in August 1943 when her group was combined with the Women's Flying Training Detachment to form the Women's Airforce Service Pilots (WASP), under the command of Jacqueline Cochran. Love was appointed executive of the Ferrying Division of the Air Transport Command, based in Cincinnati, Ohio, and continued to fly. She achieved several firsts; in 1943, she was the first woman to fly a P-51 Mustang fighter plane, and she was one of the first women to qualify as a B-17 pilot. After the war, she continued to work in the field of aviation.

References

Deborah G. Douglas, *American Women in Aviation, 1941–1985* (1991); Sally Van

Wagenen Keil, *Those Wonderful Women and Their Flying Machines* (1979).

Loyalist Women

People who supported the British cause against the rebellious colonists in the American Revolution were known as loyalists. Loyalist women were not as numerous or active as members of the Daughters of Liberty, those who supported the rebellion, however. As one of their activities, a group of loyalist women in New York State raised money to buy a ship, *The Fair American*, which was outfitted for use against the Patriots during the war. In some cases, women from both groups assigned individuals and committees to keep an eye on the activities of the other side and report their findings to military officials.

See also

Brant, Mary (Molly); Daughters of Liberty; Espionage.

References

Patricia Edwards Clyne, *Patriots in Petticoats* (1976); Selma Williams, *Demeter's Daughters: The Women Who Founded America* (1976).

Ludington, Sybil (1761–1839)

As a 16-year-old, Sybil Ludington made a nighttime ride to alert the people in the area of Danbury, Connecticut, that British troops were coming. The daughter of Colonel Henry Ludington, Sybil was a resident of Fredericksburg, New York.

On the night of 26 April 1777, she rode 40 miles on her horse, Star. As she passed various homes, Ludington banged on the doors. The awakened men then rose and rode to Danbury, an important location of stored supplies for the patriots.

As a result of Ludington's courage, the men were able to reach the storage center in time to guard the supplies. They waited at the home of Colonel Ludington until 2,000 British and loyalist soldiers arrived there. Colonel Ludington then ordered the British troops to go back to their ships.

References

Patricia Edwards Clyne, *Patriots in Petticoats* (1976); Selma Williams, *Demeter's Daughters: The Women Who Founded America* (1976).

M

McAfee, Mildred Helen (1900–1994)

A distinguished educator, Mildred Helen McAfee left her position as a college president to become the first director of the Navy's Women Accepted for Voluntary Emergency Service (WAVES) during World War II.

Born in Parkville, Missouri, McAfee graduated from Vassar College in 1920. From 1923 to 1926, she taught at Tusculum College in Greenville, Tennessee. She then served as dean of women at Centre College in Danville, Kentucky. After earning a master's degree at the University of Chicago in 1928, she returned to Vassar to serve as executive secretary of the alumnae association from 1932 to 1934. Moving to Ohio, McAfee was named dean of women at Oberlin College, a position she held from 1934 to 1936. In 1936, she become president of Wellesley College in Massachusetts.

McAfee was part of the committee that designed the Naval Reserve program for women after World War II began. When the WAVES was formed in 1942, McAfee agreed to head this women's auxiliary unit for the Navy while also serving as special assistant to the chief of naval personnel. She had advocated that her group be known as women in the Navy rather than receive an acronym such as WAVES, but she was overruled on this matter.

On 3 August 1942, McAfee became the first woman sworn into the Naval Reserve as an officer. She rose to the rank of captain, directing the WAVES as it grew to about 86,000 women by 1945.

McAfee was known for her outstanding communication skills, her ability to work well with others, and for finding outstanding people for recruitment, training, and administration roles in the WAVES. Known as "Captain Mac," she was a popular director who discovered innovative ways to solve problems.

McAfee received the Distinguished Service Medal after the war. She returned to Wellesley to resume her position as president, and after resigning in 1949, she promoted a number of important social causes and served on several corporate boards of directors. She was president of the National Social Welfare Assembly from 1950 to 1953, then president of the American Board of Commissioners of Foreign Missions from 1959 to 1961. In 1962, she was appointed a U.S. delegate to the United Nations Educational, Scientific, and Cultural Organization (UNESCO). From 1963 to 1964, she cochaired the National Women's Committee on Civil Rights.

See also

"Battle of the Black Stockings"; Women Accepted for Voluntary Emergency Service (WAVES).

References

Marie Bennett Alsmeyer, *The Way of the WAVES: Women in the Navy* (1981); Joy Bright Hancock, *Lady in the Navy: A Personal Remembrance* (1972); Jeanne Holm, *Women in the Military: An Unfinished Revolution* (1992); Phyllis J. Read and Bernard L. Witlieb, *The Book of Women's Firsts* (1992); Nancy Wilson Ross, *The WAVES: The Story of the Girls in Blue* (1943).

McBride, Maggie (b. 1767)

As a 14-year-old farm girl in Guilford County, North Carolina, Maggie McBride became a heroine of the American Revolution. In 1781 she helped a group of patriot soldiers locate a Tory camp hidden in a dense pine forest. She rode along with the leader behind his saddle until they reached the camp. As the first shots rang out, McBride leaped off the saddle and ran home, a distance of several miles.

McCauley, Mary

See Hays, Mary Ludwig.

McGee, Anita Newcomb (1864–1940)

Physician Anita Newcomb McGee organized nursing services for the Army during the Spanish-American War and promoted the formation of the Army Nurse Corps (ANC) in 1901.

A native of Washington, D.C., she was married to a geologist. While rearing two children, McGee completed her M.D. degree in 1892 at Columbian (later George Washington) University, then did postgraduate work in gynecology at Johns Hopkins University.

Known for her management skills and her association with the Daughters of the American Revolution (DAR), she was asked to serve as acting assistant surgeon general during the Spanish-American War of 1898, a position she held until 1900. McGee succeeded in organizing nurses needed to care for the servicemen in the Army and Navy. These soldiers were not only wounded but stricken in large numbers with yellow fever.

During the war, McGee came into conflict with officials from the American Red Cross, since they viewed her as encroaching upon their role of procuring nurses for the military. McGee's successful recruitment methods resulted in less federal funding to the Red Cross for its efforts.

The year after the war ended, McGee became the head of the Society of Spanish-American War Nurses, a position she held until 1904. Along with others from that organization, she aided Japanese nurses during the Russo-Japanese War of 1904–1905.

McGee's wartime work demonstrated the value of an organized group of military nurses, and it spurred the creation of the Army Nurse Corps. By 1900, the government was keenly aware of the ongoing need for professional nurses in the military, in times of both peace and war. McGee was asked to draft the Army Reorganization Act of 1901, which set up the nursing corps as a permanent part of the Army.

As a physician rather than a nurse, McGee was not eligible to become director of the ANC. She continued to practice medicine and was a member of the American Association for the Advancement of Science as well as the Women's Anthropological Society of America.

References

Ruth J. Abram, ed., *"Send Us a Lady Physician": Women Doctors in America, 1835–1920* (1985); Edward T. James et al., *Notable American Women II* (1971); Dorothy and Carl J. Schneider, *Into the Breach: Women in World War I* (1991).

"Mae West"

During World War II, servicemen used the nickname "Mae West" for the vest-like, inflatable life preservers used by pilots and sailors. It was named after the voluptuous blonde Mae West (1893–1980), a popular actress and comedienne of the day.

Manhattan Project

In 1939, after hearing about German research on atomic energy, President Roosevelt authorized a secret research project in the United States. The research was aimed at building atomic weapons that would enable the Allies to win World War II. Under the direction of the United States Army, with General Leslie R. Groves as military director, this effort became known as the Manhattan District Engineer, or Manhattan Project for short.

An early, vital part of the project was the development of a controlled nuclear chain reaction. The group that finally achieved this, under the direction of Italian-American physicist Enrico Fermi at the University of Chicago, included a woman physicist, Leona Wood. On 2 December 1942, along with 19 male scientists, Wood watched this unprecedented scientific event, which later enabled scientists to build atomic bombs. The bombs were eventually used on two Japanese cities, Hiroshima and Nagasaki, in August 1945, and Japan surrendered shortly after the second bomb was dropped.

At Los Alamos, New Mexico, where the bombs were being built and tested, members of the Women's Army Corps (WAC) provided many services for the Manhattan Project. WAC-member Mary Lehman was among those who chauffeured the scientists, including Enrico Fermi, from place to place. She later said, "It took a long time to figure out what they were doing." While at Los Alamos, she met her future husband, Joe Lehman, who was a master sergeant in the Army Special Engineer Detachment. Another woman working at Los Alamos, Miriam Campbell, was asked to do technical drawings for the project. Women physicists Maria Goeppart Mayer and Chien Shiung Wu also worked on the project.

Women also served in many other roles that aided the project. This included working in plants in Oak Ridge, Tennessee, and Hanford, Washington, to process enough plutonium and uranium to construct the bombs.

See also
Corps of Engineers.

References
Bonnie Bell et al., "Witness at Trinity Site," *Newsweek* (17 July 1995): 68–75; Laura Fermi, *Atoms in the Family: My Life with Enrico Fermi* (1954); Leslie R. Groves, *Now It Can Be Told* (1962); William L. Laurence, *Dawn over Zero: The Story of the Atomic Bomb* (1947).

Marble, Alice (1913–1990)

A champion tennis player, Alice Marble served as the director of physical fitness programs for women in the military during World War II and played in tennis exhibitions for servicepeople.

Born in California, Marble was one of the first women tennis players to use an aggressive, hard-hitting style. She won four U.S. women's titles and the Wimbledon Championship (1939). Sportswriters named her the Woman Athlete of the Year in 1939 and 1940.

When the war broke out, tournament play in Europe was suspended. In 1941, Marble enlisted with the Hail American Movement and played exhibition matches to entertain servicepeople stationed at training stations and camps throughout the United States. It was during this time that Marble began directing physical fitness programs for military women.

Alice Marble

Marble resumed her tennis career after the war, moving from amateur to professional tournaments. She taught tennis, encouraged a number of up-and-coming young players, and supported the rights of African-American tennis players, such as Althea Gibson, to enter tournaments that had been closed to them before the 1950s.

References

Bud Collins, ed., *Bud Collins' Modern Encyclopedia of Tennis* (1994); George Sullivan, *Queens of the Court* (1974).

Marier, Rebecca (b. 1974)

In 1995, Rebecca Marier became the first woman to graduate at the top of her class at the United States Military Academy (USMA) at West Point, New York.

Marier grew up in New Orleans, the daughter of Robert Marier, a physician and associate dean of the medical school at Louisiana State University, and Joanne Marier, a lawyer. In high school, Rebecca was a National Merit Scholar and served as president of her senior class. An outstanding athlete, she lettered in soccer, tennis, and volleyball.

The 1995 graduating class at West Point was made up of 858 men and 130 women. Marier's academic average was 3.95 out of a possible 4.0, and her cumulative scores for academics, military performance, and physical fitness made her the top-ranking senior. She then became the second West Point graduate to enroll at Harvard Medical School.

Reference

"Class of the Class," *People Magazine* (19 June 1995): 59.

Marine Corps, United States

See United States Marine Corps.

Marine Corps Reserves

During World War I, the Marine Corps recruited women in August 1918, shortly before the war ended. Three hundred women enrolled as Marine (F)—female—and were nicknamed "Marinettes." Facing a manpower shortage, the Marines decided that women could fill a number of clerical roles so men could be released for other duties, mainly combat. These women were accorded full military status as members of the Marines.

In 1918, Opha Johnson became the first woman to join the Marine Corps Reserve. The secretary of the Navy had authorized the Marine Corps to accept women reservists only one day earlier, on 12 August. Johnson served as a clerk, with the rank of private, in Washington, D.C., and remained in the Marines until 1919. Eventually, 1,277 women served in the Marines in World War I.

Mariner, Rosemary Conatser (b. 1953)

Captain Rosemary Mariner, the first woman to qualify in high-performance jet aircraft, was also known as a staunch advocate of equal opportunities for women in military aviation.

A native of California, Mariner grew up in a military family. Her father, an Army Air Force pilot, was killed in a crash when she was three years old, and her mother had served as a Navy nurse during World War II. While in high school, Mariner decided she would become an airline pilot, but during the late 1960s, no women were being hired for such jobs. Neither were there any women pilots in the military.

At Gillespie Field, near her home, she swapped flying lessons for washing

Three Marine Corps Reserve members, nicknamed "Marinettes," pose in their new uniforms in 1918.

airplanes and doing other odd jobs, earning her license by age 17. Her instructor, Fred Priest, had taught members of the Women's Airforce Service Pilots (WASP) during the war when they trained at Avenger Field in Sweetwater, Texas. Priest shared with Mariner many inspiring stories of these pioneer women fliers. Mariner later earned her multiengine rating under a former WASP, "Mac" Huntington. When Mariner entered Indiana's Purdue University as the first woman ever enrolled in the aviation program, one of her main instructors was another former WASP, Jill McCormick.

While Mariner was finishing college, the chief of Naval Operations was Elmo Zumwalt, a Vietnam War veteran who had been greatly impressed by the fighting ability of the North Vietnamese (Vietcong) women during that war. Zumwalt concluded that women had the ability to perform additional roles in the U.S. Armed Forces and that they would be needed more than ever when the All-Volunteer Force (AVF) took effect. Under his direction in 1972, the Navy decided to train its first group of women pilots. Zumwalt also directed that women be allowed to serve in command capacities at shore stations.

Excited by the opportunity to become a military pilot, Mariner finished her college degree at age 19 and joined the group of Navy flight trainees at Pensacola, Florida. These women received a great deal of publicity as they went through their arduous flight school training. Mariner later recalled the biases against women pilots that they encountered:

> It wasn't enough that women had been flying since the beginning of aviation, that they had flown all the airplanes of World War II without benefit of hydraulically boosted flight controls, that the Russians had three squadrons of women fly in combat during that same war, or that by this time, the airlines had hired women pilots. . . . One commander told me that women were physically incapable of flying high-performance jets because 'they can't wear G-suits.' When I informed him that Jackie Cochran had broken the sound barrier in 1953 in an F-86, and that Cochran and Jackie Auriol had volleyed speed records back and forth in excess of Mach 2—both while wearing G-suits—he looked at me as if I were an outright liar.

Despite the odds, Mariner and five other women completed the training and received their commissions in 1973. As part of Oceana, a jet composite squadron, Mariner towed targets that ships used during gunnery practice. Among her colleagues were male pilots in their twenties who had been highly decorated for their service in the Vietnam War. Mariner was the only woman aviator in the squadron during those years.

In 1975, her squadron commander, Captain Ray Lambert, selected Mariner, along with several male pilots, for jet-pilot training. Her assignment was not approved until eight months later, while male pilots were cleared within two weeks. Later, Mariner praised Lambert, an African-American officer, as a role model for skillfully combating discrimination. In the years that followed, she continued to overcome barriers against women in the military.

Cleared to "go jets," Mariner went on to fly more than 3,500 hours in 15 types of naval aircraft, including the A-4L, the A-4E, and the A-7E. Working at the Naval Weapons Center in China Lake, California, Mariner flew in research and development test and evaluation projects. She tested new weapon systems, dropped bombs in the desert, and fired guns.

From 1990 to 1991, Mariner was the first woman ever to command an operational aviation squadron when she headed a Navy tactical electronic warfare squadron. She showed her ability to land a jet on an aircraft carrier, one of the first women to "carrier qualify." When women were at last permitted on the *Forrestal*, an aircraft carrier—but one that did not go on full-length deployments—Mariner served onboard the training carrier *Lexington*.

In 1994, Rosemary Mariner and her husband welcomed their first child, a daughter. The next year, they left Washington, D.C., for Meridian, Mississippi, where Mariner became the first woman to command a naval air station. Throughout her long and active naval career, Mariner had achieved many firsts and had inspired and helped numerous other women to become Navy pilots.

References

Jeanne Holm, *Women in the Military: An Unfinished Revolution* (1992); "Women at Sea: Navy Traditions Being Rewritten," *Washington Post* (25 February 1979): 1; Jean Zimmerman, *Tailspin: Women at War in the Wake of Tailhook* (1995).

"Marinettes"

See Marine Corps Reserves.

Marshall, Leona Wood

See Manhattan Project.

MASH

See Mobile Army Surgical Hospital (MASH).

May, Geraldine Pratt (b. 1895)

In 1948, Colonel Geraldine May became the first woman director of Women in the Air Force (WAF). Born in Albany, New York, she graduated from the University of California at Berkeley in 1920 and later became a social worker and administrator with the Camp Fire Girls of America.

After marrying Albert May in 1928, Geraldine May moved to Oklahoma. Years later, in 1942, she returned to California and joined the newly established Women's Army Auxiliary Corps (WAAC). May was among the first women to graduate from the WAAC training school in Des Moines, Iowa, at which time she was commissioned as a second lieutenant. In 1943, she served as staff director for the Air Transport Command. Promoted to major and then lieutenant colonel, May became staff director of the Army Ground Forces in 1947.

The next year saw the passage of the Women's Armed Services Integration Act of 1948. This made the women's Air Force part of the regular Air Force, rather than an auxiliary component. May was named director of the WAF and promoted to the rank of full colonel.

Reference

U.S. Department of the Army, "Geraldine P. May," Fact Sheet (1970).

Medals

Women in the military have received numerous medals for their achievements and services. The first woman to receive a Purple Heart, given to servicepeople who have been wounded, was a Canadian-born nurse, Ann Leah Fox, who was head nurse at Hickam Field, Hawaii, when Pearl Harbor was bombed.

In 1943, Edith Greenwood became the first person to receive the Soldier's Medal. Greenwood was a nurse at an army hospital in Yuma, Arizona. During a fire, she and an attendant safely evacuated all the patients on their ward.

See also
Army Nurse Corps (ANC); Corregidor; Decorations; Hobby, Oveta Culp; SPAR; United States Coast Guard; Vietnam War; Women's Army Corps (WAC); Women Accepted for Voluntary Emergency Service (WAVES); Women Marines; World War I; World War II.

Mellette, Nancy (b. 1978)

In 1995, 17-year-old Nancy Mellette made news headlines when she applied to the all-male Citadel, a military college in South Carolina that had gone to court asking that women not be admitted. That same year, in August, Shannon Faulkner, the first woman to be admitted to the Citadel, had dropped out for health reasons, including the mental stress she experienced as the only female cadet.

Mellette is the daughter of a Citadel graduate and career military officer, Army Lieutenant Colonel Bland Mellette; her mother is a psychiatrist. Nancy Mellette's older brother, James Bland Mellette III, graduated from the Citadel in 1996.

In June 1996, the U.S. Supreme Court handed down a ruling that requires the Virginia Military Institute (V.M.I.) to admit women. This ruling was viewed as applicable to other military colleges, and the Citadel announced that it would now accept women students.

Mellette attended a private high school, Oak Ridge Military Academy, where she was in the Reserve Officer Training Corps (ROTC). About 80 percent of the students at Oak Ridge were men. A strong athlete, Mellette earned varsity letters in basketball, cross-country running, and softball. She told reporters she planned to enter the military and pursue a career in electrical engineering.

See also
The Citadel; Faulkner; Shannon; Virginia Military Institute (V.M.I.).

Memorials

Some states and organizations in local communities have built memorials to honor women in the military. For example, the Minneapolis Nurses Project funded the statue of an American Army nurse serving in Vietnam; it was completed in 1984 and now stands in Landmark Center in St. Paul, Minnesota. The statue was commissioned by two Army nurses, Diane Carlson Evans and Donna-Marie Boulay, who were also Vietnam veterans. They also raised the funds for the memorial.

The Minneapolis group then had a larger version of the statue built for Washington, D.C., which was officially unveiled on Memorial Day, 1995. Forty nurses, all Vietnam veterans, attended the ceremony.

See also
Casualties; Hart, Nancy; Hays, Mary Ludwig; Vietnam Veterans Memorial; Vietnam Women's Memorial.

Menopause

Menopause, the stage of life when a woman's menstrual cycles cease and she can no longer become pregnant, has at times been cited as a reason to limit women from serving in the military or to discharge them before they reach their mid-forties and fifties, the age at which menopause usually occurs.

Symptoms can include mood swings, fatigue, hot flashes, night sweats, and other physical and emotional changes. Symptoms vary in severity and from one woman to another, however, so a policy has evolved through the years that treats menopause like any other health condition that might require temporary treatment or, in rare and severe cases, medical discharge. Medical consultants to the military have also pointed out that men undergo similar hormonal shifts at midlife, and it would therefore be discriminatory to treat women as a group differently from men for reasons of hormonal changes.

See also
Craighill, Major Margaret D.

Menstruation

See Craighill, Major Margaret D.

Military Academies

The four U.S. military service academies provide the most highly trained commissioned officers to the various branches of the service. Women were not admitted to military academies until 1976, a reflection of the viewpoint that few women were expected to become officers or have lifetime careers in the military. In 1975, the first women were admitted to the Coast Guard Academy, actually classified as a federal academy rather than a military academy, since the Coast Guard is only under the authority of the Department of Defense during war or a state of emergency. The next year, women enrolled in the three other military academies—those of the Air Force, Navy, and Army.

See also
Public Law 94–106; United States Air Force Academy (USAFA); United States Coast Guard Academy (USCGA); United States Military Academy (USMA); United States Naval Academy (USNA).

Military Band

See Women's Military Band.

Military Occupational Specialties (MOS)

Military occupational specialties (MOS) are specific job assignments within broader occupational fields. For instance, in the field of aviation, women could pursue jobs in the specialties of air traffic control, radar, and weather service.

Training for MOS takes place after basic and combat training. Trainees are schooled in the type of work they intend to pursue—for example, chemist, typographer, airplane mechanic, dog trainer. Through the years, more and more MOS have been opened for women. In 1972, the Army permitted women officers and enlisted women to train for all MOS except those requiring combat training or assignment.

Minerva Center

The Minerva Center was founded by historian Linda Grant De Pauw, a historian and author of numerous books and articles about women and the military. The center studies women in the military and publishes *Minerva's Bulletin Board*, a magazine that addresses these issues and reports on the results of important studies.

In Roman mythology, Minerva was the goddess of wisdom and the patron of warriors. Born to Jupiter, king of the gods, and Juno, she was full-grown at birth, springing from her father's head dressed in armor. Besides being the symbol of defending the home and state, Minerva was the patron of artisans and the trades.

Mitchell, Brian

See *Weak Link: The Feminization of the American Military.*

Mitchell, Elyse (1919–1945)

On 5 May 1945, Mitchell became the first and only known woman to die on American soil during World War II as the result of an enemy bomb. Mitchell, the wife of the Reverend Archie Mitchell, was living in Bly, Oregon, where her husband was serving with the Christian and Missionary Church. The couple had embarked that morning on a fishing outing with five children from the church. Near the place they had chosen for a picnic, Mrs. Mitchell and the children went for a brief walk along a stream.

A few minutes later, her husband heard an explosion and rushed to the scene. He found all the children dead and his wife on fire, which he unsuccessfully tried to put out with his bare hands. Elyse Mitchell was five months pregnant with her first child at the time of her death. When local Forest Service workers arrived, they found pieces of a Japanese balloon bomb, pieces of shrapnel, metal rings and clips, and an unexploded incendiary bomb.

The U.S. government kept news of these deaths quiet, fearing it might cause widespread panic throughout the country and, in addition, let the enemy know they had succeeded with one of their planted bombs. Investigating the incident, military officials were unsure whether the balloon bombs were being launched from submarines or if they had drifted onto American soil.

Nobody could determine how many other balloon bombs might exist, but those that were found had not exploded upon making contact with the ground. It was later found that about 9,000 such bombs had been launched, and about 340 were found in North America, in places as diverse as Nebraska, Texas, Michigan, and parts of Canada. The Japanese had hoped the bombs would cause deaths and destruction as well as frighten and demoralize the American people.

Reference

Archie Satterfield, *The Home Front: An Oral History of the War Years in America: 1941–1945* (1981).

Mobile Army Surgical Hospital (MASH)

First created in 1942, Mobile Army Surgical Hospital (MASH) units were designed to follow troops into battle zones. These teams, made up of a surgeon, physicians, nurses, and medical corpsmen, were able to provide soldiers with more rapid care than if they had to be transported to distant hospitals. Designed for mobility, units could be assembled and dismantled quickly to move where they were needed. Helicopters were used to evacuate the wounded quickly to MASH locations.

MASH units were regarded as highly effective and became a standard part of Allied military procedures. They were also employed during the Korean War and Vietnam War. A popular feature film (1970) and a later television series dramatized the experiences of a MASH unit.

Women in the Army Nurse Corps (ANC) have always been part of MASH units, and the first Army nurse to be wounded in Italy during the war was a MASH nurse. Nurses were also part of the crews on helicopters used to evacuate the wounded from battle areas. The work of women serving as medics in MASH units, conducted under dangerous combat conditions, was often exhausting, demanding, and emotionally draining.

See also
Post-Traumatic Stress Disorder; Vietnam War.

Montgomery GI Bill

An amended version of the GI Bill of Rights passed after World War II, the Montgomery GI Bill set up a system by which veterans can receive aid for their college educations. For example, Marines who allocated $100 a month of their pay for a period of 12 months could later receive government funds amounting to $300 per month for 36 months to be used for their college expenses.

Moon, Lottie and Ginnie (n.d.)

Lottie and Ginnie Moon were Tennessee-born sisters who worked as a spy and courier team for the Confederacy during the Civil War. One of their best sources of information about the locations and movements of Union troops came from their many suitors. The sisters were both engaged to more than a dozen Union soldiers at once and received letters from them at camp. They relayed this information to Confederate officers, often carrying messages themselves through enemy lines.

Near the end of the war, Lottie Moon married Judge Clark and moved to New York City. She worked as a reporter in New York and later in Europe. Returning to the United States, she lived in Hollywood, California, where she embarked on a new career as an actress.

References
Penny Colman, *Spies! Women and the Civil War* (1992); *Encyclopedia of the Civil War* (1986).

Moore, Beth (n.d.)

As a teenager during the American Revolution, Beth Moore carried an important message to Captain Wallace of the colonial army. The captain and his troops were upriver from Charleston, South Carolina, when British forces planned a surprise attack on Wallace's men. Moore avoided suspicion by devising a clever plan. With her brother and a girlfriend, she set out on a canoe ride, paddling into the night as if for recreation. Warned ahead of time, Wallace's group was able to relocate before the Redcoats arrived.

"Mop Commando"

Women in the military during World War II scornfully referred to their position as "mop commando" when their duties did not use their skills and training. The term was most used in the medical services and Corps of Engineers, where some women reported being assigned to baby-sit, clean, or serve food and drinks in base recreation centers rather than perform the war-related tasks that they had learned in training.

Motherhood

Before the 1970s, women could be terminated from military service because they were pregnant or because they were responsible for a minor child. Being a mother, stepmother, foster mother, or guardian for a child under age 18 prevented many women from joining the military or continuing their careers.

Few people questioned the practice of barring pregnant women from the military before the 1950s since, traditionally, most women remained home with their children in socially acceptable domestic roles.

As Jeanne Holm points out in *Women in the Military: An Unfinished Revolution*, there were other barriers for mothers in the military:

> Moreover, without child care facilities, it would be impossible to care for an infant and remain in the services. The low military pay at that time would have made remaining out of the question, since the cost of paying for the services of a full-time babysitter would have been prohibitive.

A number of women with children, however, were willing and able to serve and objected to being forced out of the military. Executive Order 10240, signed in 1951, gave military officials a legal basis for discharging any woman who had a minor child living in the household for 30 days or more a year. Holm calls this law "arbitrary, . . . inexplicable and totally unjustified" and found applying it to stepmothers particularly incomprehensible, since the children may have spent years living with only their fathers. (The service would discharge a military woman who became a stepmother "without regard to her personal desires, her investment in her career, the taxpayers' investment in her training, or the criticality of her skills to the service.")

Through the years, Holm, as director of Women in the Air Force (WAF), and some military officials had urged that this policy be changed, while others, including Women's Army Corps (WAC) Director Elizabeth P. Hoisington, supported it. Opponents of the automatic discharge policy pointed out that men could remain in the military while being the sole guardians of minor children, whether through divorce, adoption, or the death of a spouse.

In rare cases, the services would grant women a "waiver" to remain in the military. She had to prove that she

A member of the 139th Aeromedical Evacuation Flight of the New York Air National Guard hugs her infant daughter after returning from a two-week tour of duty in Saudi Arabia in August 1990.

had made arrangements to provide care for the child so she would not be prevented from fulfilling her duties.

In 1969, officials in the Air Force were considering revoking this policy. In September 1969, Captain Tommie Sue Smith, an attorney with the Air Force in Washington, D.C., challenged the legality of Executive Order 10240 in federal district court. That same week, the Air Force, which had been considering revoking the rule, announced it was officially changing the discharge policy.

By that time, Major Lorraine R. Johnson, a member of the Army Nurse Corps since 1958 and a reservist who had been teaching intensive nursing care to military corpsmen, also challenged the law in a U.S. district court. The Army chose to grant Johnson a waiver to remain in the service and began to grant these waivers routinely. In 1975, the Pentagon ordered that the military end the practice of discharging women under the old rule.

More recently, the branches of service have gone further to implement programs that help parents and support family life through family housing, child care, family activities, and counseling centers. These quality-of-life matters, as they are called, can include a broad range of support programs, depending on the military base.

Should mothers go to war? This controversial issue received more attention throughout the 1980s and in 1991 during the Persian Gulf War. By that time, military policy stated that women who had given birth could be granted maternity leave, then return to duty. Department of Defense policies required joint-service couples to have a designated guardian and child-care plan in case they were ever both deployed.

The media carried stories of women who were leaving children and husbands behind as they headed for the Gulf. Although a much larger percentage of servicemen had children than did servicewomen, the media focused more on the newer phenomenon of "mothers going to war." *People* magazine (10 September 1990) featured a cover story called "Mom Goes to War" with a photograph of an Air Force captain leaving her young daughter.

Among those who oppose the idea of mothers fighting in a war is the conservative author, activist, and attorney Phyllis Schlafly, who supports traditional roles for men and women. In a 1991 speech to the Heritage Foundation, Schlafly asserted, "Pregnancy and motherhood are simply not compatible with military service. It is wrong to pretend that a woman who is pregnant or who has a baby is ready to ship out to fight a war. She is not ready. . . . The present policies are contrary to combat readiness, common sense and respect for family integrity."

An Associated Press poll conducted in February 1991 showed that Americans opposed the policy of sending mothers to the Persian Gulf War by a 2 to 1 margin. Some Americans said that any serviceperson, male or female, was making a sacrifice by leaving their family to go to war and that mothers should not receive special treatment over fathers.

See also

Cornum, Rhonda; Pregnancy; Women's Army Corps (WAC).

References

Elaine Donnelly, "Children Are Harmed When Mothers Serve in the Military," *Human Events* (16 March 1991); Cynthia Enloe, *Does Khaki Become You? The Militarization of Women's Lives* (1988); Jeanne Holm, *Women in the Military: An Unfinished Revolution* (1992); Phyllis Schlafly, "The Combat Exclusion Law Is Necessary," in Carol Wekesser and Matthew Polesetsky, *Women in the Military* (1991); Dorothy and Carl J. Schneider, *Sound Off! American Military Women Speak Out* (1988).

Motte, Rebecca

See American Revolution.

Mutter, Carol A. (b. 1945)

On 25 July 1996, Lieutenant General Carol A. Mutter of the Marine Corps became the first female three-star general in the U.S. military. Born in Greeley, Colorado, Mutter graduated from Northern Colorado University with a degree in mathematics education, then earned a master's degree in business from Salve Regina College and another master's degree in national security and strategic studies from the Naval War College.

She completed officer's basic training at Quantico, Virginia, in 1967, then worked in data processing installations at that base and at Camp Pendleton in California. She returned to Quantico in 1971 as a platoon commander and instructor for women officer candidates. From 1973 to 1984, Mutter completed various assignments—as project officer for Marine Corps Air Command and Control Systems (Pendleton), as a financial management officer (Quantico), and as a deputy controller at Headquarters, Fleet Marine Force Atlantic (Norfolk, Virginia). She served as deputy program manager, then as program manager after being promoted to colonel.

In 1988, Mutter joined the U.S. Space Command (Operations) Directorate, working in Colorado Springs. During this assignment, she qualified as a space officer. She then served in Okinawa, Japan, beginning in August 1990, with the III Marine Expeditionary Force as assistant chief of staff, controller. June 1994 brought another promotion, this time to major general, and a position directing the Marine Corp Systems Command. Mutter advanced to lieutenant general in July 1996, at which time she became deputy chief of staff for Manpower and Reserve Affairs at headquarters.

Reference

United States Marine Corps, Division of Public Affairs, "Lieutenant Carol A. Mutter, USMC" (22 August 1996).

Myers, Caroline Clark (1888–1980)

Caroline Clark Myers was the first woman to be hired as a teacher by the United States Army. In 1917, the Army hired Myers and her husband, Gary C. Myers, to teach illiterate soldiers how to read, using special methods and materials they had developed for this purpose.

After the war, Myers and her husband operated the popular children's magazine *Highlights for Children*, based in Boyds Mill, Pennsylvania. Myers served as managing editor and became chairman of the board in 1971 after her husband's death.

N

National Defense Authorization Act for Fiscal Years 1992 and 1993

Signed into law by George Bush in December 1991, the National Defense Authorization Act for Fiscal Years 1992 and 1993 enabled Congress to retain or repeal the part of the Women's Armed Services Integration Act of 1948, the law that barred women from combat-related duties, including flying combat missions.

This authorization act set up a presidential commission to study women's roles in the military and make recommendations. In November 1992, the 15-member commission announced that it had voted 8 to 7 against permitting women to fly combat aircraft.

See also
Combat; Combat Exclusion Law; Pilots; Sea Duty; United States Air Force; United States Navy; Women's Armed Services Integration Act of 1948.

References
Presidential Commission on the Assignment of Women in the Armed Forces Report to the President, U.S. Government Printing Office, Washington, DC (November 1992).

National League for Women's Service

Formed during World War I, the National League for Women's Service aimed to supplement the work of the Army, Navy, and Red Cross. Local chapters trained women in first aid, home nursing, and other skills that would help them deal better with the absence of professional health-care givers and national calamities, including fire, floods, famine, and war-related problems.

Reference
Dorothy and Carl J. Schneider, *Into the Breach: Women Overseas in World War I* (1991).

Native Americans

Native-American women were involved in military activities before white settlers reached North America, and they have played a role in the various wars that have taken place since. Traditionally, Native-American men were assigned to defend villages or serve as warriors, while women often had domestic roles as mothers, homemakers, and farmers. Some Native-American tribes, however, gave women leadership positions. Women in certain groups had a voice in whether or not their tribe would fight.

Among the Plains Indians in particular, many women knew how to use weapons to defend themselves and their villages in case of an attack by other Indians, whites, or U.S. Army troops. In the Nez Percé War of 1877, some women fought alongside men against U.S. soldiers.

During the American Revolution, Polly Cooper, an Oneida Indian, served as the cook and housekeeper for General George Washington. Throughout those seven years, the patriotic Cooper refused to accept any payment for her work. Working as a spy and aid to the British during this war was a Mohawk woman, Mary (Molly) Brant. When Indian men fought with both sides during the Civil War, women supported them as did women in white society, through nursing, cooking, doing laundry, and other tasks.

During the 1800s, the United States moved against various Indian groups

National League for Women's Service member A. B. Baylis cranks the car prior to delivering various government packages in December 1917.

and claimed their lands. Native-American women suffered displacement, injury, and death from these armed conflicts, as well as the loss of their husbands and male children. A few, like the Nez Percé women, took up arms themselves during these battles.

About 800 Native-American women enlisted in the armed forces during World War II, while others worked in service and relief organizations. An estimated 12,000 Native-American women worked in war-related jobs. On the West Coast, hundreds of these women worked in the aircraft industry, taking jobs as machinists, riveters, and inspectors.

As the armed services were opened to minorities and became an All-Volunteer Force (AVF), Native-American women have joined and served on the same terms as others for the same variety of reasons—patriotism, career and educational opportunities, and the chance to travel.

See also
Brant, Mary (Molly); To-Ka-Mappo; Volunteers; Winema (Tobey Riddle).

References
Allison R. Bernstein, *American Indians and World War II* (1991); Penny Colman, *Rosie the Riveter: Women Working on the Home Front in World War II* (1995).

Naval Academy

See United States Naval Academy (USNA).

Naval Reserve Act of 1916

The Naval Reserve Act of 1916 changed the wording of Navy enlistment policies so the service could enlist qualified *persons* instead of only qualified *men*. The Navy made this change on 19 March 1917 and proceeded to recruit women as Yeoman (F)—female—as a source of additional personnel needed during World War II.

See also
United States Navy; World War I; Yeomen (F).

Naval Reserve Act of 1938

The Naval Reserve Act of 1938 allowed women to be enrolled in the Navy during World War II, and more than 27,000 women had joined by July 1942. As Public Law 689, signed by President Franklin D. Roosevelt, the act was amended in 1942 to include the women's auxiliary reserve, known as the Women Accepted for Voluntary Emergency Service (WAVES).

See also
McAfee, Mildred Helen; United States Navy.

Navigators

See Sea Duty; United States Coast Guard; United States Navy; World War II.

Navy, United States

See United States Navy.

Navy Medical Corps

Like other branches of the military, the Navy refused the services of women physicians, permitting only men in the medical corps, until the twentieth century. Only a few women were hired as physicians during World War II. In 1950, the Navy assigned the first women physicians to shipboard duty. Bernice M. Walters, a graduate of Woman's Medical College of Pennsylvania, served with nine other medical officers on the hospital ship USS *Consolation*. At that time, only four other women physicians were on active duty with the Navy's Bureau of Medicine and Surgery.

Navy Nurse Corps (NNC)

Although not an official part of the Navy for many decades, nurses began serving at Navy hospitals as early as 1811, after Navy doctors requested that they be hired. During the War of 1812, nurses served as contract employees aboard Navy ships.

During the Civil War, women again served as nurses for the Navy in hospitals and aboard ships. Nuns from the Sisters of the Holy Cross, a nursing order, served aboard the *Red Rover*, the Navy's first hospital ship. Nurses, some from the Red Cross, were also employed to take care of wounded and sick men during the Spanish-American War (1898).

The Navy Nurse Corps (NNC) was established in 1908, with 20 nurses making up the first corps. The NNC had auxiliary status, which meant that nurses did not receive full military rank or benefits. Many complained that although they had large responsibilities, their authority was quite limited. Expected to direct the medical corpsmen who served with them, they had no officer's rank to give weight to their authority.

During World War I, the NNC grew from 460 to 1,400 women. Navy nurses served in the United States, the British Isles, in field hospitals in France, and on transport ships. They were called upon to treat more serious wounds and other conditions than most had anticipated. They served on blood transfusion teams and gave anesthesia, often providing care in crude buildings with inadequate supplies.

Navy nurses had been accustomed to assignments at base hospitals in ports located far from combat, but in World War I, many served as close as three miles from the front. They performed surgery during air raids, with packing crates for instrument tables and operating tables made from two sawhorses with a stretcher placed across them. Like Army nurses, they were understaffed, and one nurse, working long shifts, might be responsible for more than a hundred patients.

Mary Elderkins, a Navy nurse stationed overseas, later said, "I don't believe one of us had ever imagined men could be so absolutely 'shot to pieces.'. . . I cannot describe those nights . . . the intense suffering of the wounded; the ghastly sights and nauseating smells when gas gangrene was present."

In 1920, military nurses were granted what was called "relative rank." They were allowed to wear insignia for ranks from second lieutenant to major but did not receive base pay in line with that given to males of the same rank, nor did they have certain other rights and privileges.

Some of those who served during World War I continued as members of the NNC after the fighting ended. Joining in 1917, Sue S. Dauser was chief nurse of Base Hospital No. 3 in Edinburgh, Scotland, and then served as chief nurse in naval facilities at sea, in the United States, and abroad. Dauser was appointed superintendent of the NNC in 1939, the first woman to wear the four gold stripes of a captain in the U.S. Navy. She retired from active duty in November 1945, having been awarded the Distinguished Service Medal.

World War II witnessed another large expansion in the NNC. It numbered 430 members before the war began, but by mid-1942, there were about 1,800 Navy nurses. Some 14,000 nurses served in the NNC during the war and were exposed to hazards and combat conditions in the Atlantic and Pacific theaters, as well as in Africa and other locations. They served aboard 12 hospital ships and during air evacuations. Jane Kendleigh became the first Navy flight nurse to serve on a battlefield.

Eleven Navy nurses were among those captured by the Japanese at Corregidor early in 1942. They remained in prison in Manila for 36 months. Five Navy nurses captured at Guam spent months in a Japanese military prison before they were repatriated on the exchange ship *Gripsholm.*

One of those who escaped by submarine from Corregidor to Australia was Lieutenant Ann A. Bernatitus, the first person in the naval service to receive the Legion of Merit. Bernatitus, a member of Surgical Unit #5, was cited for meritorious conduct during the Japanese bombing of the Philippines from December 1941 to April 1942. During this time she and her fellow nurses continued to care for their patients while under siege. Later, Bernatitus served as chief nurse on the USS *RELIEF*, a hospital ship that treated and evacuated the wounded during the Allied invasion of Okinawa.

The NNC became a permanent staff corps of the Navy as a result of the Army-Navy Nurse Act (Public Law 36-80C), enacted in April 1947. From then on, female nurses could be integrated into the officer ranks of the regular Navy, up to the grades of lieutenant colonel and commander.

After Public Law 90-130 was enacted in 1968, women in the Navy could be promoted to the rank of admiral. In July 1972, Alene B. Duerk, chief of the Navy Nurse Corps, became the first female rear admiral (lower half).

Navy nurses served in Southeast Asia in the 1960s after the United States became involved in the conflict in Vietnam. By then, male nurses were also accepted in the corps, but the vast majority were still women. Navy nurses served at hospitals in Saigon, often as instructors to Vietnamese people who were learning nursing. They also cared for those servicepeople who were assigned to duty in the region.

In 1965, 29 Navy nurses traveled with the hospital ship USS *Repose* to Vietnam; another 29 sailed with the USS *Sanctuary* the following year. During the Vietnam War, about 300 Navy nurses served on ships off the coast, as well as in field hospitals and evacuation hospitals. Four Navy nurses injured during a bombing in 1965 became the first women in this war to receive Purple Hearts.

In peacetime, Navy nurses serve for the benefit of Navy personnel and their dependents and have cared for civilians during times of disaster. In 1961, members of the NNC aboard combat ships aided victims of a hurricane in Texas, and in 1962, they joined a special naval medical mission to Honduras where an epidemic of gastritis had overwhelmed the resources of local public health resources. They have also accompanied earthquake relief teams to Iran, Yugoslavia, and Alaska.

See also

Corregidor; Public Law 36-80C; Public Law 90-130.

References

Mabel T. Boardman, *Under the Red Cross Flag at Home and Abroad* (1917); Bobbi Hovis, *Station Hospital Saigon: A Navy Nurse in Vietnam, 1963–1964* (1991); U.S. Department of the Navy, "History and 'Firsts' of Women in the Navy" (1995); U.S. Department of the Navy, *White Task Force: History of the Nurse Corps, United States Navy* (1946).

Neuffer, Judy (b. 1949)

In 1973, Judy Neuffer became the first woman assigned to military pilot training, making the Navy the first service branch in the U.S. Armed Forces to offer pilot training to women.

The daughter of a fighter pilot, Neuffer earned a degree in computer science from Ohio State University in Columbus. She proceeded to the Navy's Officer Candidate School for Women at Newport, Rhode Island, and was then assigned to work as a computer programmer at a naval base in San Diego, California.

Shortly after Neuffer was chosen to take part in the 18-month naval pilot training program, seven other women were also admitted to the course, which was conducted at Pensacola, Florida. The eight women were trained to fly transport aircraft and helicopters, but none of them were later assigned to aircraft carriers.

In August 1974, Neuffer made history again when she became the first

Navy pilot ever to fly into the eye of a hurricane. Flying a P-3 Orion, Neuffer was attempting to measure the wind speeds (around 150 miles per hour) and ascertain the exact location of the eye of Hurricane Carmen off the coast of Florida.

See also
Pilots.

Nevius, Colleen
See Test Pilots.

Nichols, Ruth (1901–1960)
Ruth Nichols was one of the first women pilots in the United States and the first to receive an international hydroplane license (1924). She later was the first woman to fly nonstop from New York City to Miami (1928), and the first woman pilot hired by a commercial airline (1932).

A native of New York, Nichols started flying while she was a student at Wellesley College in Massachusetts. In 1927, she earned her pilot's license and was the only woman among 37 New York pilots on the list published by the U.S. Department of Commerce. That year, she became the second woman to earn a transport pilot's license. In 1929, during two transcontinental flights, Nichols broke speed records in both directions.

In 1932, Nichols began working for New York and New England Airways as a commercial pilot, and seven years later, she began training other women to fly in a school she founded in Garden City, New York. During these years, Nichols competed in numerous events, such as the Bendix Race of 1933, and worked to promote flying for women.

By the time World War II began, Nichols had amassed numerous records and won several races. In 1940, she founded Relief Wings, Inc., a civilian air service that performed ambulance and disaster relief by air. The organization offered to assist the U.S. government after the war began. From this group developed the Civil Air Patrol, with Nichols serving as director from 1940 to 1949. During that time, she qualified as a flight instructor for multiengine aircraft.

Throughout the rest of her life, Nichols continued to support women and flying while working for numerous charitable organizations, many of them to benefit underprivileged children.

References
Deborah G. Douglas, *United States Women in Aviation, 1940–1985* (1991); Henry M. Holden, *Ladybirds: The Untold Story of Women Pilots in America* (1991); Claudia M. Oakes, *United States Women in Aviation, 1920–1939* (1991).

Ninety-Nines
In 1929, a group of pilots from the New York area, led by Betty Huyler, decided to form a national organization for women aviators. About 20 women met that November at Curtiss Airport to plan the organization, which attracted 99 charter members, thus giving it its name. These determined women made plans to promote aviation among women and to gain the flying experience they would need to prove themselves in this male-dominated field. A number of Ninety-Nines served as ferrying pilots and instructors during World War II.

See also
Earhart, Amelia; Huyler-Gillies, Betty; Pilots; Women's Airforce Service Pilots (WASP).

References
Deborah G. Douglas, *United States Women in Aviation, 1940–1985* (1991); Henry M. Holden, *Ladybirds: The Untold Story of Women Pilots in America* (1991); Claudia M. Oakes, *United States Women* in *Aviation, 1920–1939* (1991); Sally Van Wagenen Keil, *Those Wonderful Women in Their Flying Machines* (1990).

North Atlantic Treaty Organization (NATO)

The North Atlantic Treaty Organization (NATO) was formed in 1949 when the United States joined 14 allies in North America and Western Europe to form a pact to defend all members against military threats. Member nations include Belgium, Canada, Denmark, France, Germany, Greece, Italy, Luxembourg, the Netherlands, Norway, Portugal, Spain, Turkey, the United Kingdom, and the United States. In the postwar years, members were particularly concerned about the threat of military aggression by the Soviet Union in Western Europe.

NATO has also served as a forum in which military leaders share ideas about the most effective ways to operate and achieve goals of national and allied defense. Members of NATO have different laws and attitudes regarding women in the military, and the members have been able to observe how these differences have played out.

During the early 1970s, military nurses were among the highest-ranking officers in the North American and European nations that participate in NATO. These women led an effort to form the Senior Women Officers Committee, based in Brussels. Together, women leaders in the military urged the military to provide more opportunities for women to serve in expanded roles. Nursing leaders pointed to the need for medical care as a critical part of planning for NATO.

NATO also created a Committee on Women in the NATO Forces to assess the status of women in the alliance and to provide an annual report on this subject. This committee reports information such as the numbers of women serving in the military forces of each member country and the ways in which women serve. Military analysts say that NATO members have often used the experiences of others in the organization to determine whether or not to make changes in their own systems.

In 1973, Captain Reba C. Tyler became the first woman to command a NATO unit. Stationed in Mannheim, West Germany, Tyler commanded the Army NATO unit there, which included 34 men, part of the 48th Adjutant General Postal Detachment.

References
Cynthia Enloe, *Does Khaki Become You? The Militarization of Women's Lives* (1988).

O

Officer Candidate School (OCS)

In order to prepare servicepeople for the roles and duties of commissioned officers, each branch of service created Officer Candidate School (OCS) programs. When the women's corps were first developed, Army, Navy, and Marine women had separate OCS programs, just as they were separated into women's corps. At times, a ceiling was put on the number of women who could become officers, such as in 1943 when the Army directed that only 200 women a year could take part in the WAC Officer Candidate School at Fort McClellan, Alabama.

In 1948 at Lackland Training Center in San Antonio, Texas, women in the Air Force became the first to attend Officer Candidate School with men. After the Air Force became separate from the Army in 1947, it was free to develop new policies and ways of operating. Officials decided that having qualified women and men train together would be best. In January 1949, the first group of 19 women entered the OCS in this integrated program, and 16 were graduated in July.

Women who had served in some other branches of the service during World War II joined the Air Force during these years, and a number of them became officers. A number of problems had to be resolved as women were integrated into the OCS, since some men resisted the change and the program was breaking new ground.

In 1967, the Army ended its separate officer training program for women, the WAC Officer Candidate School. Women were then integrated into the OCS at Fort Benning, Georgia, and, by 1972, could come up the ranks through college Reserve Officer Training Corps (ROTC) programs as well. By 1976, women could prepare to be commissioned as officers by attending the United States Military Academy (USMA) at West Point, New York, as well as the Navy and Air Force service academies. The Coast Guard had also opened its academy to women.

In 1973, women in the Navy were integrated with men at the Naval Officer Candidate School. The coeducational program included studies in leadership, management, administration, seamanship, and navigation.

Women in the Marines had access to integrated OCS as of 1977, when 22 women took part. Before that time, the women's officer training course was shorter than men's—12 weeks instead of 26. Today, the Marine Officer Candidates Class lasts ten weeks and is conducted at the Basic School in Quantico, Virginia. The candidates also attend college.

References

Army Center of Military History, "History of the Women's Army Corps, 1942–1978" (1989); Marie-Beth Hall, *Cross Current: Navy Women from World War I to Tailhook* (1993); Jeanne Holm, *Women in the Military: An Unfinished Revolution* (1992); Mary V. Stremlow, *A History of the Women Marines* (1986); Mattie E. Treadwell, *U.S. Army in World War II: Special Studies—The Women's Army Corps* (1954).

Operation Desert Shield

For several months beginning in September 1990, women served in the Persian Gulf, deployed to Saudi Arabia with military units that were preparing for the possibility of war in that region. The operation was launched after Iraqi leader Saddam Hussein invaded the small, oil-rich nation of Kuwait in the Gulf. Thousands of women, mostly members of the Army, took part in the operation. Among other jobs, women pilots transported fuel to Iraq in preparation for the tanks that would be brought there later.

See also
Persian Gulf War.
Reference
Jeanne M. Holm, "The Persian Gulf War Proved That Women Can Serve in Combat," in Carol Wekesser and Matthew Polesetsky, *Women in the Military* (1991).

Operation Desert Storm

See Persian Gulf War.

Operation Petticoat

A popular 1959 feature film, starring Cary Grant, Tony Curtis, and Dina Merrill, *Operation Petticoat* portrayed a naval crew in the South Pacific. Featured in the story were women serving in the Navy as nurses and in traditional supportive roles. The film, later adapted into a television series, showed the different roles played by men and women in the military during that era. Many of the comments made by men in the movie might be viewed as sexist by today's viewers.

Operation Yellow Ribbon

A support group for soldiers and families, Operation Yellow Ribbon was organized by Gaye Jacobson, whose son Derek, a Marine, was sent to the Persian Gulf War as a medic. The project eventually developed into dozens of chapters in different states with more than 5,000 members.

It began as Jacobson set up counseling sessions in the San Francisco Bay Area for families who had loved ones in the service. Operation Yellow Ribbon asked companies to donate money, food, and other items that could be packaged, then sent them to people serving in the war. Other activities of this operation included a massive letter-writing campaign for GIs and a volunteer-run 24-hour hotline for relatives. Jacobson believed that these efforts would show those serving in the Gulf that other Americans cared about them and appreciated their efforts.

In Caroline, New York, volunteers Barbara Kone and Sandy Clary set out to show their support by tying yellow ribbons around every house in their rural community of 3,055. Kone, who had a son in the reserves, and Clary, whose son was serving on the Kuwaiti border, spent three weeks on their project and used about 11 miles of ribbon.

References
"Emotions of War," *People* (Spring/Summer 1991): 44; Barbara Maddux, "A Thing for Ribbon: Two Women Tie up Their Whole Town," *Life* (25 February 1991): 75.

Ordnance

About 700 enlisted Wacs (members of the Women's Army Corps) and 80 WAC officers served in ordnance during World War II. Some served in clerical services in the ordnance department, while others took on less routine duties such as ballistics testing. Wacs computed the velocity of bullets, measured the weight of bomb fragments in order to calculate the degree of fragmentation that occurred with a particular bombing, mixed gunpowder, and loaded shells. Some women were

A female Marine carries her combat gear and two bottles of water after arriving at a Saudi air base on 22 August 1990 during Operation Desert Shield.

trained in ordnance engineering; others worked as draftsmen, mechanics, and electricians within the ordinance department.

As more jobs were opened to women in the military after World War II, women could train in different ordnance specialties in the various branches of service.

See also
Corps of Engineers; Hopper, Grace Murray; Manhattan Project; United States Air Force; United States Army; United States Marine Corps; United States Navy; World War II.

References
M. C. Devilbiss, *Women and Military Service: A History, Analysis, and Overview of the Key Issues* (1990); Monro MacCloskey, *Your Future in the Military Services* (1979); Mattie E. Treadwell, *U.S. Army in World War II: Special Studies—The Women's Army Corps* (1954).

Over Here

Over Here was a publication produced and distributed by the Women's Overseas Service League, an organization made up of women who had carried out volunteer work overseas during World War I. The women saw themselves as being united by a common experience that was unusual for women of their day. *Over Here* was developed after the war, keeping women abreast of the activities of those whom they had known while working in the league.

Reference
Dorothy and Carl J. Schneider, *Into the Breach: American Women Overseas in World War I* (1991).

Overseas Theater League

See Young Men's Christian Association (YMCA).

Owens v. Brown

This case arose after Yona Owens, a naval interior communications electrician, was denied a chance to serve aboard an oceangoing survey ship in 1974. The Navy justified its position by applying Section 6015 of Title 10, which gives the secretary of the Navy the power to "prescribe the kind of military duty to which such women members may be assigned and the military authority which they may exercise." Section 6015 further stated that women were not permitted to be assigned to duty in combat aircraft or Navy vessels other than hospital ships and transports.

Owens and three other women who felt they had been the victims of sex discrimination by the Navy filed a class action suit, *Owens v. Brown*, challenging the constitutionality of Section 6015 and claiming that the Navy denied women equal protection under the law. The Navy offered to amend Section 6015 to allow women to be assigned to certain noncombatant ships. The proposed amendment would have allowed women to serve on auxiliary ships—tenders, repair ships, research ships, and rescue vessels—but not on combat vessels.

A ruling on *Owens* was handed down on 27 July 1978 by District Court Judge John J. Sirica. The court struck down Section 6015 on the grounds that it denied women as a group the right to equal protection under the laws. The Navy was ordered to take the necessary steps to end this discrimination and base decisions on each individual's fitness for a particular job.

As a result of this ruling, women in the Navy were finally considered for sea duty. The ruling also set a precedent that the military could not exclude women as a group from certain kinds of jobs.

See also
Sea Duty.

References

Marie-Beth Hall, *Cross Current: Navy Women from World War I to Tailhook* (1993); Jeanne Holm, *Women in the Military: An Unfinished Revolution* (1992); *Owens v. Brown*, 455 F. Supp. 291 (D.D.C. 1978); "Women at Sea: Navy Traditions Being Rewritten," *Washington Post* (25 February 1979: 1).

P

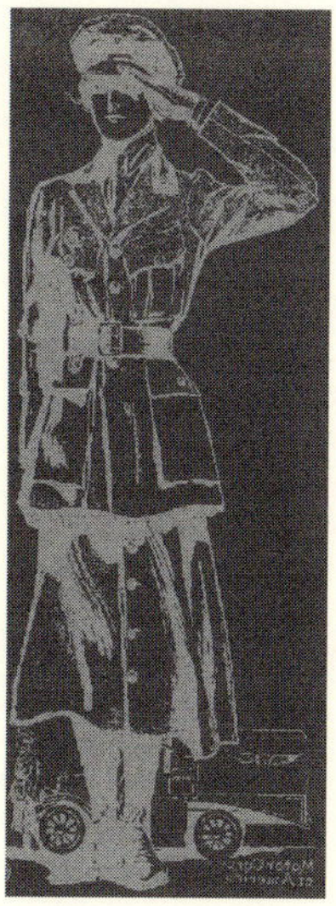

Pallas Athene

A rendering of the Greek goddess Pallas Athene was chosen for the insignia of the Women's Army Corps (WAC), which was established in 1943. A life-sized statue representing Pallas Athene stands in the garden of the WAC Museum at Fort McClellan in Alabama.

Panama, Invasion of

Called "Operation Just Cause," the U.S. invasion of Panama took place in 1989 in the intent to oust Panamanian dictator Manuel Noriega. Military women served in a variety of noncombat positions during the invasion. About 800 Army women served in combat support jobs, including logistics, communications, supply, transportation, military police, and members of helicopter crews. More than a hundred of these servicewomen may have been in areas where fighting took place. Women in the Air Force served on aircrews that airlifted troops and supplies to Panama. Two female helicopter pilots who delivered troops to combat areas received medals for bravery.

During the invasion, two other women commanded troops in a combat situation where they met enemy soldiers on the ground. In the wake of this event, people again debated whether or not women should serve in military roles involving combat.

A Women's Army Corps member poses with the crew of a newly christened bomber, which bears the insignia of the Greek goddess Pallas Athene, the symbol of the WAC, in this undated photograph.

See also
Bray, Linda L.
References
Phyllis Schlafly, "The Lesson of Women in Combat in Panama," *Conservative Chronicle* (7 February 1990); Carol Wekesser and Matthew Polesetsky, eds., *Women in the Military* (1991); Women's Research and Education Institute, *Women in the Military: 1980–1990* (1990).

Paratroopers

See Broadwick, Georgia ("Tiny"); Cornum, Rhonda.

Passing

Prior to the 1900s, American women who wished to serve as soldiers often resorted to "passing," or disguising themselves as men in order to enlist. These women wanted to take part in the military for a variety of economic, political, and personal reasons. Some wanted to serve their country more actively than was commonly possible for women at the time, while others sought to escape dull lives. Still others joined to be near their husbands or fiancés.

In those days, recruits were badly needed, and military physicals usually were quick and superficial. Many resourceful women were able to enlist and serve without fanfare. Their identities might go undiscovered, at least until a woman was wounded, at which time doctors learned the truth.

Among the best-known women who passed as men during the American Revolution was Deborah Sampson, who disguised herself as a man named Robert Shurtleff.

As many as 400 women may have tried to pass during the Civil War alone. Sarah Emma Edmonds was perhaps the best-known woman soldier of this era. Another who passed was Frances Clalin, who became a trooper with the cavalry of the Missouri militia. A New Jersey woman, Franny Wilson, fought for 18 months with the Union Army before she was wounded at the Battle of Vicksburg. Anny Lillybridge of Detroit joined the 21st Regiment as a soldier in order to be with her fiancé. Jennie Hodgers fought in an Illinois regiment for four years, disguised as "Albert Cashier," an identity she continued to maintain after the war ended. In 1911, Hodgers was injured in an auto accident and doctors realized her true gender.

See also
Benefits; Civil War; Edmonds, Sarah Emma; Pensions, Veterans'; Revolutionary War; Sampson, Deborah; Velasquez, Loreta Janeta; Veterans.
References
Elizabeth Anticaglia, *Heroines of '76* (1975); Ina Chang, *A Separate Battle: Women and the Civil War* (1991); Sarah Edmonds Edwards, *Nurse and Spy in the Union Army* (1865); Lucy Freeman and Alma H. Bond, *America's First Woman Warrior: The Courage of Deborah Sampson* (1992); Richard Hall, *Patriots in Disguise: Women Warriors of the Civil War* (1993).

Pensions, Veterans'

Pensions for male veterans of the American Revolution were promised as an incentive for enlisting and staying in the Continental Army. In 1818, Congress set up payments for veterans, based on need. Widows of officers who died in that war had been receiving pensions as of 1780; widows of other men who were killed in the war were finally granted pensions in 1836. Margaret (Molly) Corbin, a woman who accompanied the troops and was disabled after being wounded in battle, received a military pension and other benefits.

Anna Maria Lane, who had disguised herself as a soldier and then worked as a nurse after the war, was badly hurt during the Battle of Germantown in Pennsylvania. During the 1807–1808 session of the Virginia Legislature, Governor William H. Cabell asked that Lane be granted a pension, saying, "Anna Maria Lane is very infirm, having been disabled by a severe wound, which she received by fighting as a common soldier in one of our Revolutionary battles, from which she never has recovered, and perhaps never will recover." In granting the pension ($100 a year, more than the usual amount of $40), the lawmakers noted that Lane had "in the garb and with the courage of a soldier performed extraordinary military services. . . ."

After the Civil War, the federal government approved veterans' benefits only for Union soldiers. Veterans' homes and employers tended to favor Union veterans as well. Confederate soldiers were pardoned nearly a century after the war, in 1958.

See also
Benefits; Edmonds, Sarah Emma; Corbin, Margaret; Hays, Mary Ludwig; Sampson, Deborah; Veterans.

References
Elizabeth Anticaglia, *Heroines of '76* (1975); Patricia Edwards Clyne, *Petticoat Patriots* (1976); Lucy Freeman and Alma H. Bond, *America's First Woman Warrior: The Courage of Deborah Sampson* (1992); Richard Hall, *Patriots in Disguise: Women Warriors of the Civil War* (1993); June A. Willenz, *Women Veterans: America's Forgotten Heroines* (1983).

Pepper Board

Chaired by Robert H. Pepper, a retired lieutenant general, the Pepper Board studied the Women Marines program in 1964 to determine how the Marines could make optimal use of female personnel in peacetime. As a result of its study, the board recommended that the program be expanded by 70 percent within a year, bringing the number of women in the Marines to about 1 percent of the total force, or 2,750. New jobs were also opened to women, and they were given assignments on a larger number of Marine bases than before.

See also
Women Marines.

Perkins, Frances (1880–1965)

The first woman ever to serve in a president's cabinet, Frances Perkins was appointed secretary of labor under President Franklin D. Roosevelt from 1933 to 1945 and worked to improve working conditions for women in defense plants, as well as for all American workers.

Born to a well-to-do Boston family on 10 April 1882, Perkins graduated from Mount Holyoke College in South Hadley, Massachusetts, and became a teacher and social worker in Chicago. She began working for social and labor reforms that would help the poor. In 1907, she moved back east, where she began graduate studies at New York City's Columbia University in economics and sociology. She also served for two years as secretary of the New York Consumer's League.

In 1911, Perkins was visiting the Lower East Side of the city when she witnessed the devastating fire at the Triangle Shirtwaist Factory, one of New York's notorious sweatshops. The

Frances Perkins

workers, mostly young immigrant women, were trapped on the top three floors of the ten-story building, which lacked stable fire escapes and other safety features. Many jumped to their deaths rather than stay in the blazing building. The final death toll was 146, the victims having burned to death or died when they hit the pavement after jumping to avoid the flames.

After the fire, Perkins worked for the Committee on Safety of the City of New York and fought for legislation to improve safety conditions in factories. She continued working to increase the minimum wage, abolish child labor, and advocate laws and policies to improve the lives of women workers during the Depression of the 1930s. When she was appointed to the New York State Industrial Commission in 1919 by Governor Al Smith, Perkins became the highest paid state employee, with an annual salary of $8,000.

From 1933 to 1945, Perkins served as secretary of labor. During World War II, Perkins fought for laws, including the Wages and Hours Act, that would protect women workers in defense plants and other settings. She resigned from her position in May 1945. Perkins then served under President Harry S. Truman in the Civil Service Commission. She wrote and lectured widely. From 1957 to 1965, Perkins taught at the Cornell University School of Industrial and Labor Relations.

References

Philip S. Foner ed., *Women and the American Labor Movement: From Colonial Times to the Present* (1979); Elaine Tyler May, *Pushing the Limits: American Women 1940–1961* (1994); Lillian Holmen Mohr, *Frances Perkins: "That Woman in FDR's Cabinet!"* (1979).

Persian Gulf War

Called "Operation Desert Storm," the 1991 Persian Gulf War marked the first time in which men and women served in integrated units in a war zone over a period of months. Women made up a larger percentage of troops and served in more different capacities than in any previous conflict involving the United States.

A total of about 37,000 women comprised about 6.8 percent of the troops in the Gulf. Many were from National Guard units. About 26,000 were members of the Army, while 3,700 represented the Navy, 2,200 the Marines, and 5,300 the Air Force. Thirteen Coast Guard women were also sent to the Gulf since the Coast Guard came under the authority of the Navy during the war. These women served in Port Security.

As in past wars, women served in communications, medical, administrative, and clerical positions and as crew members on medical evacuation teams. They flew jets and helicopters and operated POW (prisoner of war) camps. Some transported POWs and wounded servicemen from place to place, while others patrolled borders.

For the first time, women directed artillery fire and served with Patriot missile crews stationed in Turkey, Saudi Arabia, and Israel, all allies of the United States. One Army woman was highly praised for her work at a computer station in Saudi Arabia, from which she launched Patriot missiles to intercept incoming enemy SCUD missiles.

At sea, women served on support and repair ships. In the air, they piloted aircraft and served on the flight crews of both helicopters and other planes, delivering supplies and personnel to the front lines and behind enemy lines and taking part in rescue missions. Air Force women piloted airlift, transport, reconnaissance, and tanker planes, and filled other positions on these planes as well.

Twenty-one women were wounded in action in the Gulf, and 13 women were killed, 4 from hostile causes and 9 from other causes. Two Army women became prisoners of war: Major Rhonda L. Cornum, a flight surgeon, was captured during a helicopter rescue mission, and Melissa Rathbun-Nealy was taken with a male soldier after their truck was stopped by Iraqi soldiers.

Carol Barkalow, a 1980 graduate in the first class of women at West Point, later told an interviewer for the *New York Times* that the strong performance of women in the Gulf War improved male officers' attitudes about women in the military. Interviewed on the ABC News program "20/20" in March 1991, General H. Norman Schwarzkopf, who commanded the allied forces during the Gulf War, said the women in the Gulf had done "a magnificent job."

See also
Cornum, Rhonda; Rathbun-Nealy, Melissa; Treloar, Theresa Lynn.

References
Carol Barkalow, "Women Really Are an Integral Part of the Military," *Army Times* (27 May 1991); Rhonda L. Cornum as told to Peter Copeland, *She Went to War: The Rhonda Cornum Story* (1992); Jeanne Holm, *Women in the Military: An Unfinished Revolution* (1992); Molly Moore, "Women in the Battlefield—Gulf War Helps Bring Shift in Attitude," *Washington Post* (16 June 1991): A1; Tom Morgenthau, "The Military's New Image," *Newsweek* (11 March 1991): 50–51.

Phipps, Anita (n.d.)

In 1921, Anita Phipps, a member of an Army family, was appointed director of women relations, United States Army. Her major job was to serve as a liaison between the Army and various women's organizations, many of them related to the military. At that time, this post did not entail full military status and Phipps had to devise her own uniform, among other things. She worked for the next ten years to get official recognition for her position, sending memoranda and complaining that other directors did not consult with her about decisions that affected her division. Often, she developed extensive studies and recommendations that were later ignored by male officials.

In 1929, Phipps finally gained tentative approval of a plan that would create a well-defined role for women in the Army, based in large part on what had been learned from women's participation in World War I. The plan provided for women civilian aides in different branches of the military and had the support of important women's groups such as the League of Women Voters, Daughters of the American Revolution, and the National Federation of Business and Professional Women's Clubs.

Secretary of War James W. Good, however, cancelled the plan after receiving a deluge of letters from clergymen, congressmen, and others protesting the idea of giving women this kind of military status. In 1930, Phipps tried again to have her position defined and given military status but was refused by Chief of Staff General Douglas MacArthur.

In ill health by that time, Phipps had to resign, but she had left behind a complete, well-researched plan for a women's army corps. Among her recommendations was that women be fully trained and receive a uniform, discipline, housing, and courtesies commensurate with service in the military. She advised that they be assigned to specific units and subject to military regulations, serving under the command of women officers. She also suggested that, in addition to the usual Army regulations, special ones might apply to women as needed.

In 1926, Army officials and the General Staff studied Phipps's plan for what she called a Women's Service Corps, and they praised its thoroughness and ideas. They rejected implementing it at that time, however, suggesting it be used in future studies. After the United States entered World War II, the Army took a fresh look at Phipps's proposal and used it as a foundation for creating the Women's Army Corps (WAC) in 1942.

References

Betty J. Morden, *The Women's Army Corps, 1945–1978* (1990); Mattie E. Treadwell, *U.S. Army in World War II: Special Studies—The Women's Army Corps* (1954).

Physical Therapists

Women served as physical therapists for the armed forces beginning with World War I. This health-care field, which aims to help people recover mobility and function after injuries to bone and muscle or the loss of a limb, was developing during the early 1900s. Women who went overseas as therapists were hired as civilian employees with the military. They wore uniforms made of heavy navy blue material with long skirts, jackets, and capes, along with beaver hats.

Once they reached their hospital assignments in Europe, these professionals often helped the nursing staff when they were not conducting physical therapy sessions with patients.

Some therapists were wounded or injured during the war. In 1931, Congress voted to award therapist Harriet MacDonald compensation for a disability she suffered while on duty during an air raid.

Reference

Dorothy and Carl J. Schneider, *Into the Breach: American Women Overseas in World War I* (1991).

Physicians

Starting with the Civil War, women physicians sought the opportunity to serve as doctors in the military. Only one, Mary Walker, succeeded in joining the Army Medical Corps, after first serving as a nurse.

During World War I, women physicians were still not being used officially in the U.S. Armed Forces. Yet, when a committee of women physicians surveyed their colleagues, they found that 40 percent of the 8,000 women polled would agree to serve if asked.

Some women physicians volunteered to work overseas with the French and Belgian armies. Others were hired by the U.S. Army as contract employees, which meant they would provide needed services but not have any military rights or privileges. This was in contrast to women physicians with the British army who had military rank. Some American women physicians worked independently as free-lance doctors, moving where they were needed overseas, often on a temporary basis.

One prominent physician serving overseas during World War I was Dr. Alfreda Withington, an expert in tuberculosis. The Red Cross appointed Withington, then 57 years old, to head a hospital in France, the Franco-American Dispensary, which provided care for both soldiers and civilians. Her competent management led to offers from both the Red Cross and the Rockefeller Foundation for her services in Europe.

See also

Army Medical Corps (AMC); Barringer, Emily Dunning; Blackwell, Elizabeth Bradwell; Cornum, Rhonda; Craighill, Major Margaret D.; Hawks, Esther Hill; Reed, Dorothy; Sparkman Bill; Walker, Mary; Willoughby, Frances L.; Women's Overseas Hospital of the U.S.A. (WOH).

References

Ruth Abram, *"Send Us a Lady Physician": Women Doctors in America, 1835–1920* (1985); Esther Pohl Lovejoy, *Women Doctors of the World* (1957); Dorothy and Carl J. Schneider, *Into the Breach: Women Overseas in World War I* (1991).

Pickersgill, Mary Young

See War of 1812.

Pilots

American women were interested in flying planes from the time Wilbur and Orville Wright first flew a plane off the coast of Kitty Hawk, North Carolina. Through the years, they faced prejudice from those who thought flying was too difficult, strenuous, and risky for women.

During World War I, there were well-qualified women pilots in the United States, but no service branch would accept them for military duty. Aviator Katherine Stinson (1891–1977) was known as the "flying schoolgirl" for her stunt-flying. When the armed services rejected women pilots during the war, Stinson joined a Red Cross ambulance service. Her sister, Marjorie Stinson (1895–1975), was also a pilot and worked in the Washington, D.C., offices of the U.S. Navy's Aeronautical Division.

Cost was a major barrier that kept many women from flying during the early 1900s. Few women had money of their own to pay for flying lessons. Only heiresses or women with wealthy parents or spouses could afford to fly.

In 1938, the U.S. government began financing the Civilian Pilot Training Program (CPTP) under the Civil

Aeronautics Administration (CAA). Flight schools were having problems attracting enough students during those years of the Depression. In addition, the government was alarmed by the deepening political conflicts in Europe. If the United States had to go to war, there were only about 30,000 pilots in the nation.

The CPTP enabled young men and women in college to learn more about flying and the field of aviation. Within a year, more than 9,000 students, about 900 of them women, had paid the $40 fee required to begin flight instruction. But in 1941, the CPTP program was suddenly limited to men.

Many people protested this new policy, including First Lady Eleanor Roosevelt. The CAA explained that with war imminent, male pilots must be trained for combat. Women argued that they would gladly use their flying skills to benefit the military. A few women were hired as flight instructors in charge of training male pilots to fly military aircraft.

Through the Women Flyers of America (WFA), a number of women were able to take inexpensive flying lessons. In 1941 alone, membership in the WFA rose by 900 percent as more women took to the air for personal and patriotic reasons.

Some female pilots went to England to volunteer their services after World War II began there in 1939. American women worked for the British Air Transport Auxiliary (ATA), in which about 25 percent of the pilots were women. ATA pilots carried combat planes, such as Tiger Moths, from their place of manufacture to military bases and were in charge of moving aircraft off the ground and keeping it aloft in case of an enemy attack on an air base.

In 1941, the ATA asked American pilot Jacqueline Cochran to help them recruit more pilots. To publicize the program, Cochran joined a crew of two men to ferry a bomber across the Atlantic from Canada to Great Britain, where it would be used by the military. Twenty-four women responded to Cochran's request for more ATA pilots.

After the United States entered World War II, people discussed whether women pilots should be allowed to fly in various capacities for the armed services. Once again, support came from Eleanor Roosevelt who said, "We are in a war and we need to fight it with all our ability and every weapon possible. Women pilots are a weapon waiting to be used." Yet a number of men still vehemently rejected the idea of women military pilots.

President and Mrs. Roosevelt met with Jacqueline Cochran to examine how women pilots were aiding the war effort in England. They asked her to develop a proposal for the use of women in the U.S. military, which led to the formation of the Women's Airforce Service Pilots (WASP). There were 1,830 pilots in the first WASP training program set up at Howard Hughes Air Field near Houston, Texas. Even before the program was implemented, General Henry Arnold of the Army Air Corps said he could use women pilots to ferry planes to military bases. These women would not, however, receive full military status.

Another pilot, Nancy Harkness Love, developed the plan that led to the Women's Auxiliary Ferrying Squadron (WAFS). Love, who operated an aircraft sales company with her husband, had begun ferrying planes from Canada to France early in 1940. The WAFS training school was located near Wilmington, Delaware. Candidates had to have at least 500 hours of flying time, more than twice what the military required of male pilots.

During the war, more than 1,000 women pilots flew for the military. They logged 60 million miles in the air and transported more than 75 percent of the aircraft. In addition, they tested new planes, delivered cargo, and towed targets in the air that soldiers on the ground used for target practice. Thirty-eight women pilots died in wartime. In some cases, sabotage was suspected as the cause of an accident. (The cause of at least one crash was traced to sugar clogging a gas tank.)

In the years that followed the war, woman attained positions as pilots as part of the regular armed services. In March 1966, Gale Ann Gordon became the first Navy pilot to fly solo—in a propeller-driven T-34 trainer. Ensign Gordon, a member of the Medical Service Corps, had begun flight training in February, the only woman in a squadron of 999 men.

Women continued to make new firsts as more and more positions as pilots were opened to them. In 1973, the first six women became designated as naval aviators. The Army's aviation program was opened to women in 1973, and in June 1974, Lieutenant Sally Murphy became the Army's first female helicopter pilot. Within six years, 16 women officers and 25 warrant officers had entered Army flight training programs, with 2 earning honors and all but 6 finishing the programs.

In the 1970s, women began flying transports, Awacs, jet refueling tankers, and high-altitude reconnaissance planes in various branches of the military. They were attending schools to receive Top Gun–style training and had become combat-qualified instructors. Women were finally cleared by Congress to fly warplanes (combat aircraft) in 1992 after years of debate, which did not end even after Congress lifted the ban. Within two years of the ban, however, the services had begun training women for combat flying.

Those who objected to women flying in combat argued that they might be shot down or captured and that pilots often have to cross-train as air controllers, a job so demanding that most men in the Air Force who attempt it do not complete the training. Opponents also said that women were not able to "pull Gs"—withstand quick turns without blacking out—as well as men. Some American women pilots had already proven this theory wrong by 1992, however, as had Canadian women who were permitted to fly fighter planes.

See also

Cochran, Jacqueline; Combat; Combat Exclusion Law; Fighter Pilots; Fort, Cornelia; Hultgreen, Kara S.; Love, Nancy Harkness; Mariner, Rosemary Conatser; Neuffer, Judy; Nichols, Ruth; Ninety-Nines; Rainey, Barbara Allen; Richey, Helen; Top Gun; United States Air Force; United States Air Force Pilots; United States Navy; Women Flyers of America (WFA); Women's Airforce Service Pilots (WASP); Women's Auxiliary Ferrying Squadron (WAFS).

References

Kathleen Brooks-Pazmany, *United States Women in Aviation, 1919–1929* (1991); Jean H. Cole, *Women Pilots of World War II* (1992); Deborah G. Douglas, *United States Women in Aviation, 1940–1985* (1991); "Girl Pilots," *Life* (19 July 1943): 7–9; Henry M.

Holden, *Ladybirds: The Untold Story of Women Pilots in America* (1991); Sally Van Wagenen Keil, *Those Wonderful Women in Their Flying Machines* (1990); Claudia M. Oakes, *United States Women in Aviation, 1930–1939* (1991); Marianne Verges, *On Silver Wings: The Women Airforce Service Pilots of World War II, 1942–1944* (1991).

Pinups

During World War II, many American servicemen prized photographs of attractive actresses or models, which they carried with them while stationed away from home. The photos, pinned up in footlockers or on the walls of barracks, were viewed as an inspiration to America's fighting men, a reminder of what they were protecting and defending on the home front.

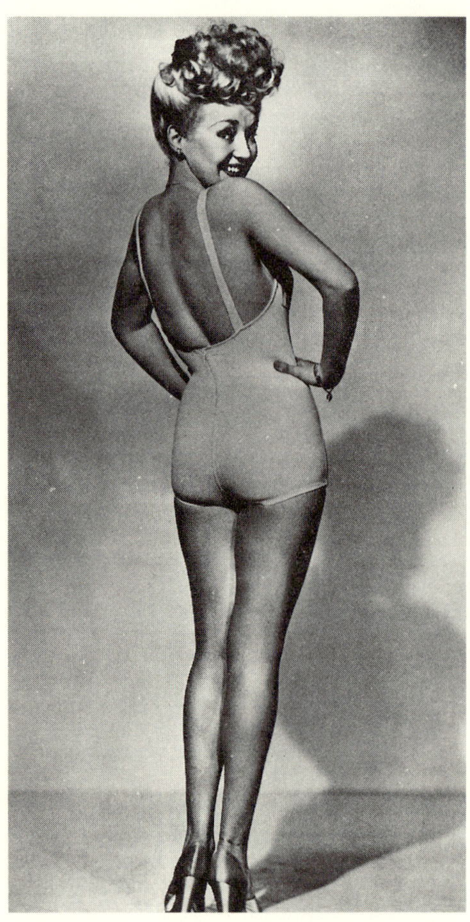

Famous wartime pinup Betty Grable

Among the most popular pinups of this era was actress Betty Grable, known for her shapely legs. More than 3,000 GIs requested a photo showing a smiling Grable wearing short shorts and peering over her shoulder. Grable received thousands of marriage proposals from servicemen and letters saying her picture reminded them of what they were fighting for back home.

The barracks of servicewomen differed in this respect. Observers noted that women were more likely to hang decorative pictures or maps and other job-related items on their walls, perhaps because they feared not being taken seriously.

References

Stan Cohen, *V for Victory: America's Home Front during World War II* (1991); Susan M. Hartmann, *The Home Front and Beyond: American Women in the 1940s* (1982); Elaine Tyler May, *Pushing the Limits: American Women 1940–61* (1994).

Pitcher, Molly

See Hays, Mary Ludwig.

Pope, Barbara

See Tailhook.

Post-Traumatic Stress Disorder

Sometimes called post-traumatic stress syndrome, post-traumatic stress disorder (PTSD) occurs when fear, anger, and depression result from a traumatic experience suffered in the past, sometimes years earlier. It can manifest itself in nightmares, depression, flashbacks, and episodes of rage or extreme guilt.

War veterans have been diagnosed as suffering from PTSD, which in the past was sometimes called "shell-shock" or "soldier's heart." People who have survived rape, childhood abuse, traumatic loss, or a natural disaster have also been diagnosed with PTSD.

PTSD became more widely recognized and understood after it was found in large numbers of men and women who served in the Vietnam War during the 1960s and early 1970s. The disorder was also used as a legal defense in some criminal trials involving explosive outbursts of rage in Vietnam veterans. In 1980, the disorder was listed in the official diagnostic manual compiled by the American Psychiatric Association.

Nurses who served in Vietnam have experienced a high incidence of PTSD. Women have reported suffering from uncontrollable crying spells and nightmares, including recurring, repetitive dreams in which they relive particularly traumatic war experiences, sometimes decades after the events themselves. A number of nurses were devastated by the incredible suffering and death they witnessed during that war and by the need to stifle their own emotions while caring for patients under those conditions. According to PTSD expert Joan Furey, herself a Vietnam veteran, while male veterans tend to experience and express more anger, female veterans have experienced more depression: "Women tend to internalize much more than men do. You see more depression."

In 1979, the Readjustment Counseling Program was set up to help women veterans who were suffering from PTSD. Three years later, the Women's Working Group became a part of this program. Women veterans could receive counseling from other women, and staff members at veterans' centers were trained to recognize PTSD and help patients deal with it.

The Veterans Administration set up the V.A. National Center for Post Traumatic Stress Disorder in Menlo Park, California. A 90-bed inpatient unit for male veterans was set up there in 1978, and the 10-bed Women's Trauma Recovery Program, an inpatient treatment unit, was opened in 1992. The center works with women who have not been able to overcome their problem with other, more conservative treatment.

The Vet Center program for women veterans estimates that 2,000 female veterans were treated for PTSD between 1980 and 1993, but others think the number is closer to 2,500. Many affected women have not come forward, possibly because they were too traumatized or embarrassed to discuss the problem. Others feared they might lose their jobs as nurses if they were viewed as unstable or suffering from a health problem.

In an interview with author Shelley Saywell, Lynn Bower, a nurse who served in Vietnam, said, "All those faces of boys, mostly boys. I don't think I saw many men die; I saw boys die. It was so futile. It was as though everyone had forgotten them. I had awful feelings of frustration and anger."

See also

Van Devanter, Lynda; Vietnam Veterans of America (VVA) Women's Project; Vietnam War.

References
Laura Palmer, "The Nurses of Vietnam: Still Wounded," *New York Times Sunday Magazine* (7 November 1993): 36ff; Shelley Saywell, *Women in War* (1985); Winnie Smith, *American Daughter Gone to War* (1992); Lynda Van Devanter, *Home before Morning* (1983).

Pregnancy

Until 1975, women in the U.S. Armed Forces could not serve while they were pregnant and might even face a dishonorable discharge for pregnancy. A ban against serving while pregnant was viewed as a way to protect women's health. Also, many people assumed pregnant women could not perform their jobs adequately. The fact that women *could* become pregnant was also cited as a reason to keep women out of the military completely by those who supported such a ban.

Pregnancy served as the basis for excluding women from particular jobs, especially those related to combat. Those who opposed permitting women to fly combat aircraft said that it would not be economical to invest in training women if they later became pregnant and stopped flying.

From the outset, the military nursing corps banned women from serving while pregnant and discharged anyone who became pregnant while in the service. In the Women's Army Auxiliary Corps (WAAC) (later the Women's Army Corps—WAC) during World War II, members who became pregnant were discharged. Married servicewomen received an honorable discharge, while a single woman in this condition or a woman who had an abortion to end a pregnancy was dishonorably discharged. During the 1940s, unwed pregnancy was regarded as scandalous, and abortions were outlawed except in order to save a woman's life.

Both women and men supported these regulations. In those days, women who were pregnant were less active than in later decades and more likely to stay at home. They were not often seen in the workplace or taking part in sports and other strenuous activities. At one time, women schoolteachers and those in various professions had to resign when they became pregnant.

The rate of pregnancy in the WAC remained low during the war, varying from 0 to 7 per 1,000 women per month. As the war ended and husbands returned home, the rate rose to about 48 per 1,000 per year as compared to 117 per 1,000 among civilian women. A number of pregnant Wacs hoped to leave the service when their husbands came home, while others sought to start their families before they grew any older.

Throughout the years, military women and their supporters complained about the policy banning pregnancy and were upset that becoming a natural mother automatically ended one's career. They suggested ways that women could be permitted to take time off for pregnancy and maternity leave. Some men also supported these ideas. In 1949, Rear Admiral Clifford A. Swanson suggested that women could remain in the military while raising families and recommended maternity leave and other programs to make this possible. Swanson's proposals were rejected, however, even by some top-ranking women in the military.

In 1951, President Harry Truman signed Executive Order 10240, which permitted the service branches to discharge any woman in the regular or reserve forces who became pregnant or responsible for a minor child as the result of birth, adoption, or becoming a stepparent. There were no comparable policies for men.

Two Supreme Court cases in 1974 challenged policies that required pregnant women to leave certain civilian jobs. By this time, the medical profession was describing pregnancy as a normal process rather than a health problem. The women who brought these suits claimed that the employer's restrictions were arbitrary and that they assumed all women were affected the same way by pregnancy and all women experienced the same physical limitations or were incapacitated by pregnancy.

Threatened with similar lawsuits, the Pentagon changed its policy in 1975. The Department of Defense (DOD) stated that the armed services would permit women to remain on active duty while pregnant and to return to their jobs after giving birth. Women who adopted children or acquired stepchildren as a result of marriage were also permitted to remain on duty.

As of the 1990s, pregnant servicewomen were free to remain on duty unless they required medical leave for health reasons or if their particular job would pose clear hazards to mother or child. Women received four weeks of leave at the time of the birth and could return to their jobs without any loss of rank, salary, or opportunities for advancement. The services are also implementing what they called quality of life programs—such as child care, family centers, and counseling—to enhance the lives of servicepeople and their families.

See also

Crawford v. Cushman; Excutive Order 10240; Flores, Anna; Pregnancy Discrimination Act (PDA) of 1978; Women's Armed Services Integration Act of 1948.

References

Helen Rogan, *Mixed Company: Women in the Modern Army* (1981); Dorothy and Carl J. Schneider, *Sound Off! American Military Women Speak Out* (1988); Mattie E. Treadwell, *U.S. Army in World War II: Special Studies—The Women's Army Corps* (1954); Doris Weatherford, *American Women and World War II* (1990).

Pregnancy Discrimination Act (PDA) of 1978

The Pregnancy Discrimination Act (PDA) of 1978 amended Title VII of the Civil Rights Act of 1964, adding pregnancy to the list of ways in which people might face discrimination on the basis of sex. The PDA was written to clear up misunderstandings among employers and employees and to set clear guidelines for all states. It bans discriminating against women because of pregnancy, childbirth, or related medical conditions. Businesses with 15 or more employees are required to treat pregnant women who are unable to work the same way they would treat other workers with a temporary disability. Employers have the right to exclude elective abortions from the health insurance coverage they give their employees, presuming the woman's life is not threatened, but they must provide sick leave and disability benefits to women who are recovering from an abortion.

Presidential Commission on the Assignment of Women in the Armed Services (1992)

In March 1992, President George Bush established the Presidential Commission on the Assignment of Women in the Armed Services to study laws and military policies as they applied to women. The president asked the panel to evaluate the combat exclusion clauses of the Women's Armed Services Integration Act of 1948, which integrated women in the military.

Made up of nine men and six women, the commission conducted fact-finding missions in the United States and abroad. It held hearings to receive testimony from civilian and military experts and studied research reports by the Department of Defense and social scientists who have studied related matters.

The report was handed down on 15 November 1992. The most controversial area covered in the recommendations dealt with women and combat. The commission said that limits in their physical strength might make it unwise for women to take part in combat, and that mixed combat units (those containing members of both sexes) might not work well together. They also expressed concerns about the possibility that women prisoners of war might be tortured and raped.

Based on these considerations, the commission recommended that women not be assigned to ground combat duty or combat aircraft. It suggested, however, that women be assigned to the crews of combatant vessels other than submarines and amphibious craft. In the case of these latter vessels, the commission said that privacy and living space were key considerations, since modifying the crowded spaces to accommodate women would be expensive.

The commission noted that women in the Air Force had already taken part in jobs that supported combat efforts, such as working in missile silos and Army air defense units. The commission favored reenacting the 1948 restriction against women on combat aircraft.

See also

Combat Exclusion Law; Cornum, Rhonda; Motherhood; Panama, Invasion of; Persian Gulf War; Pilots; Sea Duty; Submarines; Top Gun.

References

Carolyn Becraft, *Women in the Military, 1980–1990* (1990); E. A. Blacksmith, ed., *Women in the Military* (1992); Jeanne Holm, *Women in the Military: An Unfinished Revolution* (1992); Helen Rogan, *Mixed Company: Women in the Modern Army* (1983); Carol Wekesser and Matthew Polesetsky, *Women in the Military* (1991).

Prisoners of War (POWs)

Although some women were captured during the American Revolution and Civil War, they were usually given light penalties and released quickly. Some female spies during the Civil War were placed under house arrest or in prisons where they were not harshly treated. Male POWs were treated more severely, in some cases being hung. In all, during World War II, 81 women were prisoners of war. They included 67 Army nurses, 11 Navy nurses, 2 dieticians, and a physical therapist.

During World War II, 82 women were taken as prisoners of war, mainly by the Japanese. One Army nurse,

Reba Zitella Whittle, was captured by Germans. All the women were eventually released, but 66 Army nurses and 11 Navy nurses were imprisoned for 37 months at the San Tomas prison in Manila after being captured at Bataan and Corregidor. The 4,000 civilian prisoners at San Tomas suffered in numerous ways before being released in 1945.

The chance that women might become prisoners of war has been used as a reason for banning women from jobs in areas related to combat. Those who support such bans have said that women might be tortured, raped, or killed if they became prisoners. Women who disagree with such bans have pointed out that male POWs have endured these burdens, including being tortured and raped, and that military women were prepared to face such ordeals as well.

The debate became more heated during the Persian Gulf War, when two American women, both serving with the Army, were captured by Iraqi forces and held as POWs for several days.

See also
Army Nurse Corps (ANC); Bataan; Brantley, Hattie Rilla; Cornum, Rhonda; Corregidor; Medals; Rathbun-Nealy, Melissa; Veterans.

References
Brian Mitchell, *Weak Link: The Feminization of the American Military* (1989); Charles Moskos, "Women's Experiences in the Military: An Overview," in Carol Wekesser and Matthew Polesetsky, *Women in the Military* (1991); Helen Rogan, *Mixed Company: Women in the Modern Army* (1981); Paul E. Roush, "Women Serving in Combat Would Strengthen America's Defense," in Carol Wekesser and Matthew Polesetsky, *Women in the Military* (1991); June A. Willenz, *Women Veterans: America's Forgotten Heroines* (1983).

Private Benjamin

A 1980 feature film starring actress Goldie Hawn, *Private Benjamin* tells the story of a pampered woman in her late twenties who enters the Army and gains skills and independence in the process. The film shows Hawn and other women in basic training, on bivouac, and on assignment for NATO in Europe. A television series by the same title was later developed.

Promotion

When the women's corps in the various service branches were first formed, women were promoted within their own ranks, separately from men. Women thus competed against each other for promotions and job assignments. Women were also limited in terms of what rank they could achieve, because laws had set ceilings on those ranks. For example, a woman could not rise to the rank of general.

When this issue was discussed after World War II, military psychiatrists said that if women were to achieve full participation in the military, men would have to overcome long-standing attitudes about women and the feminine role, as well as accepting the idea of women as generals.

In 1967, President Lyndon B. Johnson signed legislation that set in motion a new policy. Public Law 90-130 removed restrictions on the promotion of women in the Air Force, Army, Marines, and Navy. This law opened the way for women to be promoted to senior grades—higher ranks than before, including the rank of general. Before this law took effect, it had

Oveta Culp Hobby, director of the Women's Army Auxiliary Corps (WAAC), pins gold leaves on the shoulder of Betty Bandel, the first field director of the WAAC. Prior to 1980, women from various service branches could only be promoted from within their own ranks and were limited as to the rank they could achieve.

been possible for women to be replaced in their jobs by men of higher rank but less experience.

In 1973, the Department of Defense developed a system to integrate men and women into the same officer structures and implement a unified promotion system. At that time, only the Air Force had integrated promotions. After facing some opposition from Congress, the Defense Officer Personnel Management Act (DOPMA) was passed in 1980.

More women also could become officers and rise in the ranks of the various branches after Reserve Officer Training Corps (ROTC) programs and military service academies were opened to them during the 1970s.

By the early 1990s, all the service branches claimed to promote women at the same rate as they did men. Yet few women were eligible to compete for the top command assignments, and the jobs open to women encompassed fewer command positions. Combat exclusion policies remained the major obstacle, according to the 1988 report issued by the Research Division of the Department of Defense.

See also
Affirmative Action; Army Nurse Corps (ANC); Defense Officer Personnel Management Act (DOPMA); Discrimination, Sexual; Hays, Anna Mae; Hoefly, Ethel Ann; Hoisington, Elizabeth P.; Holm, Jeanne; Reals, Gail; Sea Duty.

References
Jeanne Holm, *Women in the Military: An Unfinished Revolution* (1992); Dorothy and Carl J. Schneider, *Sound Off! American Military Women Speak Out* (1992).

Prostitutes

Among the women who were camp followers in the American Revolution were prostitutes who accompanied the troops. One contemporary author described them as "filthy, slutty toothless women following behind the supply wagons, hair caked with mud, lice-ridden, cursing, emitting a stench and words so foul that prudent women along the route closed their doors and windows and covered the ears and eyes of their children."

Some military historians believe that old perceptions—that women who associated with the military were prostitutes or women of low repute—have continued to haunt women in the modern military. To combat such prejudices, there were strict rules governing the personal conduct and appearance of women who joined the women's corps during both world wars. The women who joined tended to be older and more mature than enlisted men. The directors of the various women's corps also stressed the need for "ladylike" behavior and high moral standards.

See also
Appearance; Discrimination, Sexual; Hazing; Sexual Harassment, Sexual Preferences; SPAR; Tailhook; Uniforms; Women Accepted for Voluntary Emergency Service (WAVES); Women Marines; Women's Army Corps (WAC).

References
Linda Grant De Pauw, *Founding Mothers: Women of America in the Revolutionary Era* (1975); Elizabeth Evans, *Weathering the Storm: Women of the American Revolution* (1975); Olga Gruhzit-Hoyt, *They Also Served: American Women in World War II* (1995); Mattie E. Treadwell, *U.S. Army in World War II: Special Studies—The Women's Army Corps* (1954).

Public Law 629

See Naval Reserve Act of 1938.

Public Law 36-80C

Known as the Army-Navy Nurse Act, Public Law 36-80C was enacted in April 1947 to set up permanent nurse corps in both service branches. Women in the corps were to be integrated into the officer ranks of the regular Army and Navy, and could rise up to the grade of lieutenant colonel or commander.

Public Law 90-130

Signed by President Lyndon B. Johnson on 8 November 1967, Public Law 90-130 amended Titles 10, 32, and 27 of the United States Code "to remove restrictions on the careers of female officers in the Army, Navy, Air Force, and Marine Corps and for other purposes." It removed the ceilings that had been placed on women's promotions to higher ranks, as well as the arbitrary percentages of women who were permitted to reach certain middle grades. For the Navy, it eliminated the 2 percent ceiling on enlisted women.

This 1967 act marked the first time since 1948 that a major policy change regarding women in the military had taken effect. As Johnson signed the bill, he commented, "There is no reason why we should not some day have a female Chief of Staff or even a female Commander-in-Chief."

See also
Hays, Anna Mae; Hoisington, Elizabeth P.; Holm, Jeanne; Promotion; Rank.

Reference
Jeanne Holm, *Women in the Military: An Unfinished Revolution* (1992).

Public Law 94-106

Passed by Congress in 1975, Public Law 94-106 stated that women would be allowed admission into the military service academies of the Navy, Army, and Air Force. The first coeducational classes entered the following year.

See also
Discrimination, Sexual; Sexual Harassment; United States Air Force Academy (USAFA); United States Coast Guard Academy (USCGA); United States Military Academy (USMA); United States Naval Academy (USNA).

Public Law 95-202

Passed by Congress in 1977, Public Law 95-202 gave veteran status to the women who had served six decades earlier in the Signal Corps of the Army during World War I.

Purple Heart

The Purple Heart medal is awarded to individuals in the service who are wounded or who die as a result of hostile enemy action. During World War II, 16 women stationed in England with the Women's Army Corps (WAC) received this medal when they were injured during German bombing attacks on London.

See also
Army Nurse Corps (ANC); Decorations; Medals; Navy Nurse Corps (NNC); Vietnam War; World War II.

Quigley, Robin L. (n.d.)

Captain Robin L. Quigley became assistant for women in the Navy, a position that also had been referred to as director of WAVES, in 1971. Known for her candor, Quigley had let it be known that she disliked the acronym WAVES, referring to it as "that cute little designator." In Quigley's opinion, women in the Navy should simply stop using the designation of WAVES. She expressed her thoughts in a memorandum sent out on 23 February 1972, saying that the term gave the impression that women in the Navy were part of a "women's auxiliary." She recommended that women drop the word from their titles, calling themselves simply officers rather than WAVE officers, in order to gain full recognition in the Navy.

During this time, a number of changes for women were taking place in the Navy. Women became part of the same personnel bureau as men. Quigley supported a number of changes being introduced by Chief of Naval Operations (CNO) Admiral Elmo Zumwalt to open more jobs to women. Quigley also recommended that the office of Assistant for Women be eliminated as women became more and more a part of the same services as men.

In 1973, Quigley was reassigned as commander of the Service School Command in San Diego, California, and the office she had held, established 31 years before during World War II, was abolished.

See also
Sea Duty; Women Accepted for Voluntary Emergency Service (WAVES).

Reference
Jeanne Holm, *Women in the Military: An Unfinished Revolution* (1992).

R

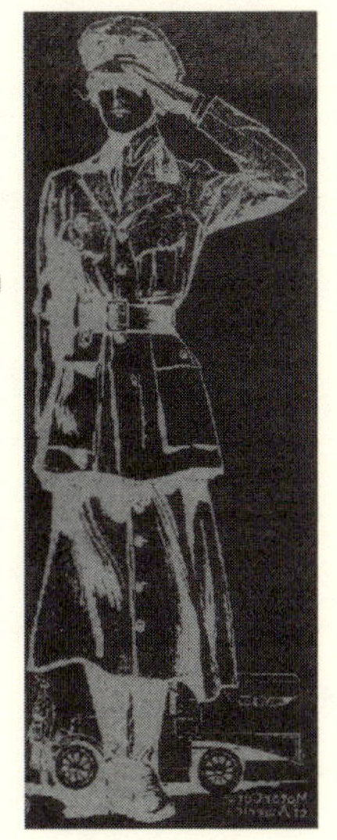

Rainey, Barbara Allen (1948–1982)

In 1974, Lieutenant Barbara Allen Rainey became the first woman pilot in the U.S. Navy. A native of Long Beach, California, who graduated from Lakewood High School, she received her bachelor of arts degree at Whittier College in Whittier, California.

In only one year, Rainey completed her flight training to become a Navy pilot. She was also the first woman to receive the prestigious Wings of Gold flying insignia from the Navy. Rainey served with the Pacific Fleet Squadron in California, flying passenger/cargo transports.

In 1977, when she became pregnant, Rainey decided to resign from the Navy. She had been frustrated at not being able to fly the same kinds of missions that were assigned to her male colleagues, even though her training and experience equaled or surpassed theirs. Rainey joined her husband, who was a Navy flight instructor at Whiting Field in Florida.

It was at Whiting that Rainey died suddenly at age 34. The Navy did not officially release the cause of her death. Rainey was buried with military honors at Arlington National Cemetery.

References

"Limits on Career, Not Pregnancy, Moved Female Pilot to Quit Navy," *The Ledger Star* (26 November 1977); Phyllis J. Read and Bernard L. Witlieb, *The Book of Women's Firsts* (1992).

Rank

When the first women entered military service, rules did not permit them to be commissioned as officers. The matter of rank became a serious issue as the armed services hired nurses and expected them to give orders to the lesser-trained aides and orderlies who cared for the sick and wounded under their direction.

After World War I, nursing leaders asked that nurses be commissioned as officers rather than having a noncommissioned status. Having praised the performance of nurses during the war, General John Pershing and several other prominent military leaders supported this idea. They argued forcefully against those who opposed giving nurses any rank in the military.

The Army Reorganization Act of 1920 gave nurses the standing of relative rank. Army nurses could then wear the insignia of relative rank but did not have the privileges, rights, or pay that went along with their rank. A similar change took place in the Navy Nurse Corps (NNC). In 1947, Congress passed Public Law 36-80C, which finally gave nurses commissioned officer status.

On 8 November 1967, Congress approved Public Law 90-130, which ended promotion restrictions that had applied to women officers in the armed forces. From that point, women could be promoted as high as the rank of general. In 1996, Carol Mutter became the first female three-star general.

See also

Bailey, Mildred; Clarke, Mary E.; Hays, Anna Mae; Hoisington, Elizabeth P.; Holm, Jeanne; Mutter, Carol; Promotion; Public Law 36-80C; Public Law 90-130.

Reference

Maj. Edith Aynes, A.N.C., *From Nightingale to Eagle: The Army Nurses History* (1973); E. A. Blacksmith, ed., *Women in the Military* (1992); Helen Rogan, *Mixed Company: Women in the Modern Army* (1981); June A. Willenz, *Women Veterans: America's Forgotten Heroines* (1983).

Rathbun-Nealy, Melissa (b. 1970)

In January 1991 at age 20, Melissa Rathbun-Nealy became the first American female listed as missing in action (MIA). Captured by Iraqi soldiers, she was one of three women to become prisoners of war (POWs) during the Persian Gulf War.

Rathbun-Nealy grew up in Grand Rapids, Michigan, and was the only child of a former nun and former Catholic brother. An outgoing person, she was described by friends as "feisty" and "carefree" during her teen years. Rathbun-Nealy joined the Reserve Officer Training Corps (ROTC) during high school but dropped out.

With her best friend, LaTanua Ivy, she joined the Army in 1988, and completed basic training at Fort Leonard Wood, then was stationed at Fort Bliss, Texas, with the 233rd Transportation Company. During this time, she was briefly married and divorced.

In October 1991, Rathbun-Nealy's unit was deployed to Saudi Arabia as part of Operation Desert Storm. While serving in the Persian Gulf War, Rathbun-Nealy drove heavy supply trucks. She was captured along with Specialist David Lockett after their truck became stuck in the sand and was stopped by Iraqi soldiers. Rathbun-Nealy was held as a prisoner of war for 34 days in Basram and Baghdad. She later reported that she was not mistreated. During her captivity, however, air raids caused explosions nearby.

After returning home, Rathbun-Nealy married fellow Gulf War veteran Michael Coleman in 1991 and became a homemaker with two daughters in Grand Rapids, Michigan. In the years that followed, both she and her husband reported experiencing symptoms such as aching joints and migraine headaches, symptoms associated with Gulf War Syndrome.

See also
Cornum, Rhonda; Gulf War Syndrome; Persian Gulf War.

Reference
Lisa Grunwald, "MIA," *Life* (25 February 1991): 42–46.

Rationing

During 1942 and 1943, the government passed laws limiting civilian use of certain foods, fuels, and other materials that were needed in large quantities by the military or were too difficult to ship over dangerous waters. Shortages of gasoline meant that women defense plant workers had to form carpools or take public transportation to get to work.

Foods that were rationed included butter, meat, sugar, coffee, and a number of canned fruits and vegetables. Homemakers, almost all of them women, had to use books containing ration stamps to buy these foods, and they learned to "make do" with shortages of various foods. Many planted victory gardens to increase the supply of produce available to their families. Women also served as assistants to rationing boards or were hired at ration centers to give out coupon and point books, but they were rarely members of ration boards.

See also
Victory Gardens.

Reference
Stan Cohen, *V for Victory: America's Home Front during World War II* (1991); Archie Satterfield, *Home Front: An Oral History of the War Years in America, 1941–1945* (1981); Ann Starrett, "Rationing Is a Woman's

Melissa Rathbun-Nealy (far right) and three other former prisoners of war receive medals for their outstanding service in the Persian Gulf War on 13 March 1991.

Job," *Independent Woman* (May 1942): 137–138.

Readjustment Counseling Program

See Post-Traumatic Stress Disorder.

Reals, Gail (b. 1937)

In 1985, Gail Reals was promoted to brigadier general, the first woman to reach that rank after the military began its new policy of promoting women in competition with men.

Reals began her career in the Marines shortly after she graduated from high school. She finished Officer Candidate School (OCS) in 1961, at which time she was commissioned as a second lieutenant. In 1968, she was stationed in Lebanon, where she served as personnel officer in the Marine security guard battalion in Beirut.

Back in the United States during the 1970s, Reals served as commanding officer for the Woman Recruit Training Battalion in Parris Island, South Carolina. In 1988, she moved to Quantico, Virginia, serving as commanding general of that large Marine base until 1990, when she retired from the Marine Corps.

See also
Promotion; Rank.

Recruitment

Women have always served in the military as volunteers, enlisting of their own free will rather than having been drafted. At various times, when the need for military personnel increased, concerted efforts were made to recruit women.

During World War II, recruitment efforts were increased greatly to attract women to serve as military nurses and in the women's corps of the Army, Navy, Marines, and Coast Guard. A two-pronged approach to recruitment was often employed. Appeals were made to women's patriotism, with posters that urged women to "Free a Man To Fight" (Marines) and "Make a Date with Uncle Sam." Nurses were urged to join the Cadet Nurse Corps in order to receive free training and stipends in exchange for service after graduation. Measures for drafting nurses were also considered.

The military rejected one recruitment advertisement that showed a wounded soldier dying on a battlefield while a group of women played cards. The caption read, "Men are dying on the battleline. Can you live with yourself on the sideline?" The accepted official policy was not to show pictures of dead U.S. soldiers to the public. One poster that was acceptable to military officials showed a group of gravestones with the caption: "They can't do any more—but you can."

Most ads, many designed by a large professional ad agency, pointed out the benefits of serving with the women's corps. They described material advantages—salary, free clothing, food, and health care, and the training and military status women would receive. There were many interesting and appealing jobs to be had in the military, the ads maintained. In addition, the "Release a Man" campaign asked women to enlist so fewer married men with children would have to be drafted and leave their families.

In cities with large defense plants that also needed workers, these recruitment stations were not welcome. Defense plant owners and military recruitment personnel both turned to the War Manpower Commission for guidance. In areas where defense industries did not want local women lured into the military, recruiters often had trouble getting radio and newspaper publicity.

Efforts to increase the number of women in the Women's Army Corps (WAC) were stepped up again when the Korean War began in 1950. As the All-Volunteer Force (AVF) took shape in the early 1970s, research studies were conducted to analyze how to attract more women to different branches of service and expand their military career opportunities.

The number of women on active duty grew to 173,450 by 1980, and the military aimed to increase that number by another 91,000 within six years. In 1981, however, officials in the Army and Air Force asked that recruitment goals be held steady until they could study what impact women were having on the overall strength and readiness of the military.

Recruitment procedures are now the same for men and women, all of whom join as volunteers. Among the criteria considered are educational level, mental abilities, background information, and physical abilities, the latter differing somewhat for the two genders. To help them understand what to expect, potential enlistees are often shown films of basic training and other aspects of military life.

See also
Army Nurse Corps (ANC); Defense Plant Workers; Draft; Women Accepted for Voluntary Emergency Service (WAVES); Women Marines; Women's Army Auxiliary Corps (WAAC); Women's Army Corps (WAC).

References
Karen Anderson, *Wartime Women: Sex Roles, Family Relations, and the Status of Women during World War II* (1981); Judith Bellefaire, *The Army Nurse Corps in World War II* (1976); Maureen Honey, *Creating Rosie the Riveter: Class, Gender, and Propaganda during World War II* (1984); John A. Tilley, *A History of Women in the Coast Guard* (1996); Mattie E. Treadwell, *U.S. Army in World War II: Special Studies—The Women's Army Corps* (1954); Doris Weatherford, *American Women and World War II* (1990).

Red Cross
See American Red Cross (ARC).

Red Rover
See Civil War.

Reed, Dorothy (1874–1964)
In 1898, Ohio native Dorothy Reed and a fellow medical student, Margaret Long, became the first two women ever hired to work in a U.S. Navy hospital. A graduate of Smith College in Northampton, Massachusetts, Reed went on to study medicine at Johns Hopkins University in Baltimore. It was as medical students that she and Long worked in the operating room and bacteriological laboratories of Brooklyn Navy Yard Hospital in New York City.

A gifted scientist, Reed won a fellowship in pathology, the study of disease processes, and went on to make important findings about Hodgkin's disease. Her work showed that Hodgkin's was not a type of tuberculosis, as some scientists had mistakenly thought. Reed also devised a method of diagnosing the disease by means of a blood test.

In 1902, Reed accepted a position as resident at the New York Infirmary for Women and Children in New York City, later transferring to New York's Babies Hospital. She married physicist Charles E. Mendenhall in 1906 and moved to Madison, Wisconsin, where she became a lecturer in home economics at the University of Wisconsin. During her years in Wisconsin, Reed organized that state's first clinic for infant care in 1915, served as a medical officer for the U.S. Children's Bureau, and worked with the Visiting Nurse Association, serving as chair for 21 years. Among her publications were books about child health and midwifery. Reed bequeathed her scientific papers to Smith College, where a building was named in honor of her and fellow alumna Dr. Florence R. Sabin.

Reference
Ruth Abram, *"Send Us a Lady Physician": Women Doctors in America, 1835–1920* (1985); Phyllis J. Read and Bernard L. Witlieb, *The Book of Women's Firsts* (1992).

Reed, Esther
See American Revolution.

"Release a Man" Campaign
See Recruitment.

Reserve Officer Training Corps (ROTC)
The programs of the Reserve Officer Training Corps (ROTC), set up on

college campuses, aim to train future servicepeople, especially officers. Women were permitted to join ROTC units for the first time in 1969 (Air Force) and 1972 (Army and Navy). As of May 1981, about 40,000 women were enrolled in ROTC programs throughout the United States.

In 1972, the Army also set up a Junior ROTC program for young women aged 14 or older. Based in high schools, the programs had enrolled more than 32,000 teenaged girls as of 1981.

Reference

Dorothy and Carl J. Schneider, *Sound Off! American Military Women Speak Out* (1992); Carol Wekesser and Matthew Polesetsky, *Women in the Military* (1991).

Revolution, American

See American Revolution.

Rhoads Dress

During World War I, a New York City designer named May Rhoads invented and patented a practical outfit for women workers. After arriving at her job, the woman worker could unbutton the outer, skirted smock that concealed bloomer-type overalls. The overdress was considered both ladylike and practical, since it could be easily removed and stored during work hours. The innovative Rhoads dress was widely used by women workers during the two world wars.

Reference

Anne L. Macdonald, *Feminine Ingenuity: Women and Invention in America* (1992).

Rice, Andrea

See Top Gun.

Richey, Helen (1910–1947)

Helen Richey served as a pilot during World War II, ferrying planes for the military from the United States to Canada and other places they were needed. Later, she was the first woman hired as a commercial airline pilot (for Capital Airlines).

Born in McKeesport, Pennsylvania, Richey completed 1,000 hours of solo flying to earn a transport pilot's license in 1933. In December of that year, she and Frances H. Marsalis set a record for endurance. They piloted *The Outdoor Girl* for 9 days, 21 hours, and 42 minutes, stopping only to refuel.

Richey was hired by Capital Airlines in 1934, but the airline then asked her to resign because passengers complained about having a female pilot in the cockpit.

In 1936, Richey went on to set records for speed (in a Class C light plane over a 100-kilometer course) and altitude (in a midget plane). In 1940, she became the first woman ever given an instructor's license by the Civil Aeronautics Administration.

Richey began aiding the war effort in 1942, going to England as a member of the Aviation Transport Auxiliary (ATA), an organization of American women pilots assisting the British Women's Ferry Command. Among other assignments, Richey transported planeloads of bombs from munitions plants to air bases. During those years, she and other women disproved the theory that women could not pilot heavy planes in adverse conditions.

Returning to the United States, Richey served as an Army flight instructor until the end of the war. She had achieved the rank of major when she left the Army in 1944. She died three years later.

Reference

Sally Van Wagenen Keil, *Those Wonderful Women in Their Flying Machines* (1979); Marianne Verges, *On Silver Wings: The Women Airforce Service Pilots of World War II, 1942–1944* (1991).

Rinehart, Mary Roberts (1876–1958)

Mary Roberts Rinehart was one of the first American journalists to report from the battlefront in World War I. A native of Pittsburgh, Pennsylvania, Rinehart first began a career in nursing, then married Dr. Stanley Rinehart, with whom she had three sons. The hard economic times of 1903 led her to begin a new career as a writer. She sold a number of mysteries and humorous stories, becoming one of the most popular fiction writers in the country.

By the time World War I began, Rinehart was a regular contributor to the *Saturday Evening Post*, a magazine with a readership of more than two million people. She was determined to become a war correspondent, and although most newspapers and magazines refused to send women to cover the war, Rinehart received credentials and funding to go abroad.

Arriving in England in January 1915, Rinehart found that the British were refusing to send correspondents to the front. Friends put her in touch with the Belgian Red Cross, which arranged for Rinehart to reach Belgium and France. Shortly thereafter, as the only woman journalist in the group, she witnessed a night attack by German zeppelins on Dunkirk, France. Rinehart interviewed Belgian and French troops and reported on the action at the front. In February, after having come within 300 yards of German lines, Rinehart wrote, "I have done what no woman has done before, and I am alive."

With the help of French Marshal Ferdinand Foch, Rinehart was able to reach the French front, where she reported on the use of poisonous gas by the Germans. Rinehart was dismayed by the lack of organized nursing services for Belgian and French soldiers who had been wounded in battle. In those years, the United States and Great Britain were the only nations to have organized groups of military nurses.

Rinehart returned home that year, but after the United States entered the war in 1917, she vowed to go back overseas as a nurse. Her application was accepted by the American Red Cross (ARC), but the War Department would not permit Rinehart to go, since she was a correspondent and no women journalists were being accredited to report from the front. Unable to serve as a nurse, Rinehart took assignments from the military to report on the conditions of Navy and Army training camps.

As a result of these efforts, Rinehart once again was permitted to go overseas, this time on an assignment from the War Department to determine the needs of U.S. soldiers. The armistice ending the war was signed the week she arrived, but she traveled through France and Belgium to report on the problems people faced after the war.

Edith Nourse Rogers looks on as President Truman signs a bill that she proposed for war service amputees in 1946. Rogers was responsible for introducing the bill that created the Women's Army Auxiliary Corps, which specified the rights of women serving in the Army, in 1941.

Back home, Rinehart fought for the right of women to vote while continuing her writing, selling millions of books during her long career. Although she was in her sixties when World War II began, the Army and Navy offered to transport her to Europe. She declined to embark on this new adventure, however, because of her age.

See also
Correspondents, War.
References
Jan Cohn, *Improbable Fiction: The Life of Mary Roberts Rinehart* (1980); Julia Edwards, *Women of the World: The Great Foreign Correspondents* (1988); Mary Roberts Rinehart, *My Story: A New Edition and Seventeen New Years* (1948).

Rogers, Edith Nourse (1881–1960)

In May 1941, as a Republican congresswoman from Massachusetts, Edith Nourse Rogers introduced H.R. 4906, the bill that created the Women's Army Auxiliary Corps (WAAC).

Born in Saco, Maine, Edith Nourse was privately educated at home and abroad. In 1907, she married attorney John Jacob Rogers, who was elected to Congress in 1912. The couple traveled in Europe during World War I inspecting military field hospitals, and Edith served as a representative of the Women's Overseas Service League. She then served as a volunteer at a veterans' hospital. Her service at home and abroad during the war strengthened her interest in politics and veterans' affairs. In 1922, she became an inspector of veterans' hospitals, an appointed job that paid one dollar per year.

Rogers won the congressional seat of her husband, John Jacob Rogers, after his death in 1925, the first of 18 victories. She was the first woman from her region to serve in Congress. As a second world war loomed, Rogers worried that if women served, they might once again be put in an ambiguous position, lacking military status as they did in World War I. She informed Army officials that she planned to introduce legislation specifying the rights of women serving with the military. In turn, they offered suggestions for a proposal the War Department would support. She hoped the military would accept women as part of the regular Army, not merely as people serving alongside it.

When Rogers proposed the WAAC bill in 1942, there was some resistance. Army General George Marshall needed clerical workers to free up more men for combat and pushed for the bill's passage. Supporters pointed out that women already had skills in typing and other areas that would relieve the Army from having to train men. Across the country, patriotic women's groups also lobbied for the passage of Rogers's bill.

The WAAC bill was passed in 1942. Two years later, Rogers helped draft the GI Bill of Rights. After the war, she was among those who supported legislation that would make a women's corps a permanent part of the Army. In 1950, the American Legion presented Rogers with its Distinguished Service Medal. She continued to serve Congress until her death from a heart attack in 1960.

See also
H.R. 4906; GI Bill of Rights.

References
Army Center of Military History, "History of the Women's Army Corps, 1942–1978" (1989); "Edith Nourse Rogers" (obituary), *New York Times* (11 September 1960); G. J. Barker-Benfield and Catherine Clinton, *Portraits of American Women* (1991); Dorothy and Carl J. Schneider, *Into the Breach: American Women in World War I* (1991); Mattie E. Treadwell, *U.S. Army in World War II: Special Studies—The Women's Army Corps* (1954).

"Rosie the Riveter"

Rosie became the symbol of women who worked in factories and defense plants during World War II while most male workers had joined the armed services. By doing jobs previously held by men in metalwork and on machinery, including the building of aircraft and ships, women kept the nation's factories operating.

Rosie was popularized in the song "Rosie the Riveter," written by Redd Evans and John Jacob Loeb. It was first heard in February 1943, performed by a male singing group, the Four Vagabonds. It became a popular selection on the radio and was featured in the motion pictures *Follow the Band* (1943) and *Rosie the Riveter* (1944).

According to Evans and Loeb, they chose the name Rosie because it sounded good with *riveter* and not because they personally knew a woman worker by that name. Throughout the nation, real-life Rosies worked in the factories—riveter Rose Bonavita of Peekskill, New York, among them.

Pictures of sturdy-looking women wearing overalls and building planes and ships appeared on posters and billboards. American artist Norman Rockwell painted a romanticized version of Rosie for a *Saturday Evening Post* cover issued on 29 May 1943. A 19-year-old telephone operator from Arlington, Vermont, posed for Rockwell's painting, which has been reproduced numerous times since then.

Some historians have noted that it is misleading to focus on Rosie as a typical wartime woman, since most American women remained homemakers during the war. Thousands of riveters and others helped build the hundreds of thousands of airplanes, tanks, pieces of artillery, warships, and munitions used by the armed forces during those years, however, and they changed public attitudes about what work women could successfully do.

See also
Defense Plant Workers; Kaiser Shipyard; Rhoads Dress.

References
Karen Anderson, *Wartime Women: Sex Roles, Family Relations and the Status of Women during World War II* (1981); Penny Colman, *Rosie the Riveter* (1995); Miriam Frank, Marilyn Ziebarth, and Connie Field, *The Life and Times of Rosie the Riveter* (1990); Ruth Milkman, *Gender at Work: The Dynamics of Job Segregation by Sex during World War II* (1987); Sheila Tobias and Lisa Anderson, "Whatever Happened to Rosie the Riveter?," *Ms.* (June 1973).

Ross, Betsy (1752–1836)

Legend has it that Betsy Ross made the first American flag, but this has never been proven. Born Elizabeth Griscom, Betsy married John Ross in 1774. After his death two years later, she ran their upholstery shop, sewing to earn money. Betsy Ross continued to work as a seamstress throughout her life and may have sewn some flags used by the government.

Ross remarried in 1776, but her second husband, Joseph Ashburn, died in 1782. Eliza, one of her two children by Ashburn, survived childhood. In 1783, Ross was married again, this time to John Claypoole, with whom she had five daughters. After a long illness, Claypoole died in 1817.

The story about Ross making the first American flag apparently emanated from her descendants. Addressing the Pennsylvania Historical Society, William J. Canby, Ross's grandson, said that Ross had told this story to him while she was on her deathbed. Other descendants testified that she had told them the same story, but nobody had actually seen her make the flag.

No official records could be found to verify the story. It was discovered that George Washington, who is said to have asked Ross to make the flag, was not in Philadelphia during the time he was alleged to have visited her at the upholstery shop.

A painting depicting Ross sewing the first "Stars and Stripes" was created by Charles H. Weisberger during the 1890s. Called *Birth of Our Nation's Flag*, it shows Ross displaying the flag she has made to a committee from Congress. Historians have noted that, until recent decades, the story about Ross and the flag has dominated other fact-based and extraordinary contribu-

Betsy Ross shows the first American flag to General George Washington (left). The story that Ross sewed the nation's first flag is legendary in American history even though no records have ever verified the claim.

tions women actually made in the Revolutionary War effort.

Reference

Selma Williams, *Demeter's Daughters: The Women Who Founded America* (1976).

Rossi, Marie T. (1969–1991)

One of the first women to fly in a combat area, Major Marie T. Rossi was killed in the Persian Gulf War when her Chinook helicopter crashed on 1 March 1991, killing Rossi and three crew members. It was the day after a cease-fire had been declared, bringing an end to the conflict.

A native of Oradell, New Jersey, Rossi graduated from high school in 1976 and attended Dickinson College in Carlisle, Pennsylvania, as a psychology major. A natural leader, she joined the Army ROTC program and found that she enjoyed the military. When she graduated in 1980, Rossi was commissioned as a second lieutenant.

Rossi's first duty station was Fort Bliss, Texas, where she served as an artillery officer before completing a rotary-wing flight program. She became a pilot in 1986 and flew Chinook helicopters in South Korea. Promoted to major in 1990, she married John Cayton, a special-operations pilot in the Army. Cayton was assigned to the Gulf, too, but in a different location than Rossi.

In the Persian Gulf War, Rossi was one of the first pilots to go into enemy territory, ferrying ammunition, troops, supplies, and fuel to the battlefront. On the night of the crash, flying her helicopter in bad weather, she hit the side of an unlit microwave tower in northern Saudi Arabia. She was later buried with honors at Arlington National Cemetery, the only woman casualty (out of 13) from that war to receive such recognition.

Reference

Molly Moore, "Women in the Battlefield—Gulf War Helps Bring Shift in Attitude," *Washington Post* (16 June 1991): 1, A16.

Rostker v. Goldberg

In 1980, Bernard Rostker brought this case before the Third Circuit U.S. Court of Appeals, asking them to stop a planned registration of men for the draft since it excluded women. The United States Supreme Court agreed to hear the case to determine whether excluding women from the military registration and draft violated the equal protection clause of the Fourteenth Amendment to the U.S. Constitution.

Rostker had argued that the government should "ask young people to serve in the most fair and equitable way" and that by excluding women, the Selective Service System had excluded a part of the population that could make a "substantial contribution" to America's defense effort. Opposing Rostker, witnesses for the Selective Service and Department of Defense said they should be free to design their own system, one that allowed them to determine how to use individuals and attain military efficiency.

In 1981, in a decision written by Justice William H. Rehnquist, the Court upheld this sex-based classification by a vote of six to three. The Court said that the government could draft men and require them to register with the Selective Service without requiring the same of women.

The decision was criticized by many, including the National Organization for Women (NOW), which said that the obligation to serve should be borne by both men and women, rather than allowing women alone to serve only as a matter of choice. Some analysts believe that the *Rostker* decision, made at a time when women's roles in the military were more limited, would not survive after various combat restrictions were lifted in the 1990s.

See also

All-Volunteer Force (AVF); Discrimination, Sexual; Draft.

S

Salvation Army

The Salvation Army, an international religious organization founded in 1865, has been involved in many charitable efforts that aim to help people regardless of race, color, or religion. The American branch, started by a group of members from England, began operating in 1880 in New York City.

During World War I, the Salvation Army provided various services to Allied military personnel, including operating mobile canteens throughout Europe from which women volunteers served doughnuts and coffee. The workers also mended clothing, consoled those in need, and provided religious services for people who wished to attend.

After the war, President Woodrow Wilson presented Commander Evangeline Booth, daughter of the British founder of the organization, with a Distinguished Service Medal for the Salvation Army's contributions.

The American branch of the Salvation Army ran more than 3,000 war service units during World War II. Among these were 1,000 mobile canteens on 26 battlefronts in Europe, many staffed by women.

See also
Booth, Evangeline; Volunteers.

References
Evangeline Booth and Grace Livingstone Hill, *The War Romance of the Salvation Army* (1919); Dorothy and Carl J. Schneider, *Into the Breach: American Women Overseas in World War I* (1991).

Sampson, Deborah (1760–1827)

During the American Revolution, Deborah Sampson posed as a man and joined the Continental Army. Blonde, blue-eyed, and large-boned, she had a muscular build after years of helping her widowed mother with farm chores at their home in Plympton, Massachusetts. At age ten, Deborah was placed as a domestic servant with a family in Middleboro, where she received an education as well as room and board.

At age 19, Sampson began working as a teacher, but by 1782, she felt drawn to serve her country in the Revolution. With her hair cut short and wearing a brown man's suit she had sewn, Sampson walked 70 miles to Worcester, where she enlisted as Robert Shurtleff.

Knowing her family would worry, Sampson wrote a letter saying she was fine and had joined "a large but well-regulated family." She fought with the Fourth Massachusetts Regiment (known as the Massachusetts Regiment of Foot) for 18 months. The regiment marched to West Point and fought near New York City, still in British hands at the time, even though colonial troops had won the Battle of Yorktown. Near the Tappan Zee in Westchester, Sampson was stabbed in the head. Her comrades later said that Sampson had been brave, shooting and swinging her musket during the skirmish. She went into the woods alone to treat her own wound.

At an ambush in nearby New Rochelle, Sampson was shot in the thigh and lay in the field as surgeons began treating the wounded. To avoid being found out, she crawled toward a woody ravine where she lay for several days, washing and bandaging her own wound. The musketball remained in her leg as she went on to fight in other battles.

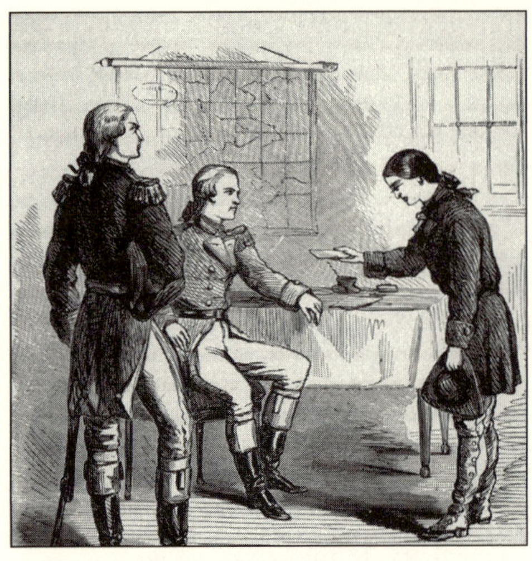

Deborah Sampson, dressed in male attire, presents a letter to George Washington during the Revolutionary War. Sampson fought with the Fourth Massachusetts Regiment for a year before her true identity was discovered.

Impressed by Sampson's performance, General Patterson chose "Private Shurtleff" as his orderly. While in Philadelphia with Paterson, she contracted a high fever and complications from the musketball that remained in her leg. The doctor who treated her realized she was a woman but agreed to keep her secret and later moved her into his house. Local women, however, smitten with "Mr. Shurtleff," were interested in marrying the houseguest.

The doctor then told her commander who Sampson really was. General Patterson was somewhat amused and asked Sampson to stand with him, dressed in an ordinary woman's gown, as he reviewed her regiment. The men did not recognize her.

Honorably discharged on 23 October 1783, Sampson went on to marry Benjamin Gannet, and they reared three children on their New England farm. In 1802, Sampson took to the lecture circuit wearing her military uniform and gave public talks about her experiences. She may have been the first paid woman lecturer in the nation.

Although Sampson suffered from war-related health problems, she was not entitled to the $4-a-month pension that was given to male veterans. Paul Revere was among those who wrote to Congress on Sampson's behalf. In 1805, she was finally granted the pension, along with two years of back payments. After she died on 29 April, 1827, Congress passed a special act to grant her husband the $80 annual pension customarily given to the widows of wounded veterans.

See also
Combat; Passing.

References
Elizabeth Anticaglia, *Heroines of '76* (1975); Elizabeth Evans, *Weathering the Storm: Women of the American Revolution* (1975); Lucy Freeman and Alma H. Bond, *America's First Woman Warrior: The Courage of Deborah Sampson* (1992); Edith Patterson Meyer, *Petticoat Patriots of the American Revolution* (1976); Beth Millstein and Jeanne Bodine, *We, the American Women, a Documentary History* (1977); R. B. Morris, ed., *The American Revolution 1763–1783* (1985); "Private Robert Shurtleff, Well-Camouflaged Fighter," *New York Times* (15 August 1992); Mollie Somerville, *Women of the American Revolution* (1974); Selma Williams, *Demeter's Daughters: The Women Who Founded America* (1976).

Scouts

Women acted as scouts during the American Revolution and Civil War. Often, they knew the countryside of frontier areas well enough to inform military officers or to lead them through. In 1777, Jinnie Waglum led Washington's troops along an uncommon route from Trenton to Princeton, New Jersey, in order to avoid British patrols on the main roads. The group arrived with Waglum in the lead, dressed in military hat and coat. On 3 January, Washington's forces surprised British troops in Princeton and were able to push the enemy back toward New Brunswick. During later frontier days, other women scouts aided U.S. troops who were fighting groups of Native Americans.

See also
Bailey, Anne; Tubman, Harriet.

References
Edith Patterson Meyer, *Petticoat Patriots of the American Revolution* (1976); Mollie Somerville, *Women of the American Revolution* (1974).

Sea Duty

One of the longest and most controversial debates in the military has been over whether women should be assigned to sea duty. In the Navy, assignments at sea have been pivotal in receiving promotions and building a successful career. Being banned from sea duty was thus a long-standing barrier to women's naval careers.

The ban on sea duty was written into Section 6015, Title 10, of the Women's Armed Services Integration Act of 1948. Written by the Armed Services Committee and reflecting attitudes then prevalent in society and the military, the law stated that women would not serve on naval vessels except hospital and transport ships.

In 1961, the first woman in the Navy received an assignment as an assistant transportation officer on a naval transport ship. During the Vietnam War, more than 300 Navy nurses served on hospital ships, but by 1971, opportunities for women to go to sea had vanished. That year, women became more insistent about sea duty. During the 1970s, they found an ally in the progressive chief of Naval Operations, Admiral Elmo Zumwalt, who was opening other doors for women. The Defense Advisory Council on Women in the Services (DACOWITS) and others urged Zumwalt to let women serve aboard Navy ships.

Women soon began training in seagoing specialties, for example as boatswain's mates and signalmen, and in 1972, the Navy assigned an integrated crew to the former hospital ship, USS *Sanctuary*, to give women a chance to develop their skills. Besides serving as nurses, corps members, and in other health-related jobs, women on the *Sanctuary* worked in supply, operations, and administration, among other departments, demonstrating they could perform these jobs well. Plans called for the ship to provide health care for Navy dependents overseas, but it was only at sea a short time before anchoring in Florida. Used only for training thereafter, the *Sanctuary* was removed from service in 1975.

Opposition to posting women at sea came from both men and women, including Zumwalt's colleague, Assistant Chief of Naval Personnel for Women, Captain Robin L. Quigley. Writing in the May 1977 issue of *Seapower* magazine, Quigley said that young American women, accustomed to comforts and conveniences, would have trouble tolerating "the uncommodious, spartan, unrelieved, and physically demanding life of months aboard a destroyer or a fleet oiler. . . ." The Navy also received complaints from the spouses of men in the Navy who objected to their husbands being assigned to ships that included women in their crews.

In 1974, Yona Owens filed a lawsuit on behalf of herself and three other Navy women who considered themselves victims of sex discrimination. Owens had been denied a position on a naval survey ship, despite the fact that her superiors had recommended her as the best-qualified for the job. In 1978, a district court ruled in Owens's favor, saying that Section 6015 was unconstitutional.

In the meantime, the Coast Guard had mixed crews serving on two cutters, the *Morgenthau* and *Gallantin.* Female officers and enlisted women began their tours of duty on these ships in 1977 and made up about 13 percent of each crew. That year the Navy sponsored an amended Title 10 of the U.S. Code, Section 6015, to allow permanent assignment of women to noncombatant ships, which Congress approved the following year.

Going to sea on 1 November 1978 as part of the Women in Ships program, eight ensigns became the first Navy women assigned to duty aboard ships (in both the Atlantic and Pacific). Within months, 55 women officers and 375 enlisted women had been assigned to sea duty on repair ships and other vessels not related to combat.

By mid-1982, there were 193 women officers aboard 30 Navy ships from a total of 2,185 female military personnel on 37 ships. Submarine duty remained closed to women, along with other combatant vessels, but in 1988, a woman was selected for command at sea for the first time. In 1989, the Navy assigned its first female command master chief at sea, and 24 Combat Logistics Force (CLF) ships were opened to women.

There were more gains for women during the 1990s. In 1990, Darlene Iskra became the first woman to assume command of a ship, the USS *Opportune.* In October 1994, the carrier USS *Eisenhower* was deployed with women permanently assigned to the crew—another first. Of the 5,500 people on board, 500 were women. The ship left Norfolk, Virginia, and spent six months in the Mediterranean.

See also
Combat; Combat Exclusion Law; *Owens v. Brown*; Quigley, Robin L.; United States Navy.

References
Jeanne Holm, *Women in the Military: An Unfinished Revolution* (1992); U.S. Department of the Navy, "History of 'Firsts' of Women in the Navy" (1995); Jean Zimmerman, *Tailspin: Women at War in the Wake of Tailhook* (1995).

Selective Service

See All-Volunteer Force (AVF); Draft; *Rostker v. Goldberg*.

Service Medal

See Medals.

Serviceman's Readjustment Act of 1944

Known as the GI Bill of Rights, or simply the GI Bill, the Serviceman's Readjustment Act of 1944 was intended to give ex-servicemen benefits to help them resume their lives after World War II. The text of the bill stated that educational allowances and financial assistance in obtaining loans for homes, farms, and businesses would help ex-GIs "make up for time and opportunities lost." They included tuition and allowances for books, supplies, and living expenses at a college or vocational school.

Some women who had served during the war took advantage of the GI Bill, but the majority did not. The Veterans Administration did not keep complete statistics regarding women's use of GI benefits. It is believed that married women often chose not to use their benefits because they returned home to raise families, while single women may have had to forgo college in order to make a living.

See also
GI Bill of Rights.

Sexism

See Discrimination, Sexual.

Sexual Harassment

Sexual harassment has been defined as the making of unwanted, uninvited remarks or physical advances of a sexual nature. Such behavior in the workplace may be most threatening when perpetrated by a person of higher rank or position who has power over the victim's job security or opportunities for promotion. Harassment can also impair job performance by causing embarrassment and humiliation to the victim. Harassment may be directed toward individuals or women as a group, in which case it may create a hostile work environment for the women in a particular setting.

All branches of the military have rules forbidding sexual harassment and provide for the punishment of offenders. The various services have also developed sexual harassment programs that are used during training and have stated a "zero tolerance" policy regarding sexual harassment in the military.

Even so, sexual harassment has continued to be a problem as people struggle to define it clearly and understand its root causes. Researchers conclude that sexual harassment may occur because of the confined nature of military life and the fact that people share close quarters. They also think this is one way in which men express hostility about the presence of women in a formerly all-male arena.

Throughout the years, sexual harassment may have caused numerous women to leave the military. According to author Cynthia Enloe, "The higher attrition rates that women display may have little to do with pregnancy and a lot to do with frustration at being the targets of sexually harassing jokes, innuendos, and retaliations on the job."

Although women had complained about such harassment for decades, the first military study of sexual harassment was conducted in 1980. Other studies were conducted during the 1980s, but many women complained that changes were implemented slowly or not at all.

Women in the military have different ideas about what constitutes sexual harassment and how to cope with it. After interviewing a number of women in the Army after the invasion of Panama in 1989, sociologist Charles Moskos wrote that enlisted women tended to define harassment "in terms of sexual propositions and actual touching." Officers saw the problem as more broad, including sexist remarks and sex-based definitions of suitable work in their description of sexual harassment.

Complaints of sexual harassment increased dramatically in all service branches during the 1990s, as women complained about incidents involving both sexes, as well as homosexual overtures. The most notorious sexual harassment incidents took place at a convention of naval officers in 1991. The annual "Tailhook" convention, which was first held in the 1950s, had been described as a three-day drinking and sex binge. At the 1991 meeting, at least 83 women claimed they were abused while trying to walk through the hotel corridors. The resulting scandal, known as Tailhook, led the secretary of the Navy and chief of naval operations to resign. Officers who had been at the convention suppressed information, however, and nobody was court-martialed afterwards.

In *Fall from Glory*, author Gregory L. Vistica states that between 1992 and 1996, the Department of the Navy recorded more than 1,000 new sexual harassment complaints and more than 3,500 charges of sexual assault. The assault charges ranged from undesired touching to rape. This is almost three times the national rate for such charges, and Vistica also believes many incidents go unreported because women have learned to fear reprisals if they file complaints.

In 1994, Congress held hearings on sexual harassment in the military. Women who testified at these hearings later complained that they had been subjected to retaliation, both after reporting incidents of harassment and then after they began testifying. Air Force Sergeant Zanaida Martinez contended that in 1990 and 1992, she had been subjected to harassment in which two different sergeants in her unit urged her to engage in unwanted sexual relationships. After refusing and then reporting their behavior to her superiors, she said she had experienced reprisals in the form of slashed car tires and poor evaluations, among other things.

In June 1994, Martinez told the *New York Times* that when she returned to her base after meeting with lawyers prior to a scheduled March 9 hearing before the House Armed Services Committee, she was interrogated by base officials. Martinez cited lawyer-client privilege as a reason not to divulge information. Shortly thereafter, she was told she was under criminal investigation related to her travel expenses—the use of a taxi rather than a bus on a recent business trip.

At a naval training center in San Diego, 16 women trainees complained that seven instructors had demanded sexual favors in return for passing grades. The Navy began investigating these charges in October 1994.

Democratic Congresswoman Pat Schroeder of Colorado, a member of the House Armed Services Committee, said, "This is astounding . . . ; I can't believe this just goes on and on and on."

Women at military service academies have also complained of sexual harassment. During the 1980s, seven faculty members at the United States Naval Academy, led by Associate Professor of History Jane Good, conducted a study at the school and determined that sexual harassment was the main reason most female students left before graduation. Two-thirds of the women midshipmen identified harassment as a major problem. They described many incidents that created what would come under the definition of a "hostile environment"—the viewing of pornographic movies in common areas of the academy, obscene electronic mail messages, and the use of language that degraded women. The study was widely publicized, but no actions were taken along the lines recommended by the research team.

In October 1994, women cadets at the United States Military Academy (USMA) at West Point alleged that they had been fondled improperly by members of the Army's football team during a pep rally. Lieutenant General Howard Graves, superintendent of the academy, ordered an internal investigation and reported the situation to the press, saying, "Openness and candor are best not only for America, but for the cadets, too. We've learned the lesson of Tailhook." Early in November, USMA officials announced that, for their inappropriate behavior, three male cadets had been suspended from the team for the remainder of the football season, restricted to the grounds of the academy for 90 days, and given 80 hours of marching discipline.

Critics, including Representative Pat Schroeder, found this punishment too lenient. There were also complaints that only a few of the perpetrators were being punished. Superintendent Graves said the investigators had interviewed hundreds of football players and cadets. He told reporters, "Many of the women involved in this incident made it clear they didn't want their classmates expelled. They just wanted the behavior to stop."

See also
Coughlin, Paula; Hazing; Tailhook.

References
Francis X. Clines, "Army Cadets Face a Charge of Harassment," *New York Times* (1 November 1994): A1, B2; Cynthia Enloe, *Does Khaki Become You? The Militarization of Women's Lives* (1983); Nina Gilden, *Countering Sexual Harassment: Theory and Applications for the Department of Defense* (March 1981); Raymond Hernandez, "3 Suspended for Groping at West Point," *New York Times* (5 November 1994): 25–26; Tom Morgenthau et al., "The Military Fights Its Gender Wars," *Newsweek* (14 November 1994): 35–37; Kenneth B. Noble, "Closing Arguments in Tailhook Lawsuit," *New York Times* (28 November 1994): A22; Eric Schmitt, "Air Force Sergeant in a Sex Complaint Tells of Reprisals," *New York Times* (10 June 1994): A1, A21; Gregory L. Vistica, *Fall from Glory* (1996); Jean Zimmerman, *Tailspin: Women at War in the Wake of Tailhook* (1995).

Sexual Preferences

Military regulations have long banned homosexuals from enlisting and remaining in the service. Men and women who were known to be homosexuals have been discharged. Others who were not known have served, often achieving outstanding records. Until the mid-1990s, revealing homosexuality meant the loss of one's military career, so the vast majority of homosexuals in the military, male and female, did not openly state their sexual orientation. Thus there are no accurate statistics about how many homosexual women have served in the military.

Throughout history, women in the military have had to deal with social prejudices and biased attitudes about appropriate female roles. Men who resent their presence and have trouble coping with the idea of strong, independent women have sometimes said that servicewomen must be either lesbians or whores. Women were sometimes put in a bind in which men would label them as "lesbians" if they resisted their advances and "loose women" if they acquiesced. These attitudes impeded the recruitment of qualified women during World War II, and the Army even undertook an investigation to track down the source of negative rumors about women in the Army.

Their morals questioned, military women have often been expected to prove they were feminine, presenting a certain type of appearance while performing difficult jobs with strength, courage, and competence. Writing about the confusing and ambivalent attitudes toward homosexuals in the military, Cynthia Enloe asks,

> Is it safer to have women who will "fraternize with", "use their charms on" men, get pregnant, and taint the masculine force with their traces of lipstick? Or is it better to have women who will pursue their military careers out of self-generated enthusiasm but who will also use the military as a place to develop emotional attachments among themselves, threaten the male soldiers' sense of masculine sexual self-confidence and offend civilian society?

The debate over this issue reached a new peak during the 1992 presidential campaign, with many people arguing that bans against homosexuals serving in the military were unconstitutional and patently unfair. Performance of duties, not sexual preferences, should be the issue, they claimed.

Bill Clinton, who was elected president that year, supported the idea of lifting such bans. He pointed out that homosexual men and women had long served in the military and that sexual orientation was irrelevant to one's ability to serve.

After Clinton took office, Congress held new debates on this divisive issue, with heated arguments about whether or not gay and lesbian individuals should be banned from the military. A compromise—the "don't ask, don't tell" approach—was reached.

See also
Appearance; Cammermeyer, Margarethe; Hollen, Andrea; Sexual Harassment.

References
Margarethe Cammermeyer, *Serving in Silence* (1994); Cynthia Enloe, *Does Khaki Become You? The Militarization of Women's Lives* (1983); Elaine Tylor May, *Pushing the Limits: American Women 1940–1961* (1994); Randy Shilts, *Conduct Unbecoming: Lesbians and Gays in the U.S. Military: Vietnam to the Persian Gulf* (1993); Carol Wekesser and Matthew Polesetsky, eds., *Women in the Military* (1991).

Sexual Quota

At various times, the military has set quotas to reach a certain number of women in various divisions or to limit the number of women to a certain percentage of the people in the service. The Women's Armed Services Integration Act of 1948 integrated women into the armed services but set a 2 percent ceiling on the number of women who could serve. This limit was finally changed in 1967, and since the introduction of the All-Volunteer Force (AVF) in the 1970s, women are enlisted in the same way as men.

The use of quotas to attain a certain number of any group in a given position also has been controversial in other areas of American life, such as jobs and education. In the early 1990s, Colonel Patrick Toffler, a spokesman for the U.S. Military Academy (USMA) at West Point, stated that the USMA tried to attain a certain number of women cadets and, in order to reach that number, it compared women applicants to each other rather than to male applicants. The same system of comparing women to women was being used at graduation to plan assignments.

See also
Affirmative Action; Women's Armed Services Integration Act of 1948.
Reference
Carol Wekesser and Matthew Polesetsky, eds., *Women in the Military* (1991).

She Went to War

The 1992 book *She Went to War*, by Rhonda Cornum with Peter Copeland, describes Cornum's capture by Iraqi soldiers during the Persian Gulf War and her subsequent experiences as a prisoner of war. Cornum, an Army flight surgeon, was one of three survivors when her search-and-rescue helicopter was shot down over Iraqi territory on 27 February 1991. She became one of only two women to be captured as a prisoner of war since World War II.

See also
Cornum, Rhonda.

Signal Corps

In October 1917 during World War I, General John J. Pershing requested that French-speaking American women telephone operators be sent to France to fill an urgent need for bilingual operators to aid the American Expeditionary Forces (AEF) under his command. In answer to his request, 200 went overseas to serve with the AEF as civilian contract employees in the Signal Corps. Their status and benefits resembled those of women in the Army Nurse Corps.

During World War II, a larger number of women served with the Signal Corps as clerks, telephone operators, and those in charge of raising carrier pigeons. These women were members of the Women's Army Corps (WAC), so their status was that of veterans when the war ended.

See also
Public Law 95-202.
References
Dorothy and Carl J. Schneider, *Into the Breach: American Women Overseas in World War I* (1991); June A. Willenz, *Women Veterans: America's Forgotten Heroines* (1983).

Slater, Sarah (n.d.)

Sarah Slater became a Confederate spy during the Civil War and then managed to disappear after the war ended, although her family and government investigators tried to find her.

Slater was born in Connecticut, but her family, of French ancestry, later moved to North Carolina. There Sarah married a dance instructor, Rowan Slater, who enlisted in the Confederate Army after the war began. He left for the North Carolina infantry just 11 days after their wedding on 12 June 1861.

In January 1865, Slater decided to move to New York City where her mother was then living. Secretary of War John Alexander Seddon asked her to become a spy and courier, working with Confederate agents in Canada. Her ability to speak French and her northern ties made Slater a prime candidate for such a role.

During the early months of 1865, Slater completed two missions for the Confederacy. She embarked on the third mission in April. After leaving Richmond, she stopped to visit friends, including John Wilkes Booth, in Washington, D.C. She left the city with instructions to retrieve a large sum of Confederate money being held in Canada and take it to England for safekeeping.

From that day on, however, nobody reported hearing from or seeing Slater ever again. Had she met with foul play or decided to vanish on her own? Did she fear she might be implicated in Booth's assassination of President Lincoln? Did she keep the money herself and start a new life under a new identity? Historians have speculated about Slater's fate, but nobody has ever answered these questions.

References
John W. Headley, *Confederate Operations in Canada and New York* (1906); Harnett T. Kane, *Spies for the Blue and Gray* (1954); John E. Stanchak, *Historical Times Illustrated Encyclopedia of the Civil War* (1986).

Spanish-American War

The Spanish-American War, in which U.S. forces ousted the Spanish military government from Cuba, took place during 1898. The cause of Cuban independence had gained broad support in Congress, although two presidents, Grover Cleveland and William McKinley, opposed U.S. intervention. An explosion on the USS *Maine* on 15 February 1989 caused 266 deaths and brought the United States into the war, although the cause of the explosion was never found.

During the war, 5,000 more men died from disease than in battle, where the casualties numbered fewer than 1,000. Although the Army did not plan to utilize women, the spread of typhoid fever and yellow fever meant that there were not enough male nurses to deal with the crisis, and women were recruited. The surgeon general hired 1,158 women nurses under contract as civilians to serve in Army hospitals for $30 per month. They came from civilian hospitals as well as the Red Cross, religious orders of nursing sisters, and other organizations. These nurses served in the United States, Cuba, Puerto Rico, the Philippines, Hawaii, and China.

Medical officers praised the skill and devotion shown by the nurses who served in this capacity. Twelve nurses died of typhoid fever while in the service. One nurse, Clara Louise Maass, died of yellow fever in 1901 after volunteering for an army medical research experiment being conducted in Cuba.

The war led to a formal role for women in the armed services of the United States. After the war, the military decided to give nurses a quasi-military status (neither commissioned nor enlisted) as uniformed personnel under the Army Reorganization Act of 1901. Nurses continued to serve with the military around the world and on the hospital ship *Relief*. The Army nurses, as well as those who became part of the Navy when its nurse corps was organized in 1908, were appointed, not commissioned, into the service.

See also
Army Nurse Corps (ANC); Coleman, Kit; McGee, Anita Newcomb.

References
Maj. Edith Aynes, A.N.C., *From Nightingale to Eagle: The Army Nurses History* (1973); Mary A. Gardner Holland, ed., *Our Army Nurses* (1895); U.S. Army Department of Information, "Facts on the U.S. Army Nurse Corps, 1775–1983" (1989).

SPAR

Formed during World War II, SPAR was the name given to the Women's Reserve of the Coast Guard. The name stands for the Coast Guard motto, *Semper Paratus* ("always ready"). Public Law 772, signed by President Franklin D. Roosevelt on 23 November 1942, created the SPAR, which modeled itself on the Navy's Women Accepted for Voluntary Emergency Service (WAVES) and enlisted its first members, including director Dorothy C. Stratton, from the Navy.

Within weeks, posters urging "Enlist in the Coast Guard SPARs" and "Don't Be a Spare—Be a SPAR" could be seen on telephone poles and at post offices throughout the United States. Recruiters actively went about in mobile units seeking candidates. Applicants had to be between 20 and 36 years of age (age 50 was the limit for officers) and have no children under age 18. Officers must have completed two years of college, while two years of high school was the minimum educational requirement for enlisted women.

To combat social prejudices against women in uniform, SPAR officials made it clear that the women would be conducting themselves according to the highest standards while serving their country. Posters showed attractive, smiling young women wearing well-tailored uniforms. A SPAR facility located in Palm Beach was a major lure for young women who wanted to "train under the Florida sun," while those trained in New York City were able to experience the life of a large U.S. city. After their basic training, SPAR recruits received specialty training at other centers throughout the country.

Spars were allowed to serve outside the continental United States after 27 September 1944, and 200 corps members were sent to Alaska and Hawaii. Besides working in clerical positions and as storekeepers, the women served as machinist's mates, drivers, pharmacist's mates, assistants in sick bays, parachute riggers, chaplains' assistants, air control tower operators, boatswains' mates, coxswains, ship's cooks, and radiomen, among other roles.

African Americans had been kept out of both the SPAR and WAVES, but after a ruling by the secretary of the Navy in October 1944 reversed this policy, the first black woman Spar, Olivia Hooker, was recruited. Other African-American women completed Officer Candidate School (OCS) and were commissioned as ensigns.

The war was coming to an end, and in December 1944, recruitment efforts stopped. The SPAR also was in its last days. Most of the 12,000 Spars then serving returned to civilian life, but a few remained to complete projects they had already begun. As the SPAR was demobilized after the war, its records were not even kept.

A group of Spars, the Women's Reserve of the Coast Guard, sit on a boom of a Coast Guard schooner in Boston Harbor in 1943. In order to serve in the SPARs program, women had to be between the ages of 20 and 36 and could not have any children under 18.

Former Spars asked to return to duty during the Korean War, but the Women's Reserve was basically inactive until the late 1950s. By the 1960s, women were working toward a permanent role in the Coast Guard, which finally became a reality in 1973.

See also
Stratton, Dorothy C.; United States Coast Guard; World War II.

References
John A. Tilley, *A History of Women in the Coast Guard* (1996); U.S. Coast Guard Public Information Division, *The Coast Guard at War, Vol. XXII: Women's Reserve* (1946); Doris Weatherford, *American Women and World War II* (1990).

Sparkman Bill

Signed into law on 16 April 1943, the Sparkman Bill permitted women physicians to serve in the military for the first time. Congressman John Sparkman of Alabama had introduced the bill in an effort to increase the number of qualified physicians available to serve in the military during World War II.

Women physicians, led by supporters such as Emily Dunning Barringer, had worked for such a bill for more than two years. Opposition came from people who believed it would embarrass men to be examined and treated by women doctors and those who said women doctors could not handle the stresses of combat duty.

See also
Army Medical Corps (AMC); Barringer, Emily Dunning; Physicians.
References
Ruth Abram, *"Send Us a Lady Physician": Women Doctors in America, 1835–1920* (1985); Esther Pohl Lovejoy, *Women Doctors of the World* (1957).

Spying
See Espionage.

Standing Committee on Women in the Navy and Marine Corps
See Tailhook.

Stinsin, Kathrine
See Pilots.

Strategic Air Command (SAC)
Created in 1947 as a key part of U.S. defense operations, the Strategic Air Command (SAC) is under the direction of the Air Force and is made up of missile warning and space surveillance systems.

Until 1974, women had not been part of any missile crews with the SAC. Opponents said that mixed crews might lower morale and upset the spouses of men on the crews. In addition, they said it would be expensive to change the underground silos where the two-person crews stayed during their shifts. A few years later, in 1979, positions as launch officers and missile crew members were opened to women, when the first women entered Titan missile training and were assigned as combat crew commanders and deputy commanders.

Reference
Jeanne Holm, *Women in the Military: An Unfinished Revolution* (1992).

Stratton, Dorothy C. (b. 1898)
Born in 1898 in Brookfield, Missouri, Dorothy Stratton was graduated from Ottawa University in Kansas with a bachelor of arts degree in 1920. She taught in high schools while pursuing her master's degree in psychology (from the University of Chicago) and her doctorate (from Columbia University). Stratton joined the faculty of Purdue University in Indiana in 1933, in the position of dean of women and professor of psychology.

At the start of World War II, Stratton was serving as lieutenant in the Naval Reserve, but she left that branch of service to become the first director of SPAR (Women Reserves in the United States Coast Guard) on 24 November 1942 as Captain Stratton.

The SPAR was established on 24 November 1942 when President Franklin Roosevelt signed Public Law 772, which stated that, in order to release more men for duty at sea, women would replace them "in the shore establishment of the Coast Guard and for other purposes." It was Stratton's idea to give the women's corps its name, which comes from the Coast Guard motto—*Semper Paratus*—"Always Ready."

After the war, in recognition of her service, Stratton received the American Theater and Victory Ribbons along with the Coast Guard Legion of

Dorothy Stratton

Merit medal. She worked in the federal Retraining and Reemployment Administration, assigned to make sure women veterans received consideration as they returned to their former communities and jobs, then returned to her former positions at Purdue. Later, Stratton served as director of personnel for the International Monetary Fund (IMF) and spent ten years as national executive director of the Girl Scouts.

Stratton was at hand in 1992 when the Coast Guard marked the fiftieth anniversary of the founding of SPAR, which brought women oficially into the Coast guard. Stratton said, "we note with awe and respect, the widened opportunities the current women who are serving in the Coast Guard have."

See also
SPAR; United States Coast Guard; World War II.

References
Robin J. Thomson, *The Coast Guard & Women's Reserve in World War II* (1992); John A. Tilley, *A History of Women in the Coast Guard* (1996); U.S. Coast Guard Public Information Division, *The Coast Guard at War, Vol. XXII: Women's Reserve* (1946); U.S. Department of the Army Fact Sheet, "Dorothy C. Stratton" (1989); June A. Willenz, *Women Veterans: America's Forgotten Heroines* (1983).

Streeter, Ruth Cheney (1895–1990)

Colonel Streeter was named director of the Women's Marine Corps Reserve when it was mobilized on 13 February 1943 to meet the increased needs for Marine personnel during World War II.

Prior to her appointment, Streeter had been active in health and social welfare work and had served on the New Jersey State Defense Council. She also was an experienced pilot who had worked for a commercial airline and held a private license as well. The mother of four children, Streeter had three sons serving in the armed forces, two in the Army and one in the Navy.

As director of the Women Marines, Streeter had the rank of major and planned and organized the women's corps, integrating it into the basic structure of the overall United States Marine Corps. Streeter supervised the selection, training programs (which included firing antiaircraft guns and dropping from parachute towers), and assignments of the women. Streeter promoted the idea that not only did women learn valuable skills while serving but they also developed important aspects of their personalities that would enhance whatever they did in the future.

In December 1945, Colonel Streeter resigned from the military to resume civilian life. She received the Legion of Merit Award for outstanding performance of duty.

See also
United States Marines; World War II.
References
Judy Barrett Litoff and David C. Smith, *We're in This War, Too: World War II Letters from American Women in Uniform* (1994); "Our Hand of Fellowship to Returning G.I. Janes," *Independent Woman* (July 1945): 203ff; Peter A. Soderburg, *Women Marines: The World War II Era* (1992).

Stringer, Ann (1909–1988)

A World War II correspondent for the United Press International (UPI) News Service, Ann Stringer managed to file a number of exclusive stories from Europe during that war, including news of the arrival of Russian troops at the Elbe River in April 1945.

The Texas-born Stringer graduated from the University of Texas in 1940 and hoped to work for UPI, as did her husband William (Bill) J. Stringer. After proving her skills as a reporter on the staff of Ohio's *Columbus Citizen*, Stringer got the job she wanted.

Ann and Bill Stringer were both foreign correspondents for UPI in New York City and Buenos Aires, and they planned to cover World War II together. Bill Stringer went overseas first but was killed by a sniper's bullet while driving his jeep through Versailles, France, shortly before Ann arrived in Paris.

Although grief-stricken, Ann Stringer decided to go on with her work as planned. By April 1945, she had blasted a number of rules and overcome stiff opposition in London in order to get to the front. She had been assigned to the First Army press camp in Germany and went on to other areas before military officials ordered her to head back to Paris.

Instead of returning to Paris, Stringer joined photographer Allan Jackson to fly over the Elbe River area of Germany. They landed, took pictures, and found out that Russian troops were on their way, another sign that an Allied victory was imminent. Stringer was able to get to Paris and file her story, which was a headliner back in the United States. She later recalled, "I had been under enemy fire, and it can be terrifying. Why I didn't get scared to death, I don't know. But there was a sense of friendship, exhilaration, and joy."

While still in Europe, Stringer witnessed the joyous victory celebrations held in France after Germany surrendered, as well as the grim sights at a former Nazi death camp, Nordhausen. While accompanying Allied troops that liberated the camp, Stringer saw people who had been buried alive under piles of bodies and others who were starving and near death. She moved on to Vienna, then drove herself to Budapest to report on postwar life there before moving on to Yugoslavia. Stringer also covered the war crime trials at Nuremberg and reported on conditions in other German cities after the war.

In 1949, Stringer married Hank Ries. Their book, *German Faces*, with photographs by Ries and text by Stringer, was published in 1950. Stringer gave up her writing career during the marriage, but after divorcing 30 years later, she returned to writing and was active in the Overseas Press Club.

See also
Correspondents, War.
References
Julia Edwards, *Women of the World: The Great Foreign Correspondents* (1988); Ann Stringer and Henry Ries, *German Faces* (1950).

Submarines

For women in the Navy, submarine duty remained one of the few duty assignments off-limits after the combat exclusion rules were abolished by Congress in 1992. As of 1995, women could not serve on SEAL (SEa Air Land) commando units or on submarines and minesweepers, but were able to serve in other Navy combat positions.

See also
Sea Duty; United States Navy.
Reference
Jean Zimmerman, *Tailspin: Women at War in the Wake of Tailhook* (1995).

Tailhook

Named for the aircraft landing hook that catches onto carrier-deck cables during carrier landings, the nonprofit Tailhook Association, founded in 1957, is a group of naval aircraft-carrier aviators. Tailhook's annual three-day convention, which features lectures, symposia, and display booths, has gained a reputation for being a hell-raising affair, with heavy drinking, strippers, prostitutes, and property damage to hotels sponsoring the convention.

The 1992 Tailhook convention made news headlines and provided a scandal. About 2,500 Marine and Navy fighter pilots attended the convention in Las Vegas that September, some of them women pilots. Analysts have since concluded that the mood at the convention was influenced by the fact that in the weeks before Tailhook, the Senate had passed a bill asking a presidential commission to review combat restriction laws as they applied to women and another bill to remove combat restrictions for female pilots. Male pilots at the convention who strongly opposed women combat pilots may have been feeling especially resentful toward women during those weeks, according to author Jean Zimmerman and others.

Women reported that while walking down the third-floor corridor of the Las Vegas Hilton Hotel on Saturday, 7 September (the last night of the convention), they were assaulted by dozens of servicemen. Women's clothing was pulled or removed and their breasts and other body parts were touched, and several were drenched when drinks were poured on their faces and bodies. Although women reported that they objected and fought off the men, the assaults continued. Several women said they were terrified, fearing they would be gang-raped.

Two civilian women filed a police report the next day and complained to a hotel security guard about the incident, but they felt these officials did not show much concern. Lieutenant Paula Coughlin, an accomplished naval pilot then serving as an admiral's aide, also decided to report her experience on the third floor. Coughlin reported trying desperately to fight off male attackers who grabbed her rear end, breasts, and other parts of her body, pinching, pushing, and biting her. People stood by and ignored Coughlin's pleas for help.

It was also discovered that an underage girl who became drunk that night and passed out was stripped of her clothing. A photograph of this girl later turned up during an investigation of Tailhook.

As 26 women came forward with their stories, the Navy launched an investigation that was completed in May 1992. The results did not satisfy some critics, including Assistant Secretary of the Navy Barbara Pope. Pope was among those who were astonished that the report, which contained more than 2,000 pages of exhibits and weighed more than 15 pounds, identified only two perpetrators against whom charges could be brought. Among those who had testified were two naval aviators who tried to steer women away from the male gauntlet on the third floor, only to be accosted by another man who told them they should leave if they didn't like what was going on.

Secretary of the Navy Lawrence Garrett sent memos stating that more of the men involved in the assaults should be referred to the chain of command for "appropriate action." Garrett stated that a number of naval officers had violated the standards of conduct and behaved inappropriately. He also asked that squadron commanders be questioned about how these events could have been allowed to unfold. In addition, Garrett proposed setting up what became the Standing Committee on Women in the Navy and Marine Corps.

Another Navy investigation was ordered, and the Department of Defense decided to conduct an investigation of its own. Congress ordered yet a fourth investigation, run by the House Armed Services Committee, whose members included Congresswoman Pat Schroeder of Colorado, an outspoken opponent of sexual harassment and supporter of opening more combat positions to women in the military. The press also was taking an active interest in Tailhook.

In the wake of the scandal, some top-ranking Navy officials resigned, including Secretary Garrett. President George Bush, a former Navy pilot and war hero himself, was disturbed after hearing about Tailhook and subsequently meeting with Paula Coughlin. He appointed Sean O'Keefe as the new secretary of the Navy. O'Keefe announced that he intended to take further action on Tailhook.

In the meantime, while he was serving as acting secretary, Under secretary of the Navy Dan Howard made a speech citing the need to "dismantle a decaying culture, a residual fabric of counter-productive and unworthy attitudes." He went on to state to this group of officers that "anyone who still believes in the image of a drunken, skirt-chasing warrior back from the sea is about half a century out of date." He further criticized the way people had looked on during the Tailhook incident and "turned a blind or bemused eye to the crude, alcohol-inspired antics of a few idiots in our ranks." According to journalist and author Jean Zimmerman, Howard was among those to publicly view Tailhook as the symptom of deep-rooted problems and arrogance in the Navy that reflected long-standing attitudes about the inferiority of women.

Paula Coughlin, who had been described as "the best of the best" in one of her naval fitness reports, eventually resigned from the Navy, citing the pressure she faced in the wake of Tailhook. She sued the Tailhook Association, which settled with Coughlin for an undisclosed amount, and then waged another lawsuit against the Hilton Hotel, claiming they did not have adequate security measures in effect during the convention. A jury awarded Coughlin $6.7 million in that case. Other women also reached settlements in suits against the association and the hotel.

See also

Coughlin, Paula; Hazing; Title VII of the Civil Rights Act of 1964; Sexual Harassment; United States Naval Academy (USNA).

References

Kenneth B. Noble, "Closing Arguments in Tailhook Lawsuit," *New York Times* (28 October 1994): A22; Kenneth B. Noble, "'I Got Attacked by a Bunch of Men': Tailhook Whistleblower Testifies about Her Fear of Being Raped," *New York Times* (4 October 1994): A12; "2 Women Settle Tailhook Suits," *New York Times*

(6 November 1994): 46; Jean Zimmerman, *Tailspin: Women at War in the Wake of Tailhook* (1995).

See also
Coughlin, Paula; Pilots; Women's Airforce Service Pilots (WASP).

Taylor, Susie King (1848–1912)

A former slave, Susie King Taylor traveled with the Union Army as a nurse and spy during the Civil War. Taylor was born in Georgia where she worked as a plantation slave. When the war began, she wanted to be near her husband and other male relatives who had managed to cross Union lines and reach the North, where they were now fighting against the Confederacy.

While accompanying her husband's regiment for more than four years, Taylor worked without pay, cooking and doing laundry and nursing the wounded and sick. She also spent hours teaching illiterate soldiers in the regiment how to read and write. After the war, Taylor wrote her autobiography, *Reminiscences of My Life in Camp*, which she published herself.

Reference
Susie King Taylor, *Reminiscences of My Life in Camp* (1968).

Test Pilots

As restrictions against women in the military were lifted during and after the 1970s, women took on new roles in aviation, including the role of test pilot. In the Army, Captain Michelle Yarborough became a top helicopter test pilot, with the job of checking the Cobra attack and OH-58 scout helicopters at Edwards Air Force Base in California. In the course of their work, Yarborough and other women became proficient in flying all types of helicopters, including those used in combat.

Tet Offensive

On 31 January 1968, during the Vietnam War, the North Vietnamese forces (Vietcong) launched a coordinated attack on Saigon, the capital of South Vietnam, which was being supported by the U.S. military. Women serving in Vietnam, including Army and Navy nurses and some members of the Women's Army Corps (WAC), Women Marines, and Women's Air Force (WAF), were under fire from helicopters, jets, rockets, and snipers during the offensive, making them the first women to experience combat conditions since World War II. Buildings, tents, and hospitals were hit, but the women continued their jobs, saying they did not want to leave.

See also
Army Nurse Corps (ANC); Boulay, Donna-Marie; Combat; Vietnam War.

Thomas, Jane (n.d.)

During the American Revolution, Jane Thomas courageously carried a message to colonial soldiers at Cedar Spring, North Carolina, warning them that loyalist troops planned to attack their camp. Thomas rode on horseback for two days, covering a distance of 60 miles. As a result, the rebel soldiers were able to hide and await their attackers, winning the battle that followed.

Thomas also had to defend her family's home against a group of Tories (British loyalists) who tried to break in and take her husband's ammunition.

Together with a servant inside the house, Jane Thomas kept firing a gun while her daughters reloaded the muskets. The Tories left the scene, fearing a large number of armed people were inside. The ammunition stored at the house was later used by Sumter's troops when they fought in the battles of Rocky Mount and Hanging Rock, North Carolina.

References

Linda Grant De Pauw, *Founding Mothers: Women of America in the Revolutionary Era* (1975); Beverly Utley, *Brave Women* (1968).

Title VII of the Civil Rights Act of 1964

In 1964, under President Lyndon B. Johnson, Congress passed the Civil Rights Act, which aims to protect people from discrimination on the basis of race, color, religion, or gender. Title VII of the act deals with equal opportunity in federal employment. The act bans discrimination in the workplace and says that neither women nor people who belong to a particular racial, religious, or ethnic group can be treated differently in regard to the terms, conditions, or privileges of their employment.

The Equal Employment Opportunity Act (EEOA) of 1972 amended Title VII, adding gender to the list of reasons that employers may not discriminate against employees. That same year, Congress amended Title VII and specified that military departments were included in the list of federal agencies that may not discriminate against anyone on the basis of race, religion, national origin, or gender. In order to justify excluding women or treating them differently from men, an employer is required to show that a gender-based classification is necessary as a "bona fide occupational qualification reasonably necessary to normal operation of that particular business."

Under Title VII, two kinds of sexual harassment are also covered. First, employers may not demand sexual favors as a condition for employment, called a "quid pro quo" situation. Second, people in the workplace may not create a "hostile work environment" by engaging in sexually offensive or intimidating behavior, including both verbal behavior and overt actions. Employers are required to remedy these situations.

Women have filed cases individually and in groups. In 1986, the United States Supreme Court ruled that sexual harassment on the job constitutes discrimination and is therefore illegal. In a 1991 case, the Court determined that within this definition of harassment, it was illegal to permit nude pictures of women in a factory or other workplace. The law in this area continues to evolve.

Advocates of opening combat jobs to women in the military used Title VII as one of the legal bases for their position. They said that under this law, such restrictions should be illegal. As of 1990, courts had not applied Title VII to the uniformed military. While developing Title VII, Congress had not specifically addressed how it would apply to combat jobs in the military, During the early 1990s, a number of women and others urged Congress to amend Title VII so that it definitely applied to the military, providing clear, objective criteria for assignments and a legal remedy for women who believe they have been the victims of unfair discrimination.

See also
Discrimination, Sexual; Sexual Harassment.
References
Martin Eskanazi and David Gallen, *Sexual Harassment: Know Your Rights* (1992); Barbara A. Gutek, *Sex and the Workplace* (1985).

Toavs, Ina J.
See United States Coast Guard.

To-Ka-Mappo (n.d.)
To-Ka-Mappo is one of the few women who fought against the U.S. Army during the 1877 Nez Percé wars. During this famous series of battles, the Wallowa Valley Nez Percé, led by Chief Joseph, fled across nearly 2,000 miles of rough terrain from Idaho to the Bear Paw of Montana. The Nez Percé, who were being driven from their homelands in Oregon and Idaho, were trying to reach Canada before being overtaken by cavalry. The tribe finally surrendered and was then moved onto a reservation in Washington State where To-Ka-Mappo lived until the late 1970s.

Tomara, Sonia (1897–1982)
As a correspondent for the *New York Herald Tribune*, Sonia Tomara was one of the top journalists reporting from Europe during World War II.

Born in Russia to a wealthy and prominent family, Tomara witnessed the tumultuous Russian Revolution before she and her sister Irina escaped from the war-ravaged nation. Sonia went to White Army territory to serve as an interpreter for the British forces involved in World War I. In 1920, she joined 4,000 other refugees fleeing to Turkey, where conditions were grim. She then managed to get to Paris where she worked as a secretary at a French newspaper for six years.

Tomara's writing career began in 1927 when the Paris editor of the *Herald Tribune* hired her for the news staff. By 1935, she had proven herself so competent that she was named Rome correspondent. From Italy, Tomara reported on the growing alliance between Germany and Italy, who formed the Rome-Berlin Axis in 1936.

For a year, Tomara worked in her paper's New York office, returning to Europe when it was clear that war was imminent. She was in Warsaw in 1939 when she heard an explosion and the sound of air raid sirens. The first bombs were being dropped on Poland as Germany proceeded to invade that country on 1 September 1939, thus starting the world war. During the war, Tomara found ways to get around in Europe, filing stories under difficult conditions from Hungary, Yugoslavia, Rumania, Greece, Syria, and various cities in Western Europe. She investigated stories that Jews were being sent to prison camps where it was rumored they would be killed.

In May 1940, Tomara reported the fall of France and managed to escape to Spain, from which she made her way back to New York. She returned overseas in 1943, this time covering the war from Chungking, the wartime capital of China, and then from North Africa. In 1944, she joined the Fifth Army, which was fighting in Rome that spring. Her daring ventures into combat areas made headlines but upset several military officials.

After the war, Tomara married Colonel William Clark, a judge, and lived with her husband in Germany where he had been assigned to reform the German court system. She continued to write for the *Herald Tribune*. After Clark's death in 1957, Tomara lived with her sister in Princeton, New Jersey, until she died in 1982.

See also
Correspondents, War.

References
Julia Edwards, *Women of the World: The Great Foreign Correspondents* (1988); John Hohenberg, *Foreign Correspondence: The Great Reporters and Their Times* (1964); Edward T. James et al., *Notable American Women* (1971).

Tompkins, Sally Louisa (1833–1916)

In 1961 during the Civil War, Sally Louisa Tompkins was commissioned as an officer in the Confederate Army in recognition of her management of a private hospital. A native of Virginia, Tompkins led a staff of six people at her Robertson Hospital, located in Richmond. During the war, 1,333 wounded men received care at Robertson Hospital and all but 73 were saved, possibly because Tompkins worked hard to maintain sanitary conditions and prevent the spread of infection.

Confederate President Jefferson Davis ordered all private hospitals for soldiers to be closed in 1861, but Tompkins kept hers operating. Davis then militarized the hospital, giving Tompkins an official appointment as captain of the cavalry in the Confederate Army. Tompkins devoted a great deal of her own fortune to the hospital, which claimed a higher percentage of survivors than any other medical facility in the nation during the war.

Sally Louisa Tompkins

Tompkins remained busy after the war, devoting herself to church and charity work and occasional nursing jobs. In 1916, Tompkins was buried with military honors.

References
Katherine M. Jones, *Heroines of Dixie: Confederate Women Tell Their Story of the War* (1955); Joan and Kenneth Macksey, *The Book of Women's Achievements* (1975); Stewart Sifakis, *Who Was Who in the Civil War* (1988).

Top Gun

This prestigious Navy Weapons Training School, known as Top Gun, prepares top jet pilots at Miramar Naval Air Station. The name Top Gun was taken from a gunnery contest dating back to the 1950s. The first women were admitted to the Top Gun program at Miramar during the early 1980s. Pilots Andrea Rice and Lucy Young were the first women to complete Top Gun training. In her book *Women in the Military*, Jeanne Holm notes that Rice and Young both later became air-to-air adversary pilots for the program. Young then became an instructor pilot, and Rice went on to the Navy's advanced training command in which she helped to train fighter pilots by assuming the role of an aggressor ("enemy") pilot.

The Top Gun program was dramatized in a profitable feature film by the same name starring popular actor Tom Cruise as pilot Pete "Maverick" Mitchell. Cruise's love interest in the film is an instructor and scientist named Charlotte Blackwood, played by actress Kelly McGillis. Flying scenes in the film were done by actual Top Gun flight instructors.

See also
Combat; Pilots.
References
Jean Ebbert and Marie-Beth Hall, *Crossed Current: Navy Women from World War II to Tailhook* (1993); Jeanne Holm, *Women in the Military: An Unfinished Revolution* (1992); Jean Zimmerman, *Tailspin: Women at War in the Wake of Tailhook* (1995).

Training, Basic

An initial military training period, often called boot camp, is required by all branches of the service. Since women have become part of the regular military and are integrated with men, the merits of different kinds of training programs, whether coeducational or single-sex, have been debated and discussed.

During the 1960s, before men and women trained together, women's basic training was not as strenuous as the men's. Women were required to be competent in swimming, and they took part in several drill classes a week. They did not carry rifles or learn to fire guns.

In the fall of 1977, the Army began training men and women together, slightly modifying the women's physical training. From 1977 until 1982, women were integrated into basic training programs at Fort McClellan (Alabama), Fort Jackson (Tennessee), Fort Dix (New Jersey), and Fort Leonard Wood (Missouri).

In 1982, a decision was made that women would once again be trained separately from men. Critics of joint basic training complained that the programs had become too easy in an effort to accommodate women.

By the late 1980s and early 1990s, that trend was again reversed and coed training was taking place at most bases. Some adjustments in training had been made in physical requirements, such as giving women a bit more time to climb a wall than men and letting them run slightly fewer miles or a shorter distance within a specified period of time. In some cases, women are not required to do as many pull-ups.

Studies show that women's physical performance in training has been improving since the 1960s. Many analysts believe that this has occurred as more young women take part in organized sports in high school and college and spend more time on fitness and exercise.

A number of critics have said that training programs should not be made easier to accommodate women and that these programs reward people for making an equal effort rather than for their actual achievement. They believe that lowering standards in this area weakens the military, slows the training process, and prevents men from reaching their physical potential.

See also
Coed Training; United States Marines; Weapons Training.
References
Cynthia Enloe, *Does Khaki Become You? The Militarization of Women* (1983); Brian Mitchell, *Weak Link: The Feminization of the American Military* (1989); Helen Rogan, *Mixed Company: Women in the Modern Army* (1981); Carol Wekesser and Matthew Polesetsky, eds., *Women in the Military* (1991).

Treloar, Theresa Lynn (n.d.)

During the Persian Gulf War, Sergeant Theresa Lynn Treloar carried out a top-secret assignment that brought her closer to the Iraqi battlefront than any other U.S. servicewoman. Treloar was part of a group that included 23 men, all of whom took part in the mission by choice. Army officials initially opposed placing a woman in such a situation, but her team leader was able to overcome their objections. When the war ended, the mission remained classified, and the Army would not release photos of those who took part.

Bilingual (French and English) and the mother of a seven-year-old at the time, Treloar was known for her proficiency with weapons and her courage in tense situations, which earned her the nickname Ice Lady. Prior to serving in the Persian Gulf War, Treloar had wanted to take part in Operation Just Cause, the 1989 invasion of Panama, but Army policy kept her at home in Fort Bragg, North Carolina.

References
Jeanne Holm, *Women in the Military: An Unfinished Revolution* (1992); Philip Shenon, "At Combat's Doorstep," *New York Times* (24 February 1991).

Trotta, Liz (n.d.)

When Liz Trotta was assigned to cover the Vietnam War for her television network, NBC, the bureau chief in Saigon was so opposed to the idea of a woman covering the war that he threatened to quit. The bureau chief eventually was replaced, and Trotta finally received the assignment. For her work in Vietnam, she won the 1968 Overseas Press Club Award for the best television news reporting from abroad.

This controversial war divided the press corps as it did other Americans. Trotta was a supporter of U.S. military action in Vietnam, while a number of other correspondents bitterly opposed American involvement.

See also
Correspondents, War.
References
Julia Edwards, *Women of the World: The Great Foreign Correspondents* (1988); Virginia Elwood-Akers, *Women War Correspondents in the Vietnam War, 1961–1975* (1988).

Trumbull, Faith (b. circa 1717)

During the American Revolution, Faith Robinson Trumbull, who lived in Lebanon, Connecticut, became famous for giving up a costly, elaborate cloak she was wearing during a church collection for the Continental Army. The cloak had been a gift from Count de Rochambeau of France.

During the winter that Washington's troops were encamped at Valley

Forge, Pennsylvania, the soldiers needed many things. Ministers called upon their congregations for donations. After Trumbull stepped up to the altar and laid down her cloak, the rest of the congregation responded to the minister's request with numerous gifts. It was said that the cloak was used to trim the uniforms of dozens of American soldiers.

Trumbull was known for other courageous deeds during the war. Later, her son Jonathan became governor of Connecticut, while another son, John, became a famous artist.

Reference

Lynn Sherr and Jurate Kazickas, *The American Woman's Gazetteer* (1976).

Tubman, Harriet
(circa 1820–1913)

An escaped slave herself, Harriet Tubman began leading people to freedom in 1850, the year after she became free. The great black antislavery activist Frederick Douglass would later say of Tubman, "The midnight sky and silent stars have been the witnesses of your devotion to freedom and of your heroism."

Born in Maryland, Tubman was named Araminta at birth, but she later adopted her mother's name, Harriet, instead. In 1849, she managed to escape from Maryland to Philadelphia and then Canada. She then proceeded to risk that freedom while making numerous trips to help others escape. It is believed that she made at least 19 trips to and from the South during the next decade, bringing some 300 slaves with her to the North, including her own parents, sister, brothers, and their families.

By planning carefully and using new, unexpected routes, Tubman managed to elude captors. A small woman (about 5 feet tall) but tough and brave, Tubman preferred to travel at night and hid her groups in barns, swamps, or the homes of people who were part of the antislavery network called the "Underground Railroad" along the route to Canada. She cleverly used disguises and forged passes for some of her runaways. Slaveowners were eager to stop her activities and offered a reward for her capture that at one time reached $40,000. Later, Tubman would tell audiences who came to hear about her experiences, "I never lost a passenger."

During the Civil War, Tubman, whom John Brown called General Tubman, served as a nurse and spy for the Union Army. To help with her spying activities, Tubman organized a group of ex-slaves, who went into Confederate camps to gather information from local black residents. They often found out valuable information about troop movements in the coastal states of Florida, Georgia, and the Carolinas.

Tubman also took part in raids upon Confederate troops. In 1863, she and some of her scouts joined Colonel James Montgomery and 150 African-American soldiers for a gunboat raid along the Combahee River in South Carolina. Before the raid took place, Tubman and her scouts found out from local slaves where explosives were located on the water. As the Union gunboats moved along the river, they were able to surprise bands of Confederate soldiers and set fire to plantations and stored supplies. Fleeing slaves clamored to grab whatever belongings they could carry and board the boats for a ride north.

When the war ended, Harriet Tubman settled with her elderly parents on land she had bought in Auburn, New York. The government refused to grant Tubman a pension for the services she had performed for the Union until 1898, when it began paying her about $20 a month.

Tubman set up schools for black citizens and, in 1908, established a rest home for the elderly poor. Until the end of her life, Tubman continued to help former slaves and to speak out for the rights of women and African Americans to vote. She died when she was about 93.

References

Susan Altman, *Extraordinary Black Americans* (1989); Marianna Davis, *Contributions of Black Women to America* (1982); Dan Elish, *Harriet Tubman and the Underground Railroad* (1994).

U

Uniforms

At various times since women have been enlisted in the military, uniforms were either inadequate for the job or there was an inadequate supply. Before the 1900s, unless they had successfully passed as men and enlisted as soldiers, women were left to their own devices to find clothing they could wear on the battlefields as they nursed soldiers or undertook other duties. Later, regulation clothing in some cases interfered with their ability to do their jobs.

During World War II, the Women's Army Corps (WAC) had numerous problems with their uniforms, which were late in arriving and often did not fit properly. Critics said that uniforms for nurses and Wacs seemed to have been designed with men's bodies in mind.

Providing enough uniforms for the Army women was difficult. The Army needed thousands of uniforms quickly and had no stockpiles of women's clothing, as it did of men's. Uniform shortages were apparent when the first women's classes graduated from their training programs in 1942.

Some women were given ill-fitting uniforms and lacked winter uniforms, using their coats to cover summer clothing in cold weather. Coats had been ordered for the fall of 1942 but did not arrive on time, so men's coats, which did not fit well, were sent as substitutes.

When the Army issued them brown underwear, many Wacs chose to wear their own underwear except on inspection day. Hemlines were a standard 16 inches from the ground so that all hems would be even when the women marched. They were modest, in keeping with the image of the WAC as a respectable, businesslike organization. Some women considered the uniforms unfeminine, but most enjoyed being able to wear them. They were proud of this visible symbol of their patriotic service.

When women from the WAC were assigned to the Southwest Pacific theater during World War II, it was discovered that women assigned to New Guinea were required to wear slacks both on and off duty in order to meet the malarial control regulations. Nurses in the Pacific had been purchasing mosquito-proof khaki slacks and shirts through civilian dealers in Australia. It was expected that each Wac would need at least six pairs of slacks and shirts, but these were not in adequate supply. The Wacs had only heavy coveralls, and these did not cover their legs.

Later in the war, when a group of Wacs landed on the beaches of Normandy on 14 July 1944—38 days after D Day—they set up camp on the cold, damp beaches and wore uniforms that included leggings, trousers, combat jackets, and long underwear.

When the Women Accepted for Voluntary Emergency Service (WAVES) was established, a well-known New York designer named Mainbocher created the blue WAVES uniforms. Conformed more to a woman's body, they were widely viewed as the most attractive uniform for women in the service at that time. A variation of this uniform was adopted by SPAR women in the Coast Guard Reserve.

The uniforms of Women Marines were similar to those of men. Women were also part of the regular Marines rather than an auxiliary unit and had more strenuous physical training than some women's corps. *Newsweek* magazine described the Marine uniform as the most colorful of the lot and said the visor-style hat was better suited to women's hairstyles than some military hats for women.

A conflict arose at the end of the war when the Army chief of staff considered allowing civilian women employees overseas to wear the WAC uniform. WAC Director Oveta Culp Hobby thought this was unwise and potentially damaging to the morale of the Wacs. Other officials, however, thought that using the same clothing would reduce storage and supply problems. It was decided that the civilian employees would wear additional trim and a blue overcoat that showed their different status. Compared to the Wacs, these civilians enjoyed higher pay, more privileges, and the opportunity to socialize with male officers.

The color of WAC uniforms was changed from khaki to taupe in 1951. The year 1954 brought a beige-colored uniform, which changed to blue in 1957. In 1960, women began wearing Army green uniforms with black accessories, with a mint-green summer uniform arriving in 1975. Women's attire included skirts, shirts, jackets, hosiery, and oxfords or pumps until the Tet Offensive (1968) of the Vietnam War, when pants were finally instituted.

See also

Appearance; "Battle of the Black Stockings."

References

Army Department of Military History, "History of the Women's Army Corps," (1989); Mattie E. Treadwell, *U.S. Army in World War II* (1954); Doris Weatherford, *American Women and World War II* (1990); June A. Willenz, *Women Veterans: America's Forgotten Heroines* (1983).

United Services Organization (USO)

In 1941, several religious organizations formed the United Services Organization (USO) to provide recreational facilities and programs for servicemen. Throughout World War II, USO centers were set up on military bases, at transportation centers, and at other areas where soldiers might congregate. Women who wished to volunteer at USO centers as hostesses and dance partners were carefully screened and expected to be of high moral character, according to the standards of the day.

After the war, the USO continued to operate its centers around the world. It sponsored touring shows, especially during the Christmas holidays, featuring popular entertainers. These shows included female singers, dancers, actresses, comediennes, and beauty pageant winners.

United States Air Force

Originally part of the Army, the U.S. Air Force became a separate service branch in 1947 and maintained bases throughout the world by the 1990s.

In June 1948, Geraldine P. May was named director of the WAF—Women in the Air Force. A WAF training center was set up at Kelly Air Force Base near San Antonio, Texas, then at nearby Lackland Air Force base. Analyzing various career opportunities, the Air Force identified 43 career fields with 349 different specialties. Thirteen fields were deemed "fully suitable" for women, 14 "partially suitable," and 16 "unsuitable." "Suitable" fields included meteorology, air traffic control, finance, and camera repair.

Women applying to the WAF had to meet high school educational and mental standards and tended to be older and better educated, on average, than male recruits. Standards for officers were especially high, and during some years, there were few commissions, for example, a total of 15 in 1954. When recruitment standards were raised even higher during the early 1950s, under Mary J. Shelly who became director of the WAF in 1951, even fewer women enlisted.

During the 1960s, under director Jeanne Holm, the Air Force opened more jobs to women in the WAF. Holm also became the first brigadier general in the Air Force (1971). During the Vietnam War, WAFs served in Southeast Asia. One of them was Major Norma A. Archer, who, as Operations Officer for the 600th Photographic Squadron at Tan Son, conducted air strike briefings. However, many Air Force women, trained and experienced in intelligence, communications, and logistics, among other fields, resented not being sent to Vietnam to perform jobs which they felt highly qualified to do.

In 1976, after military service academies opened their doors to women, ten female lieutenants began pilot training

Soldiers flock around an improvised stage to witness the first USO camp show in France in July 1944.

at Williams Air Force Base in Arizona. The following year, women began taking part in navigation training. Within ten years, it was possible to make up an entire flight crew with women.

Air Force women had opportunities to serve during conflicts that took place during the 1980s and 1990s. During the invasion of Grenada, women served on the crews of airlifters and tankers. When the raid on Libya took place in 1987, women served on the crews of KC-135s, planes that refueled the F-111s that carried out the raid. For Operation Just Cause in Panama (1990), women Air Force pilots flew in troops and supplies.

During Operation Desert Storm, 12,500 women from the U.S. Air Force served in tanker, transport, and medical evacuation aircraft, as well as in aircraft maintenance and as munitions experts.

By 1990, women were eligible for 97 percent of all jobs in the U.S. Air Force. It had the largest percentage (14.7) of women on active duty in the armed forces, and women made up 19 percent of the Air Force Reserves. Women worked in maintenance and repair, air traffic control, health care, and administration. Some took part in fire fighting and intelligence.

Between 1975 and 1995, the number of women in the Air Force increased from 33,000 to 64,546, and by 1994, 24 percent of all Air Force recruits were women. In 1995, women made up 16 percent of those in the Air Force—15.4 percent of all officers and 16.2 percent of all enlisted people. Women comprised 2 percent of all Air Force pilots and 1.7 percent of all navigators.

Between 1989 and 1995, the number of women training to be Air Force pilots nearly doubled. Women were piloting aircraft, flying support missions, and performing other flying tasks. During those years, there were 300 women pilots, 100 navigators, and nearly 600 enlisted aircrew members. By 1995, there were also 10 women flying combat aircraft and 3 more in training to do so. Women pilots now fly bombers, helicopters, fighters, and space shuttles.

In 1993, the Air Force opened jobs as combat pilots to women and also appointed the first female missile squadron commander. A number of other firsts occurred: Lieutenant Jeanne Flynn became the first F-15 fighter pilot; Major Jacquelyn Parker, a graduate of the Air Force Test Pilot School, became the first Air National Guard F-16 fighter pilot; SrA. Lisa Wilson began training to become a loadmaster on HC-130s; and Lieutenant Colonel Susan Helms became the first Air Force astronaut, going on to orbit the Earth 96 times and deploy a satellite. In 1995, Lieutenant Colonel Eileen Collins was the first woman pilot of the Space Shuttle, lifting off in an STS-63. That same year, Lieutenant Colonel Patricia Fornes assumed command of the 740th Missile Squadron at Minot Air Force Base in North Dakota.

In 1995, 99 percent of all Air Force jobs were open to women. The few positions that remained closed to women involve a high potential for direct ground combat, positions such as combat controller, air liaison officer, and pararescue.

See also
Ashcraft, Juanita; Harris, Marcelite J.; Holm, Jeanne; Pilots; Recruitment; United States Air Force Academy (USAFA);

United States Air Force Pilots; Widnall, Sheila E.

References

Jeanne Holm, *Women in the Military: An Unfinished Revolution* (1994); Sheila E. Widnall, "Women in the United States Air Force: Passages of Time" (U.S. Air Force Speeches, June 1995).

United States Air Force Academy (USAFA)

Located in Colorado Springs, Colorado, the United States Air Force Academy (USAFA) first admitted women in 1976. Air Force officials had been considering admitting women since the 1960s, when they asked for a study that supported it. Opposing the idea of enrolling women were officials at the academies themselves, other military officials, some politicians, and some members of the public.

The traditional means by which young men were admitted to military service academies was the nomination of a member of Congress. In 1972, Congress debated a resolution stating that a woman nominated to a service academy should not be denied solely on the basis of her gender. While the Senate passed the resolution, it was defeated in the House of Representatives.

In September 1973, a lawsuit was brought against the Air Force by a woman who wished to enter the academy. She charged that there was sex discrimination in the nominating process used by members of Congress to recommend those who would attend the academy.

In April 1974, the Departments of the Army, Navy, and Air Force wrote official statements opposing the admission of women to their academies. The Department of Defense agreed with them. One of their main reasons was that it was essential to use the expensive training opportunities for those who might be called upon to serve in combat and to serve in leadership roles in combat situations. Air Force Academy Superintendent Lieutenant General Albert P. Clark said,

> The environment of the Air Force Academy is designed around these stark realities [of combat]. The cadet's day is filled with constant pressure. His life is filled with competition, combative and contact sports, rugged field training, use of weapons, flying and parachuting, strict discipline and demands to perform to the limit of endurance mentally, physically, and emotionally.

Among those who agreed that women should not be enrolled at military academies was retired Colonel Jacqueline Cochran (Air Force Reserve), who had led women pilots in the WASP during World War II. She said that since women should not be in combat situations, they should not receive the special training given at the service academies.

Supporters such as Congresswoman Patricia Schroeder, however, said that women should go to the academies for the same reasons that men did—to pursue military careers and receive fine educations. She and others pointed out that the academies did not exist solely to train people for combat. They cited statistics showing that of those who graduated from the USAFA between 1964 and 1973, fewer than 40 percent had specialized in combat jobs. All but 3 of the 24 career fields open to graduates were open to women. In April

1975, a report showed that of the 8,880 Air Force Academy graduates on active duty as of October 1974, 29 percent had not had any combat assignments. More than 10 percent of the graduates from all the service academies combined had not had any combat assignments. Supporters also claimed that women were denied equal opportunities in the Air Force by not being allowed to attend the academy because, unlike graduates of officer training and reserve programs, academy graduates receive regular, rather than reserve, commissions.

The passage of Public Law 94-106 directed that women be allowed into all the service academies. The schools developed new facilities for women and modified gymnasiums and other areas to accommodate them.

The Air Force took a proactive stance at that time and made an effort to meet with high school students and counselors in order to recruit talented cadets.

On 28 June 1976, 155 women registered at the academy to begin training, comprising about 6 percent of the entering class. The academy assigned 13 women lieutenants to serve as training officers and role models for the new cadets. It was clear that some male upperclassmen and members of the faculty and administration resented the presence of women. Jeanne Holm writes, "Much of this resentment centered not just around preconceived ideas of what a woman is for, but around the perception that women are not fully a part of the team and, hence, do not really belong at the academies."

When the first class of women graduated from the academy in 1980, a higher percentage of the women who had entered in 1976 graduated than did men. Women also experienced fewer academic failures, with men having one in five and women having one in ten.

The rate of attrition of women cadets at the USAFA was lower than that for men and also lower than the attrition rate for women cadets in the Army and Navy academies. The attrition rate for women cadets remained lower than the men's through the graduation of that first class. By the early 1990s, women made up about 11 percent of the entering class at the USAFA.

See also

Military Academies; Public Law 94–106; United States Coast Guard Academy (USCGA); United States Military Academy (USMA); United States Naval Academy (USNA).

Reference

Jeanne Holm, *Women in the Military: An Unfinished Revolution* (1992).

United States Air Force Band

The United States Air Force Band remained all male until 1972, when Airman Karen Riale became the first female member. Riale, a clarinetist, joined the group, of which her husband was also a member. In 1973, she made headlines when she said she could not join her fellow band members to play at the presidential inauguration of Richard Nixon because the uniform had not yet been properly tailored to fit a woman, a situation that was then remedied.

United States Air Force Pilots

The first group of women pilots who earned their wings in the Air Force received the title United States Air Force Pilot. Ten women who qualified as official Air Force pilots were honored on 2 September 1977 at a ceremony at William Air Force Base, Arizona. Since there was a legal ban against women flying in combat at the time, the pilots were assigned to fly cargo or medical evacuation planes or tankers, rather than working on bombers or fighter planes.

United States Army

The first women to serve officially in the Army were nurses. They served as contract employees until the Army Nurse Corps (ANC) was established in 1901 after nurses had proven indispensable during the Spanish-American War.

During World War I, no women's army corps was established, although women served as nurses, occupational and physical therapists, and telephone operators with the Signal Corps of Engineers.

The need for manpower surged during World War II, and the Army recruited nurses to fill its urgent needs, enlisting thousands of young women in the Cadet Nurse Corps (CNC). Eager to use women to replace men who could join combat units, the Army agreed to establish an auxiliary corps in the form of the Women's Army Auxiliary Corps (WAAC). Congresswoman Edith Nourse Rogers introduced a bill to create the WAAC, which faced numerous opponents. Among the supporters of the bill was Army General George Marshall. The bill passed on 15 May 1942 by a vote of 249 to 83 in the House of Representatives and 38 to 27 in the Senate. WAAC recruits did not receive the same rank, pay, or other benefits as men, however. The WAAC unit was viewed as temporary.

Heading the WAAC was Oveta Culp Hobby, a successful executive, journalist, and civic leader. Hobby recruited and trained women who could become officers and instructors for the corps. The first class began at Fort Des Moines, Iowa, on 20 July 1942 and included 440 women whose average age was 30. They were highly educated, many with years of work experience as teachers, social workers, executive secretaries, and magazine and newspaper editors.

Applicants had to pass rigorous physical examinations and a written entrance exam, along with presenting strong character references. A police check was run before any applicant was admitted to the four-week training program at Fort Des Moines.

In all, about 140,000 women joined the WAAC during the war and served as clerks, secretaries, cartographers, drivers, and switchboard operators. As in the men's divisions, African-American and white WAAC units were segregated.

In March 1942, the first WAAC unit was sent overseas. Their assignment was to fulfill clerical duties in North Africa, where troops had been arriving from the Italian peninsula. That December, a boat carrying five WAAC captains to Africa to set up the process was torpedoed by a German submarine. The women survived, but the disaster prompted new objections about sending women overseas.

Nonetheless, WAAC units, and later WAC units, were sent to England, Italy, Egypt, Australia, China, and elsewhere. Eventually, about 5,000 American women served in Asia and more than 8,000 went to Africa and Europe. They sometimes came within 20 miles of battle lines, and hundreds earned combat decorations.

On 1 July 1943, President Franklin D. Roosevelt signed the law that reorganized the WAAC as a regular part of the Army named the Women's Army Corps (WAC), effective 1 September 1943. No longer an auxiliary, the WAC offered its members military status with veterans' benefits. A 1948 law made the WAC a permanent part of the military.

Throughout the 1950s and 1960s, women in the Army steadily gained ground as an increasing number of jobs were opened to them and the rules that discriminated against women and limited their numbers or ranks were eliminated. During the 1970s, women were admitted to Reserve Officer Training Corps (ROTC) and the United States Military Academy (USMA). The creation of an All-Volunteer Force (AVF) enabled more women to join the military on an equal basis with men, often taking part in the same training programs and entering fields related to combat and aviation that had previously been off-limits.

As of 1991, women in the Army could serve in 52 percent of all positions. They made up 12.2 percent of the total number of people on active duty and 20.6 percent of the reserves. After Congress revoked the Combat Exclusion Law in 1993, still more jobs opened to women. As of 1994, women were still being kept out of units that were likely to be involved in direct ground combat, but they had been admitted to new positions in the military police, military intelligence, forward maintenance support teams, and engineer companies.

See also

Adams, Charity; Army Nurse Corps (ANC); Cadet Nurse Corps (CNC); Cadoria, Sherian Grace; Clarke, Mary E.; Combat; Cornum, Rhonda; Defense Advisory Council on Women in the Services (DACOWITS); Hays, Anna Mae; Hobby, Oveta Culp; Persian Gulf War; Pilots; Pregnancy; Presidential Commission on the Assignment of Women in the Armed Services (1992); Promotion; Rank; Rogers, Edith Nourse; United States Military Academy (USMA); Veterans; Vietnam War; Walker, Mary Edwards; Women's Army Auxiliary Corps (WAAC); Women's Army Corps (WAC); World War II.

References

Army Center of Military History, *History of the Women's Army Corps (1942–1978)* (1 January 1989); Jeanne Holm, *Women in the Military: An Unfinished Revolution* (1992); Helen Rogan, *Mixed Company: Women in the Modern Army* (1983); Dorothy and Carl J. Schneider, *Sound Off! American Military Women Speak Out* (1992); Mattie E. Treadwell, *U.S. Army in World War II: Special Studies—The Women's Army Corps* (1954); Doris Weatherford, *American Women and World War II* (1990).

United States Coast Guard

The United States Coast Guard is responsible for protecting the United States coastline and inland waterways. Among its myriad functions during peacetime are enforcing customs and fishing laws, combating drug smuggling, conducting search and rescue missions, maintaining lighthouses and other navigational aids, protecting marine wildlife, fighting pollution, promoting boating safety, and monitoring harbor traffic.

Prior to becoming an official part of the United States Coast Guard, women had been performing many of this organization's functions. For example, a number of distinguished lighthouse keepers were women, some of whose husbands or fathers were keepers.

The Coast Guard was established on 28 January 1915 when Congress combined the Revenue Cutter Service and Life Saving Service. During World War I, it became part of the Department of Defense. It now operates under the Department of Transportation during peacetime, switching to the Department of Defense during times of national emergency.

Although a few women were employed at headquarters to do clerical work during World War I, there was no recruitment program for women. The first two uniformed Coast Guard women were 19-year-old twins, Genevieve and Lucille Baker, who had been in the Naval Reserve. Like the Navy's women reservists, these women were called Yeomanettes.

The Women's Reserve of the Coast Guard was created on 23 November 1942, when President Roosevelt signed Public Law 772. The law was intended to release more servicemen for duty by replacing them with women.

The women's corps was organized like that of the Navy's Women Accepted for Voluntary Emergency Service (WAVES), and women's corps did not serve overseas or give orders to any male serviceman. Dorothy Stratton, a former university dean, was appointed director of the Coast Guard Women's Reserve, called SPAR.

After the war ended, the SPAR was virtually disbanded. The Women's Armed Services Integration Act of 1948 made women part of the other branches of service but did not apply to the Coast Guard, which during peacetime, was under the jurisdiction of the Department of the Treasury at that time.

About 200 former Spars enlisted during the Korean War, then left the Coast Guard when the war ended. Some women worked to revive the SPAR during the 1950s so that the Coast Guard women could serve in peacetime. Some reserve units were operating by the 1960s, but no Spars served in Vietnam.

Like the other branches of service, the Coast Guard changed in response to the civil rights movement and the women's movement. In 1973, Congress passed laws requiring women to be incorporated into regular and reserve services. This allowed women to serve on active duty with both the Coast Guard and Coast Guard Reserve alongside men. That same year, the Coast Guard became the first branch of service to open its Officer Candidate School (OCS) to women.

Women in the Coast Guard were first assigned to seagoing ships in 1977. The idea of "mixed crews" was controversial, but the people aboard the cutters *Gallatin* and *Morgenthau* were able to work together as a team without major problems.

Today, women in the Coast Guard might find themselves rescuing boats that have run into treacherous weather, aiding vessels that are disabled at sea, or breaking ice in bodies of water in order to permit traffic flow. They deal with boat safety matters, aids to navigation, search and rescue, commercial shipping, smuggling, drug trafficking, marine science, marine safety, environmental concerns, customs, and tariffs—anything to do with water and the law.

About half of the Coast Guard's time and 40 percent of its annual budget are devoted to enforcing federal laws regarding drugs, conservation, fishing rights, and international treaties. Toward that end, members of the Coast Guard perform inspections of commercial seagoing vessels.

The top commander in the Coast Guard is an admiral, the commandant of the Coast Guard. Vice admirals command two areas—the Atlantic (from Governor's Island in New York Bay) and the Pacific (at Alameda on San Francisco Bay). The Atlantic region includes the East Coast to the Midwest, from the Great Lakes in the North to the Gulf of Mexico in the South. The Pacific region includes the Pacific Ocean all the way to Korea and Japan, as well as the ten westernmost U.S. states, including Alaska and Hawaii.

The Coast Guard accepts applications from people between 17 and 26 years of age, preferring that they have high school diplomas. A tour of duty lasts four years, starting with eight weeks of basic training at Cape May, New Jersey. Only about 80 percent of those in training complete this difficult course. Afterwards, they may choose advanced training at a service school featuring specialties such as marine science technician, sonar technician, and public affairs.

Since this branch of service is the least involved with actual combat, women have been free to choose from many jobs. By the 1990s, no jobs in the Coast Guard were closed to women. Women made up 7.4 percent of the active-duty personnel and 11.3 percent of the Coast Guard Reserves. Of approximately 30,000 enlisted members of the Coast Guard, 2,300 are women.

Among the Coast Guard women who have distinguished themselves is Seaman Ina J. Toavs. In 1979, Toavs was awarded the Coast Guard medal for extraordinary heroism after she rescued an unconscious fisherman who had washed overboard during a severe storm off the coast of Bodega Bay, California, on 13 April 1979. Maneuvering a 16-foot craft in the heavy surf, Toavs risked her own life to save the man, whom she delivered to the Coast Guard Station at Bodega Bay for emergency care.

The first woman to serve as a pilot with the Coast Guard was Janna Lambine, a geologist who had graduated from the Naval Air Station at Whiting Field in Florida. She conducted search-and-rescue missions from the air and surveillance to enforce antipollution laws.

Lieutenant Sandra L. Stosz became the first woman ever to command a U.S. icebreaker. During the early 1990s, Stosz and her crew operated the *Katmai Bay* in the Great Lakes during the ice-breaking season, from November to May.

By the 1990s, about 300 of the Coast Guard officers were women. The Coast Guard was also the first branch of the U.S. military to place women officers in command of an armed ship.

The Coast Guard Reserves, about 12,000 strong by the early 1990s, included both men and women who train with monthly drills and other activities to prepare them for active duty in the event of a war. Volunteers also help the Coast Guard perform its many duties. During World War II, as men went to active duty, thousands of women volunteers patrolled the nation's coastline, searching for enemy submarines.

In 1990, the Coast Guard conducted a study, Women in the Coast Guard, to identify their concerns and problems and set up the Women's Advisory Council to examine those concerns and make recommendations. Nine officers and senior enlisted women serve on the council. Efforts to address women's concerns have led to various changes, among them the development of the Care of Newborn Child Program. It gives new mothers and fathers the option to take a year off from the service with no loss of rating or rank when they return. In addition, classes on sexual harassment are required for all personnel in the Coast Guard.

See also
Kelley, Beverly Gwinn; Lighthouse Keepers; Sea Duty; SPAR; Stratton, Dorothy C.; United States Coast Guard Academy (USCGA).

References
Robert Erwin Johnson, *Guardians of the Sea: History of the U.S. Coast Guard: 1915 to the Present* (1987); Corinne J. Naden and Rose Blue, *The U.S. Coast Guard* (1993); Robin J. Thomson, *The Coast Guard & the Women's Reserve in World War II* (1992); John A. Tilley, *A History of Women in the Coast Guard* (1996); U.S. Coast Guard Public Information Division, *The Coast Guard at War, Vol. XXII: Women's Reserve* (1946).

United States Coast Guard Academy (USCGA)

Located in New London, Connecticut, the United States Coast Guard Academy (USCGA) is at Fort Trumbull on the shores of the Thames River. The original school was set up in July 1876 by an act of Congress.

The first class at what was then called the Revenue Cutter School of Instruction included nine male cadets who concentrated on courses in science and mathematics. They trained aboard the schooner *J. C. Dobbin.* The school closed down between 1879 and 1894. A new site near the Curtish Bay Coast Guard Yard was chosen at Arundel Cove, Maryland, in 1900. The academy moved again, to its current location in Connecticut, in 1910.

Congress did not fund any new programs for Coast Guard cadets during those years, and there were only five students at the academy in 1914. In 1915, the Revenue Cutter Service was merged with the Life Saving Service and the school was renamed the U.S. Coast Guard Academy (USCGA).

Women were admitted to the USCGA in June 1976. By 1994, women made up 17 percent of the entering class at the academy. In the 1990s, there were between 800 and 900 students at the USCGA, with about 300 entering freshmen each year. Applicants are required to be U.S. citizens between 17 and 22 years old and unmarried. They vie for spots at the academy by taking the Scholastic Aptitude Test (SAT) or American College Testing Assessment (ACT).

Once admitted, cadets study for a bachelor of science degree in one of seven major areas: civil, electrical, or marine engineering; marine, mathematical, or computer science; or government and management. They receive full tuition, training, and a monthly stipend and must fulfill a minimum six-year commitment to the

Coast Guard after graduation. Most officers in the Coast Guard are academy graduates.

Reference
John A. Tilley, *A History of Women in the Coast Guard* (1996).

United States Marine Corps

The United States Marine Corps was created on 10 November 1775, shortly after the beginning of the American Revolution, just one month after the Navy was organized. The Marine Corps was intended to work with the Navy to protect American interests at home and abroad. Marines were to be amphibious, able to move from naval ships to enemy soil.

Until World War I, the corps was limited to men. During that conflict, about 300 women served with the Marines, primarily as clerks. They were not allowed to remain in the Marines after the war ended.

The Marine Corps Women's Reserve was created on 7 November 1942. Women could then serve as Marines in World War II. These women Marines also served in clerical positions, but in some new areas, including recruiting and air traffic control. Again, women were dismissed and encouraged to resume their traditional roles as wives and mothers after the war. Fewer than 100 women were on active duty with the corps when the war ended.

The Women's Armed Services Integration Act of 1948 required all branches of the military to enlist women on active-duty status, banning them from any combat jobs. By the 1960s, about 2,700 women were Marines. Some were involved in the Vietnam War, again in supportive roles only and not in many jobs that men had traditionally held. That changed again in 1972, when a new law stated that women in the military could not be kept from noncombat occupational fields and assignments.

The modern-day Marines, who serve as an expeditionary force in readiness, might be sent anywhere in the world and serve on naval ships, as security guards at embassies, in the White House, at Camp David, or at the National Security Agency. They pilot planes and helicopters, drive armored vehicles, gather intelligence, and maintain and repair vehicles, aircraft, weapons, and equipment. Among the types of jobs open to Marines are accounting, audiovisual support, auditing, data processing, food service, heavy equipment operations, intelligence, journalism, law, law enforcement, motor transport, personnel administration, public affairs, and weather service.

About 2,000 female Marines were among the 33,300 women who served in the Persian Gulf War. They were involved in communications, intelligence, reconnaissance, and surveillance operations. In addition, women Marines delivered trucks full of supplies behind enemy lines, bringing them near combat situations. Drivers also delivered enemy prisoners of war to allied territory.

Marine recruits must be U.S. citizens, have a high school diploma or equivalent, and for women, be no shorter than 4 feet, 10 inches and no taller than 6 feet, 6 inches, with weight in proportion to height. They are required to have excellent health with no record of drug abuse or serious crime. Those under age 18 must have the consent of both parents or their legal guardian.

Women who have become Marines say they appreciated the team spirit and job training, as well as the chance to learn discipline and build a career. Some come from military families and are carrying on the tradition. Women considering joining the corps are advised to maintain the proper weight and be in top physical condition, since injuries and lack of endurance lead many to drop out of basic training. Recruiters advise a thorough physical exam and tell potential Marines to run about three miles a day and learn to swim or improve their swimming skills before starting basic training.

As of 1991, about 20 percent of all jobs in the Marines were open to women. Women were still not accepted in Marine aviation jobs, and only 4.7 of all Marines on active duty were female, possibly because the primary function of the Marine Corps is combat readiness. In 1992, the Marine Corps announced that women officers would receive full combat training, including learning to fire M-16 rifles and launch grenades.

Women and men Marines receive their basic training at Parris Island, South Carolina. Sergeant Wayne Moore told journalist N. R. Rowan, "I've been in the Marines for 14 years and I can tell you, the females listen up! They make better recruits overall than the males. They are better motivated, adapt better, take instruction better, and seem to retain what they learn better. I've never had a female recruit refuse to jump off the 45-foot rappeling tower. So far three males have refused to jump."

One special challenge of Parris Island is to stand at attention for several minutes for outside inspection. The area is infested with sand fleas, and these irritating insects bite exposed body parts, such as hands, ears, and necks.

The three phases of the training include I) orientation, military drills, and physical training, during which recruits learn to complete obstacle courses and hike with heavy backpacks; II) instruction with weapons on the rifle range, which includes target shooting and handling live grenades; and III) Basic Warrior (Combat) Training, during which recruits learn how to use a gas mask and withstand time in a gas chamber that contains chemical smoke.

Despite the difficulties and challenges, one woman in training told Rowan, "This recruit would like to say that everything here builds your self-confidence and ability."

As of 1994, about 2,000 female recruits were coming to Parris Island each year and about 75 to 80 percent were completing basic training. Some left for medical reasons, others because of what the military calls FTA—failure to adjust.

After boot camp, Marines go on to receive on-the-job training or to enter one of 500 specialized schools run by the service. They may train for one month to a year or more. The Marines then receive assignments stateside or at an overseas base.

See also

"Marinettes"; Mutter, Carol A.; Women Marines.

References

Nancy Loring Goldman, ed., *Female Soldiers—Combatants or Noncombatants?* (1982); N. R. Rowan, *Women in the*

Marines: The Boot Camp Challenge (1994); Peter A. Soderburg, *Women Marines: The World War II Era* (1992).

United States Merchant Marine Academy (USMMA)

Located in King's Point, New York, the United States Merchant Marine Academy (USMMA) was established in 1943. In July 1974, it became the first service academy to admit women cadets. Fifteen women joined that year's class along with 333 men—8 of them graduating from the USMMA in 1978.

United States Military Academy (USMA)

The oldest of the nation's military service academies, the United States Military Academy (USMA), located at West Point, New York, was established in 1802 by an act of Congress. Women were first admitted as cadets in 1976, with 119 women entering a class of 1,480 freshmen that year. Of these women, 61 graduated in 1980. The change from the long-standing all-male admission policy was the result of congressional action in the form of Public Law 94-106, which required military service academies to admit women.

In 1976, the first women cadets were integrated into 12 of the companies; the remaining two-thirds remained all male. Women have been part of every entering class at the USMA since that year. By 1992, they made up about 11 percent of the entering class.

Shortly after women were first admitted to the USMA, one West Point officer commented about which women gained the most acceptance. He said, "Women cadets are accepted by male cadets largely according to how well they do in physical training. The women who are best able to compete and compare with the men receive the most support and consideration."

See also

Barkalow, Carol; Marier, Rebecca; Military Academies.

References

Carol Barkalow with Andrea Raab, *In the Men's House: An Inside Account of Life in the Army by One of West Point's First Female Graduates* (1990); Janice Kaplan, *Women and Sports* (1990); Carol Wekesser and Matthew Polesetsky, eds., *Women in the Military* (1991).

United States Naval Academy (USNA)

Established in 1845 in Annapolis, Maryland, the United States Naval Academy (USNA) is the service academy for both the Navy and Marines. The academy maintained an all-male admission policy until Congress passed Public Law 94-106, requiring the admission of women beginning in 1976.

The process of making military service academies coeducational had begun in earnest in 1972. Senator Jacob Javits nominated a woman to the Naval Academy but she was denied admission. The Navy had then opened its Reserve Officer Training Corps (ROTC) programs to women, but not the Naval Academy. Congress then decided to consider how the academies might be integrated with both men and women students. Then, in 1973, a woman who had been denied admission to the academy sued the Navy. Congress continued to debate the matter, culminating in its controversial decision in 1976.

The matter was the subject of heated debates, and some top-ranking Navy women opposed women cadets at Annapolis. Captain Robin L. Quigley, then the women's director for the Navy, said women need not be trained at that level for seagoing or warfaring specialties. The director of the Women's Army Corps (WAC) also opposed admitting women, but directors of the women's Air Force and Marine Corps supported the idea.

The first group of women, 6 percent of the freshman class, entered the academy in 1976. The academy had developed facilities and uniforms for women and determined how haircuts and other matters would be handled in respect to this change. Adjustments in physical training were also made to reflect the different capacities of women, especially in upper-body strength. Some changes were made in terms of the treatment of new cadets (plebes), although they still had a harsh existence.

Cadet Kirsten Bailer, the first West Point female brigade commander, stands at the head of her division during the graduation ceremony in 1991.

Resentment was expressed toward female cadets at the USMA as in the other service academies. Problems have continued into the 1990s; women have complained of sexual harassment and hazing scandals, making news headlines. Marsha Evans, who later became a member of the Standing Committee on Women in the Navy and Marine Corps, had been assigned to the academy in 1986, its first woman battalion officer. Evans later said that although women had been attending the academy for a decade, they were still being "treated badly." She said, "I couldn't believe the sexism, the lack of respect for me as a woman." She spent over three months studying conditions at the academy and then reported her findings, believing that unless graduating men learned to accept and get along with women, they would not be fit to be leaders in the modern Navy.

In 1992, a former history professor at the academy, Carol Burke, published an article describing academy traditions that were demeaning to women. She had recorded jokes and marching songs sung by male cadets that described graphic violence against women and sexual abuse. She catalogued what she called the WUBA jokes. (WUBA was a tag given to women cadets, based on the name of the first uniforms for females called

"Working Uniform Blue Alpha." Some men had changed the phrase to a new and widely used slang version: "Woman used by all.")

Others believe that having women at the academy has diluted its ability to develop strong leaders who are able to withstand severe physical and emotional strain. In a 1979 article he wrote for *The Washingtonian* called "Women Can't Fight," academy graduate (1968) and former secretary of the Navy, James Webb, bemoaned changes at the academy. He said that not being able to inflict the physical and mental punishment that characterized his own education weakened the cadets, who would therefore not be as well prepared for combat. Webb claimed that his experiences had helped prepare him for the horrors of the Vietnam War.

See also

Gallina, Julianne; Hazing; Military Academies; Reserve Officer Training Corps (ROTC); Sexual Harassment.

References

Jean Ebbert and Marie-Beth Hall, *Crossed Current: Navy Women from World War I to Tailhook* (1993); Jean Zimmerman, *Tailspin: Women at War in the Wake of Tailhook* (1995).

United States Navy

The United States Navy uses sea power and air power to protect the rights of the United States and its allies to move about freely at sea. Women have been part of the Navy officially since the formation of the Navy Nurse Corps (NNC) in 1908.

The nurse corps was thus already in place when the United States entered World War I. About 13,000 women served as part of a female reserve unit called Yeoman (F). Nicknamed Yeomanettes, they did mostly clerical work for the Navy. A few Yeoman (F) women were sent to work in these jobs at naval hospitals in France.

Women served in World War II as part of the Women Accepted for Voluntary Emergency Service (WAVES). Directed by Mildred A. McAfee, the WAVES sent its members for training to campuses such as Smith College and Mount Holyoke in Massachusetts and Hunter College in New York City. Waves were known as highly qualified women who were called upon to carry out complicated jobs, some requiring intelligence testing and security clearance. They became air traffic controllers, aviation machinist mates, metalsmiths, instrument workers, gunnery specialists, and parachute riggers, among other things.

After the war, the WAVES remained a part of the Navy, but with far fewer women serving. The Women's Armed Services Integration Act of 1948 set a ceiling of 2 percent on the number of women who could serve in the U.S. military and limited women to certain ranks.

Limitations for women in the military were eliminated steadily after the late 1960s. By the 1970s, the Navy was admitting women to its Reserve Officer Training Corps (ROTC) programs, the United States Naval Academy at Annapolis, training programs for pilots, and in other arenas that had previously been closed to women.

In 1992 a presidential commission recommended to the Department of Defense (DOD) that women be allowed to serve on combat naval vessels except submarines and amphibious craft, which transport personnel to land-based military operations. Secretary of Defense Les Aspin asked Congress to repeal the Combat Exclusion Law that had been in effect since 1948.

Thus, as of the early 1990s, women could apply for 59 percent of the jobs available in the Navy. They made up 10.4 percent of those on active duty and 15.1 percent of the Navy's reservists. More women were training and serving in nontraditional roles. They were stationed to sea duty and piloting aircraft, as well as commanding aviation squadrons and serving as test pilots for fighter planes. Top female pilots were being promoted as instructors in flight training schools.

By 1995, there were 55,548 women on active duty in the Navy, about 11 percent of the force. Of these, 47,563 were enlisted women and 7,985 were officers. Women were serving aboard 40 combatant vessels and 72 noncombatants, numbers that were expected to increase by the end of 1996. These combat ships included amphibious assault vessels, guided missile craft, destroyers, aircraft carriers, and dock-landing ships. Also as of 1995, there were 206 Navy women officers serving as pilots and 77 as naval flight officers. In addition, 43 women were training in combat aviation and 54 women pilots had reported to combat aviation squadrons. Submarine duty remained closed to women, but this, too, is being reconsidered.

See also

Bell, Barbara; Combat; Coughlin, Paula; Hazing; McAfee, Mildred Helen; Mariner, Rosemary Conatser; Pilots; Quigley, Robin L. Rainey, Barbara Allen; Sea Duty; Sexual Harassment; Submarines; Tailhook; Test Pilots; Top Gun; United States Naval Academy (USNA); USS *Dwight D. Eisenhower*; Walsh, Loretta; Women Accepted for Voluntary Emergency Service (WAVES); Yeomen (F).

References

Marie Bennett Alsmeyer, *The Way of the WAVES: Women in the Navy* (1981); Jean Ebbert and Marie-Beth Hall, *Crossed Current: Navy Women from World War II to Tailhook* (1993); Joy Bright Hancock, *Lady in the Navy: A Personal Remembrance* (1972); Jeanne Holm, *Women in the Military: An Unfinished Revolution* (1992); Helen Hull Jacobs, *"By Your Leave, Sir": The Story of a Wave* (1943); Monro MacCloskey, *Your Future in the Military Services* (1979); R. B. Morris, ed., *The United States Navy* (1992); Dorothy and Carl J. Schneider, *Into the Breach: Women Overseas in World War I* (1991); U.S. Department of the Navy, "Facts on Women in the Navy" (1995); Doris Weatherford, *American Women and World War II* (1990).

United States Sanitary Commission

During the Civil War, the Union government set up the United States Sanitary Commission in July 1861 to collect and distribute supplies needed by the army. They were also authorized to hire nurses and maintain healthy, sanitary conditions in military camps and hospitals. Although under the direction of men, most staff members and some regional directors of the commission were women. They set up supply stations and hospitals and sent inspectors to evaluate conditions in military facilities. Volunteers demonstrated how to store and prepare food safely and how to prevent diseases from spreading.

See also

Civil War; Livermore, Mary.

USS *Dwight D. Eisenhower*

The USS *Dwight D. Eisenhower* was the first aircraft carrier to which women in the Navy were assigned, a landmark event that took place in 1993. The debate over whether or not women should be assigned to combatant vessels such as this one had been raging for years. It continued to spark controversy after the first women on combat vessels embarked on their tours of duty.

See also
Combat Exclusion Law; Discrimination, Sexual; Sea Duty; United States Navy.

USS *Sanctuary*

See Sea Duty.

V

Van Devanter, Lynda (b. 1947)

A surgical nurse and veteran of the Vietnam War, Lynda Van Devanter was asked to form a women's committee for the Vietnam Veterans of America in 1979.

Born and raised in Arlington, Virginia, Van Devanter graduated from the Mercy Hospital School of Nursing in Baltimore, Maryland. Having been moved by television reports about Vietnam, she wanted to use her nursing skills to help soldiers who were there risking their lives. She joined the Army Nurse Corps (ANC) upon graduation and pursued specialty training in operating room nursing after basic training.

Van Devanter volunteered to go to Vietnam and arrived on 8 June 1969, a few hours after Sharon A. Lane became the first nurse to be killed in that war from enemy fire. Soon, Van Devanter heard stories of other nurses who had died in Vietnam, at least six of whom were killed in helicopter crashes. She was stationed as a surgical nurse at a place known for heavy casualties: the 71st Evacuation Hospital, a Mobile Army Surgical Hospital (MASH) facility in Pleiku, located in a mountainous region near the border of Cambodia. The year that followed was harrowing, as Van Devanter and her colleagues worked to save lives and repair torn bodies, working understaffed and often under combat conditions.

After returning home, Van Devanter continued to practice nursing as a civilian. She found she had been traumatized by her experience and suffered from bouts of depression and other symptoms, at times feeling suicidal.

She married Bill Blackton, who made a radio documentary about Vietnam veterans in which Van Devanter was interviewed. At that time, she met Bobby Muller, the executive director of the Vietnam Veterans of America (VVA), who asked her to head the VVA Women's Project.

Van Devanter went on to earn an advanced degree in psychology and worked to help Vietnam veterans who were experiencing severe emotional aftereffects of the war. She was one of the first people to discuss the problem of post-traumatic stress disorder (PTSD) and the need to offer treatment services to veterans. Her committee also studied how herbicides, such as Agent Orange, and other chemicals that had been used in Vietnam had affected women Vietnam veterans. They worked with the Veterans Administration to provide medical care for those who had health problems resulting from these causes.

Through counseling, Van Devanter was able to cope with her war experiences and she began counseling others herself. She wrote a critically acclaimed book, *Home before Morning: The Story of an Army Nurse in Vietnam*, which details her wrenching experiences in Vietnam.

See also
Post-Traumatic Stress Disorder (PTSD); Vietnam Women's Memorial.

Reference
Lynda Van Devanter with Christopher Morgan, *Home before Morning: The Story of an Army Nurse in Vietnam* (1983).

Van Lew, Elizabeth (1818–1900)

A spy for the Union Army, Elizabeth Van Lew has been described by some historians as the most successful of all spies for either side during the Civil War.

Although hailing from an aristocratic Southern family, Van Lew had

Elizabeth Van Lew

been educated in Philadelphia where she developed her opposition to slavery. Her father was a hardware merchant and the family lived in Richmond, Virginia. After he died, Van Lew and her mother freed the family's slaves, most of whom loyally remained with the family and helped Van Lew aid the Union throughout the war.

Amazingly, Van Lew had no formal preparation as a spy and operated by her own design. Deciding to spy of her own accord, she kept Union Army officials informed about activities in Richmond, the capital city of the Confederacy. One of her major activities was to hide men who had escaped from Confederate jails. The family mansion contained a secret room large enough for dozens of men.

Van Lew also gathered information by visiting inmates in prison under the guise of bringing them food and other supplies. Her messages were sent in coded form, ingeniously hidden in such places as empty eggshells. Van Lew organized a network of houses to carry messages along a route to Union territory. Her servants worked in these homes and relayed messages to locations north of Richmond. She even had one of her former slaves take a job as a servant in the home of Confederate President Jefferson Davis for the purpose of spying and reporting back to her.

Van Lew was never arrested, but she experienced a great deal of social isolation and endured the hatred of her fellow townspeople. Shortly before the war ended, a mob tried to burn down her home. Union soldiers were told to protect Van Lew and her property when they entered the defeated Confederate capital.

After the war, Van Lew was ostracized by her neighbors. She also had financial problems, since she had used so much of her own money for the Union cause. The federal government was grateful for her wartime help and appointed her postmistress of Richmond, a position she held until 1877. Congress considered paying her a cash bonus for her services during the war but failed to act. Van Lew lived in poverty until her death in 1900, aided by her former servants and the Union prisoners she had freed. Later, some descendants of a Union colonel named Paul Revere, whom she had once hidden in her home, sent a granite stone with a bronze plaque to be placed on Van Lew's humble grave.

References
Donald E. Markle, *Spies and Spymasters of the Civil War* (1994); Stewart Sifakis, *Who Was Who in the Civil War* (1988).

Velasquez, Loreta Janeta (circa 1842–1897)

Born in Cuba, Loreta Janeta Velasquez later married an American officer and disguised herself as a man in order to join the Confederate Army during the Civil War.

The daughter of a wealthy family, Velasquez grew up in New Orleans with an aunt. As a young girl, she was enthralled with the romantic stories she read about famous battles and soldiers. She later said in her memoirs, "Joan of Arc became my heroine, and I longed for an opportunity to become another such as she." Reared to be quiet and ladylike, Velasquez wished she were a man "and could discover new worlds, or explore unknown regions of the earth."

In 1861, Velasquez decided to fight for the Confederacy disguised as "Lieutenant Harry Buford." She cut her hair, applied a fake mustache and beard, and spoke in a low voice to avoid detection. She became an independent, not always attached to a particular combat unit. She fought in the fierce first battle of Bull Run on 21 July 1861, where the South was victorious.

After a few battles, Velasquez tired of camp life and tried her skills as a spy. She assumed several different disguises in order to get information from Union officials in Washington, D.C., over a period of weeks, then went back into uniform. Velasquez next became a military conductor on trains, leaving that job to serve on picket duty. By the time the Confederacy lost the battle at Fort Donelson, Velasquez concluded that a long, hard war lay ahead. In her memoirs, she describes being depressed by the sights she had witnessed.

Velasquez worked a while more as a spy but was wounded in a small battle in Tennessee. She left the army to recuperate in New Orleans, then joined the 21st Louisiana Regiment for a brief time before joining the Army of East Tennessee. In 1862, at the battle of Shiloh, her right arm was hit. Realizing the doctor treating her wound would see that she was a woman, she told him who she really was and left the army. Once again, Velasquez turned to spying, an occupation to which she brought her experiences as a soldier and finely tuned skills in disguising herself.

After the war, Velasquez would eventually marry four times and travel around the United States and to South America and Cuba. She settled in the West, living at various times in Nebraska, Nevada, California, Utah, New Mexico, Colorado, and Texas.

Velasquez's memoirs were published in 1876. Recalling her experiences in battle, she wrote, "Fear was a word I did not know the meaning of, and as I noted the ashy faces, and the trembling limbs of some of the men about me, I almost wished I could feel a little fear, if only for the sake of sympathizing with the poor devils."

References

Ina Chang, *A Separate Battle: Women in the Civil War* (1991); Richard Hall, *Patriots in Disguise: Women Warriors of the Civil War* (1993).

Veterans

In 1979, the American Veterans Committee proposed that an Advisory Panel on Women Veterans be set up at the Veterans Administration (VA) to suggest policies and programs to meet the specific needs of women veterans. It took several years for the panel to become a reality.

A 1982 report from the General Accounting Office (GAO) called

Actions Needed to Ensure That Female Veterans Have Equal Access to VA Benefits spurred Congress to hold more hearings on the subject. In 1983, women veterans testified about the shortcomings of the current system—inadequate facilities, the lack of specialized care for problems affecting women, the lack of daily physical therapy and a self-help ward for women. Experts said that women were now in military jobs where they were more likely to be hurt or disabled, working as jet mechanics and repair technicians, refueling tankers and aircraft in the air, flying helicopters and C-141s, and as paratroopers and crew members of destroyers and submarine tenders. More support also came from the Disabled American Veterans.

In 1983, Congress passed the Veterans' Programs Improvement Act of 1983, which included provisions for the women's panel. Representative Bob Edgar of Pennsylvania, a sponsor of the bill and chairman of the Subcommittee on Hospitals and Health Care of the House Committee on Veterans Affairs, said, "We intend to see that equality of military service is matched by equal rights and benefits provided through the Veterans Administration, regardless of sex, age, or race."

Women veterans have also received more coverage in military publications and in the media. In 1982, author June A. Willenz, a member of the Veterans Administration Advisory Committee on Women Veterans, began writing a weekly column for the military magazine *Stars and Stripes*. The VA developed an exhibit on women veterans, loaning it for display at conventions and in hospitals.

In 1982, the World Veterans Federation, founded in 1950, held its first session on women. Panels discussed the impact that war has on women and the many roles they play as nurses, soldiers, resistance fighters, victims, widows, survivors, wives, and prisoners of war.

In April 1983, the VA and Department of Defense (DOD) sponsored POW-MIA Day ceremonies honoring women prisoners of war and those missing in action. During the three days of ceremonies, Secretary of Defense Caspar Weinberger announced that a permanent corridor was being created in the Pentagon for displays honoring military women. The hall had been proposed in the 1970s by the Defense Advisory Council on Women in the Services (DACOWITS).

Thirty nurses who had been captured by the Japanese after the fall of Bataan and Corregidor were flown in for these ceremonies. One of them, Colonel Madeline M. Ullom, had served on the Advisory Committee on Prisoners of War set up by the VA in 1981. Women POWs from World War II were finally able to receive government help for the health problems, including serious dental needs, resulting from their years of imprisonment when they subsisted on a starvation diet and lived in unsanitary conditions.

See also

Benefits; Demobilization; GI Bill of Rights; Post-Traumatic Stress Disorder; Serviceman's Readjustment Act of 1944.

References

Lynda Van Devanter with Christopher Morgan, *Home before Morning: The Story of an Army Nurse in Vietnam* (1983); June A. Willenz, *Women Veterans: America's Forgotten Heroines* (1983).

Veterans' Preferences

The federal government and several state governments have traditionally given veterans preferences when reviewing applications for civil service positions. Their scores on civil service examinations have been upgraded by a given number, usually five to ten points.

In a 1979 lawsuit, *Personnel Administrator of Massachusetts v. Feeney*, a woman challenged the constitutionality of such preferential treatment. The United States Supreme Court upheld such laws, however. While agreeing that it had an effect on women, since women veterans were smaller in number than men, the Court said this effect was unintended. It said that such laws could be supported, since their purpose was to prefer veterans as a group, regardless of their race, color, religious affiliation, or gender.

See also
Title VII of the Civil Rights Act of 1964.

References
Susan Gluck Mezey, *In Pursuit of Equality: Women, Public Policy, and the Federal Courts* (1992); Deller Ross and Ann Barcher, *The Rights of Women* (1984).

Victory Gardens

During World War II, families were urged to plant victory gardens (V-gardens) at their homes, since food was being rationed in order to supply the military. Among the rationed foods were meat, sugar, butter, cooking oils, and canned goods. In addition, gas and oil were rationed, which made trips to the store and elsewhere more difficult. Since food preparation was still done almost solely by women, they did most of the gardening along with the canning and preserving of food. Some communities held classes to teach women how to plant their gardens and preserve food.

During the peak of this movement, there were about 20 million victory gardens in the United States, producing nearly one-third of all the vegetables being grown in the nation. Statistics showed that about 75 percent of all homemakers were canning food by 1944.

References
Penny Colman, *Rosie the Riveter: Women Working on the Home Front during World War II* (1995); Stephen J. Schlector, *The Homefront: America during World War II* (1984); Allan M. Winkler, *Home Front U.S.A.: America during World War II* (1986).

Vietnam Veterans Memorial

In 1982, the Vietnam Veterans Memorial wall was dedicated to those who served in Vietnam and erected in Washington, D.C. The names of thousands of male casualties are grit-blasted into the black granite wall, along with the names of eight nurses who were killed while serving in the war.

Vietnam veteran Jan Scruggs, who had been wounded and decorated for bravery in 1969, first envisioned a memorial in 1979. He believed it should contain the names of all American servicepeople killed in the war. Two other veterans, attorneys Robert Doubek and John Wheeler, worked with Scruggs to form the nonprofit Vietnam Veterans Memorial Fund (VVMF) to raise money and plan the memorial. The money to build the wall was donated by the American people. Congress gave the VVMF two acres near the Lincoln Memorial as a building site.

The Vietnam Women's Memorial, unveiled on Veterans Day, 1993, depicts a nurse holding a wounded soldier while another woman looks over a barrier of sandbags.

The memorial was designed by Maya Ying Lin, an Ohio woman who was attending Yale University when she read about the competition for the design. She later said that her goal had been to keep the design so simple and powerful that "the names would become the memorial." To satisfy critics who found the wall too stark, sculptor Frederick Hart was commissioned to design a statue of three men in battle fatigues to stand nearby.

The memorial, fashioned from 3,000 cubic feet of polished granite, was dedicated on Veterans Day 1982. More than 150,000 people were in Washington, D.C., for the ceremonies. During a 56-hour vigil, every name on the wall was read in a chapel at the National Cathedral in Washington. Millions of Americans have since visited the Wall, as it is often called.

See also
Vietnam Women's Memorial.

Reference
Jan C. Scruggs and Joel L. Swerdlow, *To Heal a Nation: The Vietnam Veterans* (1985).

Vietnam Veterans of America (VVA) Women's Project

The Vietnam Veterans of America (VVA) Women's Project began in 1980 as an outgrowth of the Vietnam Veterans of America, whose executive director was Bobby Muller, a Marine who had been wounded in Vietnam. The VVA had been founded to address the concerns of Vietnam veterans—including jobs, housing, drug and alcohol abuse, and marital problems—and to promote pride in their service despite the controversial nature of the war itself. Lynda Van Devanter, a nurse who had served in a tough surgical post for a year in Vietnam, was asked to head the Women's Project.

See also
Van Devanter, Lynda.

Vietnam War

During the Vietnam War, between 7,500 and 55,000 served in Vietnam with the U.S. military, mostly with the Army Nurse Corps (ANC) and Navy Nurse Corps (NNC). During the Vietnam years, around 265,000 women served in the various branches of the military around the world. A number of women were willing to accompany fighting units, but government and military officials believed it was unsafe and inappropriate for women to venture into the types of combat zones that typified this war. Besides serving as nurses and medics, women were air traffic controllers, clerks, intelligence officers, technicians, and security personnel.

A former French colony in Southeast Asia, Vietnam won its independence in 1955. Its peace agreement with France specified that free nationwide elections would be held to decide the leadership of the country. The government of South Vietnam barred these elections, however, arousing the communist guerrillas in the south and the regular troops in North Vietnam to fight a regime that was viewed as weak and corrupt. The United States was then an ally of South Vietnam and sent both economic and military aid during the late 1950s and early 1960s.

From 1962 to 1965, Army nurses served in the only existing U.S. Army hospital in Vietnam at that time, located in Nha Trang. In 1965, the first U.S. military troops landed at Da Nang. By 1966, there were 5,008 U.S. casualties.

In 1967, the passage of Public Law 90-130 ended the 2 percent limit that had been set for the number of women serving in the armed forces. It also expanded the job possibilities for women and enlarged their chances for promotion. The armed services still did not actively recruit women to serve in Vietnam, but a number of women volunteered to serve. Civilian women also served, as part of the Red Cross, the Agency for International Development (AID), and other organizations.

It is not clear exactly how many women served with the military during the war. According to author Shelley Saywell, the Department of Defense estimated that about 7,465 women served in Vietnam, but some estimates have been as high as 55,000. Author Laura Palmer, a nurse who served in Vietnam, has determined that the number was about 11,500.

Members of the Women's Army Corps (WAC) were in Vietnam from 1962 to 1972 as administrative assistants, stenographers, and clerks. In 1964, some Wacs set up training centers for South Vietnamese women who were developing their own military corps. In Vietnam, most Wacs worked 12 to 14 hours a day, yet found time to volunteer at Vietnamese orphanages. Like men, Wacs served for one year. A total of 91 WAC officers and 518 enlisted women served in Vietnam, the number of Wacs reaching a peak in 1969 with 150 enlistees and 20 officers.

Most military women in Vietnam were nurses or other medical personnel. Most of these nurses were in their early twenties, and fewer than half had been in the military for more than a year before arriving in Vietnam. About 11,000 nurses served in Vietnam itself, while thousands of others cared for soldiers who had been wounded in Vietnam at hospitals in Guam, Hawaii, Japan, and the Philippines. They served in 18 hospitals, nine dispensaries, and a number of naval ships and aircraft.

Nurses in Vietnam treated and operated on wounded soldiers who had just been evacuated from combat areas. In this war, more of the wounded were able to be airlifted and brought to field hospitals than in any previous war. As a result, nurses saw more critically wounded patients and more lives were saved, but more patients were also left permanently disabled.

During the war, more than 57,000 American soldiers died in Vietnam, as well as more than 2 million Vietnamese. About 300,000 soldiers returned home with severe disabilities. One Army nurse, Sharon A. Lane, died in 1969 as a result of enemy fire. Eight nurses who died in Vietnam are among those whose names appear on the Vietnam Veterans Memorial in Washington, D.C.

A number of these women were present in combat situations. Four Navy nurses received Purple Hearts after they were injured during a 1964 bombing in Saigon. Other women veterans returned with serious psychological wounds and found it necessary to seek psychological or psychiatric counseling as a result of their experiences.

Veteran and nurse Juddy Marron would later say, "Don't tell me women don't know anything about war because we weren't out on the frontlines. . . . There were days when the stress and strain and blood and guts almost had to equal what you experienced out on the frontlines."

See also
Memorials; Post-Traumatic Stress Disorder; Van Devanter, Lynda.

References
Army Center of Military History, "Fact Sheet: WAC's in Vietnam, 1963–1972" (1982); Bobbi Hovis, *Station Hospital Saigon: A Navy Nurse in Vietnam* (1991); Laura Palmer, "The Nurses of Vietnam, Still Wounded," *New York Times Sunday Magazine* (7 November 1993): 36ff; Al Santoli, *Everything We Had: An Oral History of the Vietnam War* (1981); Winnie Smith, *American Daughter Gone to War* (1992); Lynda Van Devanter and Christopher Morgan, *Home before Morning: The Story of an Army Nurse in Vietnam* (1983).

Vietnam Women's Memorial

In July 1993, ground was broken for a memorial dedicated to the women who served in the Vietnam War, and the memorial was unveiled on Veterans Day later that year. At the groundbreaking ceremony, speaking of the burdens women in Vietnam had carried, General Colin L. Powell, a Vietnam veteran and chairman of the Joint Chiefs of Staff at that time, said,

> I realized for the first time that for male soldiers, the war came in intermittent flashes of terror, occasional death, moments of pain; but for the women who were there, for the women who helped before the battle and for the nurses in particular, the terror, the death and the pain were unrelenting, a constant terrible weight that had to be stoically carried.

A memorial bronze statue designed by Glenna Goodacre, the Vietnam Women's Memorial portrays a nurse holding a wounded soldier while another woman looks out over a barrier of sandbags.

See also
Vietnam Veterans Memorial.

References
Laura Palmer, *Shrapnel in the Heart: Letters and Remembrances from the Vietnam Veterans Memorial* (1993); Laura Palmer, "Still Wounded: The Nurses of Vietnam," *New York Times Sunday Magazine* (7 November 1993) 36ff.

Virginia Military Institute (V.M.I.)

On 26 June 1996, the United States Supreme Court ruled that women had a legal right to be admitted to the Virginia Military Institute (V.M.I.), an all-male school that received both state and federal funds. The institute had waged a legal battle to avoid becoming coeducational since 1990, when the U.S. Justice Department sued the

State of Virginia on behalf of women who had been denied admission.

In a 1993 decision, the United States Court of Appeals for the Fourth Circuit in Richmond, Virginia, said that the state might be able to retain its single-sex program if it provided a program for women comparable to that provided for men at V.M.I. The State of Virginia had argued that single-sex education was valuable and should be maintained. They hoped the court would accept the alternative program they had developed for women at the Virginia Women's Institute for Leadership.

In the meantime, the Justice Department pursued its case to the Supreme Court, which declared that barring women students from the V.M.I. denied them equal protection under the law as guaranteed by the United States Constitution. The decision, written by Justice Ruth Bader Ginsberg, was supported by six other justices, with Justice Antonin Scalia dissenting. Justice Clarence Thomas abstained from the decision because he had a son attending V.M.I.

This decision marked the first time the Court had ruled on the legitimacy of single-sex military academies that receive state or federal funding, thus setting a precedent for similar situations.

See also
Citadel, The; Faulkner, Shannon; Mellette, Nancy; Virginia Women's Institute for Leadership.

Virginia Women's Institute for Leadership

The Virginia Women's Institute for Leadership was set up as a result of the Supreme Court decision that compelled the State of Virginia to establish a program for women that could provide them the same educational experiences that men received at the Virginia Military Institute (V.M.I.).

The U.S. Justice Department sued the State of Virginia in 1990 after an unidentified woman complained she had been banned from attending V.M.I. because of her gender. A federal district court judge ruled in 1991 that it was possible to justify single-sex education for public policy reasons.

The Justice Department appealed this ruling. In 1993, the United States Court of Appeals for the Fourth Circuit in Richmond, Virginia, said that it could uphold the district court ruling if the state provided a program for women that was comparable to that provided for men at V.M.I. A task force was set up to develop a program and find a women's college to implement it. When the plan was approved by the appeals court in April 1994, it was seen as a model for other situations in which the courts have authorized a separate-but-equal approach to educational disputes.

The Virginia Women's Institute for Leadership is run by Mary Baldwin College, a 153-year-old private women's school in Staunton, Virginia. It includes a demanding health and physical education program and four years of Reserve Officer Training Corps (ROTC) training in the service branch chosen by the student. For some activities and programs, the students travel to the Virginia Military Institute (V.M.I.) 35 miles away in Lexington. The goal of the program is to prepare women for leadership roles in whatever career path they choose, be it military or otherwise.

See also
Reserve Officer Training Corps (ROTC); Virginia Military Institute (V.M.I.).
Reference
Michael Janofsky, "V.M.I.'s Partner in Leadership Training for Women," *New York Times* (1 February 1995): B-7.

Vivandieres

The term *vivandieres*, coming from the French, is a term often applied to "canteen women"—those who followed the troops in the American Revolution and Civil War, carrying food and water and selling different types of goods to soldiers. The women also sometimes performed other tasks—cooking, washing, mending, obtaining food and supplies, and nursing the sick and wounded. A number of vivandieres wore colorful outfits, often with a wide-sleeved Zouave-style jacket, short skirts over trousers, boots, and hats.

One of the best-known vivandieres of the Civil War was Marie Tebe, whose husband was in the Union Army. She was at several important battles, including the battle of Fredericksburg, and was said to have been under fire 13 times. During one battle, she was wounded in her left ankle.

See also
Camp Followers.
Reference
H. Sinclair Mills, Jr., *The Vivandiere: History, Traditions, Uniform, and Service* (1988).

Volunteers

Since women have never been drafted into the armed services, all women serving thus far have been volunteers, enlisting by choice or because they had committed themselves to serve after accepting educational funding from the military. In addition, individuals and groups of women have served in numerous service and relief organizations, large and small, during all the wars.

Women were quick to support the cause of liberty during the American Revolution. Besides the Daughters of Liberty, there were various local groups throughout the colonies that supplied the troops with clothing, blankets, and other needed items. They raised money to buy military supplies and collected pewter and other metal goods that could be made into bullets. Volunteers went with the troops to nurse the wounded and perform other tasks.

Women volunteers were similarly active during the Civil War, which saw strong involvement on both sides as women organized fund-raising events and made clothing, bandages, and other items for their respective armies. There were numerous ladies' aid societies and volunteer refreshment stations. Many of those who nursed soldiers during the war did so as volunteers.

During World War I, women took part in the Women's Committee of the Commission for Belgian Relief, the Vacation War Relief Committee, the Surgical Dressings Committee, the National League for Woman's Service, and the National Patriotic Relief Society, among others. Women set up the American Ambulance Service in Paris, and the American Women's War Relief Committee was established in London. The Red Cross estimated that 4,610 American women took part in some kind of relief work overseas during the war with around 50 U.S. and 45 foreign agencies.

Besides doing the day-to-day work of these organizations, women also coordinated and inspected their activities. National service training camps were set up in various places so women could learn skills that would be useful in volunteer organizations at home and abroad. Among other things, they studied driving, signaling, bicycling, map-reading, and camp cookery. The women involved in these activities were usually from the upper and upper-middle economic classes, since they alone had enough leisure time and money to travel to Europe for this sort of volunteer work. Most were single women.

During World War II, about 25 percent of all American women were involved in some kind of volunteer organization on the home front that aided the war effort directly or indirectly. More than three million women joined the Red Cross. These volunteers were largely involved in blood drives and manning blood banks for the thousands of pints that were donated weekly. They rolled bandages and packed kits that were sent to soldiers.

Other women worked as aircraft spotters for the Office of Civilian Defense. Since radar was often inadequate to keep track of enemy planes, many volunteers were needed. Women volunteers also worked for the Civil Air Patrol, which kept a lookout for enemy submarines along coastal waters. Women prepared themselves to deal with any emergencies in their communities. They formed volunteer fire brigades and drove ambulances.

Celebrities and athletes entertained people in the service by performing and taking part in exhibition sports events. Celebrities also devoted their time to sell war bonds.

The American Women's Voluntary Services (AWVS) recruited more than 350,000 members. Besides fund-raising and bond drives, the AWVS ran courses in air-raid work, fire fighting, map-reading, signal coding, motor mechanics, first aid, and other useful skills. The AWVS organized diverse activities throughout the United States, among them delivering hot meals to isolated Coast Guard stations, teaching Braille to servicemen who had been blinded at sea during the war, and staffing ambulances with members who had taken advanced first aid classes. Author Doris Weatherford describes efforts by the AWVS to involve women outside its original, well-to-do membership by organizing chapters in Harlem, a Chinese unit, and members of the Taos Indian tribe. African-American members were invited to join some southern chapters as well.

Among the groups who volunteered their job skills during this war were the WIRES (Women in Radio and Electric Service), WOWS (Women Ordnance Workers), and WAMS (Women Aircraft Mechanics).

In 1943, the popular women's magazine *Ladies Home Journal* said that readers should consider themselves part of a group called WINS—Women in National Service—in order to volunteer important services they could fit into their schedules as mothers and homemakers.

Millions of young women served in the Junior Red Cross, Victory Corps, and Victory Farm Volunteers, which was part of the Women's Land Army. Junior Red Cross chapters raised money for children in war-torn countries, packed kits for soldiers, and completed a first aid course that qualified them to work as hospital aides.

Girls in the Victory Corps, affiliated with high schools, ran day nurseries for women working in defense plants and other war-related industries. These young women also learned to drill and shoot rifles at targets. After graduation, some went on to join women's military service groups.

See also

American Red Cross (ARC); Blackwell, Elizabeth Bradwell; Canteens; National League for Women's Service; Salvation Army; United Services Organization (USO); United States Sanitary Commission; Women's Central Relief Association; Women's Land Army; Young Men's Christian Association (YMCA); Young Women's Christian Association (YWCA).

References

Dorothy Dunbar Bromley, "Women on the Home Front," *Harpers* (July 1941): 188ff; Mary Steele Ross, *Women in Uniform* (1943); Dorothy and Carl J. Schneider, *Into the Breach: Women Overseas in World War I* (1991); Doris Weatherford, *American Women and World War II* (1990).

WAAC Bill

In May 1941, Congresswoman Edith Nourse Rogers of Massachusetts introduced a bill to create the Women's Army Auxiliary Corps (WAAC).

There were heated debates as people spoke for and against this legislation. One major critic was Congressman Somers of New York. During the hearings on the WAAC Bill, he said, "Think of the humiliation. What has become of the manhood of America?" The bill passed on 15 May 1942 by a vote of 249 to 83 in the House of Representatives and 38 to 27 in the Senate. However, women recruits did not receive the same rank, pay, or other benefits available to men in the military. The WAAC Bill set up a corps that was viewed as temporary.

See also
Women's Army Auxiliary Corps (WAAC).

Wages

The issue of equal pay for equal work became a major one during World War II. Studies of defense plants showed that most women were not being paid the same wages as men. A 1942 survey conducted by the Women's Bureau of the U.S. Department of Labor confirmed that only 3 of 18 ammunition plants paid women the same wages as men in the same jobs. Ads in local newspapers showed the gap to be as much as 40 percent. For example, in Springfield, Massachusetts, the wages for beginning workers in the U.S. Armory were listed as $5.28 for men, $3.36 for boys, and $3.12 for women for a 48-hour week.

More women joined unions during the war. While some unions worked to aid women workers, others rejected women members and focused solely on the needs of men in the workplace. Unions that resisted the entry of women into male-dominated jobs sometimes held demonstrations to protest the hiring of women.

Wages for women in the military have changed dramatically. During the early 1900s, women were not accorded equal rank, pay, or benefits. By the time the All-Volunteer Force (AVF) was instituted in the mid-1970s, the military had developed into what most observers consider one of the most equitable employers in the nation for women and minorities.

See also
Defense Plant Workers; Rank; "Rosie the Riveter."

References
Penny Colman, *Rosie the Riveter: Women Working on the Home Front during World War II* (1995); Clarence D. Long, *The Labor Force under Changing Income and Employment* (1958); Christine L. Williams, *Gender Differences at Work: Women and Men in Nontraditional Occupations* (1989).

Waglum, Jinnie

See Scouts.

Walker, Mary Edwards (1832–1919)

Mary Edwards Walker, a native of Oswego, New York, was the first woman doctor to serve with the Army Medical Corps and the only woman as of 1989 to have received the Medal of Honor. One of the first American women to graduate from medical school (Syracuse Medical College in New York, 1855), Walker fought for the right of other women to receive a medical education.

Mary Edwards Walker

After the Civil War began, Walker was rejected by the Union Army as a physician, so she accepted a position as a nurse for three years. In 1864, she was appointed an assistant surgeon under contract to the army. For a time, she was a prisoner of war, having been captured by Confederate troops. Imprisoned for four months in Richmond, Virginia, she was then exchanged for a Confederate prisoner. Although having been captured, Walker still was regarded as a civilian since she was a contract employee.

After the war, Walker worked as a physician in Washington, D.C. She continued to fight for women's rights, especially the right to vote and the rights of women physicians. An advocate of changes in the type of dress acceptable for women, she also startled many people of her day by wearing pants. Walker also believed that capital punishment should be abolished.

Walker was the first woman to receive the Congressional Medal of Honor, which she received in November 1865 for her outstanding service during the Civil War. In 1917, Walker's award, along with the awards of 910 others, was revoked by the Army review board. In 1977, however, the secretary of the Army restored the medal.

References

Ruth Abram, *"Send Us a Lady Physician": Women Doctors in America, 1835–1920* (1985); Sara M. Evans, *Born for Liberty: A History of Women in America* (1989); George Sullivan, *The Day Women Got the Vote* (1994); Lisa Tuttle, *Encyclopedia of Feminism* (1986).

Walsh, Loretta (b. circa 1898)

On 22 March 1917, Loretta Walsh enlisted in the U.S. Navy, becoming the first woman ever to enlist in that service branch. A native of Philadelphia, Walsh was able to enlist during the brief time during World War I when the Navy was willing to hire women. A manpower shortage had occurred as men went overseas, and women were assigned to military clerical jobs in the United States.

Walsh passed the entrance examination given to all applicants, male and female, and was named chief yeoman in charge of recruiting for the Naval Coast Defense Reserve.

Reference

Phyllis J. Read and Bernard Witlieb, *The Book of Women's Firsts* (1992).

Walters, Bernice R.

See Navy Medical Corps.

War Advertising Council

During World War II, the council used advertising to promote patriotism and increase public participation in the war effort. Early in the war, the council developed ads for popular magazines that portrayed women in the various roles needed for victory. Some ads showed women working in defense plants, calling them "production soldiers." The ads also featured admiring husbands and children, along with workers who fit the standards of feminine beauty at the time. Other ads showed women working in jobs that supported the infrastructure of America and kept public works operating. Still others showed women operating farm machinery, harvesting crops, and planting victory gardens to augment the nation's food supply, since many items were being used by the military and others overseas.

Near the end of the war, when women were expected to give up their jobs to returning veterans, the council promoted magazine ads showing women carrying out domestic chores as wives and mothers. Reversing their earlier goals to move women into the work force, the council now promoted images of women in traditional roles and occupations.

See also
Victory Gardens.

War Bonds

A number of women helped to sell war bonds during World War II. These government-backed bonds cost $18.75 each and could be sold for $25 ten years from the date of purchase. Citizens who bought bonds were told that they were being patriotic by helping to pay for the war effort, as well as making a good investment, since the amount of money paid for the bonds would gain interest for the bearer.

Throughout the United States, posters and billboards urged citizens to "Buy Bonds!" Movie theaters and grocery stores were among the public places that featured bond booths.

Eight large-scale bond drives were held during the war. Among the women celebrities who promoted the sale of war bonds was the popular singer Kate Smith, who took part in the radio-sponsored War Bond Day on 21 September 1943 and sold more than $39 million worth of bonds. The total amount of money raised from war bond sales during the course of the conflict was about $100 billion.

The American Women's Voluntary Services (AWVS) also involved its hundreds of thousands of members in bond drives, selling millions of dollars' worth of bonds.

The first death of a woman attributable to the war occurred in 1943 when actress Carole Lombard, the wife of Clark Gable, was killed in a plane crash while touring the country to raise money for war bonds.

References
Ronald H. Bailey and the editors of *Life* magazine, *World War II: The Home Front* (1978); John Morton Blum, *V Was for Victory: Politics and American Culture during World War II* (1976); Doris Weatherford, *American Women and World War II* (1990).

War Manpower Commission (WMC)

Created in early 1942, the War Manpower Commission (WMC) aimed to mobilize the workers needed to fill millions of jobs in defense plants during World War II. From the beginning, the commission, headed by Paul V. McNutt, realized that thousands more women workers would be needed. Prior to the war, most working women were single and under the age of 30. These demographic figures changed dramatically as the WMC sought to draw more women into the work force; these women were older, often married and mothers.

Immediately after its creation, the WMC launched its "program for the utilization of women workers." They developed materials that advised employers how to hire, train, and supervise women employees. The WMC also used all branches of the media to change public attitudes about women and work. To counteract traditional biases against women in certain types of jobs, the WMC worked with the Office of War Information to use the press, radio, and motion pictures to influence public opinion. Women were urged to take jobs in shipyards, airplane factories, steel mills, and elsewhere in order to free men to serve in combat. Attractive images of women in work clothing appeared on posters and billboards and in magazines and newspapers. One popular poster showing a female riveter stated, "Women in the war: We Can't Win without Them." Others urged women to work in order to "free a man to fight."

Stories of women in these new roles appeared in popular women's magazines. Many were written by members of the Writer's War Board, a group created to support measures the government believed would hasten an Allied victory over the Axis nations.

The WMC also carried out a campaign to recruit women for essential civilian jobs, such as police officers, grocery store clerks, bus drivers, and telegraph operators—positions that had traditionally been filled by men. Recruitment appeals pointed out how vital such jobs were for keeping the country operating. They also pointed out that women had a patriotic duty to undertake these jobs, even if they were not glamorous.

As the war drew to a close, the WMC stated that "the separation of women from industry should flow in an orderly plan."

By early 1944, the last big WMC recruiting effort was over. Late that year, the commission began a new campaign, one that aimed to influence women to return home to devote themselves to being wives and mothers or return to more traditional occupations, such as medical, educational, secretarial, and clerical work. Magazines featured stories about women cheerfully leaving the factories at war's end with a sense of satisfaction at having contributed to the war effort and a desire to resume traditional roles.

References

Miriam Frank et al., *The Life and Times of Rosie the Riveter* (1982); Sherna V. Gluck, *Rosie the Riveter Revisited: Women, the War, and Social Change* (1987); Maureen Honey, *Creating Rosie the Riveter: Class, Gender, and Propaganda during World War II* (1984); Allan M. Winkler, *The Politics of Propaganda: The Office of War Information, 1942–1945* (1978).

War of 1812

During the War of 1812, the British blockaded many U.S. ports and stopped U.S. ships at sea. American women were thus required to be resourceful and manage their homes without certain goods and foodstuffs. Women distinguished themselves in other ways, sometimes taking up arms to defend their homes or towns near the sea.

One memorable act during the war was undertaken in 1813. Mary Young Pickersgill, a talented seamstress, managed to fulfill a request from a general at Fort McHenry in Maryland to sew a flag so large that the British would be able to "see it from a distance." With her daughter Caroline, Pickersgill spent six weeks sewing 440 yards of red, white, and blue cloth into a 36-foot-by-42-foot flag that she delivered to the fort on 19 August 1813. The flag, with its 15 stars and 15 stripes, inspired Frances Scott Key the following year to write the famous patriotic song "The Star-Spangled Banner." The flag now hangs in the Smithsonian Institution in Washington, D.C.

See also
Bates, Rebecca and Abigail.

Reference
Lynn Sherr and Jurate Kazickas, *The American Woman's Gazetteer* (1976).

Ward, Nancy (1738–1822)

A Delaware Indian by birth, Nancy Ward became part of the Cherokee tribe in what is now the state of Tennessee. After her husband was killed during fighting between Cherokee and Creek warriors, Ward took charge and was able to rout the enemy. She was then appointed to the Council of Chiefs in her tribe and given the position of "Beloved Woman." She also headed the Woman's Council of the tribe. After marrying a white man in 1760, she helped negotiate peace talks between whites and the Cherokee, continuing to advocate in the interests of her tribe. She also aided whites on several occasions, as when she convinced some of her people not to kill a white woman. Seeking peace between the two groups, she often said, "The same sky covers us all."

When Ward became too old and feeble to attend a council meeting in 1817, she sent her sacred walking cane in her place along with a message imploring the council not to cede any more Cherokee land to the whites. Ward died more than ten years before the Cherokee were removed to lands west of the Mississippi along what was called the Trail of Tears.

Reference
Lynn Sherr and Jurate Kazickas, *The American Woman's Gazetteer* (1976).

Warne, Margaret (Peggy) (1751–1840)

Called the "Florence Nightingale of New Jersey" in a poem by W. Clement Moore, Margaret ("Peggy") Warne cared for sick and wounded soldiers and civilians during the American Revolution. Warne's husband had left their home in Warren County, New Jersey, to fight with the colonial army, leaving Warne to care for their nine children.

Aunt Peggy—as she was known—was in great demand for her skills in delivering babies and caring for the sick in two counties, especially as male doctors left for the military. She rode for miles on horseback in all kinds of weather to reach those who called for her. After the war, Warne continued to work in the health-care field.

Reference

Elizabeth Anticaglia, *Heroines of '76* (1975).
Lynn Sherr and Jurate Kazickas, *The American Woman's Gazetteer* (1976).

Washington, Martha (1731–1802)

Martha Washington left her comfortable home in Virginia numerous times during the American Revolution to join her husband, General George Washington, at various camps.

In 1759, Martha Dandridge Curtis was a widow with two young children when she and Washington married. In 1776, Mrs. Washington gave her husband a miniature of herself that he wore in a locket throughout the war. During her time at home, she spent many hours knitting socks and making cloth and clothing for men in the Continental Army.

Martha Washington

She showed her love and devotion by arranging to be with her husband often during those years. During the harsh winter the general's troops spent at Valley Forge, Pennsylvania, Mrs. Washington came to the camp in deep snow throughout the winter, bringing food and supplies for the troops and visiting those who were ill. The soldiers affectionately called her Lady Washington. Her philosophy was expressed in a letter she wrote to her friend Mercy Otis Warren: "I am still determined to be cheerful and happy, in whatever situation I may be; for I have also learned from experience that the greater part of our happiness or misery depends upon our dispositions, and not upon our circumstances."

Reference

Margaret Brown Klapthor, *The First Ladies* (1979).

Weak Link: The Feminization of the American Military

This 1989 book, written by Brian Mitchell, aroused much debate with its thesis that women cannot perform many military jobs as well as men and should definitely not be assigned to combat-related duties. Mitchell believes that the "myth" that women can perform as well as men in the military threatens the national defense.

Among other things, Mitchell states that women are less capable physically than men and less willing to take risks. He cites a report from the Army that women do not have the strength to perform a high percentage of the jobs to which they are assigned. Women, says Mitchell, also are prone to more diseases than men and are more likely to seek medical aid for both physical and emotional ailments.

Mitchell is a former intelligence agent and officer in the Army infantry; he was a reporter for the *Navy Times* newsletter at the time he wrote *Weak Link*.

Reference

Brian Mitchell, *Weak Link: The Feminization of the American Military* (1989).

Weapons Training

Weapons training for women in the military is a relatively recent event. Although Women Marines handled weapons and learned to shoot rifles during World War II, other women's corps had no such training.

Between 1965 and 1975, Army women did not have weapons training, but in 1975, the Army reinstituted the training for women. Such training became a requirement as of 1 July 1975. Two years later, when women began taking their basic training with men, their program included the same weapons training as the men's.

See also

Training, Basic; United States Marines.

Weed, Ethel Berenice (1906–1975)

As an officer in the Women's Army Corp (WAC), Weed served after World War II in occupied Japan. Born in Syracuse, New York, Weed spent her teenage years in Cleveland, Ohio, and attended Western Reserve University, earning a degree in English. During her youth, her parents had encouraged her interests in journalism, travel, and social reform.

From 1928 to 1936, Weed worked as a writer on staff at the *Cleveland Plain Dealer*. After a trip to Europe, she began working in the field of public relations, doing publicity for various women's groups in Cleveland.

Weed joined the WAC in 1943 and was commissioned as a second lieutenant in August 1944, initially working in recruiting and public relations. She was invited to take a course in Japanese studies as one of 20 women the Army had chosen for assignments in the Far East. After Japan surrendered in August 1945, Weed was sent there to help set up the Allied Occupation. Under the direction of General Douglas MacArthur, the Allies would oversee the demilitarization of Japan and the development of a democratic form of government there.

As women's information officer in the Civil Information and Education Section, Weed worked with Japanese women, who were being given new political, social, legal, and economic rights, including the right to vote as of December 1945. Weed waged a large campaign urging women to vote in Japan's first postwar election in April 1946. She and her staff received credit for the large turnout—67 percent of all eligible women voters, close to the rate for male voters. Weed also helped Japanese women to organize various leagues and associations run by democratic principles and gave them information about their new rights and opportunities.

Although Weed left the WAC in 1947, she remained in her job until the Occupation ended. She returned to the United States in 1952 and took some doctoral-level courses in East Asian studies at Columbia University and later co-owned a bookshop that specialized in Asian materials. In 1971, Weed returned to Japan as the guest of women she had known during the Occupation. Government officials praised her work for Japanese women during those years. Weed died in Connecticut in 1975.

West Point

See United States Military Academy (USMA).

White House Honor Guard

The White House Honor Guard, made up of the five branches of the military—Air Force, Army, Coast Guard, Marines, and Navy—are chosen for the honor by their branches of service. The guards were required to be male until 17 May 1978. That evening, the tradition changed as five women, one from each service branch, were at the White House during a welcoming ceremony for President Kenneth Kaunda of Zambia.

Rosalyn Carter, wife of President Jimmy Carter, had worked to end the all-male tradition after receiving a letter from Air Force Sergeant Elizabeth Foreman questioning the policy. Foreman was one of the guards present on 17 May, along with Army Specialist Fourth Class Christine L. Crews, Coast Guard Apprentice Enda Dunham, Marine Private First Class Myrna Jepson, and Navy Seaman Apprentice Catherine Behnke.

Widnall, Sheila E. (b. 1939)

In 1993, Dr. Sheila E. Widnall became the first woman secretary of the Air Force, charged with conducting all Department of the Air Force matters—recruiting, organizing, training, administration, and maintenance. Other duties, such as research and development, are defined by the secretary of defense.

Widnall, a native of Washington State, graduated from the Massachusetts Institute of Technology (MIT) in 1960 with a degree in aeronautics and astronautics. She was one of 20 women in a class of 900. The next year, she earned her master's degree in her field, followed by a doctor of science degree (Ph.D.) in 1964.

Widnall then taught at MIT, moving from assistant professor to associate professor and then full professor, a position she held from 1974 to 1993. Her specialty areas included fluid mechanics and fluid dynamics research. During her last year at MIT, Widnall was associate provost. One of her strongest interests during those years was bringing more women and minorities into scientific and technical fields and encouraging people to study and learn together in an atmosphere of mutual respect.

As secretary of the Air Force, Widnall worked on many issues affecting women and thought her service branch had done more with "quality of life issues . . . family housing, dormitories, child care centers, certain medical and pay benefits . . ." than the other branches.

In March 1996, Widnall became the first woman to fly in a B-2 Spirit bomber during a visit to Whiteman Air Force Base in Missouri. At one point, she was given a chance to work the controls. Expressing enthusiasm about the trip, Widnall also commented on women's opportunities in the Air Force, saying, "I'm very happy about what the Air Force has achieved in opening up virtually all of its career fields to women. We have a lot of programs going on and I know there will be women B-2 pilots in the near future."

References

U.S. Department of the Air Force, "Biography: Dr. Sheila E. Widnall" (1995); U.S. Department of the Air Force–Air Force News Service, "Widnall Pilots B-2 Spirit" (1 April 1996); Sheila E. Widnall, "From WAFs to Warriors: A Reflection of Women in the United States Air Force" (speech given to National Archives Conference on U.S. Military Women in World War II, March 1995).

Willoughby, Frances L. (1906–1984)

A native of Harrisburg, Pennsylvania, Frances L. Willoughby in 1948 became the first woman physician to be commissioned as a regular naval officer. She enlisted in the Navy during World War II, shortly after receiving her M.D. from the University of Arkansas School of Medicine in Little Rock. At the time, the Navy was only accepting women as reservists.

Remaining in the naval reserve after the war, Willoughby was among the women whose status changed in 1948 as a result of the Women's Armed Services Integration Act of 1948. With this legislation, the WAVES became part of the regular Navy, and women moved from reserve to regular status.

Willoughby retired from the Navy in 1964 to enter private practice as a psychiatrist in New Jersey. In 1981, she received the Benjamin Rush Award, given for outstanding achievement by the American Psychiatric Association.

See also

Physicians.

Winema (Tobey Riddle) (1836–1932)

A member of the Modoc Indian tribe of Oregon and California, Winema ("Woman of the Brave Heart") served as an interpreter and negotiator between her people and U.S. military officials during the late 1800s.

Winema was born in 1836 near the Link River region of northern California. As a child, she showed independence and courage in paddling her canoe in the rough, rocky rivers near her home. In 1863, she married Frank Riddle, who had come west along with other white settlers to start farms, ranches, and mines.

When conflict broke out between whites and Native Americans in 1864, Winema translated for the parties and helped them reach a peaceful agreement. She performed the same duties as part of another peace commission in 1869. During an 1872 dispute with Pit River Indians, traditionally enemies of the Modoc, Winema led a group of Modoc warriors to recover stolen horses. On another day that year, she rode 75 miles to warn a group of Modoc warriors camped at Lost River that white soldiers were approaching. During the Modoc War that followed, Winema continued to risk her own safety in an effort to get the opposing sides to reach a peaceful agreement.

In spring 1873, Winema was present when a group of Modocs shot several white officials during a prearranged meeting. After a white man, Commissioner Alfred Meacham, was wounded, Winema wrapped him in her saddle blanket and took him to a camp to receive medical care. She later cared for him until he regained his health.

For her efforts, Winema was honored by the U.S. Army and given a medal by President Ulysses S. Grant. She toured the nation, often with fellow Modocs, to describe the Modoc War and the current problems Indians faced. In 1890, she was granted a pension of $25 a year, most of which she used to help the Modoc people. Winema died in 1932 on the Modoc Reservation, where she is buried. Winema National Forest in California was named for her. Her son, Jeff Riddle, later wrote about his mother's contributions in his book *An Indian History of the Modoc War*.

See also
Native Americans.
References
Hon. Alfred Benjamin Meacham, *Wi-Ne-Ma (the Woman-Chief) and Her People* (1876); Keith Murray, *The Modocs and Their War* (1959); Jeff C. Riddle, *An Indian History of the Modoc War* (1914).

Wings of Gold

See Rainey, Barbara Allen.

Withington, Alfreda

See Physicians.

Women Accepted for Voluntary Emergency Service (WAVES)

An auxiliary organization for women in the Navy, the Women Accepted for Voluntary Emergency Service (WAVES) was established during World War II, with Mildred A. McAfee as director. The bill authorizing the WAVES was signed on 30 July 1942, and the first group began training that October at a center set up at the all-women's Smith College in Northampton, Massachusetts. Members of the WAVES were part of the Navy reserve and thus had military status and eligibility for veterans' benefits.

Although a few hundred women had served with the Navy as Yeomen (F) during World War I, the WAVES recruited thousands of women and was ready to accept more than the number that volunteered. Women were particularly qualified for certain jobs being performed by men, who were needed for sea duty in combat positions and overseas. About 100,000 women served with the WAVES during the war in clerical, administrative, and communications positions, moving into more technical jobs by the end of the conflict. According to Doris Weatherford, Waves were involved in finance, chemical warfare, aviation ordnance, aerological engineering, navigation instruction, aviation gunner instruction, and other work that traditionally had been done by men.

By the war's end in 1945, about 86,000 women were still serving in the WAVES. The organization became part of the regular Navy and naval reserve in 1948; Joy Bright Hancock, who had served in both world wars, became the first director of women in the regular Navy.

In 1982, when the WAVES celebrated its fortieth anniversary at a reunion in Seattle, Washington, each woman received a letter from Secretary of the Navy James Forrestal, in which he wrote:

You have served in the greatest Navy in the world. No other Navy at any time has been so great. For your part in these achievements, you deserve to be proud as long as you live. The Nation which you served in a time of crisis will remember you with gratitude.

See also
"Battle of the Black Stockings"; Uniforms; United States Navy; Women's Armed Services Integration Act of 1948.

References
Marie Bennett Alsmeyer, *The Way of the WAVES: Women in the Navy* (1981); Joy Bright Hancock, *Lady in the Navy: A Personal Remembrance* (1972); Helen Hull Jacobs, *"By Your Leave, Sir": The Story of a WAVE* (1943); Alma Lutz, ed., *With Love, Jane: Letters from American Women on the War Fronts* (1945); Doris Weatherford, *American Women and World War II* (1990); June A. Willenz, *Women Veterans: America's Forgotten Heroines* (1983).

Women Employed Institute

The Women Employed Institute was founded in 1978 to improve employment opportunities for women. Its work includes promoting the availability of nontraditional jobs, many of which are found in the military. The institute developed model programs for change. It began monitoring federal agencies such as the Office of Economic Opportunity (OEO), charged with enforcing laws that prohibit discrimination on the basis of one's sex. The institute also informs women

Women Accepted for Voluntary Emergency Service students fire pistols at the Gunnery School, Naval Air Station, in Pensacola, Florida, in this undated photograph.

about the law and ways to gain equal opportunity in the workplace.

Women Flyers of America (WFA)

After World War II broke out in Europe in 1939, the Women Flyers of America (WFA), which numbered only a dozen women or so, sought endorsements from influential New York women to build its membership. The group negotiated with flight schools for discount lessons for its members.

By 1940, there were more than 3,000 women pilots in the United States. It became clear that war was probable, and the WFA urged women pilots to think of ways they could become involved. At a large WFA meeting in New York City, a speaker told potential women flyers, "Aviation offers women the chance to play a new and great role in the defense of America!" WFA members hoped they would have the chance to serve as mail pilots, pilots of passenger planes, and air ambulance pilots, among other things.

The WFA slogan was Airmindedness for Sport, Profession, and Emergency. Their signature flight cap was white leather with a deep blue lining.

See also
Pilots.

References
Henry M. Holden, *Ladybirds: The Untold Story of Women Pilots in America* (1991); Sally Van Wagenen Keil, *Those Wonderful Women and Their Flying Machines* (1979); Claudia M. Oakes, *United States Women in Aviation: 1930–39* (1991).

Women in Defense

A ten-minute filmstrip, *Women in Defense* was produced in early 1941 to encourage women workers to take jobs in industry. As defense industries increased production to ship arms to Great Britain and to bolster the U.S. military, they knew women employees would be needed in addition to men. The text of the film was written by Eleanor Roosevelt, wife of President Franklin D. Roosevelt, and was produced and distributed by the federal government. The narrator was Katharine Hepburn, a well-known actress and advocate of more rights for women. Hepburn described the capabilities of women to fill new roles in science and industry while the film portrayed women in action.

See also
Defense Plant Workers; "Rosie the Riveter."

Women in Military Service for America Memorial

In 1992, during President George Bush's administration, ground was broken for the $15 million Women in Military Service for America Memorial. The memorial was installed to honor the contributions of women who have served in the U.S. military throughout the nation's history. Public recognition of women in the military increased after the Persian Gulf War in 1991 spurred contributions for and interest in the project. Those who supported the memorial pointed out that more than 1.6 million women had been involved during the past 200 years. An act of Congress authorized the building of the memorial, the first of its kind in the United States. The site chosen was a gateway to Arlington National Cemetery.

Women in Ships

The Women in Ships program, initiated in 1978, opened assignments for women in the Navy in support and noncombatant vessels. The program was developed after Congress approved an amendment to the Women's Armed Services Integration Act of 1948, which previously had prevented women from being assigned to sea duty.

See also
Sea Duty.

Women in Support of the Citadel

The all-female Women in Support of the Citadel was organized by Sallie Baldwin in the wake of a lawsuit filed in 1994 by Shannon Faulkner. Faulkner had been accepted at the all-male military academy, but was rejected after academy personnel realized she was a woman.

The organization supported keeping the academy all male. Members appeared in federal court during the trial, passing out "Save the Males" pins and bumper stickers.

Reference
"'Save the Males' Becomes Battle Cry in Citadel's Defense against Women," *New York Times* (23 May 1994): A10.

Women in the Air Force (WAF)

Established in 1943 during World War II, Women in the Air Force (WAF) enlisted about 40,000 women, or Air-Wacs. These women served in the continental United States in clerical and support positions for the Air Force and at bases all over the world in a variety of positions. The WAF was directed by Elizabeth (Betty) Bandel, formerly a member of the Women's Army Corps (WAC). More women enlisted in this branch of service than any other, possibly because aviation seemed more exciting to women looking for new experiences and opportunities.

Women were admitted to all the Army Air Force (AAF) training schools except combat and flying schools. They could work in all jobs except those related to combat. Compared to other branches of the service, AAF male leaders tended to express the most positive attitudes about women and include them more fully in their organizations.

An act of Congress made the WAF part of the regular United States Air Force on 12 June 1949, when the Air Force became an independent branch of the service. In September of that year, four former WAF members returned to the service and were sworn in as part of the U.S. Air Force, which began to recruit more women. Geraldine P. May, who had begun her career as a Women's Army Corps (WAC) officer in 1942 before serving during the war in the Air Force Air Transport Command, became the first director of the regular Women's Air Force. Women could study a number of different specialties, including intelligence, meteorology, cryptography, finance, air traffic control, and electronics. All training schools were open to both men and women except those connected to combat and flying aircraft.

At the beginning of the Korean War, there were only 310 WAF officers on active duty, a number that rose to 1,023 by the war's end. The numbers of women then diminished again, and only 15 women were commissioned into the corps in 1954. At about this time, the Air Force began to seriously consider ways to improve the experience of women in the service and give them more opportunities. Air Force officials consulted with experts to help them find ways to attract well-qualified women. Opportunities for women in the Air Force continued to expand during the 1960s and after women and men were integrated into a single Air Force in the 1970s.

See also
Air-Wacs; Bandel, Betty; Holm, Jeanne; United States Air Force.

References
Wesley F. Craven and James L. Cate, *The Army Air Forces in World War II*, Vol. 7 (1958); Olga Gruhzit-Hoyt, *They Also Served: American Women in World War II* (1995); Sheila E. Widnall, "From WAFs to Warriors: A Reflection of Women in the United States Air Force" (speech given to National Archives Conference on U.S. Military Women in World War II, March 1995); June A. Willenz, *Women Veterans: America's Forgotten Heroines* (1983).

Women Marines

During World War I when the Navy enrolled its Yeomen (F), approximately 305 women were enrolled in the United States Marine Corps Reserve (Female), or USMCR(F). Called Marine (F) or Marinettes for short, they were the only women to receive military rank; they were considered enlisted, not commissioned. Women Marines were known for their forest green uniforms with the globe-and-anchor insignia. Male Marines who earlier had criticized the idea of women serving as clerks during the war found that fewer women could cover these jobs compared to the number of men needed previously.

During World War II, the USMCR(F) was reestablished in the same July 1942 bill that set up the Navy WAVES. The Women Marines were part of the military rather than an auxiliary, and members had military status and veterans' benefits. The first 19 officers, including Director Ruth Cheney Streeter, transferred to the Marines from the women's naval reserve where they had been serving.

The enlisted women were trained at Fort Lejeune, North Carolina, where their experiences included firing weapons and jumping from parachute towers, as well as the usual drilling and training.

To determine what jobs women could hold, the Marines carefully classified all military occupational specialties (MOS) in terms of the degree to which they were deemed appropriate for women. MOS in Class I were viewed as jobs in which women were viewed as better and more efficient than men; these included clerical and secretarial work as well as "routine" jobs and those connected with instruction and administration of the women's corps itself. Class II MOS were viewed as jobs women could do as well as men—for example, accounting, being postal messengers, and certain types of repair work and light machine operation. Class III jobs were those men did better, but women could do in times of great need—positions in motor mechanics, supervising men, and loading and reloading trucks. The Class IV jobs were those involving great physical strength, such as handling heavy cargo, and jobs related to combat.

After the war, the Marines initially planned to disestablish the women's corps or have only a women's reserve that would be ready for service in the event of an emergency. They decided, however, to retain an organized corps of women on a permanent basis like the other service branches. Women thus became part of the regular Marines when the Women's Armed Services Integration Act of 1948 was signed into law. Katherine Towle became the first director of regular Women Marines.

In 1964, the Pepper Board studied the Women Marines program to determine how this branch of service could make optimal use of women in peacetime. As a result of their study, it was recommended that the program be expanded by 70 percent within a year, bringing the number of women in the Marines to about 1 percent of the total force, or 2,750. New jobs were also opened to women, and they were given assignments on more Marine bases than ever before. Positions continued to open for women as they became integrated with men in a single Marine Corps in the 1970s.

See also
Streeter, Ruth Cheney; United States Marine Corps.

References
Linda L. Hewitt, *Women Marines of World War I* (1974); Pat Meid, *Marine Corps Women's Reserve in World War II* (1968); Peter A. Soderburg, *Women Marines: The World War II Era* (1992); Barbara A. White, *Lady Leatherneck* (1945).

"Women of the Army"

During the American Revolution, wives, female children, and widows who accompanied units of the Continental Army were known as "women of the army." They performed essential chores, such as cooking, washing, mending, and caring for the sick and wounded. Most rode from place to place in the baggage wagons. The women received rations of food and other necessities in return for their labor, but many just followed the army in order to be near their loved ones.

Women Veterans Health Program Act of 1992

See Veterans.

Women's Airforce Service Pilots (WASP)

The Women's Airforce Service Pilots (WASP) was an all-female group set up to ferry military planes from place to place within the United States and Canada. It combined two other groups, one of which was the Women's Auxiliary Ferrying Squadron (WAFS), an association of elite women flyers organized in September 1942 by pilot Nancy Harkness Love. The other group, the Women's Flying Training Detachment, had been flying domestic missions to free up male pilots for military duty overseas. The two groups were under the direction of pilot Jacqueline Cochran, who had been running the Women's Flying Training Detachment. WASP members were trained at Avenger Field in Texas.

During World War II, 1,047 Wasps flew all types of aircraft, including the heaviest fighter planes and bombers, the B-17 and B-20, but they did not fly across the Atlantic or in actual combat. Interestingly, a few male pilots had refused to fly or test some of these planes, considering them too dangerous. While serving in the WASP, 38 women died, and a number of women received medals. Barbara Jean Erikson flew 36 types of aircraft overseas and was honored for outstanding service with the Air Medal.

In June 1943, Army officials suggested that women pilots and trainees of the WASP be incorporated into the regular Army air corps. Director Cochran wanted the WASP to remain separate from the Women's Army Corps (WAC) so it would have its own administration and female colonel. The War Department disagreed, pointing out that male pilots were under the Army Air Force. They refused to authorize a separate WASP corps. Congress considered such a bill, but it was defeated in June 1944.

Some Wasps who disagreed with Cochran wrote to Congress expressing their wish to be in the WAC assigned to the Army Air Force. A decision was made not to take women pilots into the WAC, however, and in December 1944, the WASP was demobilized and relieved of duty. The end of the war was in sight, and no permanent place in the military had been made for the WASP. The demand for ferrying aircraft was no longer high, and there were enough men in the Army Air Corps to meet the need for pilots.

Despite their success and devoted service, the WASP was never made a part of the military, as had been expected at the time it was formed. There was so little publicity about the women pilots that their uniforms often were not recognized when they were out in public. After the war, they had to compete with returning male pilots for flying jobs, and the women had few options. They were not hired by commercial airlines or the military, although some were able to fly for private airports or do commercial ferrying work. Others became instructors or taught in college aviation programs.

It was not until 1979 that members of the WASP, only three of whom were still living, were finally granted military status by an act of Congress that recognized the contributions of several other civilian groups, such as the Women's Auxiliary Army Corps (WAAC), Signal Corps operators of World War II, and Merchant Marine flying instructors who had worked for the armed forces. They were then eligible for benefits from the Veterans Administration, which had long opposed giving veterans' status to the WASP. WASP members, however, did not receive GI benefits, such as educational funds, National Service Life Insurance, or loans for homes or farms.

See also

Avenger Field; Cochran, Jacqueline; Mariner, Rosemary Conatser; Pilots; Women's Auxiliary Ferrying Squadron (WAFS) of the Air Transport Command.

References

Jean H. Cole, *Women Pilots of World War II* (1992); Sally Van Wagenen Keil, *Those Wonderful Women and Their Flying Machines* (1979); Marianne Verges, *On Silver Wings: The Story of the Women's Airforce Service Pilots* (1989).

Women's Armed Services Integration Act of 1948

Passed as Public Law 625, the Women's Armed Services Integration Act of 1948 allowed women regular military status and defined certain limits on their participation. The act declared that women would be a permanent part of the Air Force, Army, Marines, and Navy. (The Coast Guard was not included.) Women were to be integrated with men in the Marines and Navy, while the Army would keep its WAC unit separate.

As the Air Force developed its programs separate from the Army, women's units were also separate. There were several restrictions regarding women's recruitment, opportunities, and family benefits. The percentage of women who could enlist or become officers was limited; a ceiling was set for no more than 2 percent women in the regular service. Women holding the same ratings as men were to receive equal pay, however.

The law stated that women would be dismissed if they became pregnant or had to take on the responsibility for minor children, whether through adoption, foster parenting, or becoming a stepparent. This controversial rule remained in effect for more than three decades.

Another provision of the act specified that women would not serve on combat aircraft or on most naval vessels. Under the act, women could serve only on naval hospital ships or on transports and other vessels not expected to be involved in combat. The Army augmented these provisions with a special policy that banned women from taking part in ground combat. The laws and policies excluding women from combat remained in effect through the 1980s; some still apply in the 1990s.

Legislation in 1967 removed the limit that had been set for the number of enlisted women and women officers. Retirement benefits for men and women were equalized, opportunities for promotion were increased, and more types of service were made available to women. Promotion systems remained segregated, and women were still not permitted to enter military service academies. Benefits for dependents of women in the military also remained unequal.

The 1970s brought more changes as the struggle for civil rights, women's liberation, and the rights of other minorities promoted awareness and concern about the inequalities in American society. The unpopular Vietnam War had increased sentiment against the drafting of men into the armed services. In 1973, under President Richard Nixon, a new law created an All-Volunteer Force (AVF).

As the services sought volunteers for the AVF, women were more welcome. More types of jobs and training became available for them in every branch of the service. Women became mechanics, served on missile crews, and were allowed to serve on more naval vessels, in some cases on permanent assignment. Women in the Navy were finally assigned to sea duty.

Other barriers gradually came down and women became naval aviators as of 1973. In the Army, women flew helicopters in 1974, moving on to other types of aircraft. As of 1977, women in the Air Force could fly tankers, personnel and cargo transport, and medical evacuation and reconnaissance aircraft. They were still not authorized to fly or use weapons in combat.

References

Monro MacCloskey, *Your Future in the Military Services* (1979); Helen Rogan, *Mixed Company: Women in the Modern Army* (1981); June A. Willenz, *Women Veterans: America's Forgotten Heroines* (1983).

Women's Army Auxiliary Corps (WAAC)

In May 1941, Massachusetts Congresswoman Edith Nourse Rogers introduced the so-called WAAC bill to create the Women's Army Auxiliary Corps (WAAC). The bill faced much resistance, but also had strong supporters, including Army General George Marshall, who needed clerical workers to free up more men for combat. Women already had skills in typing and other areas, and hiring them would relieve the Army from having to train men to fill these jobs.

The bill passed on May 15, 1942, by a vote of 249 to 83 in the House of Representatives, then by a margin of 38 to 27 in the Senate. The bill did not give WAACs the same rank, pay, or benefits as men in the Army.

From the outset until 1944, the WAAC was headed by Oveta Culp Hobby. She recruited and trained women officers and instructors at the training facility in Fort Des Moines, Iowa. The first class included 440 women, with an average age of 30. They were highly educated, and included many professional women—teachers, social workers, executive secretaries, all types of businesswomen, and journalists.

Thousands of WAACs served as clerks, secretaries, cartographers, drivers, and switchboard operators, among many other jobs. Applicants had to pass strict physical examinations and written exams. They required strong character references and police checks were run on all applicants.

At the end of 1942, a second training center was set up in Daytona Beach, Florida. New centers opened in 1943 at Fort Oglethorpe, Georgia (January); Fort Devens, Massachusetts (March); and Camp Ruston, Louisiana (March). Twelve thousand women were trained in 1942 and another 25,000 went through the program in 1943.

One of the most challenging issues regarding WAAC regulations was whether or not they could socialize with males in the military. It was decided that enlisted men and women could socialize, but Army generals declared that all socializing among officers was banned. This rule, however, was often broken.

Like the men's divisions, black and white WAAC members were segregated. The women's barracks were divided accordingly, and African-American women ate and trained in different places from whites.

In March 1942, the first WAAC unit went overseas, to Algiers in North Africa, where most of the women assumed clerical jobs. That December, five WAAC captains were en route to Africa when their boat was torpedoed by a German submarine. The women survived, but many critics used the incident as an example of why women should not be stationed overseas or in combat areas.

Nonetheless, thousands of women volunteered for overseas assignments. In July 1943, a WAAC battalion under the command of Lieutenant Colonel Mary A. Hallaren arrived in England. Soon others reached Italy, Egypt, Australia, and China, among other places. During World War II, some 5,000 WAACs served in Asia, while more than 8,000 served in Africa and Europe. As the women accompanied troops all over the world, they came within 20 miles of battle lines in some regions. Hundreds of women earned combat decorations for their courage under fire.

On 1 July 1943, President Franklin D. Roosevelt signed the WAC bill, which reorganized the WAAC as a regular part of the Army, changing its name to the Women's Army Corps (WAC). This law went into effect on 1 September 1943.

See also
Hobby, Oveta Culp; Women's Army Corps (WAC).

References
Army Center of Military History, *History of the Women's Army Corps (1942–1978)*, updated 1 January 1989; Jeanne Holm, *Women in the Military: An Unfinished Revolution* (1992); Elizabeth R. Pollack, *Yes, Ma'am: The Personal Papers of a WAAC Private* (1943); Jean Stansbury, *Bars on Her Shoulder: A Story of a WAAC* (1943); Mattie E. Treadwell, *U.S. Army in World War II: Special Studies—The Women's Army Corps* (1954); Doris Weatherford, *American Women and World War II* (1990).

Women's Army Corps (WAC)

In 1943, the Women's Army Corps (WAC) replaced the Women's Army Auxiliary Corps (WAAC) as women gained regular Army status rather than auxiliary status. Efforts to recruit members continued, since many women were drawn to the higher wages available to workers in defense plants. There was also competition from other branches of the military, but the Army was the first to make its women's corps part of the regular service.

A Women's Army Auxiliary Corps (WAAC) battalion march on the parade ground at Fort Des Moines in Iowa, 1942. Thousands of WAACs took overseas assignments and served alongside troops in Italy, China, Egypt, Australia, and Africa during the 1940s.

Periodically, the WAC was plagued by malicious rumors about women in the service—a problem that occurred repeatedly from the time women were first allowed in the military. Some slanderers spread stories that women in the service were prostitutes and that many became pregnant out of wedlock. Investigations by Army officials and the Federal Bureau of Investigation (FBI) were launched to track down the sources of such rumors. They concluded that disgruntled men were behind the attacks, men who hoped that, by verbally attacking women, they could keep them out of their male-dominated world.

During World War II, Wacs served in administrative, clerical, and personnel jobs—positions that had long been open to women in the civilian work force. Depending on their special skills and physical abilities, women also entered new jobs in intelligence, communications, and surveillance. They worked as interpreters, analysts, radio operators, mechanics, and parachute riggers, among other things. At its peak, the WAC had 100,000 women in service.

By the end of the war, the WAC unit serving in Europe had received 3 presidential citations, about 200 Bronze Stars, and many other decorations. Some Wacs had received the Legion of Merit.

As the war drew to a close, Representative Edith Nourse Rogers, a strong supporter of women in the military, lobbied to keep the WAC going. The Women's Armed Services Integration Act made the WAC a permanent part of the Army in 1948. By that time, there were about 5,000 women in the WAC, but recruitment efforts increased the number to about 7,300 by the time the Korean War began in 1950.

In the years that followed, members of the WAC served at posts throughout the United States and in every theater of operation around the world. New laws passed in 1967 removed promotion restrictions, enabling women to reach the rank of general and commander.

Recruitment efforts increased again in 1972, the year before the draft was to end and the All-Volunteer Force (AVF) would take effect. In addition, the jobs open to women increased to include combat support. From June 1973 to September 1978, the number of women in the WAC rose from 13,269 to 52,996. Then, in October 1978, these women were integrated into the Army along with men, and the WAC was disestablished.

See also

Benefits; Promotion; Rank; Uniforms; Vietnam War; Women's Army Auxiliary Corps (WAAC); Women's Army Corps Band; Women's Army Corps Memorial Chapel; Women's Army Corps Museum.

References

Army Center of Military History, *History of the Women's Army Corps (1942–1978)* (1989); Nancy Damman, *A WAC's Story: From Brisbane to Manila* (1992); Charity Adams Early, *One Woman's Army: A Black Officer Remembers the WAC* (1989); Jesse H. Johnson, *Black Women in the Armed Forces, 1941–1974* (1974); Dorothy R. Spratley, *Women Go to War: Answering the Call in World War II* (1992); Mattie E. Treadwell, *U.S. Army in World War II: Special Studies—The Women's Army Corps* (1954).

Women's Army Corps Band

In 1943, the first official Women's Army Corps band, or WAC band, was formed at Fort Des Moines, Iowa, at the WAC Training Center. Called the

Women's Army Corps members disembark at a North African port in January 1944.

400 Army Services Forces (WAC) Band, it played for military ceremonies and parades on the post and in surrounding areas, and then at war bond drives in cities around the United States. When Fort Des Moines was closed, the band moved to Camp Stoneman, California, where it often played for servicepeople returning home by ship from the war in the Pacific.

Although the band was discontinued in 1947, it was reactivated in 1948 and renamed the 14th Army Band (WAC). It was then stationed at Camp Lee, Virginia, but moved six years later to Fort McClellan, Alabama, where new headquarters for the WAC had been located. Growing in size, the band also increased its repertoire to include classical music, jazz, and dance numbers, as well as traditional marching songs for parades.

The WAC band toured the nation in 1951 to assist in the recruiting drives for the Korean War. It was also invited to play at three presidential inauguration parades, at the New York World's Fair of 1961, and at the Rose Bowl Parade in 1969. The musicians were featured in recruiting and training films, on national television, and in feature films. From 1969 through 1973, the group received top honors as the best military band at the Veterans Day Parade in Birmingham, Alabama.

From a total of 16 members in 1948, the band grew to 68 women in 1968. In keeping with changing military policies, starting in 1975 the band became integrated to include both men and women. Today, those who wish to join the band audition on their instrument during basic training. Musicians who are selected then take courses at the U.S. Naval School of Music.

Reference

U.S. Army Information Sheet: "Women Musicians—The 14th Army Band" (n.d.).

Women's Army Corps Memorial Chapel

Located at Fort McClellan, Alabama, at the site of the WAC Training Center and School, the Women's Army Corps Memorial Chapel was the site of religious services, marriages, graduations, and various other ceremonies during the fifties, sixties, and early seventies. In 1963, a stained glass window was installed with a design that includes the insignia, Pallas Athene.

Women's Army Corps Museum

The Women's Army Corps Museum was built at Fort McClellan, Alabama, where the WAC Center and School was located between 1954 and 1977. The initial funding for the museum was $400,000 raised by a private foundation made up of women in the WAC, their families, and other supporters. Funding to maintain the museum comes from the WAC Foundation and from the U.S. Army. Chronological displays in the museum describe the history of the WAC and show how women are serving today.

Women's Army Corps Service Medal

The Women's Army Corps Service Medal was established by President Franklin D. Roosevelt in 1943 to honor women who had served in both the Women's Army Auxiliary Corps (WAAC) and Women's Army Corps (WAC). About 50,000 women who fulfilled these conditions became eligible for this service medal.

Women's Army Corps Veterans Association

The nonprofit, nonpartisan Women's Army Corps Veterans Association, formed in 1947, was the only formal group for women veterans of World War II. Incorporated in the District of Columbia in 1951, the association—known as the WAC Vets—is open to women who served either in the Women's Army Auxiliary Corps (WAAC) or Women's Army Corps (WAC). The association's charter states that no person will be barred from membership because of race, creed, color, or political belief "unless such belief is contrary to the principles of the Constitution and the government of the United States of America."

Besides publishing a monthly letter, *The Channel*, the WAC Vets has held annual conventions since 1947. Members join together for social and family activities and to sponsor fund-raisers and volunteer work on behalf of veterans and veterans' hospitals.

Reference

Women's Army Corps Veterans Association brochure.

Women's Auxiliary Ferrying Squadron (WAFS) of the Air Transport Command

Organized in fall 1942 and headed by Nancy Harkness Love, the Women's

Auxiliary Ferrying Squadron (WAFS) of the Air Transport Command, a group of experienced women pilots, transported aircraft needed by the armed forces during World War II. The pilots averaged about 1,200 hours of flying experienced when they began training at New Castle Army Air Base in Wilmington, Delaware. WAFS members flew in various types of military aircraft, including some with open cockpits. In May 1943, the WAFS merged with another group of women pilots, the Women's Airforce Service Pilots (WASP).

See also
Fort, Cornelia; Huyler-Gillies, Betty; Women's Airforce Service Pilots (WASP).

References
Sally Van Wagenen Keil, *Those Wonderful Women in Their Flying Machines* (1979); Marianne Verges, *Silver Wings: The Story of the Women's Airforce Service Pilots* (1989).

Women's Central Relief Association

America's first female doctor, Elizabeth Blackwell, set up the Women's Central Relief Association to train nurses for work on battlefields during the Civil War. After training, the nurses worked with the Union Army.

See also
Blackwell, Elizabeth Bradwell.

Women's Land Army

A volunteer organization, the Women's Land Army devoted itself to farm labor, making up for the lack of farm workers when many men were in the military during World War II. These women harvested crops, sometimes moving from one assignment area to another. Crops were especially important since food was being rationed and much was sent overseas to the military. The land army, which included young people known as Victory Farm Volunteers, also did other farm chores, such as caring for livestock, milking cows, and repairing fences. About 600,000 young women are thought to have taken part in the farm volunteers program.

Women's Medical Specialist Corps

Set up by both the Army and Air Force in 1949, these two Women's Medical Specialist Corps brought the total number of women's components in the military to nine. Women serving in these corps specialized in health-care services other than nursing, such as the job of corpsman or hospital aide.

Women's Military Band

The first military band composed entirely of women was created in 1942, during World War II. Made up of women in the Women's Army Auxiliary Corps (WAAC), the band grew from 11 to 40 members within a year. They had permission to rehearse in a local resident's basement, which led them to call themselves the "Lost Battalion."

See also
Women's Army Corps Band.

Women's Overseas Hospital of the U.S.A. (WOH)

Soon after World War I began, the New York Infirmary for Women, with support from the National American Woman Suffrage Association, offered to send a mobile unit staffed by women physicians for the use of the military. The U.S. War Department, however, declined the mobile unit. The group then offered its services to France, and in May 1918, the Women's Overseas Hospital of the U.S.A. (WOH), under the direction of Dr. Caroline Finley, began aiding refugees in southern France. Some physicians with the WOH were asked to work with French doctors in French hospitals, which also served some U.S. servicemen. The United States sent the WOH a treatment unit for soldiers who had been gassed, and they also added a 100-bed hospital to treat people from the French military. WOH continued to operate until 1920.

See also
Army Medical Corps (AMC); Physicians.
Reference
Dorothy and Carl J. Schneider, *Into the Breach: American Women Overseas during World War I* (1991).

Women's Overseas Service League (WOSL)

The WOSL was founded in 1921 by and for women who had served overseas in wartime either with or for the military. These women included members of the Signal Corps, Quartermaster Corps, and about 52 agencies and relief organizations, such as the American Friends Service Committee (AFSC), a Quaker relief organization; the Red Cross, and the Young Women's Christian Association (YWCA). As time went on, the WOSL included thousands more women who served in the military during World War II, in Korea and Vietnam, and as part of the military in Cold War confrontations such as the Berlin Airlift.

Women's Relief Society

The Women's Relief Society was a volunteer group formed by women in the South during the Civil War. They collected money and supplies and gave aid to the sick and wounded. Many women in the group were nurses.

Women's Reserve of the Coast Guard

The Women's Reserve of the Coast Guard, called SPAR during World War II, was reestablished in 1949, four years after the end of World War II, during which time about 10,000 women had served in the reserves. When the Korean War began in 1950, some women who had served in World War II returned to active duty. Their numbers then dwindled after the Korean War.

By the early 1970s, so few women remained in the SPAR that the Coast Guard began actively recruiting them. This led to the organization of women in the modern Coast Guard, where they are integrated with men and are eligible to apply for any Coast Guard position.

See also
SPAR; United States Coast Guard.
Reference
Robin J. Thomson, *The Coast Guard & Women's Reserve in World War II* (1992).

Women's Reserve of the Marine Corps

See Women Marines.

Women's Working Group
See Post-Traumatic Stress Disorder (PTSD).

Wonder Woman
A cartoon character known for her amazing physical strength and courage, Wonder Woman was developed during World War II as a role model for women. During those years, women were encouraged to take up jobs in factories and join the military in order to further the war effort.

See also
Defense Plant Workers; "Rosie the Riveter"; War Manpower Commission (WMC).

Harriet Wood

Wood, Harriet (n.d.–1894)
The woman born as Harriet Wood later assumed the name Pauline Cushman while working as a spy for the Union Army during the Civil War. A native of New Orleans, Wood was nonetheless a Union supporter and decided to spy for the federal army early on. Trained as an actress, she was able to go undercover in different cities where she identified Confederate spies and discovered how they were operating.

In Nashville, Tennessee, she pretended to be an actress searching for a brother in the Confederate Army. She took up residence in the Dixie Hotel in 1863, where a large number of Rebel soldiers also lived. While pretending to romance a Confederate captain, she was able to smuggle out sketches of defense fortifications he kept in his room.

Wood was captured in May 1863 while spying inside Confederate lines in order to find out the location of the Army of Tennessee. General Bragg ordered that she be hanged as a traitor. While Wood was under guard in Shelbyville, Tennessee, Union troops arrived and the Rebel troops had to retreat in a hurry. Wood was left behind, unharmed. The grateful Union Army gave her the honorary title of "Major."

Although she escaped her punishment, she was the only woman spy to be sentenced to death by either side during the Civil War. Chivalrous attitudes on the part of both North and South had allowed women to spy without receiving strong punishment.

The publicity that followed Wood's rescue meant that she could no longer work effectively as a spy. She continued to aid the army by sharing her knowledge of the geographic areas she knew well in the South.

As Pauline Cushman, Wood returned to stage acting and later was briefly married to Jerry Fryer, who served as the sheriff of Florence, Arizona. When she died in 1893, she was living in the West, and was buried in San Francisco with military honors. More than 100 men wearing uniforms of the Grand Army of the Republic marched at the service. Her grave marker at San Francisco Cemetery, Presidio, reads: "Pauline Cushman, Federal Spy and Scout of the Cumberland."

References

Donald E. Markle, *Spies and Spymasters of the Civil War* (1994); Philip Van Doren Stern, *Secret Missions of the Civil War* (1959).

Wood, Leona

See Manhattan Project.

Woodsmall, Ruth Frances (1883–1963)

Woodsmall was very active in the Young Women's Christian Association (YWCA) for more than 30 years and served as general secretary from 1935 to 1947, which included World War II. Born in Atlanta, Georgia, she graduated from Franklin College in Indiana and earned a degree in German from Wellesley College. After working as a teacher and a high school principal, Woodsmall toured the Far East, which heightened her interest in diplomacy and social work.

She joined the YWCA in 1917 and helped to organize hostess houses near military bases in France and the United States. After the war, she visited both Germany and Poland and wrote reports on postwar conditions that were used to plan YWCA relief efforts. She served as executive secretary for the Near East YWCA (1920–1921), then as secretary for the Eastern Mediterranean. From 1928 to 1930, Woodsmall studied the conditions of women in the Middle East, issuing a report called *Moslem Women Enter a New World* (1936).

After working for the U.S. YWCA from 1932 to 1935, she left for Switzerland where she served as secretary of the World's YWCA. Woodsmall continued to report on the social, political, and legal status of women throughout the world. After the war, she worked in Asia, then as chief of women's affairs in Occupied Germany (1948–1954). From 1955 until her death in 1963, she conducted more research on Far Eastern women and wrote two key books on that subject.

World War I

It is estimated that more than 25,000 American women served overseas during World War I—the so-called Great War or War To End All Wars, which lasted from 1914 to 1918 in Europe. The United States joined the war in 1917, and American women went overseas with the military as news correspondents and as volunteers serving with relief organizations and groups providing entertainment or recreational activities for servicemen.

There were about 5,000 women in volunteer groups. They ranged in age from 21 to over 60. In the early years of the war, they worked with large relief organizations such as the Salvation Army, the Young Men's Christian Association (YMCA), the Young Women's Christian Association (YWCA), and the American Red Cross to help the Allied effort.

The war brought changes in employment for women, both in military and civilian life. As more men joined the Army, women filled a number of jobs traditionally held by men, which helped to change society's attitudes about their competence in these roles.

For the first time, women participated in wartime service as an integral part of the Army and Navy, both in the nursing corps and in clerical positions. In October 1917, General Pershing requested that French-speaking women telephone operators be sent to France, where the Army was not able to find enough bilingual operators for the American Expeditionary Forces (AEF) under his command. Two hundred women went overseas to serve with the AEF as civilian contract employees.

Women were officially recruited to serve in positions other than as nurses during the war. Referred to as Yeomanettes, a few hundred women served with the Coast Guard, and about 12,000 women enlisted in the Navy as Yeomen (F). The Navy wanted to free more men for sea duty by having women replace them in clerical and administrative jobs in hospitals. Some women served as translators and draftsmen.

Likewise, the United States Marines hired women, setting high standards for those accepted to work as Marinettes in the Marine Reserve. Approximately 305 women served for a few months from August until November 1918 as messengers, clerks, administrators, and recruiter's aides. These servicewomen were discharged without veterans' benefits after the war ended.

Approximately 36,000 American women served with the Army and Navy nursing corps from 1917 to 1918. Military nurses served on the battlefield, on ships, and at both field and base hospitals. In the European theater, only 150 nurses were available to care for 9,000 soldiers who were wounded. These women often suffered the risks and hardships endured by men, such as shelling, gassing, disease, and unsanitary living conditions. Nearly 300 nurses died during the war, most from diseases, some from wounds. A few nurses were captured by the Germans as prisoners of war. It has been estimated that 200 American servicewomen were killed during the war, in which 115,000 U.S. soldiers died. Some women remained in military service after the war was over.

During the war, African-American women faced great obstacles in joining both service and volunteer groups, as well as military organizations. Black nurses were especially frustrated that the need for nurses was so great yet they were refused positions in the Army Nurse Corps.

A few African-American women were able to reach France and work with the YWCA. These included Addie Waites Hunton, a college dean, wife of the first African-American secretary of the international YMCA, and a cofounder of the National Association for Colored Women; Miss Kathryn Johnson; and Mrs. James Curtis, widow of a U.S. ambassador to Liberia. The black servicemen who arrived at YWCA canteens were often disheartened by the problems they experienced in the military, and, as Hunton later wrote, they were eager to see someone who reminded them of home. The women set up Sunday chat hours, a reading room, and educational activities for soldiers who had had limited opportunities. During an influenza epidemic, they contrived to make space for sick soldiers, both black and white.

African-American pianist Helen Hagan was finally invited to entertain the troops in Europe near the end of the war. According to Dorothy and Carl Schneider, one black woman physician may have also practiced in France during the war.

At the end of the war, the three African-American canteen directors—Hunton, Johnson, and Curtis—were treated unjustly. They were allotted space on the ship's lower decks, below the white women passengers. They were also segregated at mealtimes and were told that these measures had been taken in order to avoid offending the southern women onboard the ship. Hunton and Johnson later wrote a book about their wartime experiences, focusing most of their attention not on their own efforts but on the problems experienced by African-American soldiers and the need to make the American military more just.

See also

African Americans; Canteens; Discrimination, Racial; *Over Here;* United States Army; United States Coast Guard; United States Marine Corps; United States Navy; Volunteers.

References

Penny Colman, *Rosie the Riveter: Women Working on the Home Front in World War II* (1995); Maureen Weiner Greenwald, *Women, War, and Work: The Impact of World War I on Women Workers in the United States* (1980); Adele Hunton and Kathryn Johnson, *Two Colored Women with the American Expeditionary Forces* (1971); Dorothy and Carl J. Schneider, *Into the Breach: American Women Overseas in World War I* (1991).

World War II

The United States became actively engaged in World War II with the bombing of Pearl Harbor in December 1941 and remained a key player until the war ended in 1945. Even before 1941, more women were needed to work in war industries, changing the face of the U.S. work force. Women quickly became involved in all aspects of the war effort, on the home front and with the armed services.

It became clear early in the war that women were needed to fill manpower shortages, to perform jobs for which they were especially qualified, and to release more men for combat. In 1942 and 1943, new service groups for women were formed in every branch of service and the Coast Guard: the Women's Auxiliary Army Corps (WAAC), which became the Women's Army Corps (WAC), Navy Women Accepted for Voluntary Emergency Service (WAVES), SPAR (Coast Guard), and Marine Corps Women's Reserve (MCWR). Some 350,000 women served in these various branches of service during the war. All enlisted as volunteers. Women were already serving as nurses in both the Army Nurse Corps (ANC) and Navy Nurse Corps (NNC).

The WAAC was created first, in 1942, under the direction of Oveta

Culp Hobby. Because reservists did not receive the same salary, benefits, or rank as those in regular military positions, the WAAC did not attract as many volunteers as other branches. In 1943, the Army changed the WAAC to the WAC to improve conditions for women and encourage enlistment. The WAVES, organized shortly after the WAAC, was directed by Mildred McAfee. The Coast Guard and Marines then set up reserve units for women under the direction of Dorothy C. Stratton and Ruth Cheney Streeter. All these organizations promoted recruitment efforts to attract more women volunteers.

Women in all service branches did not receive the same pay, benefits, or opportunities for advancement as men did during World War II. They were trained separately and served in separate units. A specific and limited number of women were permitted to enlist. African Americans faced additional barriers and limitations; they joined the WAAC, but they were not able to move into the Navy, Coast Guard, or Marines until the war had almost ended.

Women served in every theater of the war, including combat zones, and were often exposed to the perils of war. About 200 women nurses died while serving in Europe and the Pacific. It is believed that 82 women were captured as prisoners of war during the conflict. One of them, Second Lieutenant Reba Zitella Whittle, an Army nurse, was shot down and captured by Germans. Most women prisoners were captured in the Pacific where they were serving with the nurse corps. Some were returned home by their captors, but 77 nurses were kept in a Japanese prison camp in Manila for 37 months until the war's end.

More than a thousand women pilots served in the Women's Airforce Service Pilots (WASP), led by Jacqueline Cochran. Subject to military rules and procedures, WASP personnel were classified as civil service employees rather than receiving military rank and status, even though they had tested and flown in every kind of aircraft in use during the war, often in hazardous conditions. This meant they were not able to receive any veterans' benefits after the war. Thirty-eight WASP pilots lost their lives in the course of their work.

Military women were honored for outstanding service. More than 1,600 received medals for their efforts during the war. The war also changed the dynamics of the labor force throughout the country. Millions of women worked in defense plant industries while about 2 million others took office jobs. During the Depression, there was a ban on hiring women teachers, but that was lifted and women soon outnumbered men in the teaching profession. As men joined the armed services, women took numerous other jobs they had seldom held, working as auto mechanics, train conductors, taxi drivers, and lumberjacks, among other positions.

In 1942, the National War Labor Board said that women should be paid the same rates as men when they did work that was the same or substantially the same. This equal-pay principle resulted in higher wages for some women, but many companies got around the idea by using loopholes in the policy or classifying women's jobs in ways that did not require them to raise their pay.

Many jobs opened up for African-American women during the war. Before that time, they had usually worked either on farms or as domestics. With the war under way, they were hired in factories and in clerical positions, as well as for jobs in the health-care field.

See also
Air-Wacs; American Expeditionary Forces (AEF); Bataan; Cadet Nurse Corps (CNC); Canteens; Casualties; Clerical Workers; Corps of Engineers; Corregidor; Correspondents, War; D Day; Decorations; Demobilization; Guerrero, Joey; Kaiser Shipyard; Lanham Act; Manhattan Project; Pilots; Pinups; Rogers, Edith Nourse; "Rosie the Riveter"; Uniforms; United Services Organization (USO); United States Army; United States Coast Guard; United States Marine Corps; United States Navy; Volunteers; *Women in Defense.*

References
Karen Anderson, *Wartime Women: Sex Roles, Family Relations, and the Status of Women during World War II* (1981); Alice A. Booher, "A Special Salute to Women Military POWs," *Minerva's Bulletin Board* (Summer 1992): 1–4; Sherna Berger Gluck, *Rosie the Riveter Revisited: Women, the War, and Social Change* (1987); Olga Gruhzit-Hoyt, *They Also Served: American Women in World War II* (1995); Jesse J. Johnson, *Black Women in the Armed Forces, 1941–1974* (1974); Sally Van Wagenen Keil, *Those Wonderful Women in Their Flying Machines* (1979); Elaine Taylor May, *Pushing the Limits: American Women 1940–1961* (1994); Mattie E. Treadwell, *U.S. Army in World War II: Special Studies—The Women's Army Corps* (1954); Doris Weatherford, *American Women and World War II* (1990); June A. Willenz, *Women Veterans: America's Forgotten Heroines* (1983).

Wormeley, Katharine (n.d.)

As a volunteer for the United States Sanitary Commission during the Civil War, Katharine Wormeley nursed wounded soldiers on the transport *Daniel Webster No. 2*, used to move patients from the field to hospitals. In June 1862, she was among those caring for several hundred men who had been wounded in the Peninsular campaign.

Wormeley wrote that the men were carried aboard in "every condition of horror, shattered and shrieking." She set about giving others something to drink, including lemons, ice, and sherry, as well as a beverage made with molasses. The men then ate crackers and milk or tea with bread. Since there were not enough mattresses or beds, the wounded were placed wherever room for a stretcher could be found.

Reference
Katharine Wormeley, *The Other Side of the War: With the Army of the Potomac* (1889).

Worster, Ann Weaver (n.d.)

During the Persian Gulf War, Captain Ann Worster flew heavy KC-135 tankers for the Air Force. She and other women flew missions in which they refueled bombers and fighter planes in midair, although they were still not permitted to fly combat aircraft at the time. One of Worster's missions took her 250 miles into Iraqi air space, a treacherous undertaking.

Military analysts have pointed out that, unarmed and visible, tankers are easy airborne targets for enemy surface-to-air missiles. They were also vital to the winning U.S. air campaign during this war.

References
Jeanne Holm, *Women in the Military: An Unfinished Revolution* (1992); Molly Moore, "Women in the Battlefield—Gulf War Role Helps Bring Shift in Attitude," *Washington Post* (16 June 1991): A1; Molly Moore, "Women Face Combat Risk," *Washington Post* (12 September 1991): 1

Y

Yarborough, Michelle
See Test Pilots.

Yelle, Deborah (n.d.)
During the Persian Gulf War, Corporal Deborah Yelle, one of more than 170 women in the second Forward Marine Support Group, served at the large Marine support base that was located nearest to the border of Iraqi-occupied Kuwait. This group erected bunkers, drove supply trucks, and set up communications systems in the desert for the benefit of the Marine infantry units, most of which were located behind them. Yelle, a tactical satellite repairman, worked in the area of communications. After fighting began in that region, Marine infantry units relied on the second Forward Marine Support Group for ammunition, fuel, and other vital supplies.

In a speech that was delivered in May of 1991 to the Defense Advisory Council on Women in the Services (DACOWITS), Commandant General Alfred M. Gray, Jr., called these servicewomen "superb Marines." Located closer to the front than many men during the war, Yelle and her colleagues showed that women were able to perform well in combat conditions.

References

Jeanne Holm, *Women in the Military: An Unfinished Revolution* (1992); Molly Moore, "Women Face Combat Risk," *Washington Post* (12 September 1991): 1.

Yeomanettes
See World War I; Yeomen (F).

Yeomen (F)
On the verge of entering World War I, the United States Armed Forces expected to need more workers in clerical and communications jobs. The naval reserve and marine reserve corps set up a special category called USNR (F) or Yeoman (F)—the F standing for female—for women performing these jobs during the war. The public soon began calling these Navy women Yeomanettes.

Around 13,000 women served in the two yeoman (F) corps both in the United States and overseas. It was the first time American women had been accorded military status and rank (up to the rank of sergeant). The women wore uniforms and were usually assigned to clerical jobs so more Navy men could go into combat positions. Many Yeomen (F) were called upon to do other jobs that had been traditionally assigned to men, such as translating and recruiting.

Although the women's reserve was viewed as a temporary organization to last only for the duration of the war, it paved the way for broader involvement of women during World War II, when thousands of women joined the Navy. Some women served with the Navy during both world wars.

See also

United States Navy; Women Accepted for Voluntary Emergency Service (WAVES).

References

Joy Bright Hancock, *Lady in the Navy: A Personal Remembrance* (1972); U.S. Department of the Navy: "Facts on Women in the Navy" (1995).

Young, Lucy
See Top Gun.

Young Men's Christian Association (YMCA)
The Young Men's Christian Association (YMCA), established in 1844 in

Elsie Spear wraps herself in the nation's flag before being sworn in as the first yeoman (F) on 30 March 1917.

London, carries on the work symbolized in its red triangle emblem: religion, education, athletics. Because it was a large, well-developed organization, the United States Army asked the YMCA to take a major role during World War I to "provide for the amusement and recreation of the troops by means of its usual program of social, educational, physical and religious activities."

In June 1917, two prominent American women, Mrs. Vincent Astor and Mrs. Theodore Roosevelt, Jr., went abroad to begin setting up and running canteens. The YMCA established hundreds of canteens in Europe, some near battle lines. Faced with a shortage of male workers in their European canteens, the YMCA found many women eager to volunteer. In a statement to the press, the YMCA announced that it would allow women to work in canteens, kitchens, and cafes it had set up overseas for servicemen. The women were expected to be energetic, sensible, able to get along with others, and bring high ideals and useful experiences to their work. Success in a canteen required "Pep, Personality, and Persistence," according to a newspaper headline of the day. During the summer of 1918, more than a thousand women applied to work in these jobs every week.

About 3,500 American women worked in canteens, as well as in cafeterias, officers' clubs, and leave areas located in France, England, Italy, and even Siberia. Women also worked in offices in clerical jobs, handling the YMCA's mail and sending out letters.

Hundreds of entertainers went to Europe to entertain Allied troops under the direction of the YMCA, which also sponsored the Overseas Theater League for this purpose. Other women did support work for the shows or found costumes, props, and other items needed for performances. Popular entertainer Elsie Janis performed her one-woman show for thousands of servicemen. She also took part in benefits to raise money for the war. Other popular women entertainers in the Y-sponsored events included Margaret Wilson, daughter of the president, and Tsianina, the daughter of a Cherokee Indian chief who had two brothers serving in the war. The YMCA also funded a group called the "Over There Theater League."

See also
Canteens.
References
Marian Baldwin, *Canteening Overseas, 1917–1919* (1920); Katherine Morse, *The Uncensored Letters of a Canteen Girl* (1920); Dorothy and Carl J. Schneider, *Into the Breach: Women Overseas during World War I* (1991); YMCA, *Service with Fighting Men: An Account of the Work of the American Young Men's Christian Association in the World War* (1924).

Young Women's Christian Association (YWCA)

Traditionally a pacifist organization, the Young Women's Christian Association (YWCA) declared that its mission during World War I would be to help meet the needs of women involved in the war, both in America and abroad. Young women planning to go overseas could take classes in physical fitness and other skills at the YWCA. Abroad, about 350 YWCA volunteers helped women with housing, restaurant, and recreational facilities. They set up hostess houses where women could stay while visiting their husbands at bases in the United States. Women serving with the armed forces could use the YWCA facilities set up for them, such as sewing rooms, music rooms, and tea rooms. In Paris, YWCA workers provided many services for women in the Signal Corps. As part of its United War Work Campaign, the Y also published posters saying, "Back our girls over there."

See also

Ingraham, Mary Shotwell; Volunteers; Young Men's Christian Association (YMCA).

Reference

Dorothy and Carl J. Schneider, *Into the Breach: American Women Overseas during World War I* (1991).

Z

Zane, Betty (n.d.)

During the American Revolution, Betty Zane was living with her family on the West Virginia frontier. In 1782 when Fort Henry was threatened, Zane raced under fire to her cabin to fetch a store of gunpowder. The fort had been attacked by 350 Indian men, and a mere 60 people—40 of them women and children—were inside.

Wrapping it up in a carpet (some say a tablecloth), Zane carried the gunpowder back to the fort to the waiting soldiers. For risking her life to save others, young Zane was called "the heroine of Fort Henry." The battle turned out to be the last one of the war. A monument in her honor stands at the entrance to Walnut Grove Cemetery in Ohio where she is buried.

Reference

Zane Grey, *Betty Zane* (1903); Selma Williams, *Demeter's Daughters: The Women Who Founded America* (1976).

Bibliography

Books

Abram, Ruth. *"Send Us a Lady Physician": Women Doctors in America, 1835–1920.* New York: Norton, 1985.

Alcott, Louisa May. *Hospital Sketches.* New York: Sagamore Press, 1957.

Alsmeyer, Marie Bennett. *The Way of the WAVES: Women in the Navy.* Conway, AR: HAMBA Books, 1981.

Altman, Susan. *Extraordinary Black Americans.* Chicago: Children's Press, 1989.

Amott, Teresa, and Julie Matthaei. *Race, Gender, and Work: A Multicultural Economic History of Women in the United States.* Boston: South End Press, 1991.

Anderson, Karen. *Wartime Women: Sex Roles, Family Relations, and the Status of Women during World War II.* Westport, CT: Greenwood Press, 1981.

Andrews, Eliza Frances. *The War-Time Journal of a Georgia Girl.* New York: Appleton, 1908.

Anthony, Susan B. *Out of the Kitchen and into the War: Woman's Winning Role in the Nation's Drama.* New York: Stephen Daye, 1943.

Anticaglia, Elizabeth. *Heroines of '76.* New York: Walker, 1975.

Army Center of Military History. *History of the Women's Army Corps, 1942–1978.* Washington, DC: Center of Military History, 1989.

Army Times editors. *A History of the United States Signal Corps.* New York: Army Times Publishing Co., 1961.

Ayer, Eleanor H. *Margaret Bourke-White.* New York: Harper & Row, 1987.

Aynes, Maj. Edith, A.N.C. *From Nightingale to Eagle: The Army Nurses History.* Englewood Cliffs, NJ: Prentice Hall, 1973.

Bailey, Ronald H., and the editors of Time-Life Books. *World War II: The Home Front: USA.* Alexandria, VA: Time-Life Books, Inc., 1978.

Bakeless, Katherine, and John Bakeless. *Spies in the Revolution.* New York: Scholastic, 1969.

Baker, Helen. *Women in War Industries.* Princeton, NJ: Princeton University Press, 1942.

Baker, Nina Brown. *Cyclone in Calico: The Story of Mary Ann Bickerdyke.* Boston: Little, Brown, 1952.

Baldwin, Marian. *Canteening Overseas, 1917–1919.* New York: The Macmillan Co., 1920.

Barkalow, Carol, with Andrea Raab. *In the Men's House: An Inside Account of Life in the Army by one of West Point's First Female Graduates.* New York: Poseidon Press, 1990.

Barker-Benfield, G. J., and Catherine Clinton. *Portraits of American Women.* 2 vols. New York: St. Martin's, 1991.

Barton, George. *Angels of the Battlefield: A History of the Labors of the Catholic Sisterhoods in the Late Civil War.* Philadelphia: The Catholic Art Publishing Company, 1897.

______ . *World's Greatest Military Spies and Secret Service Agents.* Boston: Page Company, 1917.

Barton, William E. *The Life of Clara Barton, Founder of the American Red Cross.* Boston: Houghton Mifflin, 1992.

Becraft, Carolyn. *Women in the Military 1980–1990.* Washington, DC: Women's Research and Education Institute, 1990.

Belford, Barbara. *Brilliant Bylines: A Biographical Anthology of Notable Newspaperwomen in America.* New York: Columbia University Press, 1986.

Bellefaire, Judith. *The Army Nurse Corps in World War II.* Washington, DC: U.S. Army Center of Military History, 1976.

Bernstein, Allison R. *American Indians and World War II.* Norman: University of Oklahoma Press, 1991.

Berube, Allan. *Coming out under Fire: The History of Gay Men and Women in World War Two.* New York: Free Press, 1990.

Binkin, Martin, and Shirley J. Bach. *Women and the Military.* Washington, DC: The Brookings Institution, 1977.

Blackford, Susan Lee. *Letters from Lee's Army.* New York: Scribner's, 1947.

Blacksmith, E. A., ed. *Women in the Military.* New York: H. W. Wilson Co., 1992.

Blackwell, Elizabeth. *Pioneer Work in Opening the Medical Profession to Women.* London, New York: Longmans, Green & Co., 1895

Bliven, Bruce. *Volunteers, One and All.* New York: Reader's Digest Press, 1976.

Blum, John Morton. *V Was for Victory: Politics and American Culture during World War II.* New York: Harcourt Brace Jovanovich, 1976.

Boardman, Mabel. *Under the Red Cross Flag at Home and Abroad.* Philadelphia, London: J. B. Lippincott, 1915.

Booker, Simeon. *Susie King Taylor, Civil War Nurse.* New York: McGraw Hill, 1969.

Booth, Evangeline, and Grace Livingstone Hill. *The War Romance of the Salvation Army.* Philadelphia, London: J. B. Lippincott, 1919.

Botkin, B. A. *A Civil War Treasury of Tales, Legends, and Folklore.* Secaucus, NJ: Blue & Gray Press, 1985.

Bourke-White, Margaret. *Portrait of Myself.* New York: Simon & Schuster, 1963.

Boutwell, Elizabeth. *Daughter of Liberty.* Cleveland, OH: World Publishing Co., 1967.

Boyd, Belle. *Belle Boyd in Camp and Written by Herself.* South Brunswick, NJ: Thomas Yoseloff, 1968.

Bradley, Jeff. *A Young Person's Guide to Military Service.* Boston: Harvard Common Press, 1987.

Brewer, Lucy. *The Female Marine.* New York: Da Capo Press, 1966.

Brink, Randy. *Lost Star: The Search for Amelia Earhart.* New York: Norton, 1994.

Britt, Brink. *The Hungry War.* Barre, MA: Barre Gazette, 1961.

Brockett, L. P., and Mary C. Vaughan. *Woman's Work in the Civil War: A Record of Heroism, Patriotism, and Patience.* Philadelphia: Ziegler, McCurdy & Co., 1867.

Brooks, Geraldine. *Dames and Daughters of Colonial Days.* New York: Arno Press, 1974.

Brooks-Pazmany, Kathleen. *United States Women in Aviation, 1919–1929.* Washington, DC: Smithsonian Institution Press, 1991.

Brown, David, and W. Richard Bruner, eds. *I Can Tell It Now.* New York: E. P. Dutton, 1964.

______ . *How I Got That Story.* New York: E. P. Dutton, 1967.

Brumgardt, John R., ed. *Civil War Nurse: The Diary and Letters of Hannah Ropes.* Knoxville: University of Tennessee Press, 1980.

Bullough, Vern, and Bonnie Bullough. *The Care of the Sick: The Emergence of Modern Nursing.* New York: Prodist, 1978.

Callahan, Sean, ed. *The Photographs of Margaret Bourke-White.* New York: New York Graphic Society, 1972.

Cammermeyer, Margarethe. *Serving in Silence.* New York: Viking, 1994.

Campbell, D'Ann. *Women at War with America: Private Lives in a Patriotic Era.* Cambridge, MA: Harvard University Press, 1984.

Carse, Robert. *Keepers of the Light.* New York: Scribner, 1969.

Catton, Bruce. *The Civil War.* New York: American Heritage, 1985.

Chafe, William H. *The American Woman: Her Changing Social, Economic, and Political Roles, 1920–1970.* New York: Oxford University Press, 1972.

______ . *The Paradox of Change: American Women in the Twentieth Century.* New York: Oxford University Press, 1991.

Chang, Ina. *A Separate Battle: Women and the Civil War.* New York: Dutton (Lodestar), 1991.

Chapline, Neal. *Molly's Boots.* Detroit: Harlo Press, 1983.

Chappelle, Dickey. *What's a Woman Doing Here?* New York: William Morrow, 1962.

Chidsey, Donald Barr. *The War in the South.* New York: Crown, 1969.

Churchill, Jan. *On Wings to War: Teresa James, Aviator.* Manhattan, KS: Sunflower University Press, 1992.

Chrisman, Catherine Bell. *My War, W.W. II as Experienced by One Woman Soldier.* Denver: Maverick Publications, 1989.

Claghorn, Charles E. *Women Patriots of the American Revolution: A Biographical Dictionary.* Metuchen, NJ and London: Scarecrow Press, 1991.

Clark, Judith Freeman. *Almanac of the American Women in the 20th Century.* New York: Prentice Hall, 1987.

Clark, Timothy R., ed. *The World Wars Remembered: Personal Recollections of Heroes, Hello Girls, Flying Aces, Prisoners, Survivors, and Those on the Home Front, from the Pages of Yankee Magazine.* Dublin, NH: Yankee, Inc., 1979.

Clayton, Susan D., and Faye J. Crosby. *Justice, Gender, and Affirmative Action.* Ann Arbor: University of Michigan Press, 1992.

Clifford, Mary Louise, and J. Candace Clifford. *Women Who Kept the Lights: An Illustrated History of Female Lighthouse Keepers.* Williamsburg, VA: Cypress Communications, 1993.

Clinton, Catherine. *The Other Civil War: American Women in the 19th Century.* New York: Hill & Wang, 1984.

Clymer, Eleanor, and Lillian Erlich. *Modern American Career Women.* New York: Dodd, Mead, 1959.

Clyne, Frances. *The Coast Guard at War, Women's Reserve.* Washington, DC: U.S. Coast Guard Headquarters, 1945.

Clyne, Patricia Edwards. *Patriots in Pettycoats.* New York: Dodd, Mead, 1976.

Cochran, Jacqueline. *The Stars at Noon.* Boston: Little, Brown, 1954.

Cochran, Jacqueline, and Maryann Bucknum Brinley. *Jackie Cochran: An Autobiography.* New York: Bantam Books, 1987.

Cohen, Stan. *V Is for Victory: America's Home Front during World War II.* Missoula, MT: Pictorial Histories Publishing Co., 1991.

Cohn, Jan. *Improbable Fiction: The Life of Mary Roberts Rinehart.* Pittsburgh, PA: University of Pittsburgh Press, 1980.

Cole, Jean H. *Women Pilots of World War II.* Salt Lake City: University of Utah Press, 1992.

Collins, Budd, ed. *Bud Collins' Modern Encyclopedia of Tennis.* Detroit, MI: Gale Research, 1994.

Collins, Jean R. *She Was There: Stories of Pioneering Women Journalists.* New York: Julian Messner, 1980.

Collis, Septima M. (Mrs. General Charles H. T. Collis). *A Woman's War Record.* New York: G. P. Putnam's Sons, 1889.

Colman, Penny. *Spies! Women and the Civil War.* Cincinnati: Betterway Books, 1992.

______. *A Woman Unafraid: The Achievements of Frances Perkins.* New York: Atheneum, 1993.

______. *Rosie the Riveter: Women Working on the Home Front in World War II.* New York: Crown, 1995.

Conrad, Earl. *Harriet Tubman, Negro Soldier and Abolitionist.* New York: Paul S. Eriksson, 1943.

Cooper, Richard. *Military Manpower and the All-Volunteer Force.* Santa Monica, CA: Rand, 1977.

Cornum, Rhonda, as told to Peter Copeland. *She Went to War: The Rhonda Cornum Story.* Novato, CA: Presidio, 1992.

Craven, Westley F., and James L. Cate, eds. *The Army Air Forces in World War II.* Vol. 7. Washington, DC: Office of Air Force History, 1983.

Crites, Laura L., and Winifred J. Hepperle. *Women, the Courts, and Equality.* New York: Russell Sage, 1987.

Crozier, Emmet. *American Reporters on the Western Front, 1914–1918.* New York: Oxford University Press, 1959.

Cumming, Kate. *The Journal of a Confederate Nurse.* Savannah, GA: Beehive Press, 1975.

Damman, Nancy. *A WAC's Story: From Brisbane to Manila.* Sun City, AZ: Social Change Press, 1992.

Dannett, Sylvia. *She Rode with the Generals.* New York: Thomas Nelson & Sons, 1960.

______, ed. *Noble Women of the North.* New York: Thomas Yoseloff, 1959.

Davis, Burke. *The Civil War: Strange and Fascinating Facts.* New York: The Fairfax Press, 1982.

Davis, Curtis Carroll, ed. *Belle Boyd in Camp and Prison.* New York: Thomas Yoseloff, 1968.

Davis, Marianna. *Contributions of Black Women to America.* Columbia, SC: Kendfay Press, 1982.

Dawson, Sarah M. *A Confederate Girl's Diary.* Bloomington: University of Indiana Press, 1960.

De Beauvoir, Simone. *The Second Sex.* New York: Bantam, 1952.

De Pauw, Linda Grant. *The First Enlisted Women, 1917–1918.* Philadelphia: Dorrance and Co., 1955.

______. *Founding Mothers: Women of America in the Revolutionary Era.* Boston, MA: Houghton Mifflin, 1975.

______. *Seafaring Women.* Boston, MA: Houghton Mifflin, 1982.

Dessez, Eunice C. *The First Enlisted Women 1917–18.* Philadelphia: Dorrance and Co., 1955.

Devilbiss, M. C. *Women and Military Service: A History, Analysis, and Overview of the Key Issues.* Maxwell Air Force Base, AL: Air University Press, 1990.

Dorr, Rheta Childe. *A Woman of Fifty.* New York: Funk & Wagnall's, 1924.

Douglas, Deborah G. *United States Women in Aviation, 1940–1985.* Washington, DC: Smithsonian Institution Press, 1991.

Dulles, Foster Rhea. *The American Red Cross: A History.* New York: Harper & Brothers, 1950.

Earhart, Amelia. *20 Hrs., 40 Min.* New York: G. P. Putnam's Sons, 1928.

Earley, Charity Adams. *One Woman's Army: A Black Officer Remembers the WAC.* College Station, TX: Texas A & M Press, 1989.

Ebbert, Jean, and Marie-Beth Hall. *Crossed Current: Navy Women from WWI to Tailhook.* Washington, DC: Brassey's, 1993.

Ebener, Charlotte. *No Facilities for Women.* New York: Knopf, 1955.

Edmonds, Sarah Emma. *Nurse and Spy in the Union Army: Comprising the Adventures and Experiences of a Woman in Hospitals, Camps, and Battlefields.* Hartford, CT: W. S. Williams and Co., 1865.

Edwards, Julia. *Women of the World: The Great Foreign Correspondents.* Boston: Houghton Mifflin, 1988.

Elhstain, Jean Bethke. *Women and War.* New York: Basic Books, 1987.

Elish, Dan. *Harriet Tubman and the Underground Railroad.* Brookfield, CT: Millbrook Press.

Ellet, Elizabeth F. *The Women of the American Revolution.* New York: Baker and Scribner, 1850.

Ellis, Joseph, and Robert Moore. *School for Soldiers.* New York: Oxford University Press, 1974.

Elting, Colonel John R. *American Army Life.* New York: Charles Scribner's Sons, 1982.

Elwood-Akers, Virginia. *Women War Correspondents in the Vietnam War, 1961–1975.* Metuchen, NJ: Scarecrow Press, 1988.

Encyclopedia of the Civil War. New York: Harper & Row, 1986.

Enloe, Cynthia. *Does Khaki Become You? The Militarization of Women's Lives.* London: Pandora Press, 1988.

Eskanazi, Martin, and David Gallen. *Sexual Harassment: Know Your Rights.* New York: Carroll and Graf, 1992.

Evans, Elizabeth. *Weathering the Storm: Women of the American Revolution.* New York: Scribner's, 1975.

Evans, Sara M. *Born for Liberty: A History of Women in America.* New York: Free Press, 1989.

Fennelly, Catherine. *Connecticut Women in the Revolutionary Era.* Chester, CT: Pequot Press, 1975.

Fermi, Laura. *Atoms in the Family: My Life with Enrico Fermi.* Chicago: University of Chicago Press, 1954.

FitzGerald, Frances. *Fire in the Lake.* Boston: Atlantic–Little, Brown, 1972.

Foner, Philips, ed. *Women and the American Labor Movement.* New York: Free Press, 1979.

Frank, Miriam, Marilyn Ziebarth, and Connie Field. *The Life and Times of Rosie the Riveter.* Emeryville, CA: Clarity Educational Productions, 1982.

Franklin, John Hope. *From Slavery to Freedom: A History of Negro Americans.* New York: Knopf, 1980.

Franklin, John Hope, and August Meier, eds. *Black Leaders of the Twentieth Century.* Urbana: University of Illinois Press, 1982.

Fraser, Antonia. *The Warrior Queens.* New York: Knopf, 1989.

Fredericks, Pierce, ed. *The Civil War as They Knew It.* New York: Bantam Books, 1961.

Freeman, Lucy, and Alma H. Bond. *America's First Woman Warrior: The Courage of Deborah Sampson.* New York: Paragon House, 1992.

Gellhorn, Martha. *The Face of War.* New York: Simon & Schuster, 1959.

General Accounting Office (GAO). *Actions Needed To Ensure Female Veterans Have Equal Access to VA Benefits.* Washington, DC: GAO Office, 1982.

George, Carol V. R., ed. *"Remember the Ladies": New Perspectives on Women in U.S. History.* Syracuse, NY: Syracuse University Press, 1975.

Geyer, Georgie Anne. *Buying the Night Flight: The Autobiography of a Woman Foreign Correspondent.* New York: Dell, 1983.

Gilbo, Patrick F. *The American Red Cross: The First Century.* New York: Harper & Row, 1981.

Gilden, Nina. *Counting Sexual Harassment: Theory and Applications for the Defense*, 1981.

Gluck, Sherna Berger. *Rosie the Riveter Revisited: Women, the War, and Social Change.* Boston: Twayne Publishers, 1987.

Goldberg, Vicki. *Margaret Bourke-White: A Biography.* New York: Harper & Row, 1986.

Goldman, Nancy Loring, ed. *Female Soldiers—Combatants or Noncombatants?* Westport, CT: Greenwood Press, 1982.

Goueff, Stephane. *Manhattan Project.* Boston: Little, Brown, 1967.

Green, Anne Bosanko. *One Woman's War: Letters Home from the Women's Army Corps, 1944–1946.* St. Paul: Minnesota Historical Press, 1989.

Greenbie, Marjorie Barstow. *Lincoln's Daughters of Mercy.* New York: G. P. Putnam's Sons, 1944.

Greenwald, Maurine Weiner. *Women, War, and Work: The Impact of World War I on Women Workers in the United States.* Westport, CT: Greenwood Press, 1980.

Grey, Zane. *Betty Zane.* New York: Grosset & Dunlap, 1903.

Gribble, Francis Henry. *Women in War.* London: Sampson Low, Marston & Co., 1916.

Groves, Leslie R. *Now It Can Be Told.* New York: Harper, 1962.

Gruenberg, Sidonie, ed. *The Family in a World at War.* New York: Harper & Brothers, 1942.

Gruhzit-Hoyt, Olga. *They Also Served: American Women in World War II.* Secaucus, NJ: Carol Publishing/Birch Lane, 1995.

Gutek, Barbara A. *Sex and the Workplace.* San Francisco: Jossey-Bass, 1985.

Hall, Marie Beth. *Crossed Current: Navy Women from World War II to Tailhook.* Washington, DC: Brassey's, 1993.

Hall, Richard. *Patriots in Disguise: Women Warriors of the Civil War.* New York: Paragon House, 1993.

Hancock, Joy Bright. *Lady in the Navy: A Personal Remembrance.* Annapolis, MD: Naval Institute Press, 1972.

Harris, Barbara J. *Beyond Her Sphere: Women and the Professions in American History.* Westport, CT: Greenwood Press, 1978.

Harris, Mark Jonathan, Franklin D. Mitchell, and Steven J. Schechter. *The Homefront: America during World War II.* New York: G. P. Putnam's Sons, 1984.

Hartmann, Susan M. *The Home Front and Beyond: American Women in the 1940s.* Boston: Twayne Publishers, 1982.

Hayton-Keeva, Sally. *Valiant Women in War and Exile: Thirty-Eight True Stories.* San Francisco: City Lights Books, 1987.

Headley, John W. *Confederate Operations in Canada and New York.* New York: Neale Publishing Co., 1906.

Hechter, Holly, and Elaine El-Khawes. *Joining Forces: The Military's Impact on College Enrollments.* Washington, DC: Department of Defense, 1992.

Hewitt, Linda L. *Women Marines of World War I.* Washington, DC: History and Museum Division, Headquarters, U.S. Marine Corps, 1974.

Higgins, Marguerite. *War in Korea.* New York: Doubleday, 1951.

______ . *News Is a Singular Thing.* New York: Doubleday, 1955.

______ . *Our Vietnam Nightmare.* New York: Harper & Row, 1965.

Higonnet, Margaret Randolph, et al., eds. *Behind the Lines: Gender and the Two World Wars.* New Haven, CT: Yale University Press, 1987.

Hine, Darlene Clark, ed. *Black Women in America: An Historical Encyclopedia.* 2 vols. Brooklyn, NY: Carlson, 1993.

Hoehling, Adolph A. *Women Who Spied: True Stories of Feminine Espionage from the American Revolution to the Present Day.* New York: Dodd, Mead, 1967.

Hohenberg, John. *Foreign Correspondence: The Great Reporters and Their Times.* New York: Columbia University Press, 1964.

Holden, Henry M. *Ladybirds: The Untold Story of Women Pilots in America.* Seattle, WA: Black Hawk Press, 1991.

Holland, Mary A. Gardner, ed. *Our Army Nurses.* Boston: B. Wilkins & Co., 1895.

Hollander, Phyllis. *American Women in Sports.* New York: Grosset & Dunlap, 1972.

Holm, Major General Jeanne. *Women in the Military: An Unfinished Revolution.* Novato, CA: Presidio Press, 1992.

Holt, Rackham. *Mary McCleod Bethune.* Garden City, NY: Doubleday, 1964.

Honey, Maureen. *Creating Rosie the Riveter: Class, Gender, and Propaganda during World War II.* Amherst: University of Massachusetts Press, 1984.

Horan, James D. *Confederate Agent: A Discovery in History.* New York: Crown, 1954.

Hovis, Bobbi. *Station Hospital Saigon: A Navy Nurse in Vietnam, 1963–1964.* Annapolis, MD: Naval Institute Press, 1991.

Howe, Julia Ward. *Reminiscences, 1819–1899.* Boston, New York: Houghton Mifflin Co., 1899.

Humphrey, Mary Ann. *My Country, My Right To Serve: Experiences of Gay Men and Women in the Military, World War II to the Present.* New York: HarperCollins, 1990.

Hunton, Adele, and Kathryn Johnson. *Two Colored Women with the American Expeditionary Forces.* Brooklyn, NY: Brooklyn Eagle Press, 1971.

Jacobs, Helen Hull. *"By Your Leave, Sir": The Story of a WAVE.* New York: Dodd, Mead & Co., 1943.

Jacquette, Henrietta, ed. *South after Gettysburg: Letters of Cornelia Hancock from the Army of the Potomac, 1863–1865.* New York: T. Y. Crowell Company, 1956.

Jakes, John. *Great War Correspondents.* New York: Putnam, 1967.

James, Edward T., Janet Wilson James, and Paul S. Boyer, eds. *Notable American Women, 1607–1950: A Biographical Dictionary.* Cambridge, MA: Belknap Press of Harvard University, 1971.

Johnson, Jesse J. *Black Women in the Armed Forces, 1941–1974.* Hampton, VA: Hampton Institute, 1974.

Johnson, Robert Erwin. *Guardians of the Sea: History of the U.S. Coast Guard, 1915 to the Present.* Annapolis, MD: Naval Institute Press, 1987.

Jones, Jacqueline. *Labor of Love, Labor of Sorrow: Black Women, Work, and the Family from Slavery to the Present.* New York: Basic Books, 1985.

Jones, Katharine M. *Heroines of Dixie: Confederate Women Tell Their Story of the War.* Indianapolis, IN: Bobbs-Merrill, 1955.

______ . *Ladies of Richmond.* Indianapolis, IN: Bobbs-Merrill, 1962.

Kane, Harnett T. *Spies for the Blue and Gray.* Garden City, NY: Hanover House, 1954.

Kaplan, Janice. *Women and Sports.* New York: Viking Press, 1979.

Kaplan, Sidney. *The Black Presence in the Era of the American Revolution, 1770–1800.* Greenwich, CT: New York Graphic Society, 1973.

Keil, Sally Van Wagenen. *Those Wonderful Women and Their Flying Machines: The Unknown Heroines of World War II.* New York: Four Directions Press, 1990.

Kerber, Linda. *Women of the Republic.* Chapel Hill: University of North Carolina Press, 1980.

Kernodle, Portia. *The Red Cross Nurse in Action, 1882–1948.* New York: Harper & Brothers, 1949.

Klapthor, Margaret Brown. *The First Ladies.* Washington, DC: White House Historical Association, 1979.

Kluger, Richard. *The Paper: The Life and Death of the New York Herald Tribune.* New York: Knopf. 1986.

Laffin, John. *Women in Battle.* London: Abelard Schuman, 1967.

Landrum, John Belton O'Neall. *Colonial and Revolutionary History of Upper South Carolina.* Spartanburg, SC: Reprint Co., 1971.

Lanker, Brian. *I Dream a World: Portraits of Black Women Who Changed America.* New York: Stewart, Tabori & Chang, 1989.

Laurence, William L. *Dawn over Zero: The Story of the Atomic Bomb.* New York: Knopf, 1947.

Lederer, Wolfgang. *The Fear of Women.* New York: Harcourt Brace Jovanovich, 1968.

Lerner, Gerda, ed. *The Female Experience: An American Documentary.* Indianapolis, IN: Bobbs-Merrill, 1977.

Litoff, Judy Barrett, and David C. Smith, eds. *We're in This War, Too: World War II Letters from American Women in Uniform.* New York: Oxford University Press, 1994.

Livermore, Mary A. *My Story of the War.* Hartford, CT: A. D. Worthington & Co., 1887.

Logan, Rayford W., and Michael R. Winston, eds. *Dictionary of American Negro Biography.* New York: Norton, 1982.

Long, Clarence D. *The Labor Force under Changing Income and Employment.* Princeton, NJ: Princeton University Press, 1958.

Lovejoy, Esther Pohl. *Women Doctors of the World.* New York: Macmillan.

Lutz, Alma, ed. *With Love, Jane: Letters from American Women on the War Fronts.* New York: John Day Co., 1945.

Lyne, Mary C., and Kay Arthur. *Three Years behind the Mast: The Story of the United States Coast Guard SPARS.* Washington, DC: n.p., 1946.

McAuley, Mary. *Germany in Wartime: What an American Girl Saw and Heard.* Chicago: The Open Court Publishing Company, 1917.

McCann, Nancy Dodd, and Thomas A. McGinn. *Harassed: 100 Women Define Inappropriate Behavior in the Workplace.* Homewood, IL: Business One Irwin, 1992.

McClard, Megan. *Harriet Tubman: Slavery and the Underground Railroad.* Englewood Cliffs, NJ: Silver Burdett Press, 1991.

MacCloskey, Monro. *Your Future in the Military Services.* New York: Richard Rosen Press, Inc., 1979.

McCullough, Joan. *First of All: Significant "Firsts" by American Women.* New York: Holt, Rinehart & Winston, 1980.

MacDonald, Anne L. *Feminine Ingenuity: Women and Invention in America.* New York: Ballantine Books, 1992.

Macdonald, Sharon, Pat Holden, and Shirley Ardener, eds. *Images of Women in Peace and War: Cross-Cultural and Historical Perspectives.* Madison: University of Wisconsin Press, 1987.

Macksey, Joan, and Kenneth Macksey. *The Book of Women's Achievements.* New York: Stein and Day, 1976.

McWhirter, Norris, et al., eds. *1986 Guinness Book of World Records.* New York: Sterling Publishing Co., 1986.

Magid, Ken. *Women of Courage: The Women Airforce Service Pilots of World War II.* Lakewood, CO: K. M. Productions, 1993.

Markel, Robert, and Nancy Brooks. *For the Record: Women in Sports.* New York: World Almanac Publications, 1985.

Markle, Donald E. *Spies and Spymasters of the Civil War.* New York: Hippocrene, 1994.

Marks, Geoffrey, and William K. Beatty. *Women in White.* New York: Scribner, 1972.

Marshall, Helen. *Dorothea Dix: Forgotten Samaritans.* Chapel Hill: University of North Carolina Press, 1937.

Marshall, Kathryn. *In the Combat Zone: An Oral History of American Women in Vietnam.* Boston: Little, Brown, 1987.

Martzolf, Marion. *Up from the Footnotes: A History of Women Journalists.* New York: Hastings House, 1977.

Massey, Mary E. *Bonnet Brigades.* New York: Knopf, 1966.

May, Antoinette. *Witness to War: A Biography of Marguerite Higgins.* New York: Beaufort Books, 1983.

May, Elaine Tyler. *Pushing the Limits: American Women 1940–1961.* New York: Oxford University Press, 1994.

Mays, Joe H. *Black Americans and Their Contributions toward Union Victory in the American Civil War (1861–1865).* Lanham, MD: University Press of America, 1894.

Meacham, Hon. Alfred Benjamin. *Wi-Ne-Ma (The Woman Chief) and Her People.* Hartford, CT: American Publishing Co., 1876.

Meid, Pat. *Marine Corps Women's Reserve in World War II.* Washington, DC: U.S. Marine Corps, 1968.

Meigs, Cornelia. *Invincible Louisa.* Boston: Little, Brown, 1933.

Meltzer, Milton. *Voices from the Civil War: A Documentary History of the Great American Conflict.* New York: Thomas Y. Crowell, 1989.

Merrill, Francis. *Social Problems on the Home Front.* New York: Harper & Brothers, 1948.

Meyer, Edith Patterson. *Petticoat Patriots of the American Revolution.* New York: Vanguard Press, 1976.

Mezey, Susan Gluck. *In Pursuit of Equality: Women, Public Policy and the Federal Courts.* New York: St. Martin's Press, 1992.

Milkman, Ruth. *Gender at Work: The Dynamics of Job Segregation by Sex during World War II.* Urbana: University of Illinois Press, 1987.

Mills, H. Sinclair, Jr. *The Vivandiere: History, Tradition, Uniform and Service.* Collinswood, NJ: C. W. Historicals, 1988.

Millstein, Beth, and Jeanne Bodine. *We, the American Women, a Documentary History.* New York: Jerome S. Ozer, 1977.

Mitchell, Brian. *Weak Link: The Feminization of the American Military.* Washington, DC: Regnery Gateway, 1989.

Mitchell, Frances Robinson. *Experiencing the Depression and World War II.* Orono, ME: Bear Paw Press, 1989.

Mohr, Lillian Holmen. *Frances Perkins: "That Woman in FDR's Cabinet!"* Croton-on-Hudson, NY: North River Press, 1979.

Moore, Frank. *Women of the War: Their Heroism and Self-Sacrifice.* Hartford, CT: Scranton, 1866.

Morden, Bettie J. *The Women's Army Corps 1945–1978.* Washington, DC: Center of Military History, 1990.

Morris, Richard Brandon, ed. *The American Revolution, 1763–1783.* Minneapolis, MN: Lerner Publications, 1985.

______. *The United States Navy.* Minneapolis, MN: Lerner Publications, 1992.

Morse, Kathrine. *The Uncensored Letters of a Canteen Girl.* New York: Henry Holt and Co., 1920.

Moskin, J. Robert. *The U.S. Marine Corps Story.* New York: McGraw Hill, 1977.

Murray, Keith. *The Modocs and Their War.* Norman: University of Oklahoma Press, 1959.

Myerson, Joel, and Daniel Shealy, eds. *The Journals of Louisa May Alcott.* Boston: Little, Brown, 1989.

Naden, Corinne J., and Rose Blue. *The United States Air Force.* Brookfield, CT: The Millbrook Press, 1993.

______. *The U.S. Coast Guard.* Brookfield, CT: The Millbrook Press, 1993.

______. *The United States Navy.* Brookfield, CT: The Millbrook Press, 1993.

Norton, Mary Beth. *Liberty's Daughters: The Revolutionary Experience of American Women, 1750–1800.* Boston: Little, Brown, 1980.

Oakes, Claudia M. *United States Women in Aviation: 1930–39.* Washington, DC: Smithsonian Institution, 1991.

Oakley, Anne. *Sex, Gender, and Society.* New York: Harper & Row, 1973.

Olson, Keith. *The G.I. Bill, the Veterans, and the Colleges.* Lexington: University Press of Kentucky, 1974.

Palmer, Laura. *Shrapnel in the Heart: Letters and Remembrances from the Vietnam Veterans Memorial.* New York: Random House, 1987.

Pollack, Elizabeth R. *Yes, Ma'am: The Personal Papers of a WAAC Private.* Philadelphia: J. B. Lippincott, 1943.

Pollard, Clarice F. *Laugh, Cry and Remember: The Journal of a G.I. Lady.* Phoenix, AZ: Journeys Press, 1991.

Pratt, Fletcher, ed. *The Civil War in Pictures.* New York: Holt, 1955.

______. *Ordeal by Fire.* New York: Harper & Row, 1966.

Presidential Commission on the Assignment of Women in the Armed Forces Report to the President. Washington, DC: U.S. Government Printing Office, 1993.

Presidential Commission on the Assignment of Women in the Military, 1980–90. Washington, DC: Women's Research and Education Institute, June 1990.

Pryor, Elizabeth Brown. *Clara Barton, Professional Angel.* Philadelphia: University of Pennsylvania Press, 1987.

Putney, Martha S. *When the Nation Was in Need: Blacks in the Women's Army Corps during World War II.* Metuchen, NJ: Scarecrow Press, 1992.

Read, Phyllis, and Bernard L. Witlieb. *The Book of Women's Firsts.* New York: Random House, 1992.

The Readers Digest Association. *Secrets and Spies: Behind-the-Scenes Stories of World War II.* Pleasantville, NY: Readers Digest Association, 1964.

Redmond, Juanita. *I Served on Bataan.* Philadelphia: J. B. Lippincott, 1943.

Reifert, Gail, and Eugene Dermody. *Women Who Fought: An American History.* Norwalk, CA: Dermody, 1978.

Reit, Seymour. *Behind Rebel Lines: The Incredible Story of Emma Edmonds, Civil War Spy.* San Diego, CA: Harcourt Brace Jovanovich, 1988.

Research Division. *Women in the Military: More Jobs Can Be Opened under Current Status.* Washington, DC: General Accounting Office, September 1988.

______. *Semi-Annual Profile of the Department of Defense Active Forces and the United States Coast Guard.* Patrick Air Force Base, FL: Defense Equal Opportunity Management Institute, September 1992.

Rexford, Oscar W. *Battlestars and Doughnuts.* Tucson, AZ: Patrice Press, 1989.

Rich, Doris L. *Amelia Earhart: A Biography.* Washington, DC: Smithsonian Institution, 1989.

Richmond, Merle. *Phillis Wheatley.* New York: Chelsea House Publishers, 1988.

Riddle, Jeff C. *An Indian History of the Modoc War.* Eugene, OR: Orion Press, 1914.

Rinehart, Mary Roberts. *My Story: A New Edition and Seventeen New Years.* New York: Rinehart & Co., 1948.

Rix, Sara E., ed. *The American Woman: 1987–88: A Status Report in Depth.* New York: Norton, 1987.

Roberts, Mary M. *American Nursing: History and Interpretation.* New York: Macmillan Co., 1954.

Rogan, Helen. *Mixed Company: Women in the Modern Army.* New York: G. P. Putnam's Sons, 1981.

Roosevelt, Eleanor. *Autobiography.* New York: Harper & Row, 1961.

Ropes, Hannah Anderson. *Civil War Nurse.* Knoxville: University of Tennessee Press, 1980.

Ross, Deller, and Ann Barcher. *The Rights of Women.* Carbondale: Southern Illinois University Press, 1984.

Ross, Ishbel. *Ladies of the Press.* New York: Harper & Brothers, 1936.

______. *Child of Destiny.* New York: Harper, 1949.

______. *Rebel Rose: The Life of Rose O'Neal Greenhow, Confederate Spy.* New York: Harper & Row, 1954.

______. *Angel of the Battlefield.* New York: Harper & Row, 1961.

Ross, Mary Steele. *Women in Uniform.* 1943.

Ross, Nancy Wilson. *The WAVES: The Story of the Girls in Blue.* New York: Henry Holt and Co., 1943.

Rowan, N. R. *The U.S. Air Force.* Minneapolis, MN: Lerner Publications, 1994.

______. *The U.S. Army.* Minneapolis, MN: Lerner Publications, 1994.

______. *The U.S. Coast Guard.* Minneapolis, MN: Lerner Publications, 1994.

______. *The U.S. Marine Corps.* Minneapolis, MN: Lerner Publications, 1994.

______. *The U.S. Navy.* Minneapolis, MN: Lerner Publications, 1994.

______. *Women in the Marines: The Boot Camp Challenge.* Minneapolis, MN: Lerner Publications, 1994.

Rowbotham, Sheila. *Women, Resistance, and Revolution.* New York: Pantheon Books, 1972.

Rupp, Leila. *Mobilizing Women for War: German and American Propaganda, 1939–1945.* Princeton, NJ: Princeton University Press, 1978.

Rustad, Michael L. *Women in Khaki: The American Enlisted Women.* New York: Praeger, 1982.

Salem, Dorothy C., ed. *African-American Women: A Biographical Dictionary.* Hamden, CT: Garland, 1993.

Salzberger, C. L., and the editors of *American Heritage. The American Heritage History of World War II.* New York: American Heritage Publishing Co., 1966.

Santoli, Al. *Everything We Had: An Oral History of the Vietnam War.* New York: Random House, 1981.

Satterfield, Archie. *The Home Front: An Oral History of the War Years in America, 1941–1945.* New York: Playboy Press, 1981.

Saywell, Shelley. *Women in War.* New York: Viking, 1985.

Schilpp, Madelon Golden, and Sharon M. Murphy. *Great Women of the Press.* Carbondale: Southern Illinois Press, 1983.

Schlector, Stephen J. *The Homefront: America during World War II.* New York: Putnam, 1984.

Schleichert, Elizabeth. *The Life of Dorothea Dix.* Frederick, MD: Twenty-First Century Books, 1991.

______. *The Life of Elizabeth Blackwell.* Frederick, MD: Twenty-First Century Books, 1992.

Schnapper, M. B. *American Labor: A Pictorial History.* Washington, DC: Public Affairs Press, 1972.

Schneider, Dorothy, and Carl J. Schneider. *Into the Breach: American Women Overseas in World War I.* New York: Viking, 1991.

______. *Sound Off! American Military Women Speak Out.* New York: Paragon House, 1992.

Schultz, Sigrid. *Germany Will Try It Again.* New York: Cornwall Press, 1944.

Schultz, Sigrid, David Brown, and W. Richard Bruner, eds. *I Can Tell It Now.* New York: E. P. Dutton, 1964.

Schwartz, Gerald, ed. *A Woman Doctor's Civil War: Esther Hill Hawks' Diary.* Columbia: University of South Carolina Press, 1984.

Scott, Emmett J. *Official History of the American Negro in the World War.* New York: Arno Press, 1969.

Scruggs, Jan, and Joel L. Swerdlow. *To Heal a Nation: The Vietnam Veterans.* New York: Harper & Row, 1985.

Seth, Ronald. *Some of My Favorite Spies.* Philadelphia: Chilton, 1968.

Sherr, Lynn, and Jurate Kazickas. *The American Women's Gazetteer.* New York: Bantam, 1976.

Shilts, Randy. *Conduct Unbecoming: Lesbians and Gays in the U.S. Military: Vietnam to the Persian Gulf.* New York: St. Martin's Press, 1993.

Siebert, Wilbur H. *The Underground Railroad from Slavery to Freedom.* New York: Macmillan, 1898.

Sifakis, Stewart. *Who Was Who in the Civil War.* New York: Facts on File, 1988.

Simkins, Francis B., and James W. Patton. *The Women of the Confederacy.* Richmond, VA: Garrett & Massie, 1936.

Smith, Jessie Carney, ed. *Notable Black American Women.* Detroit: Gale Research, 1992.

Smith, Winnie. *American Daughter Gone to War.* New York: William Morrow, 1992.

Snow, Edward Rowe, *The Lighthouses of New England.* New York: Dodd, Mead, 1973.

Sochen, June. *Herstory: A Woman's View of American History*. New York: Alfred Publishing Co., 1974.

Soderburg, Peter A. *Women Marines: The World War II Era.* Westport, CT: Praeger, 1992.

Sommerville, Mollie. *Women of the American Revolution.* 1974.

Spratley, Dorothy R. *Women Go to War: Answering the Call in World War II.* Columbus, OH: Hazelnut Publishing Co., 1992.

Stanchak, John E. *Historical Times Illustrated Encyclopedia of the Civil War.* New York: Harper & Row, 1986.

Stansbury, Jean. *Bars on Her Shoulders: A Story of a WAAC.* New York: Dodd, Mead, 1943.

Sterling, Dorothy, ed. *We Are Your Sisters: Black Women in the Nineteenth Century.* New York: Norton, 1984.

Stern, Philip Van Doren. *Secret Missions of the Civil War.* New York: Rand McNally and Co., 1959.

Stiehm, Judith Hicks. *Arms and the Enlisted Women.* Philadelphia: Temple University Press, 1989.

Stremlow, Mary V. *A History of the Women's Marines.* Washington, DC: History and Museums Division, Headquarters, U.S. Marine Corps, 1986.

Stringer, Ann, and Henry Ries. *German Faces.* New York: Sloane, 1950.

Studios, Paula. *Women of Computer History: Forgotten Heroines.* Wilmington, DE: World Information Institution, 1990.

Sullivan, George. *Queens of the Court.* New York: Dodd, Mead, 1974.

______ . *The Day Women Got the Vote*. New York: Scholastic, 1994.

Tarleton, Lieutenant-General Banastre. *A History of the Campaigns of 1780–81*. London: T. Cadell, 1787.

Taylor, Susie King. *Reminiscences of My Life in Camp*. New York: Arno Press, 1968.

Terkel, Studs. *"The Good War": An Oral History of World War Two.* New York: Pantheon Books, 1984.

Thomson, Robin J. *The Coast Guard and the Women's Reserve in World War II.* Washington, DC: Coast Guard Historical Office, 1992.

Tilley, John A. *A History of Women in the Coast Guard.* Washington, DC: U.S. Coast Guard, 1996.

Tocqueville, Alexis de. *Democracy in America.* Garden City, NY: Doubleday, 1969.

Treadwell, Mattie E. *U.S. Army in World War II: Special Studies—The Women's Army Corps.* Washington, DC: Department of the Army, 1954.

Turner, Marjorie. *Women and Work.* Los Angeles, CA: UCLA Institute of Industrial Relations, 1964.

Tuttle, Lisa. *Encyclopedia of Feminism.* New York: Facts on File, 1986.

Tyler, Kathryn Richardson. *The History of the American National Red Cross. Vol. XXXII: Red Cross Negro Personnel in World War II.* Washington, DC: American National Red Cross, 1950.

United States Air Force. "Major General Jeanne M. Holm." 1973.

U.S. Army Information Sheet. "Women Musicians—The 14th Army Band." n.p., n.d.

U.S. Coast Guard Public Information Division. *The Coast Guard at War, Vol. XXII: Women's Reserve.* Washington, DC: U.S. Coast Guard, 1946.

U.S. Department of Defense. *Military Careers: A Guide to Military Occupations and Selected Military Career Paths.* Washington, DC: U.S. Government Printing Office, 1995.

U.S. Department of the Air Force. *History of Women in the Air Force.* Semiannual Reports, 1948–1976.

U.S. Department of the Army. "Facts on the U.S. Army Nurse Corps, 1775–1983." Washington, DC: U.S. Government Printing Office, 1989.

______ . "Background Information: The 50th Anniversary of the Women's Army Corps." Washington, DC: U.S. Government Printing Office, 1992.

______ . "Fact Sheet: Oveta Culp Hobby." Washington, DC: U.S. Government Printing Office, n.d.

U.S. Department of the Army, Medical Department. *Highlights on the History of the Army Nurse Corps.* 1987.

______ . "Fact Sheet: "Grace M. Hopper." 1992.

U.S. Department of the Navy. *White Task Force: History of the Nurse Corps.* Washington, DC: Bureau of Medicine and Surgery, 1946.

______. "Facts on Women in the Navy." 1995.

United States Marine Corps, Division of Public Affairs. "Lieutenant Carol A. Mutter, USMC." 1996.

Utley, Beverly. *Brave Women.* Gettysburg, PA: Historical Times, 1968.

Van Devanter, Lynda, and Christopher Morgan. *Home before Morning: The Story of a Nurse in Vietnam.* New York: Beaufort Books, 1983.

Van Doren, Carl. *Secret History of the American Revolution.* New York: Viking, 1941.

Velasquez, Loreta Janeta. *The Woman in Battle: A Narrative of the Exploits, Adventures and Travels of Madame Loreta Janeta Velasquez, Otherwise Known as Lieutenant Harry T. Buford, Confederate States Army.* Hartford, CT: T. Belknap, 1876.

Verges, Marianne. *On Silver Wings, 1942–44: The Women Airforce Service Pilots of World War II.* New York: Ballantine, 1991.

Vistica, Gregory L. *Fall from Glory.* New York: Simon & Schuster, 1996.

von Miklos, Josephine. *I Took a War Job.* New York: Simon & Schuster, 1943.

Waggaman, Mary. *Women Workers in Wartime and Reconversion.* New York: Paulist Press, 1947.

Wagner, Lilya. *Women War Correspondents in World War II.* Westport, CT: Greenwood Press, 1989.

Wandrey, June. *Bedpan Commando: The Story of a Combat Nurse during World War II.* Elmore, OH: Elmore Publishing Co., 1989.

Warren, Ruth. *A Pictorial History of Women in America.* New York: Crown, 1975.

Weatherford, Doris. *American Women and World War II.* New York: Facts on File, 1990.

Weaver, Robert. *Negro Labor: A National Problem.* New York: Harcourt, Brace, 1946.

Wekesser, Carol, and Matthew Polesetsky, eds. *Women in the Military.* San Diego, CA: Greenhaven Press, 1991.

Welter, Barbara, ed. *The Woman Question in American History.* Hinsdale, IL: Dryden, 1973.

Wertheimer, Barbara. *We Were There: The Story of Working Women in America.* New York: Pantheon Books, 1977.

White, Barbara A. *Lady Leatherneck.* New York: Dodd, Mead, 1945.

Wiley, Bell Irvin. *Confederate Women.* Westport, CT: Greenwood Press, 1975.

Willenz, June A. *Women Veterans: America's Forgotten Heroines.* New York: Continuum, 1983.

Williams, Christine L. *Gender Differences at Work: Women and Men in Nontraditional Occupations.* Berkeley and Los Angeles: University of California Press, 1989.

Williams, Juan. *Eyes on the Prize: America's Civil Rights Years.* New York: Viking, 1987.

Williams, Selma. *Demeter's Daughters: The Women Who Founded America.* New York: Atheneum, 1976.

Wilson, George C. *Flying the Edge: The Making of Navy Test Pilots.* Annapolis, MD: Naval Institute Press, 1992.

Winkler, Allan M. *The Politics of Propaganda: The Office of War Information 1942–1945.* New Haven, CT: Yale University Press, 1978.

______. *Home Front U.S.A.: America during World War II.* Arlington Heights, IL: Harlan Davidson, 1986.

Wise, Nancy Baker, and Christy Wise. *A Mouthful of Rivets: Women at Work in World War II.* San Francisco: Jossey-Bass, 1994.

Women in Congress, 1917–1990. Washington, DC: Office of the Historian, U.S. House of Representatives, U.S. Government Printing Office, 1991.

Women's Research and Education Institute. *Women in the Military: 1980–1990.* Washington, DC: Women's Research and Education Institute, 1990.

Wormley, Kathrine. *The Other Side of the War: With the Army of the Potomac.* Boston: Ticknor & Co., 1889.

YMCA. *Service with Fighting Men: An Account of the Work of the Young Men's Christian Association in the World War.* New York: Association Press, 1924.

Yost, Edna. *American Women of Nursing.* Philadelphia: J. B. Lippincott, 1947.

Young, Donald J. *The Battle of Bataan.* Jefferson, NC: McFarland & Co., 1992.

Zeinert, Karen. *Those Incredible Women of World War II.* Brookfield, CT: The Millbrook Press, 1994.

______. *Elizabeth Van Lew, Southern Belle, Union Spy.* Columbus, OH: Dillon Press, 1995.

Zimmerman, Jean. *Tailspin: Women at War in the Wake of Tailhook.* New York: Doubleday, 1995.

Zumwalt, Elmo R., Jr. *On Watch: A Memoir.* New York: Quadrangle, 1976.

Articles

Abbott, Josephine. "What of Youth in Wartime?" *Survey Midmonthly* 79 (October 1943): 265–267.

Anderson, Karen. "Last Hired, First Fired: Black Women Workers during World War II." *Journal of American History* (June 1982): 82–89.

Atherton, Jane. "Society Acts To Restore Scituate Lighthouse." *The Scituate Historical Society Bulletin* (February 1968).

Aynes, Edith A. "Colonel Florence A. Blanchfield." *Nursing Outlook* (February 1959): 78–81.

Barron, James. "Oveta Culp Hobby, Founder of WAC's and the First Secretary of Health, Dies at 90." *New York Times* (17 August 1995): B13.

Beans, Harry G. "Sex Discrimination in the Military." *Military Law Review* 67 (Winter 1975): 19–83.

Bell, Bonnie, et al. "Witness at Trinity Site." *Newsweek* (17 July 1995): 68–75.

Booher, Alice A. "A Special Salute to Women POWs." *Minerva's Bulletin Board* (Summer 1992): 1–4.

Bourke-White, Margaret. "Women in Lifeboats." *Life* (22 February 1943).

______ . "Women in Steel." *Life* (9 August 1943): 74–81.

Bromley, Dorothy Dunber. "Women on the Home Front." *Harpers* (July 1941): 188ff.

Brown, Barbara, et al. "The Equal Rights Amendment: A Constitutional Basis for Equal Rights for Women." *Yale Law Review* 80 (5 April 1971): 871–979.

"Citadel Marches on, without Female Cadet." *New York Times* (20 August 1995): 24.

"Citadel Offers Plan To Avoid Female Cadets." *New York Times* (7 October 1994).

"Class of the Class." *People Magazine* (19 June 1995): 59.

Clines, Francis X. "Army Cadets Face a Charge of Harassment," *New York Times* (1 November 1994): A1, B2.

De Pauw, Francis Grant. "Women in Combat: The Revolutionary War Experience." *Armed Forces and Society* (Winter 1981): 209–226.

Dent, David. "Women in the Military." *Essence* (April 1990).

"Designed for 24-Hour Child Care." *Architectural Record* (March 1944): 75.

Donnelly, Elaine. "Children Are Harmed When Mothers Serve in the Military." *Human Events* (16 March 1991).

"Edith Nourse Rogers" (obituary). *New York Times* (11 September 1960).

"Emotions of War." *People* (Spring/Summer 1991): 44.

Erlick, Jane Carolyn. "Women as the New War Correspondents." *Washington Journalism Review* (June 1982).

Farley, M. Foster. "Emily Geiger's Ride." *South Carolina Magazine* (May–June 1976): 10–11.

"First Day for Female Cadet Ends in Citadel's Infirmary." *New York Times* (15 August 1995): A14.

Frank, Linda Bird. "Paula Coughlin: The Woman Who Changed the U.S. Navy." *Glamour* (June 1993): 159ff.

Gardner, Harry. "A Conversation with Muriel Earhart Morrissey." *Cobblestone* (July 1990): 10–13.

"Girl Pilots." *Life* (19 July 1943): 7–9.

Grunwald, Lisa. "MIA." *Life, in Time of War* (25 February 1991): 42–46.

Heisey, John W. "'Ladies' in Our Wars." *AntiqueWeek* (29 May 1989): 12b.

Hernandez, Raymond. "3 Suspended for Grouping at West Point." *New York Times* (5 November 1994): 25–26.

Hilts, Philip. "Researchers Say Chemicals May Have Led to War Illness." *New York Times* (17 April 1996): A17.

Hoefer, Jean M. "They Called Her 'Moses.'" *Civil War Times Illustrated* (February 1988): 36–41.

Janofsky, Michael. "V.M.I.s Partner in Leadership Training for Women." *New York Times* (1 February 1995): B7.

Komarow, Steve, and Gordon Dickson. "Female Aviator, a Navy Pioneer, Killed in Crash." *USA Today* (27 October 1994).

Lancaster, John. "Nearly All Combat Jobs To Be Open to Women." *Washington Post* (29 April 1993): A1, A8.

"Limits on Career, Not Pregnancy, Moved Female Pilot To Quit Navy." *The Ledger Star* (26 November 1977).

Little, Lt. Col. Cynthia. "A Look at Women Cadets after Four Years." U.S. Air Force Academy (Spring 1980).

McInery, Nancy. "The Woman Vet Has Her Headaches, Too." *New York Times Magazine* (11 February 1946): 18.

Maddox, Barbara. "A Thing for Ribbon." *Life, in Time of War* (25 February 1991): 75.

Manegold, Catherine S. "Judge Allows Head Shaving for Woman at Citadel." *New York Times* (2 August 1994): A14.

______. "Appeals Panel Hears Case on Citadel's Ban on Women." *New York Times* (31 January 1995).

______. "Female Cadet Quits the Citadel, Citing Stress of Her Legal Battle." *New York Times* (19 August 1995): 1, 9.

Meyerowitz, Joanne. "Beyond the Feminine Mystique: A Reassessment of Postwar Mass Culture, 1946–1958." *Journal of American History* (March 1993): 1, 455–482.

Miller, Kenneth. "The Tiny Victims of Desert Storm." *Life* (November 1995): 46–52.

Moore, Molly. "Women in the Battlefield—Gulf War Helps Bring Shift in Attitude." *Washington Post* (16 June 1991): A1.

Morgenthau, Tom, et al. "The Military's New Image." *Newsweek* (11 March 1991): 50–51.

______. "The Military Fights the Gender Wars." *Newsweek* (14 November 1994): 35–37.

Murphy, Mark. "You'll Never Know." *New Yorker* (12 June 1943): 34.

"Navy Records Highly Rated Woman Pilot Who Crashed." *New York Times* (21 November 1994): A16.

Noble, Kenneth. "I Got Attacked by a Bunch of Men: Tailhook Whistleblower Testifies about Her Fear of Being Raped." *New York Times* (6 November 1994): A12.

______. "2 Women Settle Tailhook Suits." *New York Times* (6 November 1994): 46.

______. "Closing Arguments in the Tailhook Lawsuit." *New York Times* (28 November 1994): A22.

"One Way To Avoid a New Draft: Recruit More Females." *U.S. News and World Report* (14 February 1977).

"Our Hand of Fellowship Returning to G.I. Janes." *Independent Woman* (July 1945): 203ff.

Palmer, Laura. "The Nurses of Vietnam, Still Wounded." *New York Times Sunday Magazine* (7 November 1993): 36ff.

"Private Robert Shurleff, Well-Camouflaged Fighter." *New York Times* (15 August 1992).

Quick, Paddy. "Rosie the Riveter: Myths and Realities." *Radical America* (July–August 1975): 115–132.

Richardson, Sarah. "Chemicals at War." *Discover* (January 1996): 19.

Rimer, Sara. "Nation Analyzes and Agonizes over Citadel Dropout." *New York Times* (21 August 1995): A8.

Rogers, Patrick, et al. "Her War Is Over." *People* (4 September 1995): 76–80.

Rogers, Robin. "A Proposal for Combatting Sexual Discrimination in the Military: Amendment of Title VII." *California Law Review* 78, 1: 165–196.

Sack, Kevin. "A Woman Reports for Duty as a Cadet at the Citadel." *New York Times* (13 August 1995): 14.

Salhoz, Eloise. "Deepening Shame: A Newsweek Investigation into the Scandal That Is Rocking the Navy." *Newsweek* (10 August 1992): 30–36.

Salisbury, Karen. "The Women's Army Corps." *Newsweek* (21 May 1951).

"'Save the Males' Becomes Battle Cry in Citadel's Defense against Women." *New York Times* (23 May 1994): A10.

Schlafly, Phyllis. "The Lesson of Women in Combat in Panama." *Conservative Chronicle* (7 February 1990).

Schmitt, Eric. "Women Ready To Fly for Navy, or Flee It." *New York Times* (23 April 1993): A14.

______. "Pentagon Must Reinstate Nurse Who Declared She Is a Lesbian." *New York Times* (2 June 1994).

______. "Air Force Sergeant in a Sex Complaint Tells of Reprisals." *New York Times* (10 June 1994): A1, A21.

______. "Navy Facing a New Sexual Harassment Case." *New York Times Sunday Magazine* (8 November 1995): A14.

Shenon, Philip. "At Combat's Doorstep." *New York Times* (24 February 1991).

Sia, Richard H. P. "Aspin Clears Way for Women To Fly in Combat, Prepares More Changes." *Baltimore Sun* (29 April 1993): 3A.

Simpich, Frederick. "Wartime in the Pacific Northwest." *National Geographic* (October 1942): 424–436.

Starret, Ann. "Rationing Is a Woman's Job." *Independent Woman* (May 1942): 137–138.

Swartz, Lora. "Child Service Centers." *Journal of Home Economics* (February 1944): 75.

Timmerman, Kenneth R. "The Iraq Papers." *The New Republic* (29 January): 12+.

Tobias, Sheila, and Lisa Anderson. "Whatever Happened to Rosie the Riveter?" *Ms.* (June 1973).

Van Biema, David. "The Citadel Still Holds." *Time* (22 August 1994): 61.

"Women at Sea: Navy Traditions Being Rewritten." *Washington Post* (25 February 1979): 1.

"Women GIs in Granada." *Houston Post* (8 December 1983): 12A.

"Women in Combat: The Same Risks as Men?" *Washington Post* (3 February 1990).

Young, Lt. Eunice F. "Three Years outside This World." *Saturday Evening Post* (5 May 1945): 18.

Speeches

"Scituate Town Report." Paper read at a meeting of the Chief Justice Cushing Chapter D.A.R. (5 September 1908).

Widnall, Sheila. "From WAFs to Warriors: A Reflection of Women in the United States Air Force." National Archives Conference on United States Military Women in World War II speech, March 1995.

______ . "Women in the United States Air Force: Passages of Time." U.S. Air Force speeches, June 1995.

Legal Case

Owens v. Brown (455 F. Supp. 291: D.D.C. 1978).

Illustration Credits

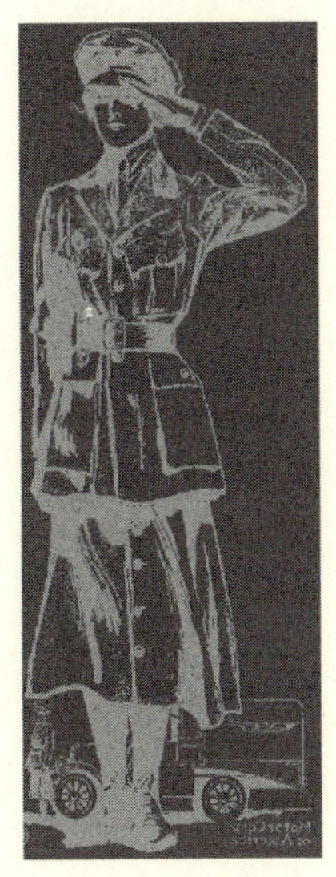

5	Gordon Parks/Library of Congress.
13	American Red Cross.
22	UPI/Bettmann.
32	National Archives A46175.
38	Illinois State Historical Society.
42	Salvation Army.
45	William L. Clements Library, University of Michigan.
56	American Red Cross.
66	American Red Cross.
74	Christopher Harris/Picture Network International Ltd.
80	Bettmann Archive.
96	UPI/Bettmann.
102	Library of Congress.
108	Library of Congress.
112	National Archives 45-WP-540.
118	Reuters/Bettmann.
127	Library of Congress.
130	Corbis-Bettmann.
136	Archive Photos.
143	Archive Photos.
146	Library of Congress.
163	UPI/Corbis-Bettmann.
170	Danbury Scott-Fanton Museum.
178	Archive Photos.
180	UPI/Bettmann.
188	UPI/Bettmann.
194	UPI/Corbis-Bettmann.
205	UPI/Bettmann.
211	UPI/Corbis-Bettmann.
214	National Archives 311A.
220	Bettmann Archive.
226	UPI/Corbis-Bettmann
237	Reuters/Mike Theiler/Archive Photos.
242	UPI/Corbis-Bettmann.
245	Archive Photos.
250	Archive Photos.
260	UPI/Corbis-Bettmann.
262	Archive Photos.
272	Museum of the Confederacy, Richmond, Virginia
281	Bettmann Archive.
293	Bill Foley/Picture Network International Ltd.
300	The Valentine Museum, Richmond, Virginia.
304	Bettmann Archive.
314	Corbis-Bettmann.
318	Archive Photos.
323	UPI/Bettmann.
331	Bettmann Archive.
333	Bettmann Archive.
337	Library of Congress.
346	UPI/Bettmann.

Index